INSIDE THE CONTEMPORARY CONSERVATOIRE

Drawing on the expertise of a wide range of professionals, *Inside the Contemporary Conservatoire: Critical Perspectives from the Royal College of Music, London*, presents fresh perspectives on the work of music conservatoires today through an in-depth case study of the Royal College of Music (RCM), London. Problematising the role and purpose of conservatoires in the context of changing cultural and societal conditions, the contributors reframe the conservatoire as a vehicle for positive change in the performing arts and society at large.

Organised into three main sections, the volume covers conservatoire identities and values, teaching and learning music at a conservatoire, and reflections on the conservatoires of the future. Diverse voices from inside and outside the RCM reflect viewpoints from professional musicians, academics, industry, and the student community, spanning topics such as arts practice, music pedagogy and education, technology, inclusion, employability, entrepreneurship, performance science, material culture, and philanthropy.

With chapters that combine interviews, case studies, analysis, critical reflection, and perspectives from inside and outside the RCM, this book offers an in-progress model for the forward-thinking conservatoire, underpinned by renewed emphasis on equitable, innovative, sustainable, and technologically enabled artistic practice.

Colin Lawson was Director of the Royal College of Music from 2005 to 2024. He has an international profile as a period clarinettist and has published widely on performance and performance practice.

Diana Salazar is Director of Programmes at the Royal College of Music. A conservatoire-trained flautist and composer, her research interests combine practice research in electroacoustic composition with exploration of conservatoire pedagogies and technology-enhanced learning in higher music education. She is a founder of the Global Conservatoire consortium.

Rosie Perkins is Professor of Music, Health, and Social Science at the Royal College of Music. She leads the RCM's Master of Science in Performance Science programme and has published extensively on music and mental health and musicians' well-being.

INSIDE THE CONTEMPORARY CONSERVATOIRE

Critical Perspectives from
the Royal College of Music, London

*Edited by Colin Lawson, Diana Salazar,
and Rosie Perkins*

Routledge
Taylor & Francis Group

NEW YORK AND LONDON

Designed cover image: © Phil Rowley

First published 2025
by Routledge
605 Third Avenue, New York, NY 10158

and by Routledge
4 Park Square, Milton Park, Abingdon, Oxon, OX14 4RN

Routledge is an imprint of the Taylor & Francis Group, an informa business

Library of Congress Cataloging-in-Publication Data
Names: Lawson, Colin (Colin James), editor. | Salazar, Diana, editor. | Perkins, Rosie, editor.
Title: Inside the contemporary conservatoire : critical perspectives from the Royal College of Music, London / edited by Colin Lawson, Diana Salazar, and Rosie Perkins.
Description: New York : Routledge, 2025. | Includes bibliographical references and index.
Identifiers: LCCN 2024040559 (print) | LCCN 2024040560 (ebook) | ISBN 9781032251066 (hardback) | ISBN 9781032251059 (paperback) | ISBN 9781003281573 (ebook)
Subjects: LCSH: Royal College of Music (Great Britain) | Curriculum change—Great Britain. | Curriculum planning—Great Britain. | Conservatories of music—England—London. | Music—Instruction and study—Great Britain.
Classification: LCC MT5.L8 R864 2025 (print) | LCC MT5.L8 (ebook) | DDC 780.71/1421—dc23/eng/20240904
LC record available at https://lccn.loc.gov/2024040559
LC ebook record available at https://lccn.loc.gov/2024040560

ISBN: 978-1-032-25106-6 (hbk)
ISBN: 978-1-032-25105-9 (pbk)
ISBN: 978-1-003-28157-3 (ebk)

DOI: 10.4324/9781003281573

Typeset in Sabon
by Apex CoVantage, LLC

CONTENTS

ACKNOWLEDGEMENTS

Many people have contributed to and supported *Inside the Contemporary Conservatoire: Critical Perspectives from the Royal College of Music, London.* Our thanks to the chapter and perspective authors, who have brought their extensive experience and expertise to the pages that follow. Thanks also to the members of the RCM community who shared their valuable viewpoints for the Preface. We are grateful for the many different voices in the volume and their enduring commitment to music and music education.

Our sincere thanks to Sarah Mennell who has provided support for this volume from inception to completion, and to Cobi Ashkenazi who has ably assisted us with preparing the manuscript and index for submission.

Thanks to Genevieve Aoki at Routledge for commissioning this book and to Sutapa Mazumder for their work in copy-editing the final manuscript.

Finally, our thanks go to the RCM community – past and present – without whom this book would not have come to fruition.

CONTRIBUTORS

Editors

Colin Lawson was formerly Director of the Royal College of Music, London, where he holds a Chair in Historical Performance. He has an international profile as a period clarinettist, with a substantial discography of concertos and chamber music. He has published widely across practice and theory, with his most recent edited volume, *The Cambridge Encyclopedia of Historical Performance in Music*, winning the C. B. Oldman Award for an 'outstanding work of music reference'.

Diana Salazar is Director of Programmes at the Royal College of Music, London. A conservatoire-trained flautist and composer, her research interests combine practice research in electroacoustic composition with the exploration of conservatoire pedagogies and technology-enhanced learning in higher music education.

Rosie Perkins is Professor of Music, Health, and Social Science at the Royal College of Music, London, where she directs the RCM's MSc in Performance Science programme. Based in the Centre for Performance Science, Rosie's research investigates two broad areas within music and mental health: how music and the arts support societal well-being and how to enhance artists' well-being and career development.

Chapter authors

Florence Ambrose is Head of Performance, Programming and Faculties at the Royal College of Music, London, where she has worked since 2007. In her role at the RCM, she manages the artistic programmes while overseeing the strategic planning and scheduling of events.

Dave Camlin teaches in music education at the Royal College of Music, London, and Trinity Laban Conservatoire, and he was Head of HE/Research at Sage Gateshead from 2010 to 2019. His musical practice spans performance, composition, teaching, Community Music

(CM), and research. As a respected practitioner and researcher, his research focuses on CM, especially group singing; music, health, and well-being; and musician education. He has pioneered the use of Sensemaker® 'distributed ethnography' as a research method for understanding artistic and cultural experiences.

Hayley Clements is Head of Learning and Participation at the Royal College of Music, London. She is responsible for the strategic vision for Learning and Participation activity at the RCM and oversees the pre-18 widening participation agenda. Hayley also oversees the role of the Learning and Participation activity as part of the BMus programme.

Jonathan Cole is a composer, teacher, and conductor. From 2009 to 2013, he was the first Composer-in-Association with the London Contemporary Orchestra, and his works have been performed and commissioned by many ensembles including BBCPO, Chicago SO, LSO, London Sinfonietta, and Tokyo Sinfonietta. He was appointed Head of Composition at the Royal College of Music, London, in 2022.

Miranda Francis is Head of Junior Programmes and Area Leader in Aural Training at the Royal College of Music, London. Miranda's research interests include performance assessment methods and comparative pedagogical approaches to aural training.

Thom Gilbert is Digital Learning Manager at the Royal College of Music, London and a music graduate and qualified teacher. Before joining the RCM, he was Head of Music and Music Technology departments in schools and colleges across East Sussex. In his last post, Thom led the development of Digital Learning strategy and practice and specialised in the application of technology in class music teaching.

Christina Guillaumier is Reader and Research Fellow in Music and Cultural Practice at the Royal College of Music, London. She is a music historian, pianist, and writer. She is a Fellow of the Royal Society of Arts (FRSA), a Senior Fellow of the Higher Education Academy, and a peer reviewer for several academic journals and publishing houses. Dr Guillaumier is an editor for Bärenreiter, specialising in critical editions of piano music.

Rachel Harris has been Director of Finance at the Royal College of Music, London, since 2019, and has over 25 years of experience in senior financial positions in the commercial and Higher Education sectors.

Lily Harriss has been Director of Development at the Royal College of Music, London, since 2015 and was Directorate lead on the More Music Campaign. She has almost 30 years of leadership experience in arts and education with a specific focus on music throughout her career. She is also a recent graduate of the RCM with an MSc in Performance Science.

Ivan Hewett is a London-based lecturer, broadcaster, and journalist. His main research interest is the reception of contemporary music, particularly in the interwar period. He is Chief Music Critic of *The Daily Telegraph*, lectures at the Royal College of Music, London, and is the author of *Music: Healing the Rift* (Continuum, 2004).

David Hockings is Head of Percussion and Timpani at the Royal College of Music, London. A performing musician who has worked with all the major London Orchestras and Chamber Ensembles, he has been Principal Percussionist for the BBC Symphony Orchestra since 1994 and since 1997 with the London Sinfonietta.

Talia Hull is Director of Communications at the Royal College of Music, London. Her experience advising high-profile, complex organisations includes previous positions as Head of Communications for BBC Radio 3 and Classical Music TV and Press Manager for Warner Classics and *National* (now Hearst) *Magazines*. Talia specialises in strategic communications, issues management, and brand positioning. She has been a trustee for the music education charity Music Masters since 2017.

Stephen Johns Stephen Johns was the first Artistic Director of the Royal College of Music, from 2010 to 2024. He read music at Trinity College, Cambridge, and went on to train at Abbey Road Studios. He has worked for over 35 years as classical record producer for a wide range of companies and with artists all over the world. He was Vice President, Artists and Repertoire for EMI Classics, and now works as a freelance recording producer and industry consultant.

Janis Kelly is Chair of Vocal Performance and Vocal Professor at the Royal College of Music, London. She is an international Soprano performing and recording Opera and Song repertoire. A renowned voice pedagogue, she has taught some of the finest young singers working today. Via RCM research, Professor Kelly has documented her vocal lineage and speech training on film.

Vanessa Latarche is Chair of International Keyboard Studies, Head of Keyboard, and Associate Director for Partnerships in Asia at the Royal College of Music, London. In addition to her managerial role, Professor Latarche is responsible for training some of the finest pianistic talents in the world.

Gabrielle Lester is a professor of violin and Deputy Head of Strings (Orchestral Strings) at the Royal College of Music, London. Gaby is recognised for chamber music and as a leader of orchestras in the UK and is often in the recording studio, playing and leading soundtracks such as Harry Potter and The Lord of the Rings. Gaby is also a mentor and coach for organisations such as the Australian Youth Orchestra, Youth Orchestra of Catalonia, and National Youth Orchestra of Spain.

Tania Lisboa is Reader in Performance Science and Digital Learning at the Royal College of Music, London, and Honorary Research Fellow at Imperial College London. Her research focuses on arts in health, expert memory, performance education, and online teaching and learning. Dr Lisboa has managed the RCM's videoconferencing programme for over 15 years, collaborating with institutions in the United States, Europe, and Asia. In parallel with her academic research, Dr Lisboa pursues an active career as a solo cellist.

Ingrid Pearson performs on both modern and historical instruments. Her publications encompass iconography, musical listening, organology, and performance practice, as well as aspects of teaching and learning in the conservatoire environment. She joined the professoriate at the Royal College of Music, London, in 2005 and is now the College's Senior Academic Tutor.

Kevin Porter is Deputy Director at the Royal College of Music, London. Previously, he worked at the Council for National Academic Awards and at universities. He has had examining and committee membership roles with organisations such as Conservatories UK and KCG internal audit. Publications include *Management in the Conservatoire of the Future: Administering or Leading?* in *Studies in Higher Education* and, with Jeffrey Weeks, the oral history '*Between the Acts: Lives of Homosexual Men, 1885–1967*'.

Diana Roberts specialises in the development of pioneering services for early-career musicians. As Head of the Royal College of Music, London's flagship Creative Careers Centre, she delivers entrepreneurial courses for undergraduate and postgraduate students. Diana is a personal and business coach and Director of the F-List for Music.

Gary Ryan was appointed to the Royal College of Music, London, in 1996 at the age of 27 and has maintained a successful freelance career as a guitarist for over 30 years alongside his educational work for the RCM and ABRSM. He was appointed Head of Strings at the RCM in 2024 after being Assistant Head of Strings since 2009 and was awarded an FRCM in 2013.

Wiebke Thormählen is Director of Research at the Royal Northern College of Music, after nine years at the Royal College of Music, London, as Area Leader in History. Professor Thormählen's research focusses on different modes of engagement in and with music as explored in key publications such as the *Routledge Companion to Music, Mind and Well-being: Historical and Scientific Perspectives* (2018, co-editor) and *Sound Heritage: Making Music Matter in Historic Houses* (2022, co-editor).

George Waddell is Performance Research and Innovation Fellow and Area Leader in Performance Science at the Royal College of Music, London. He conducts research on performance development, evaluation, and technology and oversees the design and delivery of performance science-driven undergraduate courses targeting musicians' health, skills, and careers.

Aaron Williamon is Professor of Performance Science at the Royal College of Music, London, where he directs the Centre for Performance Science. His research focuses on skilled performance and applied scientific initiatives that inform music learning and teaching, as well as the impact of music and the arts on the society.

Richard Wistreich is Professor of Music at the Royal College of Music, London, where he was Director of Research from 2014 to 2020. His research focuses on the history of performance, particularly before 1800. He has also had a long career as a professional singer, specialising in early and contemporary music.

Andrew Zolinsky is professor of Piano at the Royal College of Music, London, and at Goldsmiths, University of London. Though a noted performer of contemporary repertoire,

Andrew enjoys performing a wide range of music spanning several musical periods. His unique style of programming and his individual interpretations have secured performances at many prestigious venues and festivals.

Perspective authors

Brydie-Leigh Bartleet is an Australian Research Council Future Fellow at the Creative Arts Research Institute and Queensland Conservatorium Griffith University. Professor Bartleet has worked on 15 major grants and consultancies, held 5 prestigious fellowships, and published 180 outputs. She is President of SIMM (Social Impact of Making Music) and Associate Editor of the *International Journal of Community Music*.

Lisa Colton (University of Liverpool) is a musicologist whose publications include *Female-Voice Song and Women's Musical Agency in Medieval Europe* (Brill, 2022, co-edited with Anna Kathryn Grau). Professor Colton is Reviews Editor for the journal *Early Music*.

Sarah Connolly was made a DBE in the 2017 Birthday Honours, having previously been awarded a CBE in the 2010 New Year Honours. In 2020, she was made Honorary Member of the Royal Philharmonic Society in recognition of her outstanding services to music. She has sung at the Aldeburgh, Edinburgh, Lucerne, Salzburg, and Tanglewood Festivals, and at the BBC Proms where, in 2009, she was a soloist at the Last Night. Opera engagements have taken her around the world from the Metropolitan Opera to the Royal Opera House, the Paris Opera, La Scala Milan, the Vienna and Munich State Operas, and the Bayreuth, Glyndebourne, and Aix-en-Provence Festivals.

Afa Sadykhly Dworkin is a music industry thought leader and cross-sector strategist driving national programming that promotes diversity in classical music. Since 2015, she has served as President and Artistic Director of the Sphinx Organization, the leading organisation transforming lives through the power of diversity in the arts. She has been named one of Musical America's 'Top 30 Influencers', has received The Kennedy Center's Human Spirit Award, and has been featured in *Crain's Detroit Business* magazine's '40 Under 40'.

James Gandre is an educator and musician with a deep commitment to students and the development of American conservatory learning. He returned to Manhattan School of Music (MSM) to assume the presidency in 2013, having served the School previously for 15 years (1985–2000), concluding that first phase of his time at MSM as Dean of Enrollment and Alumni. In 2000, Dr Gandre became Dean of Chicago College of Performing Arts at Roosevelt University, where he went on to ultimately serve as Provost and Executive Vice President.

Helena Gaunt is a musician (oboist), author, and thought leader on professional education and practice in the performing arts. She was Founder Member of the Britten Sinfonia and taught at the Guildhall School of Music & Drama, London, for many years. Professor Gaunt is Principal of the Royal Welsh College of Music & Drama (RWCMD) and Chair of the Advisory Board for the National Music Service in Wales and sits on the Council of the

Royal Philharmonic Society. She has also served on many working groups for the European Association of Conservatoires and is Vice Chair of Conservatoires UK.

Wendy Heller, Scheide Professor of Music History at Princeton University, New Jersey, the United States, focuses on the study of Baroque music from interdisciplinary perspectives. As Department Chair for seven years, she partnered with the Royal College of Music in developing a programme that sends Princeton students to study at the RCM each fall.

Joachim Junghanss studied Jazz, classical piano, and pedagogy and earned his DMA degree as Fulbright grantee at the Manhattan School of Music. He serves as Deputy Director at Conservatorium van Amsterdam (CvA) heading the Jazz, Pop, and Electronic Music departments. Joachim has worked in music education worldwide, as a teacher, start-up founder, grassroots activist, and also as a BCG consultant.

Susan Madden, a longtime New York City-based development professional, is Manhattan School of Music's Vice President for Philanthropy. Prior to joining the School's executive staff, she held senior development positions at the Museum of the City of New York, the New York Restoration Project, and the Solomon R. Guggenheim Museum.

Peter Maniura is an award-winning freelance TV producer and director with more than 30 years' experience in music and arts broadcasting, formerly at the BBC as Head of Classical Music Television and at the EBU. He is Director of the IMZ Academy and also a digital media consultant and guest lecturer.

Ruth K. Minton (University of Liverpool) is a pianist and musicologist who undertakes regular performance engagements alongside her academic roles; she is a committed and passionate musician.

Lucy Noble was the first ever Artistic Director of London's Royal Albert Hall, prior to her appointment to the same role at AEG Presents, in which she is expanding the company's touring and live events business. She recently served as Chair of the National Arenas Association, which represents 23 UK arenas, including London's O2, Manchester Arena, and the SEC in Glasgow. She is an alumna of the RCM, where her principal study was the flute.

Michelle Phillips is Head of Enterprise (Academic) at the Royal Northern College of Music, Manchester, the United Kingdom. Dr Phillips has published peer-reviewed articles on music and entrepreneurship and given talks nationally and internationally. Michelle is Fellow of Enterprise Educators UK and Director of the Institute for Small Business and Entrepreneurship (ISBE).

Martin Prchal is Vice Principal at the Royal Conservatoire in The Hague. A trained musician of Czech origin, he holds teaching and performance diplomas (violoncello) and an MA degree in Musicology. He served as the first Chief Executive of the European Association of Conservatoires (AEC) from 2001 to 2011. Martin was also one of the Founders of MusiQuE – Music Quality Enhancement and has served as a peer reviewer and board member for various national quality assurance agencies in Europe. His current post includes curriculum development and innovation, research, quality assurance, and international relations.

Emma Redding is Director of the Victorian College of the Arts (VCA) at the University of Melbourne, Australia. The VCA offers a range of degree programmes in visual arts, performing arts, and screen arts. Prior to this, she was Professor in Performance Science and Head of Dance Science at Trinity Laban Conservatoire of Music and Dance, London. Emma co-wrote the first ever Master's degree in dance science and has since played a major role in developing dance science as a recognised field of study in higher education. In 2022, Emma was awarded an MBE in the Queen's New Year Honour's List for her services to dance.

James Williams was Managing Director of the Royal Philharmonic Orchestra from 2016 to 2024. Notable achievements include appointing Vasily Petrenko as Music Director of the RPO, securing the RPO a Residency at the Royal Albert Hall, and devising an international touring programme for the orchestra, embracing four continents. In 2022, James was invited by HM King Charles III to act as music advisor for the Coronation Service held at Westminster Abbey on 6 May 2023. In September 2024, James assumed the role of Director at the Royal College of Music, London.

Roger Wilson is Co-founder and Director of Operations at Black Lives in Music, an organisation working for equal opportunities for Black, Asian, and ethnically diverse people in the jazz and classical music industries. Conservatoire-trained, he has worked extensively in the commercial, jazz, and classical sector with a wide range of artists from Lesley Garett and Bryn Terfel to James Brown and Quincy Jones. As an instrumental teacher and lecturer, Roger has worked throughout the UK music education sector at all levels.

ABBREVIATIONS

ABRSM	Associated Board of the Royal Schools of Music
AEC	The Association Européenne des Conservatoires, Académies de Musique et Musikhochschulen
AEG	Anschutz Entertainment Group
AHRC	Arts and Humanities Research Council
AI	Artificial Intelligence
ARC	Australian Research Council
BAPAM	British Association for Performing Arts Medicine
BBC	British Broadcasting Corporation
BMus	Bachelor of Music
CCC	RCM Creative Careers Centre
COVID-19	Coronavirus Disease 2019 (and its ensuing pandemic)
CPS	Centre for Performance Science (a Partnership between the Royal College of Music and Imperial College London)
CUK	Conservatoires UK
CvA	Conservatorium van Amsterdam
DMA	Doctorate of Musical Arts
EBU	European Broadcasting Union
ECTS	European Credit Transfer and Accumulation System
EDI	Equality, Diversity, and Inclusion
EDIMS	Equality, Diversity and Inclusion in Music Studies
ENO	English National Opera
FRCM	Fellow of the Royal College of Music
GC	Global Conservatoire
GloCoDA	A Global Conservatoire for the Digital Age
HE	Higher Education
HEartS	The Health, Economic, and Social Impact of the ARTs project
HEFCE	Higher Education Funding Council for England
HEI	Higher Education Institution
HESA	Higher Education Statistics Agency

HMEI	Higher Music Education Institution
HPSM	Health Promotion in Schools of Music
HR	Human Resource
ICON	Innovative Conservatoires
IMZ	International Music + Media Centre
IOS	Inclusion of Other in Self Scale
IVT	Instrumental and Vocal Teaching
KPI	Key Performance Indicator
LoLa	Low Latency Audio Visual Streaming System
LSO	London Symphony Orchestra
MDW	Universität für Musik und darstellende Kunst Wien (University of Music and Performing Arts Vienna)
MIDI	Musical Instrument Digital Interface
MSc	Master of Science
MSM	Manhattan School of Music
MusiQuE	Music Quality Enhancement
NEC	New England Conservatory
NPME	National Plan for Music Education (UK)
OfS	Office for Students
PRiHME	Power Relations in Higher Music Education
QAA	Quality Assurance Agency for Higher Education
R&D	Research & Development
RA	Royal Academy of Arts
RAM	Royal Academy of Music
RCM	Royal College of Music, London
RCMJD	Royal College of Music Junior Department
RCS	Royal Conservatoire of Scotland
REC	Research Ethics Committee
ROH	Royal Opera House
RPO	Royal Philharmonic Orchestra
RSL	Rockschool Awards
SAMR	Substitution, Augmentation, Modification, and Redefinition
SIMM	Social Impact of Making Music
SRHE	Society for Research into Higher Education (UK)
SWEMWBS	Short Warwick–Edinburgh Mental Well-Being Scale
TCL	Trinity College London
VLE	Virtual Learning Environment

FOREWORD

The world of classical music is a remarkable ecosystem. A constant process of interaction between performers, composers, ensembles, venues, broadcasters, charities, businesses, administrators, educators, critics, consumers, funding bodies, governments, and countless other actors on a local, national, and global level. The result is a complex, complicated, and often downright confusing network of interdependencies where events or actions in one bit will always have an impact on another.

At the heart of this ecology sits the conservatoire – the fulcrum of musical education, dedicated to providing the highest quality musical grounding to the musicians of the future and providing a crucial pipeline for the sector.

In many ways, much about the institution of the conservatoire has stayed the same over its history. Whether it is in the organisational structure, the importance of one-to-one teaching, or the guiding principles – as Colin Lawson highlights in the opening chapter, the Royal College of Music's original three core values of access, advocacy, and excellence endure to this day – the model, methods, and core mission of the contemporary conservative bear remarkable similarity to the institutions established across Europe two hundred years ago.

This is no bad thing – indeed, the preservation and passing on of that tradition of pedagogy and cultural lineage are one of the conservatoire's greatest strengths. However, the young musicians who pass through the conservatoires of today must venture out into a musical world that is radically different – indeed, unrecognisable in many senses – from the one their forebears inhabited.

Two centuries ago, those completing a formal musical education had good prospects to secure a stable and regular income from a single employer at court or perhaps the support of a wealthy patron to sustain their career. Now, the expectation for those leaving even the most notable of institutions is of a freelance career and the often precarious professional lifestyle that entails.

For hundreds of years, a prerequisite to a stellar artistic reputation was a spell at a Western conservatoire during one's formative years. Today, you could argue that likes on your TikTok account will have more of a correlation with commercial success than lines on your educational CV. And the advent of recording and broadcasting, combined with the increased commercialisation of music, has radically changed how musicians create their art and how the public consume it.

The musical ecosystem looks very different from how it looked two centuries ago – and yet the pace of change the sector has gone through since then could be about to exponentially increase. With the onset of AI, a rapidly evolving professional landscape, a blurring of musical boundaries, and an increased focus on diversity and representation, the classical music ecosystem is poised to undergo a more intense transformation than ever before over the next two decades. The year 2025 could look as alien to the musical world of 2045 as the world of Beethoven and Schubert looks to us today.

This poses huge questions not just for the contemporary conservatoire but also for the classical music sector as a whole.

How does an art form steeped in history and tradition truly embrace innovation and make the most of the technological revolution? In an increasingly commercialised music industry, how do you balance artistry and commercial success? Is the tension between excellence and access a false dichotomy – and if so, how do you achieve both? How does classical music interact with other musical genres and other art forms? How do educational institutions link with the profession, and how do those institutions equip their students with the skills they need to succeed in the industry? What are the future funding models for the sector, and how should state funding and philanthropy interact? What are the implications of 'global pedagogy'? What role should music play in our national, civic life, and what does that mean for conservatoires?

This volume grapples with all of these issues, along with many others. Each comes with major implications for the sector, and you could devote a whole book to any single one of them. There are no easy or simple answers – and I don't think any of the brilliant thinkers, educators, and practitioners who have contributed would claim to have all the solutions – but how we respond to these challenges will have a significant and lasting impact on the whole classical music ecology.

Over recent years, I've had a fascinating vantage point on many of these issues. As a one-time music student who went on to be a policymaker in government, a trade body chief executive representing the music industry, a board member of a venue and an orchestra, a trustee of a musical charity, a National Council member of the Arts Council, and a council member of the RCM, I have watched these debates play out at every level of the sector – and it is clear to me that the response from educators and conservatoires will be one of the most consequential. The students going into a conservatoire today are the shapers and leaders of our musical ecosystem tomorrow – and how conservatoires adapt in this rapidly changing environment will therefore have an impact on the whole musical world.

So, this volume is a timely and invaluable contribution which offers not only a fascinating depiction of what the contemporary conservatoire is but also a thoughtful and provoking set of perspectives on what it needs to be going forward. In that respect, this book bears relevance not only to the future of the conservatoire but also to the future of the whole classical music ecosystem.

Jamie Njoku-Goodwin
Former Chief Executive of UK Music

PREFACE: CONSERVATOIRE AS COMMUNITY

Conservatoires are specialised institutions for the study of music or other performing arts, often in the continental European tradition. But how did the term come about? Its origins date from the early nineteenth century, when the French adapted the Italian word *conservatorio*, from late Latin *conservatorium*, which in turn derives from the word *conservare*, to preserve. As outlined in Chapter 1 of this book (which traces conservatoire values past, present, and future), curating the Western musical canon continues to loom large in the curricula of present-day conservatoires. On the other hand, the learning culture within conservatoires has recently broadened in ways that would surely have astonished past generations of music students. In effect, an accommodation of mind and spirit is allied to an emphasis on entrepreneurship and student initiative. Today's concentration on innovation to complement tradition promotes an increased interaction with the other arts and ongoing dialogue with the music profession. Furthermore, the digital world has opened hitherto unimaginable possibilities for student musicians. As implied by many of this book's contributors, the enduring label of 'conservatoire' barely does justice to the range of activity within contemporary institutions. Nevertheless, the term implies an important value shared by conservatoires large and small throughout the world, namely that technical grounding must be an absolute for young musicians aspiring to be the most complete artists they can become.

Over recent decades, a gradual waning of a culture of deference has inflected conservatoire communities in countries across the world. There is a clear parallel here with the conducting profession, where in general a more consensual approach is beginning to replace unchallenged autocracy. Respect must be earned, even (and especially) by senior institutional leaders; an equally positive development is that formal staff appointment processes have replaced the informal recruitment that in former times inevitably compromised the applicant pool. Within conservatoires in the UK and elsewhere, students have experienced ever-increasing fees, bringing new expectations from them as paying 'customers'. Student representation on committees, including governing bodies, has become *de rigeur*. Communication across committees that give a platform to student views is a delicate matter; the senior management team may spend time considering strategic policies that will have an effect 50 or even a 100 years hence, whereas a current student body will naturally focus upon matters of more immediate concern. A cohort of learners from diverse nationalities brings further institutional responsibilities. In recent years, students' mental health and well-being have become topics of great consideration, producing a range of wider pastoral obligations for those who teach. An important consequence of all this change has been to increase awareness that a broad range of professional expertise contributes to the effectiveness and success of any institution that has learning and teaching at its heart.

The work of Christopher Small has immediate resonance here; he coined the term 'musicking' to highlight music as a process and not as an object. In his book of the same title from 1998, he argued that 'to music' could mean any activity involving or related to musical performance:

> To music is to take part, in any capacity, in a musical performance, whether by performing, by listening, by rehearsing or practising, by providing material for performance (what is called composing), or by dancing. We might at times even extend its meaning to what the person is doing who takes the tickets at the door or the hefty men [sic] who shift the piano and the drums or the roadies who set up the instruments and carry out the sound checks or the cleaners who clean up after everyone else has gone. They too are all contributing to the nature of the event that is a musical performance.[1]

Transferring Small's discourse to the conservatoire, the parallels are obvious. Management of the physical spaces and associated facilities, student services, administration, marketing, finance, and fundraising all contribute vitally to the work undertaken by artistic and academic colleagues. In the UK, an additional burdensome element is of course the handling of increasingly demanding regulatory frameworks (see also Chapter 6). As outlined in Chapter 13, fitting surroundings play a key role in musicians' lives. In addition to capital investment, fundraising (see Chapter 5) is crucial to scholarship programmes, without which impecunious but talented applicants are deprived of the opportunity for specialised study. Overall sound financial management is of course a *sine qua non*, since conservatoires are effectively businesses in their own right. It follows that marketing has become more sophisticated, reflecting the global environment in which league tables are a fact of everyday life. Administration routinely involves a vast range of issues, as any perusal of agendas pertaining to audit or governance instantly reveals. As part of the academic agenda, an active research profile as discussed in Chapter 10 enables an institution to explore and demonstrate its value beyond music and can instil a vital spirit of inquiry within the community.

It is instructive that Small proceeds to emphasise the human element, noting that the act of musicking establishes a set of relationships, found not only in the organised sounds which are conventionally thought of as being the substance of musical meaning but also between the people who are taking part. Conservatoires are themselves microcosms of society, often with a strong international flavour and with a wide range of interacting age groups. Increased attention to equity, diversity, and inclusion has focused upon nurturing under-represented groups among students, staff, and visiting artists, as well as determining repertory choices. A particular challenge for many institutions is that many influential teachers spend relatively little time in the physical spaces of the institution, balancing one-to-one teaching with busy professional schedules elsewhere. Yet, these teachers are at the very heart of students' development, both as musicians and human beings. Indeed, their credibility and reputation are often significant elements in an individual applicant's choice of conservatoire. At the same time, these colleagues, most of whom in the UK are paid hourly, inevitably vary markedly in their degree of loyalty to the institution, their interest in strategic matters, and their pride in its overall achievements. Within this environment there is of course a danger that not all members of the community will know, or even be aware of, each other.

What follows is a series of responses from students and staff from the Royal College of Music (RCM), London to two questions – what it has meant to each of them to be part of the RCM community, and what their aspirations are for the future of this community. Their reflections provide an appropriate springboard for the material in this book in which the RCM acts as a case study for the range of critical perspectives from inside the contemporary conservatoire. It continues to be a substantial challenge that the complex agenda revealed within these pages remains all too invisible to the general public at large. Let us regard this as work in progress!

Community perspectives I: what does it mean to you to be part of the RCM community?

Barnaby Robson (Clarinet professor and MSc in Performance Science Student): During nearly twenty years of RCM clarinet teaching, the students have always been at the heart of my RCM community experience. As they've absorbed the expertise that the College so abundantly offers and have collaborated with their musical contemporaries, the RCM's influence on them has been profound, both as musicians and people. Many of my students have gone on to work in the profession, becoming colleagues and friends. I have found teaching each of them to be challenging, inspirational, and rewarding.

Tymon Zgorzelski (RCM graduate, composer, and RCM Students' Union President, 2022–2024): The RCM community is a collective of people intensely focused on pursuing and advancing music, both staff and students. It is a unique environment to be in, with incredible talent and dedication showcased on every turn. Belonging to it gives a sense of pride (I am among these people!) and humility (am I among these people?). Ultimately, it makes one strive for their best at a given point on their musical journey. An important feature of the RCM community is how international it is. There are many couches to crash on all over the world unlocked by studying at the RCM.

Sarah Hanratty (Head of Projects, Facilities, and Operations): I feel privileged to be part of a community that nurtures, supports, and cultivates students and staff. I am proud to have experienced the strength and commitment of the community during a major capital project that has transformed our beloved campus.

Rianna Henriques (Postgraduate Flute Student): I am beyond grateful for being a member of the RCM community. The RCM is a vibrant conservatoire full of talented musicians, each with individual excellence. I believe being an emerging professional in the classical music industry is to undergo a series of progressions: progressing in your practice, your studies, and on your instrument in general. I am so honoured to be able to experience this journey as an emerging professional with like-minded students I'll no doubt be working with for the long haul, far in the future.

Bex Herman (Performance Science PhD Student): Being part of any community, to me, means celebrating its strengths while acknowledging and challenging its limitations.

Studying in a building filled to bursting with musicians tirelessly honing their craft is inspiring and endlessly motivating. From a research perspective, I am constantly amazed by the innovative and impactful research being done by my research colleagues. Overall, it is an extraordinary privilege to be part of the RCM community. Within that, doctoral study is an inherently solitary endeavour, and it can feel isolating, navigating both the successes and the inevitable challenges, alone. To mitigate this, I have done everything possible to build a strong and supportive doctoral community. However, this raises broader questions around whose responsibility community is, such as whether community should be student-led or institution-led. Either/both is possibly fine, but an institutional commitment to community arguably requires transparent conversation around these types of issues.

Maxine Smith (Receptionist): I love my job, getting to know the students, engaging with staff, and visitors. During my years at College, it has been truly an inspiration, not forgetting the wonderful music.

Mengyang Pan (Piano professor, Module Leader and Lecturer, and Student Advisor): Being part of the RCM community means belonging to a team that embraces me for who I am. The camaraderie spirit in the College is so strong that it gives me the most pleasure to work with my colleagues and to achieve shared goals together. The College's encouragement and unwavering support propels me on the journey of personal growth and gives my professional development much fulfilment.

Rieko Makita (Constant and Kit Lambert Junior Fellow & Artistic Diploma student (Solo Piano)): Being at the RCM has allowed me to meet, learn, and play alongside talented musicians from all over the world. It has been inspiring to be here. I am thankful to those particular individuals who have been especially kind to me and have encouraged me to be bold and to realise the potential in myself. As the Constant and Kit Lambert Junior Fellow, I have been able to create and lead projects with artistic freedom in a supportive environment. The performance experiences, the facilities available for use, and the people I've been able to meet have helped me in preparing for a professional musical career. This fellowship opportunity has been life-changing for me.

Community perspectives II: what are your aspirations for the RCM community?

Barnaby Robson (Clarinet professor and MSc in Performance Science Student): The RCM's ambition to provide an increasingly diverse array of music education pathways is hugely exciting. As the music profession adapts to changing funding models and new technologies, so too must the training grounds for new artists. With creativity placed front and centre, young musicians need to be taught not only to replicate but also to innovate. Providing a musician with the skills to perform a chamber recital, then engage with their local community choir, is both enlightened and essential, as is the academic research connecting these practical activities. The RCM is perfectly placed to deliver in all these areas.

Tymon Zgorzelski (RCM graduate, composer, and RCM Students' Union President, 2022–2024): I think RCM strives for equality, which is hard, especially with how expensive and uncertain studying music is. I wish RCM could offer something like at the Curtis Institute, Harvard, or most European universities, where the tuition fee is not a barrier at all, to enable all suitable candidates to belong to the RCM. I also hope more professors will be engaged with the community, what happens here, and what the issues or successes are. The 'old guard' is venerable, but there are always new things to learn. Finally, I wish that the Students' Union continues to be useful to the RCM community.

Sarah Hanratty (Head of Projects, Facilities, and Operations): My 12 years at the College are proof that I'm sure the community will continue to grow from strength to strength. My aspirations for the RCM community are that it continues to foster creativity and maximise the determination and dedication of all students and staff.

Rianna Henriques (Postgraduate Flute Student): The RCM trains gifted musicians from all over the world for international musical careers, yet I believe it could be diversified even further still. This is my main aspiration for the RCM community, and this stems from the fact that a student's socio-economic background can influence their aspirations and sense of belonging within UK conservatoires. Although discussions around the lack of diverse representation in the music industry are gaining public attention, there is a recorded lack of diversity in classical music, and I hope music education, and therefore conservatoires, have a more inclusive future.

Bex Herman (Performance Science PhD Student): Given the multidisciplinary nature of musical study at the RCM, it would be wonderful to see more creative collaboration across disciplines and departments. We could learn so much from each other, yet tend to work in silos. I would also love for discussions around the pursuit of excellence to include (a) a more nuanced definition of excellence and (b) the cost of excellence. These are both easily overlooked, yet so important to think about. I would love for elite institutions to measure their success not only by their competition winners and internationally acclaimed soloists but also by the impact musicians make in their communities, and the joy and satisfaction graduates find in less traditionally 'acclaimed' careers. Recent times have also seen a profound cultural shift in the way women are treated in professional contexts, with the 'MeToo' movement bringing global awareness to the subtle and not-so-subtle ways in which women are overlooked or mistreated in workplaces. Within the musical community, a tidal wave of allegations over the last decade or so has shone a light on the inappropriate conduct which has been rife in our profession for so long. Across the RCM community, there is a real need for more transparent and compassionate communication, as well as greater accountability in response to failures of leadership and abuses of power.

Maxine Smith (Receptionist): To continue to support the students, staff, and colleagues with a personal touch.

Mengyang Pan (Piano professor, Module Leader and Lecturer, and Student Advisor): In addition to dedicating myself to my one-on-one students and classes, I would like to continue representing the RCM and its ethos internationally. I also aim to contribute to the College by sharing what I learn from my experience abroad.

Rieko Makita (Constant and Kit Lambert Junior Fellow & Artistic Diploma student (Solo Piano)): The RCM is making an effort to encourage and foster cultural diversity in classical music. For my fellowship projects, I have programmed and commissioned Japanese and Australian composers (as I am Japanese-Australian) to hopefully inspire others to play something of their cultural background. I hope the RCM continues its effort to support musicians of all backgrounds to discover their unique musical identity.

Where to from here?

These reflections from some members of our RCM community reveal just a few of the many views, experiences, opportunities, and challenges within the conservatoire ecosystem. We see how the conservatoire works well, with contributors highlighting principles such as collaboration, nurturing, commitment, vibrancy, camaraderie, care, inspiration, artistic freedom, and personal growth. We see aspirations for more innovation and research, for dialogue about whose responsibility it is to build and sustain a sense of community, and for more creative collaboration across various parts of the institution. And we also see areas where change needs to be forthcoming, not least in terms of addressing and preventing abuses of power and in ensuring that our conservatoire is inclusive and diverse. These topics are just some of those unpacked in the chapters that follow, as we seek to explore and critique the contemporary conservatoire.

Colin Lawson
Diana Salazar
Rosie Perkins
London, April 2024

Bibliography

Small, Christopher. *Musicking: The Meanings of Performing and Listening*. Wesleyan University Press, 1998.

Note

1 Small, *Musicking*, 9.

PART I

Rethinking conservatoire identities and values

1

INTRODUCTION

Tracing conservatoire values past, present, and future

Colin Lawson

What is a conservatoire?

In the international field of higher education, conservatoires are small and highly special-ised players; yet, despite their size, they carry significant responsibility for shaping the future of the performing arts. As selective institutions, their core purpose is to identify and develop outstanding artists who will proceed to make their mark on the profession at local, national, and international levels. However, external and mainstream attitudes towards the conservatoire usually reflect the mistrust of this specialist environment.[1] Conservatoires are often regarded as elusive, elitist, or old-fashioned. Furthermore, recent discourses, such as the spotlight on access and representation in classical music, amplify questions about the relevance and contribution of conservatoires in modern society. Conservation of tradition is nowadays part of a much wider educational context, and thus the label itself is fundamen-tally unhelpful and somewhat misleading.

Although a traditional and narrow view of the one-to-one lesson as the defining feature of conservatoire education persists, the environment in which learners develop and grow as artists is much more complex than is generally recognised. In investigating conservatoire identities and values, perspectives reflecting viewpoints from academia, professional musi-cians, industry, and the student and graduate community seem critical in addressing such topics as arts practice, music pedagogy, music sociology, digital culture, inclusion, employ-ability, entrepreneurship, performance science, and material culture. The conservatoire's unique learning culture is defined not simply by its intensity or teaching models but also by the way in which these complex (and at times extra-musical) parameters intersect with and influence each other.

Knowing and doing

Part of the misunderstanding surrounding conservatoire culture has its roots as far back in history as Boethius during the early years of the sixth century. He entrenched a view of music as *musica speculativa* (theory, as part of mathematics) versus *musica practica*

DOI: 10.4324/9781003281573-2

(the performance of music, generally linked with religious ceremonies). In *De institutione musica,* he declared:

> Now, it should be known that he is not called a musician who performs only with his hands, but he is truly a musician who knows naturally how to discuss music and to eluci-date its meaning with pure reason . . . for every art and every discipline considers reason inherently more honourable than skill which is practised with the hand and labour of an artisan. For it is much better to know what someone does than to do what one learns from another.[2]

Thus, the scene was set for the theory versus practice bifurcation, which was to linger for many centuries afterwards.

Subsequent evidence consistently signals the disjuncture between the concepts of music and musical performance. The fourth Earl of Chesterfield (1694–1773), for example, remarked:

> If you love music, hear it: go to operas, concerts and pay fiddlers to play to you; but I insist upon your neither piping nor fiddling yourself. It puts a gentleman in a very frivo-lous, contemptible light. . . . Few things would mortify me more, than to see you bearing a part in a concert, with a fiddle under your chin, or a pipe in your mouth.[3]

The challenge of healing the breech between knowing and doing has been addressed in dif-ferent ways at various times, though in certain ways, the traditional divide between univer-sity and conservatoire around the world has nowadays become somewhat blurred.

The Paris Conservatoire: reach and influence

All modern conservatoires originated from the radical developments initiated during the foundation of the Paris Conservatoire in 1795 in the wake of the French Revolution. There were of course many earlier teaching models, which have been documented in some detail, whether based in church, at court, via guilds and apprenticeships, or the Italian *ospedali*. It is especially revealing that a contemporary curriculum from outside France might in other circumstances have set nineteenth-century music education on a rather different course altogether. In 1800, Mozart's clarinettist Anton Stadler compiled a 50-page document, which was in effect a response to 16 questions contained in a letter (now lost) by Count Georg Festetics, the answers to which were to serve as the basis for a music school in Hungary on the count's estate at Keszthely on what is now Lake Balaton. Classes, rooms, staffing, grades, levels, textbooks, musical aesthetics, repertoires, and library resources were all matters for consideration. Recognising three aspects of music – theory, perfor-mance, and composition – Stadler's ambitious six-year curriculum supplemented practical matters with the observation that anyone wanting to understand music must acquire a broad knowledge of the world and mathematics, poetry, rhetoric, and several languages. All students would be required to participate in singing, piano, organ or thorough bass, violin, and wind instruments.[4] The sheer breadth of this enlightenment vision gave way to the promotion across Europe of more specialist activity that was accessible to a wider cross-section of society.

The *Conservatoire de Musique* in Paris was founded on the new democratic principle of free education for the qualified, irrespective of social status. Its development was the result of careful planning, artistic vision, and astute political action. Members of staff were to serve both as performers and teachers; students of both sexes, admitted between the ages of 8–13, were to be chosen from each geographical area by means of competitive examination. There would be prizes at the end of each school year, with regular examinations. Indeed, many features of institutional life today were set in train that continue even now to be the subject of vigorous debate. The institutional model contributed in so many ways to the development of models of training, technique, standards, repertoire, and the position of the conservatoire more generally in cultural life and society. The national festivals, for which the Conservatoire initially provided the music, were mass propaganda on a hitherto unknown scale. Everyone was expected to participate, including artists, writers, poets, painters, and musicians. As Boris Schwarz has remarked, 'Torn from the shelter of the court, the chapels and the aristocratic salons, musicians were faced with a mass of impassioned, undisciplined and largely uneducated humanity.'[5]

As opera and concert life became re-established, Conservatoire students began to set new performing standards in orchestral music. Already in 1800, the critic of the *Décade philosophique* could write: 'A numerous orchestra, consisting entirely of young people, performed with unity, precision and firmness, using intelligence and discretion in the accompaniments, which is even more difficult.'[6] Later, especially under the direction of the violinist François Habeneck, the unified and disciplined bowing of the string players won particular praise. The role of the Conservatoire in performances of Beethoven was a celebrated part of its early history. After the 'Eroica' Symphony was played in 1811, a reviewer in the *Courier de l'Europe et des spectacles* showed an equal measure of understanding and unease:

> The Symphony in E flat . . . is the most beautiful [Beethoven] has composed, aside from a few harsh Germanisms, which he used by force of habit. All the rest offers a sensible and correct plan, though filled with vehemence; graceful episodes are artfully connected with the principal ideas, and his singing phrases have a freshness of colouring quite their own.[7]

The Conservatoire was the first truly modern institution for music education, free from charitable aims and with an entirely secular, indeed, anti-clerical background. In view of the later history of the sector as a whole, it is significant that in his youth, Berlioz encountered a conservatism that is not unfamiliar within institutional environments, which blighted his difficult relationship with the Director Cherubini. Yet, teaching was taken very seriously, and so the profession as a whole was elevated to a position of unprecedented dignity and importance; the *professeur de musique*, formerly a call-boy for the nobleman, became a pillar of musical culture and tradition.[8] But, as with many such situations, not everything was as rigorous as the syllabus might imply. In 1798, the 23-year old François-Adrien Boieldieu from Rouen was appointed to the piano faculty and was described in the following way by one of his pupils, François-Joseph Fétis:

> Too occupied with his career as a dramatic composer to take interest in lessons in instrumental technique, Boieldieu was a rather bad piano teacher; but his conversation was

studded with very fine remarks on his art, full of interest for his students and not without profit for their studies.[9]

The question still resonates today as to whether an outstanding performer is automatically an outstanding teacher.

In the eighteenth century, an understanding of musical language had been an integral part of learning an instrument, but the Conservatoire published tutors that replaced verbal description with pictorial elements. The production of faculty treatises, offering systematic courses of technical and interpretative instruction for aspiring professionals, incorporated studies and exercises for advanced players. But this was at the expense of philosophy about musical rhetoric and the communication of emotion, a source of later criticism of the conservatoire model.

Institutions were bound to encourage competition, and virtuosity was an element that could easily be encouraged and measured. The instrumental tutors published by the Conservatoire offer considerable insight into technical practices of the period and soon were being used throughout Europe. By 1805, the bassoon, cello, clarinet, flute, piano, and violin had newly written manuals for them. Jean-Louis Adam's *Méthode de Piano* is significant for its advice on pedalling and for redefining the trill as a structural rather than ornamental device. In 1826, the Méthode was translated into German by Beethoven's pupil, Carl Czerny. For the violin, the Conservatoire published a multi-authored work by Baillot, Rode, and Kreutzer, which set out the performer's chief expressive means as sound quality, movement, style, taste, genius of execution, and precision. It is revealing that the flexibility of tempo was regarded as an essential musical effect, especially as this remains one of the most difficult aspects of performance to describe in words or notation.

On the Conservatoire syllabus, there was of course no opportunity to study the whole of worldly wisdom, as envisaged by Anton Stadler. In view of the immense global influence of the Paris Conservatoire wherever Western art music is learnt and taught, it is worth recalling here the serious reservations about the Paris model expressed by Nikolaus Harnoncourt.[10] He argued some 30 years ago that developments in France after the Revolution marked the beginning of a shift of music's position as one of life's moving forces to a mere adornment. From the Middle Ages, music had been one of the foundations of cultural life, and the understanding of it formed part of a general education. Undoubtedly, Harnoncourt's writings make a radical contribution to any debate about conservatoire values, past, present, and future.

Dissemination of the model

Importantly, the concept of a state conservatoire for music soon spread throughout Europe, to Prague (1811), Graz (1815), and Vienna (1817), as well as London's Royal Academy of Music (RAM, 1822). The Regio Conservatorio in Milan was established in 1824, with a curriculum that modified that of Paris and with students recruited partly on a fee-paying basis and partly by state subvention. Somewhat later, the conservatory at Leipzig proved a huge influence from its inception in 1843, with a staff that included Mendelssohn and Schumann. Other German cities soon followed suit, and there were later foundations in Italy, Russia, and the United States, as well as further developments in Britain.

Leipzig pointedly illustrated the advantages and disadvantages of the conservatoire model. It emerged from an environment in which the fascination with music-making as a domestic activity had led to a burgeoning of public, semi-private, and fully private music schools operating under varying standards, as well as large numbers of poorly trained private teachers taking advantage of the middle classes. In an environment in which the piano reigned supreme, the conservatoire existed in a symbiotic relationship with the Gewandhaus orchestra; the latter would provide teachers and exposure to high-level concert life, while the former would provide new players when members left or retired. Mendelssohn's educational vision was founded upon the idea that group teaching would provide advantages over one-to-one lessons; the initial prospectus claimed that through the participation of several students on the same elements of learning and the same studies, a genuine musical sense would be awakened among the students, which would keep them fresh, motivate them to be diligent and competitive, and protect them from insularity. Revealingly, after Schumann had met his first pupils, his wife Clara wrote in her *Tagebuch* that she had no idea how one could teach six students at once.

Mendelssohn promoted an idealistic vision of contextual study, with a three-year theory course embracing harmony, advanced counterpoint, formal analysis, instrumentation, score-reading, and musical direction, together with Italian language for singers. All students were expected to take lessons in figured bass, piano, and singing; there were also lectures in aesthetics, acoustics, and repertory old and new. It seems that Mendelssohn soon realised that the standard of the new cohort was not what he might have hoped for and that their needs were more basic than he had imagined. An over-full curriculum led to students studying as many as 60 hours a week, with a corresponding lack of discipline. By the mid-1860s, auditions had become a meaningless formality, as greater commercialisation became an imperative. Twenty years later, the conservatory was truly international, with just under half the 406 students from outside Germany and the cohort roughly equally balanced in terms of gender. A consistent problem familiar from later conservatoire models was the retention of high-profile staff; there were early resignations from Schumann, Joachim, and Mendelssohn himself.[11] The early Leipzig history is relevant in today's climate; group teaching is attracting a higher profile, many conservatoires have adopted more rigorous theoretical training, and the reliance on the profession for its workforce has the capacity to make staff retention more difficult.

Very few published articles in English bear witness to the great pedagogical traditions within the conservatories of St. Petersburg (founded, 1862) and Moscow (1866). However, the plethora of talented Russian performers and composers has ensured a wide circulation of tales relating to friction between brilliant students and the establishment.[12] In promoting the St. Petersburg Conservatory, Anton Rubinstein argued that the lack of a music profession in Russia was a consequence of the failure of musicians to persuade the state to give music the *civic status of artist.*

Rubinstein's attack on Russia's dilettantes was met by the Balakirev circle with taunts of 'German pedantry' and support for the supposed creativity and originality of Russian 'amateur' composers and performers. Until the abolition of serfdom in 1861, 'working musicians were largely serfs, former serfs, or foreigners.' Highly skilled aristocrats participated in music-making but only as amateurs; there was in fact literally no way to accommodate the professional musician in Russia's estate-based social hierarchy.[13] A respectable social status (with pension rights and state service) came only at the beginning of the twentieth century. Although women students outnumbered men, their interest in music was routinely disparaged by cultural critics, even though many did in fact pursue professional (and semi-professional) careers. A valuable insider's view of Russian ideas and teaching practice is contained in *The Art of Piano Playing* by Heinrich Neuhaus (1888–1964), who had studied in Berlin and Vienna and was Director of the Moscow Conservatory between 1934 and 1937. His declared method was to use:

> [E]very means to arouse [a student's] professional ambition: to be equal to the best; developing the imagination by the use of apt metaphor, poetic similes, by analogy with natural phenomena or events in life, particularly spiritual or emotional. It means supplementing and interpreting musical language; using every means to develop a love of other forms of art, particularly poetry, painting and architecture, and, most important of all, instilling a feeling for the ethical dignity of the artist, notably obligations, responsibilities and rights.[14]

With this progressive agenda, he followed Rubinstein's emphasis on musical characterisation as being the highest achievement of pedagogical thinking and practice. A passionate advocate of class teaching, Neuhaus considers a great failing of the system is that overloaded student schedules permit them only rarely to listen to each other, in laboratory conditions.

Founding of the Royal College of Music

A huge number of European conservatoires came into being during the latter half of the nineteenth century, each with its own funding and curriculum models.[15] For the purposes of the present volume, the fortunes of the Royal Academy of Music (RAM) are especially relevant. Following earlier unsuccessful schemes, the RAM opened in 1823 and was awarded a Royal Charter in 1830, 'more a compliment to its aristocratic supporters than testimony to its effectiveness.'[16] Although it trained such significant musicians as William Sterndale Bennett and Arthur Sullivan, finances were insecure, there was no formal curriculum, and it was roundly criticised in a celebrated 1866 Royal Society of Arts report. From that point, student numbers increased, and a more confident RAM resisted attempts at a merger with the National Training School for Music:

> In the subsequent fundraising campaign for the Royal College of Music (RCM), the RAM mounted a spirited defence of its position while denying any necessity for the college's foundation; only with the establishment of the Associated Board of the Royal Schools of Music (1889) to hold joint music exams did friendly rivalry replace bitter resentment.[17]

At a meeting on 28 February 1882, the then Prince of Wales (later King Edward VII) laid out his plans for the foundation of the RCM on a site held by the Commissioners of the Great Exhibition of 1851. He launched a national fundraising campaign for scholarships, some of which would also cover living costs. This was precipitated by the government refusal of treasury funding to establish the college, despite ever-increasing pressures to provide systematic training for British composers and performers. He observed that the additional presence of fee-paying students would ensure a union of different classes in a common and elevating pursuit, the best way of binding in one tie of common enthusiasm the different grades of society, varying alike in wealth and social influence. The Prince of Wales aspired for the RCM to:

> [B]e to England what the Berlin Conservatoire is to Germany, what the Paris Conservatoire is to France, or the Vienna Conservatoire to Austria – the recognised . . . head of the musical world. . . . There is [currently] no centre for music to which English musicians may resort with confidence, counsel and inspiration.[18]

Thus, the RCM's founding vision may be said to foreground access, advocacy, and excellence.

In its early years, the RCM was given enormous impetus by gifts of several important collections of historical material (including autographs of major works) and instruments, notably by George Donaldson in 1894. The present imposing building was opened in that year, sponsored by the Leeds industrialist Samson Fox; it already reflected the RCM's high-quality training, the musical distinction of its members, and an already established national standing. It is telling that, in relation to the foundation of the RCM in 1883, London University Registrar's Collection (RC4/18) has a bundle of correspondence from senior university figures protesting against the RCM's charter's provision for awarding degrees, a highly unusual feature for such an institution. Though no disquiet was registered officially, background communications give a sense of the indignation that was felt by the universities. Cambridge Professor of Surgery G. M. Humphry, seemingly a member of the Council of Senate, indicated to the London Vice Chancellor that he was discussing the matter with his Cambridge counterpart, arguing that 'representation from the several universities would have weight in the matter.'[19] Ironically, the RCM made only limited use of its degree-awarding powers after a further half-century had elapsed, establishing its own BMus only in 1995. Academic study and performance have continued their multifaceted relationship ever since, extending into today's debates about the nature of 'artistic research' (see e.g., Chapter 10).

David Wright's recently published *The Royal College of Music and its Contexts: An Artistic and Social History* (Cambridge, 2020) offers a critical narrative of how successive directors grappled in changing external environments with the central issues of curriculum, funding, the estate, and (increasingly) accountability. Whatever the immediate challenges, a list of alumni bears witness to the RCM's enormous influence throughout its existence; some of the earliest students included Samuel Coleridge Taylor, Holst, Vaughan Williams, and Ireland, to be followed by such seminal figures as Britten, Tippett, Colin Davis, Gwyneth Jones, Elisabeth Lutyens, Elizabeth Maconchy, Thea King, Joan Sutherland, Andrew Lloyd Webber, and Mark-Anthony Turnage. Under the leadership of the earliest directors George Grove, Hubert Parry, and Hugh Allen, the RCM, in common with other British conservatoires, focused on the core Classical and Romantic repertories as played in essentially nineteenth-century performance traditions. As David Wright observes, the adherence to a received musical tradition constrained much interest in repertories of other types and helps explain the prominence in the UK of university-trained musicians in pioneering historical performance projects and in avant-garde programming.

Global competition continued to gather momentum outside Europe, notably in the United States, with Baltimore's Peabody Conservatory (1857) and the New England Conservatory in Boston a decade later. By the 1920s, Eastman, Curtis, and Juilliard had been established. Other parts of the world were already assuming a significant presence, not least East Asia and Australasia.

The balance of theory and practice

For much of the period before 1945, formal and informal musical training existed side by side. Pupils often studied privately with teachers outside their institutions or took only part of the curriculum on offer, sometimes over relatively short periods. At the RCM, a succession of high-profile masterclasses and lectures (sometimes on subjects beyond music) revolutionised the curriculum in the 1960s, as early steps were taken towards providing guidance and career support for a lifetime in professional music. David Wright's account of this period reveals the reality of the university/conservatoire binary divide. When RCM alumnus Thurston Dart was appointed King Edward Professor at King's College London, he immediately set about creating a different sort of musical degree, which greatly reduced the emphasis on vocational training and opened out the subject to a wide range of intellectual, critical, and historical enquiry. Dart sought 'to educate *through* music, rather than in it', so as to 'quicken the perceptions, stretch the mind, and temper the judgment.'[20] Only by means of various compromises were the conservatoires able to continue to teach this London BMus degree. Dart subscribed firmly to the principle that only universities awarded degrees, while 'professional teaching institutions' (Dart's term for music colleges) awarded diplomas. Dart's successor at King's, Howard Mayer Brown, explained: 'For university students, learning to talk and write intelligently and critically about music is an activity that is central to their training, and that distinguishes it from study at music college.'[21]

As RCM Director from 1960 to 1974, Keith Falkner had to grapple with a worsening financial situation and a serious threat to independence; *Making Musicians: A Report to the Calouste Gulbenkian Foundation* (London: Calouste Gulbenkian Foundation, 1965) recommended the amalgamation of RCM, RAM, and Trinity College of Music. A quarter of a century later, the Review led by Lord Gowrie was again to recommend the joining together of RAM and RCM, which the College fiercely and successfully resisted. More positively, as David Wright observes, the government's newfound enthusiasm for less-traditional higher education institutions (HEIs) reflected its perception that the practical and vocational orientation of polytechnics and colleges made them more cost effective and so 'more in tune with the thinking of a managerial government than were the traditional scholarly citadels of unproductive, useless learning'.[22]

If UK conservatoires have manifestly been on an upward trajectory ever since, the mission of university music departments has sometimes maintained a certain awkwardness in relation to performance, even when it seemingly occupied a central role in the curriculum. For example, in an Oxford prospectus from the early years of the twenty-first century, emphasis is placed on the theoretical elements of music, incorporating some optional performance training. While performance is included within the aims and outcomes, it is listed after historical, analytical, and critical skills. The undergraduate syllabus suggests that:

A clear division between intellectual and practical skills in the domain of music may be misleading, since many so-called practical skills have a pronounced intellectual dimension, as for example interpretative and compositional skills. These by definition are forms of *non-verbal* discourse, but rich in intellectual content.[23]

The intoxicating mixture of elements in today's curricula has radically inflected the discourse.

The Royal College of Music: a global leader

The aims and objectives of the RCM remain closely descended from the ideals of its founders. In particular, its global leadership and sharing of expertise build on the international achievements of Keith Falkner, who began a series of exchanges with European conservatoires, while closely involving the RCM in the Association of European Conservatoires, a network initiated in 1953. Janet Ritterman (Director, 1993–2005) was hugely influential in bringing the RCM's governance structures and strategic management into line with the formal expectations of UK higher education. The RCM's current vision statement provides a useful context for the panorama of today's activity:

> The Royal College of Music provides music education and professional training at the highest international level, through commitment to the transformative power of music and its own founding principles of excellence, advocacy, and access. . . . It embraces the ideals of an inclusive, open, and just society, supporting students from diverse social, economic, and ethnic backgrounds. . . . A core curriculum blending theory and practice fosters critical appreciation and understanding of music as an art and a science, offering a transformative, holistic education, tailored to individual needs.[24]

Critical engagement with the music profession ensures that alumni from as many as 60 nationalities are readily employable; a vibrant research environment extends way beyond music, with the Library and Museum offering an opportunity to learn from the past that is fully integrated into the curriculum.

Inside the contemporary conservatoire

This volume applies a novel, multidisciplinary approach to investigating and mapping the artistic ecology of the conservatoire. The authors aim to reveal previously unseen layers of the complex environment in which learners develop and grow as artists. The volume is the first to adopt a comprehensive and multidimensional approach to examining the work of conservatoires today. Uniquely, it situates conservatoire learning and teaching practices in a dynamic environment that is informed by a diverse range of internal and external voices and expertise. This shift from an exclusively student-centred music education focus towards a broader ecological approach recognises that today's conservatoires are much more than sites of advanced musical performance training and serve not just their students but wider society. There is a strong argument that the focus on a monotechnic institution offers a novel route for understanding the issues faced by all HEIs providing specialist music education. Too often, becoming 'multidisciplinary' is presented as the twenty-first -century solution for innovating the conservatoire model. Yet, this approach fails to recognise the disciplinary cultures that persist within multidisciplinary institutions and the fact that cross-disciplinary experiences for students in such institutions are often located at the periphery of their 'core' studies. Indeed, the RCM has a distinctive, multidimensional approach to the study of music. Performance, composition, performance science, historical performance, musicology, composition for screen, music education, and artistic research sit side-by-side in RCM's programmes. At the nexus of these specialisms lies a rich seam for exploring what the study of music might become in the future. At the same time, examples from a monotechnic institution can help to amplify the urgency for a radical change in conservatoires to meet the needs of today's society. Thus, the RCM can serve as an ideal case study to illuminate the challenges and potential of classical music in contemporary higher education.

The following chapters offer a critically informed glimpse into the workings of the contemporary conservatoire in the digital age. They are clustered around three main themes: 1. Rethinking conservatoire identities and values; 2. Evolving the learning and teaching of music in a conservatoire; and 3. Conservatoires of the future. Between each chapter, a range of stakeholders offer their personal perspectives on the preceding chapter's material, as well as their perceptions of the conservatoire's past, present, and/or future. This variety of individual voices illuminates a diverse range of views on many of the topics touched upon within this chapter. Despite many external challenges in today's society, the conservatoire sector is undoubtedly in rude health, while at the same time demonstrating a variety of practices across the world. It remains to be asked: where do we go from here, within an exciting new world in which the communication of our art offers possibilities that would have been unthinkable in earlier times?

Bibliography

Breen, Edward. *Thurston Dart and the New Faculty of Music at King's College, London: A 50th Anniversary Biography*. London: King's College, 2015.

Brown, Howard Mayer. 'The study of music at university. 9'. *The Musical Times* 115, no. 1572 (February 1974): 123. https://doi.org/10.2307/954972.

Caizley, Scott. 'The conservatoire crisis: Suggestions from Oxbridge'. *Higher Education Policy Institute*, May 22, 2019. www.hepi.ac.uk/2019/05/22/the-conservatoire-crisis-is-oxbridge-a-model-for-widening-participation/#:~:text=A%20recommendation%20could%20be%20for,students%20to%20the%20musical%20world.

Dobreé, Bonamy, ed. *The Letters of Philip Dormer Stanhope, 4th Earl of Chesterfield. Vol. 4: Letter 1633*. London: Eyre & Spottiswoode, 1932.

Fenlon, Iain, ed. *Studies in Medieval and Early Modern Music. Vol. 18: Early Music History*. Cambridge University Press, 1981.

Fétis, François-Joseph. *Biographie universelle des musiciens*. 2nd ed. Vol. II. Paris: Didot Frères, 1860.

Harnoncourt, Nikolaus. *Musik als Klangrede*. Kassel: Bärenreiter, 1982. Translated by K. A. Leibovitch as *Baroque Music Today: Music as Speech*. London: Christopher Helm, 1988.

Lawson, Colin, and Robin Stowell, eds. *The Cambridge History of Musical Performance*. Cambridge University Press, 2012.

Lawson, Colin, and Robin Stowell, eds. *The Cambridge Encyclopedia of Historical Performance in Music*. Cambridge University Press, 2018.

Morgan, Kenneth O. *The People's Peace: Britain Since 1945*. 3rd ed. Oxford University Press, 2001.

Neuhaus, Heinrich. *Ob iskusstve fortepianoy igrï* (Moscow, 1958). Translated by K. A. Leibovitch as *The Art of Piano Playing*, 20–22. London: Barrie & Jenkins, 1973.

Pierre, Constant. *Le Conservatoire nationale de musique et de déclamation*. Paris: Imprimerie nationale, 1900.

Poulin, Pamela L. 'A view of eighteenth-century musical life and training: Anton Stadler's "Musick plan"'. *Music and Letters* 71, no. 2 (1990): 215–24. https://doi.org/10.1093/ml/71.2.215.

Prod'homme, Jacques-Gabriel. *Les Symphonies de Beethoven*. Paris: Libraire Delagrave, 1906.

Royal College of Music. *RCM Strategic Plan 2017–27*. Accessed November 2024. https://www.rcm. ac.uk/media/strategicplan22.pdf

Sargeant, Lynn. 'A new class of people: The conservatoire and musical professionalization in Russia, 1861–1917'. *Music and Letters* 85, no. 1 (February 1, 2004): 41–61. https://doi.org/10.1093/ ml/85.1.41.

Schwarz, Boris. *French Instrumental Music Between the Revolutions (1789–1830)*. New York: Da Capo Press, 1987.

Weber, William, Denis Arnold, Cynthia M. Gessele, Peter Cahn, Robert W. Oldani, and Janet Ritterman. 'Conservatories'. In *Grove Music Online*. Vol. 1. Oxford University Press, 2001. https://doi. org/10.1093/gmo/9781561592630.article.41225.

Wilson, Elizabeth A. M. *Mstislav Rostropovich: Cellist, Teacher, Legend*. London: Faber, 2007.

Wright, David. 'Grove's role in the founding of the RCM'. In *George Grove, Music and Victorian Culture*, edited by Michael Musgrave, 219–44. London: Palgrave, 2003.

Wright, David. 'Royal Academy of Music (London)'. In *The Cambridge Encyclopedia of Historical Performance in Music*, edited by Colin Lawson and Robin Stowell, 554. Cambridge University Press, 2018.

Wright, David C. H. *The Royal College of Music and Its Contexts: An Artistic and Social History*. Cambridge: Cambridge University Press, 2020.

PERSPECTIVE: CHAPTER 1

James Gandre

Introduction

I am an educator and musician with a deep commitment to students and the development of American conservatory learning. I returned to Manhattan School of Music (MSM) to assume the presidency in 2013, having served the School previously for 15 years (1985–2000), concluding that first phase of my time at MSM as Dean of Enrollment and Alumni. In 2000, I became Dean of Chicago College of Performing Arts at Roosevelt University, where I went on to ultimately serve as Provost and Executive Vice President.

I have broad knowledge of the history of the American conservatory, the subject of my doctoral dissertation: *And Then There Were Seven: An Historical Case Study of the Seven Independent Conservatories of Music that Survived the 20th Century*. I have also written about conservatories in *Music in American Life: An Encyclopedia of the Songs, Styles, Stars, and Stories that Shaped Our Culture* (ABC-CLIO, 2013) and in the *2014 Musical America Directory*.

As a performer, I have appeared as a tenor soloist with the Cleveland Orchestra, London Classical Players, Philharmonia Baroque, and members of the San Francisco Symphony. My professional choral engagements include more than 175 performances with the New York Philharmonic, Aix-en-Provence Festival, Metropolitan Opera Orchestra, Royal Concertgebouw, Israel Philharmonic, Warsaw Symphony, and San Francisco Symphony. I have appeared on more than 20 commercial recordings and on NBC's *The Today Show*, PBS' *Live from Lincoln Center*, ABC, and CBS. In these performances, I have worked under such conductors as Leonard Bernstein, Zubin Mehta, Sir Colin Davis, James Levine, Mstislav Rostropovich, Riccardo Chailly, Christopher Hogwood, and Roger Norrington.

Perspectives

The history of American conservatories begins with the founding and opening of four conservatories in 1867: New England Conservatory of Music (Boston), Boston Conservatory, Cincinnati Conservatory of Music (Ohio), and Chicago Musical College. (Note: Peabody Conservatory was founded in 1857 but did not begin operations until 1868.) Throughout

DOI: 10.4324/9781003281573-3

America's history, there have been more than 80 independent (private) conservatories of music. Only six independent American conservatories survived the twentieth century and are still in operation – Cleveland Institute of Music, Curtis Institute of Music, The Juilliard School, Manhattan School of Music, New England Conservatory of Music, and San Francisco Conservatory of Music. A seventh, the Colburn School (Los Angeles), after a long history as a community music school that was part of the University of Southern California, became an independent, degree-granting institution in 2004. Interestingly, five of these seven independent American conservatories were founded during a seven-year period between 1917 and 1924.

During the decades that followed the founding of those first four American conservatories, the institutions that did and did not survive as independent institutions became more and more like their European counterparts, growing greatly in stature and excellence just as classical music in America greatly grew in stature and excellence.[25] Indeed, like their European counterparts, a disproportionate number of great American performers were educated in independent conservatories as opposed to music schools within larger institutions. For example, if one looks at the top 20 orchestras in the United States, the vast majority of members were educated at one of the American independent conservatories. European tradition was at the heart of these conservatories, and only in the last two to three decades have American conservatories, again like their European counterparts, begun to increasingly expand their curricula and other offerings beyond the traditional classical music canon.

One critically differentiating distinction was inherent from the beginning of these institutions that separated the financial models on these two continents: unlike European institutions, independent conservatories in the United States did not directly receive any ongoing, annual government support, while European conservatories relied primarily or very heavily on government funding.

Instead, American conservatories relied primarily on two primary sources of income: student tuition and philanthropy (either gifts given and expended in their entirety annually or given as restricted endowment gifts in perpetuity, for which only earned interest upon the principal gift would be expended annually). Consequently, due to the high cost of music education and lack of ongoing government support, most of these conservatories were not financially sustainable, resulting in three primary outcomes: some schools ceased operations (e.g., Chicago's American Conservatory of Music, New York College of Music, and New York Conservatory); some become local community (non-degree-granting) music schools (e.g., Wisconsin Conservatory of Music is now a community music school); and, finally, some merged with larger institutions (e.g., Cincinnati Conservatory merged with Cincinnati College of Music and is now part of the University of Cincinnati; Chicago Musical College merged with Roosevelt University; and the Boston Conservatory merged with Berklee College of Music).

In tandem with this different funding model of tuition-based revenue came an inherently different overseeing or governing structure. In America, independent colleges and universities, including conservatories, are governed by a Board of Trustees whose members constitute the governing body of the institution who are both volunteers for and philanthropists to the institutions they serve. As a consequence, each Trustee is required to donate annually to their institution. As of this writing, the annual minimum contribution for Trustees at five of the seven conservatories is $25,000, with most members giving more than the minimum. Additionally, when there is a major Board-authorized fundraising campaign, it is expected that each Trustee will give an additional gift beyond their regular contribution to the campaign.

Two of the seven independent conservatories are outliers to the tuition/philanthropy model seen at most independent colleges and universities in the United States. Curtis and Colburn both received initial, permanent endowed funding from their original benefactors/founders (Mary Louise Curtis Bok and Richard Colburn), providing sufficient financial underpinning to be tuition-free for all students (policies that continue today, due to the original generosity of their founders and those donors who believed in their mission). The other five conservatories have operated like nearly all other independent American institutions of higher education, relying primarily on tuition, with supplementary donated monies to fund annual operational budgets. (Juilliard did begin as a tuition-free institution, charging tuition later as it moved to a new, larger location and expanded its programmes after merging in 1926 with the Institute of Musical Arts of the City of New York, which was founded in 1905.)[26]

Indeed, today, the majority of revenue for four of the seven independent American conservatories still comes primarily from tuition. The tuition 'sticker price' of these four, plus The Juilliard School, ranges from $40,000 to $57,000 per year. The 'discount rate' at these five institutions (the percentage of scholarship funding an average student receives each year) ranges from 41% to approximately 65%.

Although during the past 30-plus years, these seven American independent conservatories have embraced more career-readiness and technology-preparedness for their students, they remain to this day rooted in the traditions of the European classical model. Indeed, three of these institutions offer classical music as their only major. In addition, jazz is offered as a major at the other four, and, of those four, musical theatre is offered at one, music technology and gaming composition are offered at another, and dance and theatre at yet another. Perhaps the most impressive and significant change to these institutions has occurred during the last five years, during which there has been a significant change in repertoire programming in American conservatories, based on a growing commitment to bringing to the fore under-represented peoples and cultures. Additionally, there has been a focus on more inclusive and diverse hiring practices. All of these developments have expanded the experiences and broadened the learning of the students at these institutions and prepared them for a changing marketplace of musical ideas and in performance. Interestingly, conservatories in Europe and America have long followed and responded to the professional performance world. Perhaps for the first time in history, conservatories are leading change writ large in the classical music world. Ideally, the conservatories of today will continue to innovate and serve as a testing ground for change in the musical world, aiding professional organisations as they change to a world that embraces and relishes a broader, more inclusive musical realm.

Summary

In total, independent American conservatories once numbered more than 80, but merely 7 have survived as independently functioning institutions of higher education, due to the high cost of operating such institutions in tandem with at times insufficient financial foundations of tuition and philanthropy. Although most of the seven survivors have expanded their degree offerings beyond classical music, including jazz, dance, theatre, musical theatre, and gaming composition, classical music is still the backbone of student enrolment in these conservatories.

At present, conservatories in the Western hemisphere are undergoing the most rapid change in their collective histories, not only because of the changing landscape in society and consequently the performance world but also because of ongoing and changing financial pressures. The pressures to adhere to traditions of the past, while also moving beyond those long-held traditions to incorporate a more diverse and inclusive environment musically and socially, as well as continuing to keep up with technological and performance practice standards, can be challenging for these relatively small schools. Nevertheless, these institutions, like the rest of society, must change and adapt to the greater society in which they operate, or they risk irrelevance and anachronism. However, as Lawson notes in his introduction, 'the conservatoire sector is undoubtedly in rude health', and I posit that most if not all conservatories are ready to tackle the newest challenges for their institutions, the musical art forms they offer, and for the greater society in which they operate.

Bibliography

Gandre, James. *And Then There Were Seven: An Historical Case Study of the Seven Independent American Conservatories that Survived the Twentieth Century.* Lincoln: University of Nebraska, 2001. https://digitalcommons.unl.edu/dissertations/AAI3028657/.
Olmstead, Andrea. *Juilliard: A History.* Urbana: University of Illinois Press, 1999.

Chapter and Perspective Notes

1 See for example Caizley, 'The conservatoire crisis: Suggestions from Oxbridge'.
2 Fenlon, *Studies in Medieval and Early Modern Music*, 69.
3 Lawson and Stowell, *The Cambridge History of Musical Performance*, 169.
4 Poulin, 'A view of eighteenth-century musical life and training', 215–24.
5 Schwarz, *French Instrumental Music Between the Revolutions (1789–1830)*, 3–9.
6 Cited in Pierre, *Le Conservatoire Nationale de Musique et de Déclamation*, 461.
7 Cited in Prod'homme, *Les Symphonies de Beethoven*, 121.
8 Schwarz, *French Instrumental Music Between the Revolutions (1789–1830)*, 44.
9 Fétis, *Biographie Universelle Des Musiciens*, 3.
10 Harnoncourt, *Musik als Klangrede*.
11 For further discussion of the Leipzig, St. Petersburg, and Moscow conservatories, see Lawson and Stowell, *The Cambridge Encyclopedia of Historical Performance in Music*, 151–60.
12 For example Rostropovich failed his first-year exams in Moscow because he had somehow 'overlooked the fact that the conservatoire course involved other disciplines such as harmony, history and analysis and the obligatory political curriculum'; see Wilson, *Mstislav Rostropovich*, 31.
13 Sargeant, 'A new class of people'.
14 Neuhaus, *Ob iskusstve fortepianoy igrï*.
15 See Weber et al., 'Conservatories'.
16 Wright, 'Royal Academy of Music (London)', 554.
17 Wright, 'Royal Academy of Music (London)', 554.
18 *Report of Proceedings at the Meeting at Saint James's Palace on Tuesday February 28th, 1882.* Cited by Wright, 'Grove's role in the founding of the RCM'.
19 I am indebted to Professor David Wright for this reference.
20 Breen, *Thurston Dart and the New Faculty of Music at King's College, London: A 50th Anniversary Biography*, 31, 27.
21 Brown, 'The study of music at university. 9', 123–24.
22 Morgan, *The People's Peace*, 481.
23 Lawson and Stowell, *The Cambridge Encyclopedia of Historical Performance in Music*, 163.
24 Royal College of Music, *RCM Strategic Plan*.
25 Gandre, *And Then There Were Seven*, 6.
26 Olmstead, *Juilliard: A History*, 83.

2

PERSONAL REALITIES I

What makes an artist?

Ivan Hewett, Jonathan Cole, and Andrew Zolinsky

The question 'what makes an artist?' not only has a deep philosophical dimension but is also of vital practical relevance to a conservatoire. Becoming an 'artist' is central to the RCM's programmes in performance or composition, often accompanied by the pursuit of proficiency in other roles which may be easier to define: singer, composer, educator, mover-and-shaker. Being an artist is manifested partly by having excellent skills in specific roles such as these; one cannot be an artist in the abstract. But the word also means something that goes beyond a definable set of skills and aptitudes. It connotes an attitude, a certain stance towards a particular art form and its audience, which is as much ethical as aesthetic.

This is exactly what we would expect because the artistic practice within which any artist works is itself also an inextricable tangle of aesthetic and ethical factors. It is an interesting fact that the question 'what is art?' is very hard to disentangle from the question 'what is *good* art?', and one thing that emerges very strongly from the two meditations that follow is that the question 'what makes an artist?' soon merges with the question 'what makes a *good* artist?'

Putting that question to a philosopher of art would yield one sort of answer; putting that question to a professor of composition and a professor of piano yields a different set of answers, because it focuses on what is perhaps the nub of the issue: how the business of acquiring a proficiency in specific technical and interpretative skills can and should be shaped by an overall conception of what it means to be an artist. Interviews with those closely involved in conservatoire training can shine a light on the institution's role in shaping the artist and collective notions of 'artistry' today.

The following interviews took place in July 2022, facilitated by the first author. They have been tidied only enough to make them easily readable, with the contributors' words otherwise remaining intact. The first is with Jonathan Cole, Head of Composition at the Royal College of Music, and with over 16 years of teaching experience at the College. He came to prominence in his twenties as a composer of beautifully crafted modernist music not so far from that of Oliver Knussen and George Benjamin. He became dissatisfied with this style, and after a period of retreat, began to work in a more experimental style influenced by John Cage, Karlheinz Stockhausen, and James Tenney.

DOI: 10.4324/9781003281573-4

IH: *What makes an artist, in your view?*

JC: Well, there are many layers to this. Most obviously it's the ability to express one's ideas clearly and inventively, in an individual way. Just knowing what it is that you want to communicate in the first place is a big part of that. The ability to do that is something that we develop throughout the four years of the Bachelor of Music course; it comes both from focusing on specifically technical exercises but also simply writing pieces. Really what you're aiming for is a sense of clarity and immediacy. And also a piece that is practical in terms of the way we can realise it here at the RCM in performance.

I think there's a maturity that comes through this. I hope this won't sound too re-ligious, but I do believe it's important to develop an awareness of music as something that is immensely powerful; that is somehow beyond ourselves. And as a composer, what we're doing is tapping into this huge thing, and in a sense we're hoping to bring some energy into that stream. Our job is to provide something that can become part of that flow, maybe. That flow is something that's already there, independent of us. It's something that we can't grab hold of, we can't really put into words, but we recognise its importance and its power, and the fact that it's expressing something outside of us, that thing which is *music*. That's really important.

I really want to communicate the sense that as an artist, you are here to serve music, and it's not here to serve you. Because if you start off with the idea that music is here to serve you and to make your career you will become very frustrated, and within a very short space of time, you probably won't want to carry on writing, because it won't be serving you well enough. You'll get frustrated and ask why your career isn't going bet-ter. Whereas if you understand from the beginning that music is something that one is always aspiring to, something you try to get closer to but which will be always be just out of reach, it will always be fresh. I mean, that's a very exciting reason to jump out of bed in the morning for the next 30 years and keep working at this difficult art! So as well as giving specific skills it's about educating people to have a creative outlook on life in general as well as their work, that will inform everything they do, and hopefully bring them a fulfilling creative life as well.

The essential thrust of what I'm concerned about is the identity of each individual composer and their role within society, which is rapidly changing in a way that it hasn't done for many, many decades (see also Chapter 14). And this is very exciting, but it's also quite terrifying. It's a question of trying to predict where it's going to go, and how one can create a secure environment where students are able to find where they fit into this changing scene, and where they are able to distil or discover their own voices, without feeling they have to submit to the demands of the new music 'system'. It's easy to give way to the pressure to conform. Because they should be questioning things all the time, and not taking anything for granted.

IH: *Is part of your role helping them to find their individual voice?*

JC: The difficulty is to influence their creative personality, without changing their essential personality! With the students who have a really strong personality, you can sort of tell where they're going to be heading in the future, to some extent. And because you can see already the areas that they're particularly interested in, it's usually the case that they've developed a greater knowledge and experience of working within that particular area – for example in working within electronic music. They come from such different backgrounds and have such different levels of experience, so you have to listen, find out about their concerns, and work out what it is they value in the music they're interested in writing. I think even when you've brought their musical personalities up to a level that's more aligned with their creative aims, one can't assume that students will leave with a fully formed individual personal voice, that's too much to expect. These things take a lot of time.

IH: *What are the difficulties that stand in the way of that process?*

JC: One of the difficulties about the current situation is that the students are in a multi-layered environment, in the sense they're surrounded by so much different media and so many different sorts of musical stimulus. It's that total availability of every kind of music which just didn't exist 20 or 30 years ago. And not just availability, but the fact that everything is thrown in your face, you can't avoid things. If you go on You-Tube, then things will pop up whether you like it or not, then you will end up listening to that thing that's popped up because it caught your attention. Whereas when I was a student if you wanted to hear a new piece by Lachenmann or Alvin Lucier or whoever, it was a rare occurrence. You had to go to that particular concert or make an appointment to listen to that particular radio programme, and this created excitement and focus. It was the same situation for people who watched TV drama or sitcoms, they could see just one episode per week, and to find out what happened next, they'd have to wait the entire week. All this has changed, in a way that's not necessarily good. It's produced a sort of sweet-shop mentality where you just grab anything that looks nice, with no limits, and that means you get sick of sweets very quickly. Whereas if you're only allowed that one little treat on a Saturday evening you really appreciate it. I think the fact that everything is on tap can lead to a devaluing of culture.

IH: *What is the core of your role, would you say?*

JC: Well, a big part of my role is to create a community of ideas, an opportunity for people to share their thoughts and their music. How people relate to each other is really important, and how they then go on to relate to people in the outside world is very important. So keeping channels of communication open is essential, because every individual has their own story, and every individual is seeing the world in a particular way. Some people are less able to be part of that community, for some it doesn't come very naturally. So there has to be quite a lot of gentle encouragement, and you help them in any way you can. That's an important part of what I do. Just being supportive. And obviously within that number of people – we have around 100 composers studying at any one time – there will be occasions where things aren't absolutely tickety-boo and that's normal within any group. So you can't expect everything to be wonderful all the time.

IH: *Are there typical weaknesses of beginner composers?*

JC: A very common problem is having too many ideas, or not really seeing the interconnections between ideas, to identify for example how a cluster of ideas could be regarded as aspects of one big idea. It's very common to encounter a student piece which starts off really well and you're on the edge of your seat, and then as you turn the pages the music somehow loses its identity. There's no 'right way' and a piece of music may leave the changes that come with the passing of time to the listener rather than incorporate what the composer thinks they may be within the piece. I think you could say there are two types of composers, there are composers who create pieces out of many different sorts of thing, and there are composers who create many things from one thing, and each kind needs a different sort of guidance. Also, students don't always grasp what the limitations of the human mind are. When you compose you are creating a flow of information within time, and you have to think hard about whether that flow can be grasped by the listener at that speed. If you exceed that limit with too much variety then you can paradoxically end up writing the dullest music imaginable. You have to avoid the danger of writing paper music, so learning to really listen is absolutely essential.

I also think it's essential to communicate an idea of what musical material is and encourage students to think about how they can get as much as possible out of the material they've invented. That's pretty central to all composition, teaching a feeling for what the most characteristic aspects of the material are, what those aspects of it are that will actually speak and communicate, which parts of it can you can lose without the material as a whole losing its identity, which aspects of the material you can start to change. And to find out how to do this in a way that's in line with the material's nature, so it almost feels like it's transforming itself.

IH: *Is it part of your role to make students savvy about the marketplace?*

JC: It's funny, there are some composers who say they feel that it's almost their role to create a music industry when they leave. It's almost as if they're going to shape it – they're part of it, and so it should adapt to them! So many of the students are already savvy, they have their own websites, they're on social media, they're extremely aware of the importance of promoting themselves (see also Chapter 12). They're making their music available on online platforms, and already they're reaching a much bigger audience than pieces written for publishers 30 years ago. I remember in my time you would send pieces personally to conductors, in the hope that they would at least read them. They're already one step ahead of that. They're also very good at producing scores, they know about all the different kinds of software, and they know how to make them look impressive!

IH: *Do you find composers want to be more than composers, they want to be all-round creative artists?*

Yes, and the reverse is true. Many visual artists are working in sound now, and some do this in a collaborative way by working with composers. Some of our composers here are collaborating with students at the Royal College of Art, for instance. What's remarkable is that they don't see an enormous difference between these two worlds, and that they actually feed into each other, and support each other. I've got some students who write poetry, some who paint, others who compose songs which they sing themselves, and they take part in the performance of their own pieces, sometimes by operating the electronics, sometimes by playing in ensemble pieces. Maybe we're entering a period where specialism isn't exactly disappearing, but a different more open-minded sort of attitude is emerging towards being a composer. And I'm all for this, I think only good things can come out of it. It doesn't mean that they're exploring their own art less deeply, it's just that the exploration is happening in a wider context.

IH: *Do you have a specific skill set you want to inculcate?*

JC: Yes, I think that's important, even though it seems very old-fashioned to some people. I'm hoping that we can bring back a course for all undergraduates in species counterpoint.[1] Not because I think the composers will actually write music in that style, it's more to do with acquainting them with the experience of working within very tight limitations, you develop a certain focused mentality, and of course you develop your aural skills, because you're listening very closely to intervals as they unfold in time, and also as they sound together simultaneously. I think there are so many musical values that are timeless that come out of that, and I think just to have that basic grounding, even now at this late point in musical history, is still extremely valuable and necessary as well.

IH: *What do you hope students leave with at the end of the four years?*

JC: A growth in confidence, and a deeper understanding of themselves that will allow them to tap into their personal core and allow it to grow and blossom. And above all a certain respect for music. All of us here have certain values that we try and instil in students, often in an unconscious way. And of course we hope they will be successful in their careers, but honestly I would be much happier if by the time they leave students are writing really interesting and individual music, and perhaps because of that are not 'making it' very quickly, rather than writing music that's easily consumable in a familiar style – because that is more likely to be ephemeral. What's essential for a long creative life as a composer is that hunger to keep exploring, to be always aware of the vastness of the world they've entered. If that happens then the obsession with self shrinks, because their identity won't be so bound up with their immediate personal ambitions or successes. That's always the danger with being a composer.

The second interview is with Andrew Zolinsky, a concert pianist, piano professor, and Contemporary Piano Co-ordinator at the RCM. As a performer he has worked closely with many leading living composers and given world and UK premieres of important works by composers such as Unsuk Chin, David Lang, and Michael Finnissy. He is determined not to be pigeonholed as a 'contemporary pianist', preferring to curate programmes that bring together past and present composers.

IH: *What makes an artist, in your view?*

AZ: It is a difficult thing to absolutely define. For me, being a real artist has a lot to do with curiosity (see also Chapter 10), especially in terms of repertoire choices of works by lesser-known composers as well as embracing music by living composers. I think that this is a very important thing to try and instil in our students, the fact that if they have something distinctive about their repertoire, something that makes them stand out from the crowd, they are more likely to be able to secure a number of concerts. I also think that the ability to decode a composer's intentions is vital both as a performer and as a teacher. The ability to do this helps us to create individual interpretations based on what we understand the composer's intentions to have been.

IH: *Creativity is often named as an essential factor of artistry. How does this apply in the case of the performing artist, which is more recreative?*

AZ: It is certainly essential. To some extent, we have to think ourselves into the position of the creator in order to *recreate* the music meaningfully, to try and understand why a composer writes a staccato where they do not literally intend us to play very short, for instance. That applies to music of all periods, of course, but it is especially relevant for contemporary music, as we are often preparing the first performance of a piece; there is no performance history to refer to, it is up to us based on our knowledge of other works by a particular composer, though the problem can often be compounded by the fact that we may be playing a work by a composer for whom there is little recorded material. My work with contemporary music has really changed how I look at traditional repertoire, it has really sharpened this sense that one can start to look at a Beethoven sonata, for instance, as if it was completed yesterday, to think about it just from the score rather than allowing the many recordings of this music to shape our own interpretations (see also Chapter 9).

IH: *What can help a pianist in creating their interpretations?*

AZ: Many things. Something I am always talking to my students about is the great importance of listening to as much orchestral music as possible. I think much of the interesting difference between pianists is rooted in sound, the ability to make the listener forget they are listening to a piano and that with the piano, there is that unavoidable fact that after we have put a single note or a chord down, the sound immediately begins to die. This factor in turn presents another challenge, that of creating a sustained line. We can only really do this by having the sound of the string section of a great orchestra playing a sustained melodic line from a Brahms symphony, for example, in our heads. To achieve this at the piano requires us to create the illusion of it; a simple physical movement at a point of intensity can encourage the listener to hear in a way that just putting the notes down might not necessarily achieve.

IH: *That is partly a matter of technique isn't it? What is the level of technique nowadays when students arrive?*

AZ: We need to remember that in today's musical world, in general, the level of technical ability has increased so much. And there is so much emphasis on that now that inevitably, within the walls of College, the students very often arrive with already extraordinary techniques. That is one of the huge differences between now and when I was a student, when there was a tiny handful of students with extraordinary technique, but the general level was much lower. The problem or challenge, though, may be that the technique is way ahead of the musical understanding. It is so important to remember that the students are still very young, and just as they have big life journeys to go on, so too do they have big musical journeys to go on. It is important to stress to them, I strongly feel, that this can be a very exciting and enriching journey!

IH: *How helpful is it for them to listen to great artists of the past?*

AZ: As important as it is to be inspired by hearing great performances by pianists both past and present, as I previously mentioned, it is vital that we understand how these pianists reached their interpretive decisions rather than trying to play as they play without realising for ourselves what is on the page. By encouraging this way of working in our students, we teach them the most valuable thing, especially when they are no longer our students – the ability to think for themselves.

I often suggest to my students that once they have lived with a piece for a period of time and developed some strong ideas of their own regarding the journey of a work, this is a good point at which to listen to other performances of the same piece. We hear things that can help us going forwards but without these elements forming the basis for our own interpretation; we can also hear things, more importantly, that make us stronger in our own musical convictions.

Listening to the likes of Artur Rubinstein or Emil Gilels, you cannot help but wonder how they created such amazing sounds and singing lines. This in turn can lead you to experiment at the piano, especially with voicing and imaginative use of the pedals.

IH: *You've made a speciality of playing contemporary music. Are there particular challenges in teaching students how to play contemporary music with real artistry?*

AZ: Well, there are certain technical challenges that are unlike the ones they meet within standard repertoire, and of course there is a lot of contemporary music which involves interpreting unfamiliar forms of notation. There are forms of graphic notation in, for example, the early works of Morton Feldman or Christian Wolff that need real imagination. Because the notations are very unspecific, this can sometimes be unsettling for the students; I have to really encourage them to be bold, to just take the leap into the unknown, and that there are often no holds barred. Experimenting inside the piano, hearing the extraordinary sounds we can create by brushing the strings with our fingertips, muting the strings, to name just two of the many possibilities, can help to open up their imaginations.

But at the same time, I think it is important to remind them that playing contemporary repertoire needs as much precision and accuracy as playing any other kind of music. There is still an idea in some people's minds that performing contemporary music means you can play anything you like, because after all no one will know if you play a wrong note!

There is music, for instance, that hardly uses time signatures at all and is accompanied by the instruction to play freely – but a problem can be caused by the fact it is precisely notated, rhythmically. One explanation could be that the score is a kind of notated performance, with all the subtle rhythmic and tonal nuances one might hear in a great performance of a Chopin Nocturne.

IH: *Do you find that some students have very fixed ideas from the start of how they would like their careers to be?*

AZ: Oh definitely! Some students arrive already planning that in their fourth year they want to take part in the Leeds piano competition. That may actually be the right thing for them, but not for everyone. I aim to be positive and try to encourage my students as much as possible, but I also feel that, at a certain point, I need to paint a realistic picture of life as a professional musician (see also Chapter 12), to try to manage their expectations. I think it is very important that I equip them with how to deal with disappointment in a positive way, as well as success. Without this, they can become disillusioned, especially if they are clearly talented, but are struggling to make their way. For those keen to enter many competitions, it is important for them to realise that winning a competition does not necessarily make a long career. Winning a competition usually guarantees some engagements for about two years, but after that you are on your own unless you are fortunate enough to be taken up by a good agent. Another thing I try to instil in the students is the importance of other kinds of music-making, beyond simply being a soloist. I know my own playing has changed enormously, and I think improved, as a result of performing chamber music and as an ensemble pianist, and this is something I am keen to pass on.

IH: What makes being a real artist different from being simply a good professional musician?

AZ: I think it is important to say clearly here that being a good professional musician should be bound up with our artistic personas. The respect we have for the profession of music leads us to our desire to be creative, curious artists. I think it is to do with being honest to ourselves as to how we want to be viewed as creative or recreative artists. Maybe the most individual performers go beyond professionalism, beyond just doing a good job but not taking risks or going against people's expectations. A good example of this is my colleague Jonathan Cole, whom I know you have also talked to on this subject. I think of him as a real artist because he turned his back on the success he enjoyed in his early career. At that time he was writing in a more avant-garde, modernist style. He could have continued that way, but he realised that he was not being true to himself artistically and decided on a complete change of creative direction. He felt that he did not want to wake up one day in 25 years' time and realise he had devoted his life to writing music to please others rather than responding to his own extraordinarily creative voice. I hugely admire him for this.

There are pianists, too, who seem similarly brave to me, who stick to their own paths. I must mention Maurizio Pollini as he was so courageous (and remains so to this day) in playing often very tough contemporary works, Boulez, Stockhausen, and Nono, in major concert venues at a time when few pianists at the highest level were similarly courageous. The one pianist, artistically, who is a beacon for me is Emil Gilels. Everything he did was so personal but so true to the composer's wishes, his performances always affect me deeply. There is just the most extraordinary emotional connection with the listener and a fantastic refinement in the use of sound. I think the ability to reach the listener in that way involves a special kind of commitment which goes way beyond professionalism and marks the true artist.

This chapter has revealed two perspectives on what makes an artist. Recurring themes include the importance of students being supported to recognise their own agency as artists, especially in the fast-paced, on-demand digital world in which they are learning and working. Other points of concurrence include the importance of fostering a curious, open-minded approach, alongside technique as well as musical understanding. Also noted is the need to facilitate diverse views on what 'artistry' might mean in today's profession. This is particularly pertinent given the College's more recent programmes – for example in performance science and research – that may require a wider definition of 'artist' than we would have hitherto considered. That artistry is individualistic also comes through clearly, with authenticity at the heart, and requiring courage to truly stand apart. The conservatoire has a responsibility to provide the ideal environment for such development, where courage, risk-taking, and boundary pushing are facilitated so that each student can develop artistry in a way that makes sense for them as individuals.

PERSPECTIVE: CHAPTER 2

Sarah Connolly

Introduction

My current repertoire ranges from Renaissance music (Monteverdi) through to contemporary (Brett Dean) in all the major international opera houses and concert venues. I am passionate about chamber music and recital work and was a Wigmore Hall Artist in Residence. At the Royal College of Music (RCM), I studied joint principal piano and voice between 1982 and 1986, when Sir David Willcocks was Director. I continued my piano studies with the inspirational Patricia Carroll until I reached the top grade within the RCM and passed my piano-teaching diploma. I particularly enjoyed accompanying instrumental students; General Musicianship classes; and getting to know professors Hugh Bean, Jeremy Dale Roberts, and James Brown. But it was Sir David who told me that I was going to be a singer and he awarded me an Exhibition and postgraduate scholarship. His Chamber Choir laid the groundwork for my first job as a BBC Singer in my early twenties. I collaborated with composer Paul Edlin and sung his and other contemporary music by Robin Holloway and Peter Maxwell Davies which again prepared me for a lifetime of challenging scores. To contribute to my living expenses, I played repertoire from *The Great American Songbook* in hotel restaurants and sang ad hoc with The Sixteen, BBC Singers, and the Stephen Hill Singers. I would say that I took advantage of all that was on offer as a student and achieved milestones with my piano playing. My confidence as a singer developed many years later.

Perspectives

I would like to suggest that ideally and realistically, a conservatoire student can be given the tools to explore what might lead to being a mature artist. How to know which questions to ask of themselves while so young is a moot point. I think a teacher's role is to suggest to the student how to ask the right questions; to be shown what the parameters and expectations might be; and to be curious, open-minded, and collaborative.

I have several responses to Jonathan Cole's illuminating thoughts on composition. He is clearly a very sensitive and caring teacher. In my experience as a very modest composer, pianist, and singer, I have this inner knowledge that music is in my very being, in my DNA

DOI: 10.4324/9781003281573-5

all the time. It is not outside nor out of reach but very much a constant unconscious and conscious energy. The hardest thing is turning off the tap sometimes; as Cole asserts, one can have too many ideas. When I need to order my thoughts to prepare for and focus on a specific piece of music, it feels like I must switch off influences that are unhelpful and zone-in on a specific and related train of thought. Preparing repertory with real or fictional protagonists, such as Benjamin Britten's *Rape of Lucretia* or his cantata *Phaedra* (and indeed Jean-Philippe Rameau's role Phèdre from the opera *Hippolyte et Aricie*), Medea, Nero, Agrippina, Mary Stuart, Julius Caesar, and Dido, I visited museums, looked at every relevant painting, and read current biographies (Mary Beard's *Emperor of Rome* or *Twelve Caesars*) and plays by Euripides, Racine, Virgil, etc. This method helps focus the boundaries – and Cole touches on this in his wish to reintroduce counterpoint. I wonder if there is the possibility of linking a composing student with a singer, whereby they can learn from each other. I would not concern myself with developing a role in society or spooking myself into having an identity or standing out from the crowd. Jonathan Cole asserts that such aspirations can be 'quite terrifying', and I would have felt such pressure. My initial terror as a first-year piano student was that I wasn't good enough, and I didn't belong at the great RCM. My teacher, Patricia Carroll, helped me to believe in my musicality, while strengthening my technique and training my confidence in memorising. It was done very slowly with no concerns about identity.

Admittedly, composition requires a more obvious individuality, but I should imagine that teaching composition is very much a part of therapy and encouragement. I ask my students for a detailed analysis of their vocal music and why they have chosen it; then we discuss how personal it can become. It helps them make their own choices and teaches them how to ask those questions of themselves without prompting.

I think Jonathan Cole is very astute to advise his students to be broadminded and collaborative with students from other art colleges with regard to future prospects and to equip students with the ability to orchestrate and construct a coherent musical form. I would also encourage them to go to as many live concerts as possible and listen to archived performances. I have performed many new recently published scores from all centuries: Peri's *Euridice*; Ivor Gurney's unpublished songs; contemporary songs and operas by Mark-Anthony Turnage (*The Silver Tassie*) and Brett Dean (*Hamlet*); and world premieres of songs by Torsten Rasch, Sally Beamish, and Turnage. Because one is literally in the dark with no reference to another's performance, this experience has taught me to treat well-known music in the same forensic and yet instinctive manner. Listening to recordings is very important, but there comes a time when listening to recordings can interfere with one's own unique set of thoughts.

I have often talked about and shared with students how I keep repertoire fresh. This might be Bach's *Erbarme dich* (*St Matthew Passion*) or *Frauenliebe und Leben* by Schumann with text by Chamisso. Particularly in this song cycle, I put myself in the composer's world: Schumann's wedding gift to Clara. Immersing oneself this way also keeps the period-style of singing in check. It is not so much Chamisso's poetry, which I feel is dated and a little gauche, but Schumann's response to it. From his position, Clara, his idol, is the person he was writing for, and it is my job to find that ecstatic energy that he must have felt. I feel the same about Britten's opera *The Rape of Lucretia*. Ronald Duncan's libretto is at times comically clunky, but Britten elevates every word so that one almost doesn't notice. Another method to reinvent the context is to apply an emotion that one has experienced recently which is relevant – for example compassion would work for *Erbarme dich*. I find students respond very well to anything which personalises a song and through which they can express genuine considered feeling.

Finally, I'd like to address Louis Andriessen's statement that 'Music is greater than we are'. That gives it an outside, unattainable iconic status which isn't connected to ourselves. I prefer Plato's assertion that 'Music gives a soul to the universe, wings to the mind, flight to the imagination and life to everything.'

Summary

It has become very clear that the political decisions of recent years have reduced work opportunities for British students, both at home and abroad. This situation may not remain in such a dire state, but, nevertheless, it is much harder to make a living as a professional musician. Rather than pressure students to find their individuality when they haven't discovered who they are, I would say the responsibility is very much on the teachers to equip them with relevant skills: solid technique, orchestration, transposition, sight-reading, ensemble playing, choral singing, interesting repertoire, difficult, testing contemporary music skills, jazz, collaboration, and technology skills/networking. I believe that music is within all of us like a loving companion. It is what makes us compassionate, vulnerable, introspective, and capable of producing something extraordinary. I don't believe that music is a higher power but sits like soul food within us. Sometimes, we can be too harsh on ourselves and too self-critical, but I think that's inevitable given what we're trying to achieve.

Chapter Note

1 A method of teaching strict counterpoint by the addition of a part or parts to a simple *cantus firmus* in long even notes, proceeding from the simplest, purely consonant note-and-against-note counterpoint to florid lines involving dissonances.

3

PERSONAL REALITIES II

How does the conservatoire link with the profession?

Stephen Johns and Janis Kelly

Training for the music profession

Widely recognised as one of the great singing actresses of her generation, Professor Janis Kelly has performed on the major stages of the concert and opera world and has been a singing professor at the RCM for over 16 years. An internationally recognised teacher, vocal consultant, and artistic researcher, she holds a Chair in Vocal Performance and teaches one-to-one lessons from undergraduate level through to the College's most advanced students in the RCM Opera Studio. She also directs and performs in projects with students. Here, she reflects on the interrelationship between her own professional experience and her approach to teaching in the conservatoire:

JK: The profession has given me a platform on which to craft a successful career doing what I love most: to sing, act, and perform, and create in the moment through drama, words, and music. As both a professional and a teacher in the College, I am constantly aware of the myriad elements necessary to obtain work and cultivate a career as a singer.

Since joining the RCM Faculty, I have balanced the demands of being an active professional singer with my teaching. I regularly give masterclasses, adjudicate competitions, offer consultations, and present talks and lecture-recitals. These simultaneous roles as both teacher of voice and professional singer are important for my credibility and visibility within the profession. But the priority is my students; to train them with all the elements required to be a professional today.

Conservatoires exist to facilitate each student's unique artistic journey, enabling them to achieve the highest level that the profession demands. However, training musicians through specialised bespoke musical and performance training is a careful process that requires long-term commitment to my students.

In our multifaceted classical music field, we need to develop those skills which are relevant for the profession of today. For singers, this is especially complex. The teaching of singing and preparing for the profession has many facets including modern languages, music theory, ensemble work, chamber music, opera, and recitals, as well as TV, film and media work, and recording.

DOI: 10.4324/9781003281573-6

These skills are bound together by musical intelligence, which involves adaptive and creative skills including analysis, practice, and wisdom. Transforming those elements into a singer's performance involves aspects including technique, imagination, memorisation, managing original interpretation, mindful practice, questioning and knowing your strengths and weaknesses, as well as artistic spontaneity. Singers also need a vast corpus of practical abilities. I encourage developing psychosocial skills, which produce positive interactions with other people in the profession. Life skills come with time, and include emotional awareness, tenacity and resilience, confidence-restoring skills, and social skills.

Appropriate self-promotion and finding new ways to reach audiences are essential today if one is to thrive in the profession. Working and performing with the spoken word is vital to the development of your voice and your ability as a genuine actor. It completes the elements necessary to enable you to stand out in the crowd. Knowing how to develop your strengths, technique, and repertoire, and capitalising on these, will help develop an emerging artist's unique contribution to the world of music. Questioning oneself on these aspects promotes lifelong learning and continuous self-evaluation, which are personally and musically rewarding while enriching the musical world.

My instruction aims to draw upon all of these factors necessary for a career as a professional singer. I begin by working on the necessary support of the speaking voice, followed by a secure and flexible vocal technique and advice on appropriate repertoire covering several different languages.

This is more than a one-way process of instruction. It is essential, too, that I encourage students to teach themselves and be able to articulate with discerning ears what they hear in others. The ability to critique themselves in a mature, professional way is an investment in their professional development. Similarly, I encourage recording and filming one's practice; it is crucial that students understand fully what audiences see and feel.

To create acting in the moment I use spoken word subtext, imagery, memory, spontaneity, colour, and vulnerability. It is critical to understand how to construct acting in the moment to perform at the deepest level. My lessons, group talks, and workshops address topics including self-motivation and practice, concert programming, and the continued value of observing (and critiquing) live performance.

Beyond developing a healthy vocal technique for professional work, there is evidence that singing also contributes to improved health and psychological well-being.[1] Longevity as a professional singer is a testament to hard work and healthy technique, but also the power and joy of being able to continue learning about oneself and the world around us in a way that goes far beyond language.

Like most conservatoire professors, Janis is a practitioner with an international performance career and profile. Her own career began much like her current students. Practice-led learning at a conservatoire led to professional performance engagements in recitals and opera companies, culminating in the international stage. For other professors, their professional story may centre on solo concert careers in professional concert halls, membership in chamber ensembles and orchestras internationally, or compositions commissioned and performed in a variety of public arenas. At the RCM, these professional stories increasingly extend to professional areas of research, music education, entrepreneurship, and cultural leadership.

Where conservatoire students once aspired to follow closely in the footsteps of their professors, in recent decades graduates have increasingly found themselves following 'portfolio careers': combinations of freelance performance and longer-term employment, workshop leadership, teaching, administration, and a wide variety of other activities, creating a rich and varied, if potentially precarious, professional life. Chapter 12 discusses this in more depth.

This shift reflects diversification in the music profession, which is increasingly global in opportunity and activity. Areas that were once exclusive or clearly delineated are now more porous. Recording, broadcasting, and streaming have all changed the way that audiences experience music, and methods of presentation and public engagement have also developed rapidly. At the core, conservatoire-trained musicians must still be able to perform with elite levels of skill and craft, but as Janis notes, they need to be able to do so in different environments. This might include non-traditional environments and diverse audiences who bring a wide range of personal and sociocultural experiences.

In the classical music industry, further developments include a welcome and overdue focus on equality and diversity.[2] Challenges to traditional 'canonical' programming create space for new and progressive approaches to audience development, participation, and accessibility (see Chapter 15). Across conservatoires and the wider profession, there is an aspiration for conservatoire students, graduates, and the audiences of the future to better reflect society. Conservatoires including the RCM are increasingly cognisant that our art form needs to be accessible and attainable if we wish to retain the right to be considered relevant and essential.

Each year, the RCM sees around 370 students graduate, many having studied for up to 8 years at degree level. But the profession they are entering is vastly different to that which their professors experienced. It is therefore essential that conservatoire students' learning and teaching take them far beyond the mastery of their instrument. While the principal study remains at the core of any performance or composition-based programme, the conservatoire-teaching environment must be open and agile enough to equip students with deep understanding of a dynamic profession. To explore this professional interplay in greater depth, we explore insights from three more RCM professors and professional musicians: David Hockings (DH), Head of Percussion; Dr Jonathan Cole (JC), Head of Composition; and Gabrielle Lester (GL), Deputy Head of Strings (Orchestral).

A changing profession

David and Jonathan acknowledge the range of routes into professional work today, and a tendency for these to diverge from the traditional model of the full-time orchestral musician or published composer:

DH: Graduates need to buy their own instruments, be versatile, and be able to read not just the standard works. The jobs they get include orchestras, the West End, session drumming, and teaching.

JC: It used to be seen as a really important aspect of being a composer that you had a publisher. Authorship is more ambiguous today as new works might incorporate indeterminate notations, collaboration with performers, and self-published scores. In terms of getting your music noticed, harnessing social media, websites, networking, and personal connections is key. Today's composition students are aware of the need to apply hybrid professional skills, and it's important to offer a learning environment that values and nurtures these.

One of Jonathan's former students exemplifies the hyper-versatile musician with an entrepreneurial spirit:

JC: They're a composer, cellist, successful journalist, performing with the BBC, LPO, running a contemporary music group, and running a record label. It's exciting to see less reliance on the 'powers that be', for example, waiting patiently for that big BBC commission. Instead, the musician can be their own gatekeeper; the one with the agency to make things happen.

Each of the three professors describe how carefully designed learning activities can promote professional attributes:

DH: For several years we've been travelling to schools and music hubs to promote conservatoire study. It's about encouraging new talent. Current RCM students perform in and lead workshops alongside me, giving them first-hand experience of learning and participation activity. This works both ways, as the RCM students are benefiting as much as the participants.

JC: We get the composition students to write pieces for each other to perform in fortnightly classes. This is great experience for them to workshop new pieces with a large group of people of different abilities, a skill that will be essential for them to respond to new commissions for young or amateur ensembles. And it encourages them to see themselves as composer-performers.

GL   Our orchestral performance module relies on input from the 'here and now' of the profession. By still playing professionally, I know what orchestras are currently looking and asking for in players. This informs the excerpts we set and the way we conduct the module assessment, a mock orchestral audition at the end of the year.

A recurring theme in these activities is the replication of professional conditions. This runs through all aspects of learning, teaching, and performing at the RCM and many other conservatoires. In this way, the College can instill in its students the positive habits of professional life, along with the expectations and experiences of professional levels of performance. In this vocational educational arena, contact with real-life situations and current practitioners is essential.

   The artistic programme is an area of the College's learning culture where the concept of 'becoming a professional' is especially important. The RCM prides itself on its extensive and high-quality performance programme, with up to 500 events each year, ranging from grand opera to solo performance to live film music showcases. Central to this programme are two overriding principles: providing each student with performing opportunities appropriate to their level of development, and presenting all performances under professional-standard conditions. In response, students' feedback contributes to the evaluation of these learning experiences and informs College decision-making on invited artists and the structure of activities. The following section of this chapter explores some of the proto-professional models found in the RCM's artistic programme.

Artist interactions in the conservatoire

Close collaboration with leading international artists is a signature characteristic of conservatoire study and an essential vehicle for students to engage with the profession and professional standards. Where long-term relationships can be embedded, the experience both ways – student to artist – is highly enriching.

The simplest form of engagement is the traditional masterclass, usually involving a visiting artist, a number of student performers, and an audience of students and external visitors. The visits are occasional, often high-profile, and might be streamed to audiences internationally. Although the value of such a visit can be enormous in itself, particularly for those playing in the class, there are other ways to widen the impact of visiting artists.

Increasingly, the RCM has been deepening relationships with performing artists to facilitate ongoing dialogue between artists and students. Visiting Professorships allow for more regular visits. Embedding artists into the life of the College provides opportunities for a wider range of immersive activities: masterclasses, faculty classes, side-by-side performances, and professional engagements.

In a similar way, visiting conductors provide rich artistic feedback to aspiring orchestral musicians. In addition to guiding a student orchestra for a public performance, visiting conductors are role models who set the perceived professional standards for musical leadership and communication. The care taken to select appropriate professionals for this type of hybrid artist-educator role should not be underestimated. The RCM also places a great emphasis on building relationships with a younger generation of conductors, ensuring students are exposed to fresh ideas and diverse role models. Similar principles apply in the selection of opera directors, who spend long, intensive periods creating productions with students. There is an important benefit to these interactions, too: visiting established artists are working directly with student emerging artists and, in doing so, strengthening the students' professional networks.

'Side-by-side' activities provide opportunities for students to work alongside professionals as peers. These take place in two ways: visiting artists to the College and sit-in schemes with professional ensembles. The RCM offers side-by-side opportunities with all the major London orchestras.

The schemes provide regular opportunities for students to experience a snapshot of life in the profession. Students are continually surprised and challenged by the physicality and stamina required to perform in these professional conditions. In addition, exposing advanced students and their all-round skills – as performers, collaborators, team players – to their professional counterparts can nurture lasting relationships that lead to vital opportunities post-graduation.

Many of the professionally focused experiences in the conservatoire revolve around *people* – communities of practice that exhibit particular working dynamics. Students observe and interact with more experienced people in the field; emerging and established artists work together to build shared understandings of what professional practice is.

Around this is a need for conservatoires to uphold a culture of professionalism. In practice, this means that the expectations of students in rehearsal and performance are to reach professional standards. Timekeeping, preparation, attention, and commitment are not negotiable in the professional world and are basic expectations in all College projects. Heads of Faculties (instrumental departments, e.g. strings, woodwind, composition), all of whom have extensive, often still current, professional performing experience, provide feedback and support for students and the teams who deliver rehearsals and performances. There is an awareness that professional expectations must be balanced with the development needs of individual students. By ensuring that students are placed in projects suitable for their abilities and stage of development, activities can provide appropriate challenge and promote positive artistic growth.

Finally, professional environments are shaped by physical as well as relational spaces. As explored in more detail in Chapter 13, the RCM seeks to provide inspiring and well-equipped performance spaces that promote the highest possible performance standards and facilitate a smooth transition into professional environments. The Amaryllis Fleming Concert Hall and the Britten Theatre both set new standards of provision for student performers when they opened. These were complemented by the building of the RCM Performance Hall and Performance Studio in 2020. Quality acoustics, stage design, lighting, and ambience all contribute to an environment of professional aspiration.

Views from the professional world

The modern conservatoire measures its programmes and strategies against current practice in the professional music world. Its students need to be ground breakers and iconoclasts, prepared to move the art form forwards.

The vast range of stakeholders in the music industry include directors and managers of large performing organisations, agents, managers, performers, conductors, composers, and entrepreneurs, not to mention educators, publishers, health professionals, and promoters. There is much for conservatoires to learn from all of these roles, but we are limited here to providing a snapshot based on a performance lens. In this final section, we present the views of three industry representatives: Debbie Wiseman (DW), composer for films and television, conductor, and radio and television presenter; James Williams (JW), at the time Managing Director of the Royal Philharmonic Orchestra; and Martyn Brabbins (MB), renowned conductor and teacher, and at the time of writing Music Director of English National Opera. These three professionals, each a leader in their respective field, identify the critical ingredients for graduates to thrive in the UK classical music performance industry:

MB: Young musicians upon leaving the nurturing environment of a conservatoire, should, at the very least, have acquired a technical mastery of their craft, be they singer, orchestra player, pianist, composer, or conductor. The level of skill demanded by the profession is breathtakingly high, and in my experience, young musicians lucky enough to gain a foothold in the profession are very much up to scratch. This is a testament to both the commitment and standing of the teachers developing these musicians, and of the young musicians themselves. This being the case, it is also true to say that post-conservatoire musicians have rarely acquired sufficient experience to enable a seamless, stress-free passage to an immediately successful career.

DW: They should leave with a comprehensive command of their principal study but also possessing an excellent overall knowledge of repertoire and music-making skills. They should be ready to enter the profession having gained enough of a grounding in their chosen area of music-making as well as the relevant social skills, and should also be prepared to tackle the inevitable ups and downs of the profession.

The strength of character to deal with rejection – especially early on in a career – is just as important as the ability to deal with success.

JW: The profession is changing and evolving constantly, and therefore we need graduating students who have creativity and entrepreneurship to help drive and lead this evolution. It's a given that we need students who have the highest levels of performance skills but fundamental to realising these fully is an ability to be able to communicate this talent to an audience in a meaningful and relevant way, whether that be from the concert platform, on digital media platforms, or in a classroom. The profession is taking a much more holistic view to its programmes of work, with community, audience engagement, and social prescribing work more deeply embedded into its core programmes. Therefore, a working knowledge and experience of engaging in wider community engagement programmes is fundamental.

There is a consensus that technical mastery is essential for all conservatoire graduates, but alongside this is the recognition of the importance of mental resilience, imaginative communication with audiences, and a commitment to one's own self-development post-graduation. These themes continue as all three contributors reflect on the relationship between the profession and conservatoires:

DW: When students enter the professional world, they are generally expected to behave as if they already have a complete set of social and professional skills and are ready to tackle all the uncertainty and pressure of a career in music. Although many professionals will be open to nurturing young talent, this doesn't apply across the board, so the more prepared a student can be on leaving a conservatoire, the better. Confidence, willingness to learn and ask for advice, and not being afraid of occasionally making mistakes are all extremely useful qualities to develop early on in one's career.

JW: It's vital that there is a direct connection between the professional world and a conservatoire's students. This can be direct (through practical side-by-side schemes) or indirectly through engaging teachers via their respective professional performance ensembles. Funding is often a barrier to achieving long-term and meaningful collaboration, and the fluid schedule of orchestras versus the often-rigid structures and timetables of conservatoires make timetabling challenging. That said, there are schemes beyond side-by-side and more traditional professional performance development classes that the professional world should be doing more to offer, which serve as 'enrichment' rather than perhaps 'educational'. For example, making students aware of the administration and artistic roles available within the industry and leading careers workshops for students interested in exploring wider career opportunities in the performing arts.

MB: My personal passion as a teacher of conducting is to teach students in collaboration with a professional orchestra. There is absolutely no comparable experience for the young conductor – a student or an amateur orchestra will not come close to the responsiveness, to the sound, or the flexibility of a professional orchestra. For the emerging conductor to gain first-hand experience of this uniquely thrilling truth is a crucial developmental opportunity.

Undoubtedly, close relationships between conservatoires and the professional ecology provide a critical training ground, but increasingly, a broader conception of the 'industry' beyond performance may be beneficial for expanding students' professional horizons. This poses the question of whether conservatoires are sufficiently engaged or, more precisely, engaging in the *right ways*, with the profession:

DW: They [conservatoires] certainly make every attempt to engage, and every conservatoire can only benefit by constantly monitoring the profession and assessing how best to equip their students for entering it. Music is a most rewarding and satisfying career, but it is also extremely demanding both on a professional and social level, and it's essential for all graduates to both accept and prepare for these demands.

JW: There is always more than can be done, but this relies on a symbiotic partnership between conservatoires and the profession. I believe there is more that can be done through the talents and connections of individual professors and tutors at the conservatoires who are perfectly placed to become the conduit to facilitate better engagement between conservatoires and the profession.

MB: As the musician advances along the creative pathway, inevitably, for the majority at least, their focus becomes narrower and more specialised. For this reason, I would encourage students to embrace as varied a diet of musical experiences as are available. Unexpected and inspiring possibilities can be discovered in the most unlikely places.

As later chapters will explore, there is great potential for conservatoires to embed emerging technologies as tools for shaping future performance:

DW: It's important to move with the times as well as look towards the future. Students need to be able to work comfortably with ever-developing technology. Computer skills are now almost as important as social skills.

MB: Living in the digital age allows access to an astonishing range of online performances. This vast and instructive resource can be mined by the young musician to help gain insights into a plethora of audiovisual delights, both historical and contemporary. That said, the most valuable piece of advice I received as a student came from the highly respected Bach scholar and performer, Paul Steinitz. It was very simple advice: 'attend as many LIVE performances as possible'. I would certainly echo that advice, and add, particularly for young conductors, attend rehearsals as well. There is no substitute for the live experience.

JW: It's clear that whilst there is a place for the traditional concert formats of core repertoire performed in the solemnity of a concert hall, there is a growing appetite particularly amongst new and younger audiences to experience classical music in a more diverse range of venues and bite-size formats. It's also clear that musicians of the future have to be open to devising new formats of programming (mixing more traditional repertoire with crossover or more contemporary music) and prepared to perform in non-traditional venues which may require a degree of compromise. Furthermore, there is the opportunity to explore more extensively music's role in presenting or collaborating with other artforms (visual arts, dance, theatre). What was termed 'added value', for example, pre- or post-concert meet/greet of audiences or donors, or devising online content, is now core for attracting new audiences and stewarding donors, and we need to ensure that graduate musicians are confident in and upskilled to deliver this valuable work.

There is a growing sense of self-awareness in the classical music profession that survival will depend on fresh approaches, new ideas, and relevance for new audiences. It is possible that conservatoire students offer the key to this renewal:

DW: Today's graduates will bring their own enthusiasm and youthful exuberance to the music industry. Constantly inviting new and passionate performers, composers, and music directors into the business is vitally important to keep the music profession alive, vibrant, and prospering.

JW: Conservatoires such as the RCM are doing a great deal to expand students' musical horizons, diversifying the repertoire and upskilling them to become musical citizens who can make a positive contribution to the society they live in. I would like to see these graduates challenge the traditional and often restrictive barriers the industry has created for itself, reprioritising the traditional and perceived hierarchy of work, valuing audiences equally, and stretching the music world to diversify its repertoire. With the advancement of social media, there's an opportunity for individual players to share online their own personalities and interests and to help demystify the music world to new audiences. Equally, I would like to see graduates influencing and leading programming and formatting of performances, unafraid to take risk and understanding the value of R&D in performance and the learning opportunity this offers. I believe graduates have valuable insight into the health and potential barriers of the musical world; some form of feedback loop back to the conservatoires on recent graduates' experience, which could then be shared wider with the industry, would provide invaluable data on what the music world is getting right, but equally what needs to change.

Reflections

JK: This need to develop a high level of skills is no different from, for example, the professional world of sports, where striving to be *elite* is appropriate as a status, as opposed to the self-appointed attitude that *elitism* implies. Today, a greater breadth of skills and diverse musical styles are opening up the conservatoire model to include a broader professional education whilst maintaining the expert teaching lineages which account for much of the reputation of these institutions.

It is clear that the modern conservatoire cannot survive, nor train its students, without active collaboration and dialogue with the music profession. This relationship must be more than simply providing *exposure* to existing practices or *transferring* knowledge that has been passed through generations of professionals. Today's students are experiencing a profession in flux. Whether they know it yet or not, they are agents for change, with great potential (and responsibility) to advance their art form in a rapidly changing artistic world. As societies reconsider how and what they subsidise, and audiences become increasingly selective in how they consume their art and culture, tomorrow's musicians need to fulfil the roles of both curators and creators. The future of the art form is in their hands, and it is the conservatoire's role to help students locate their role and influence in this future.

JK: While this education is specialised it is not narrow. Our goal is to cultivate connections, at a local level through proactive dialogue with professors who are practising musicians, and at a global level with the professional environment internationally.

The future for the conservatoire, like any other vocational, practice-led institution, must therefore be outwards-looking. Our horizon-scanning must engage with and reflect trends in the music profession, but it will also benefit from looking beyond the traditional sphere of classical music partners, towards the wider cultural industries and society at large. With our extended communities of practising professional musicians (teachers, graduates, and the students themselves), conservatoires are uniquely poised to cultivate meaningful dialogue with the profession. Equally, there is an untapped capability for conservatoires and our students to influence the profession in positive ways, securing the future of classical music as a relevant and persuasive art form for all society.

Bibliography

Daykin, Norma, Louise Mansfield, Catherine Meads, Guy Julier, Alan Tomlinson, Annette Payne, Lily Grigsby Duffy, Jack Lane, Giorgia D'Innocenzo, Adele Burnett, Tess Kay, Paul Dolan, Stefano Testoni, and Christina Victor. 'What works for wellbeing? A systematic review of wellbeing outcomes for music and singing in adults'. *Perspectives in Public Health* 138, no. 1 (2018): 39–46. https://doi.org/10.1177/1757913917740391.

PERSPECTIVE: CHAPTER 3

James Williams

Introduction

I was Managing Director of the Royal Philharmonic Orchestra (RPO) between 2016 and 2024, and, prior to that, I worked at the Philharmonia Orchestra and Royal Northern College of Music. Alongside my fiduciary responsibility for overseeing the RPO's wider business, my role encompassed artistic planning (in conjunction with the RPO's Music Director Vasily Petrenko) and shaping the strategy for the Orchestra's education and community engagement work. As an orchestra that receives under half the level of public funding compared to its UK counterparts, the RPO has to remain tenacious and fleet-of-foot to adapt its business model in order to maintain earned income and ensure that its artistic and education programmes evolve to remain relevant to the diverse range of communities the Orchestra serves. I had the privilege to be a member of the Royal College of Music (RCM)'s Council between 2020 and 2024, providing a direct insight into the challenges and opportunities that face today's young musicians.

I was fortunate to study an undergraduate and Master's degree at the University of York. The most valuable learning for me came from the freedom to create my own performance projects and events, facilitated by a culture that encouraged innovation, exploration, and risk-taking.

Perspectives

It is clear that the professional music industry has recently become a greatly changed landscape and one that feels both fluid and fragile. Multiple headwinds, ranging from the recovery from the COVID-19 pandemic, Brexit, the cost-of-living crisis, and the challenges emerging from an increasing demand to address the Equality, Diversity, and Inclusion (EDI) deficit, can feel overwhelming both to those already working in the industry and to those soon to enter. And yet, with every challenge there comes an opportunity, and it is the 'adaptive and creative skills' that Professor Janis Kelly references when teaching her students that the music industry now needs to draw upon in order to evolve to better serve and remain relevant to the diverse communities it serves.

DOI: 10.4324/9781003281573-7

However, it is often these creative skills from emerging artists that are hardest to capture and realise, frequently as a direct result of the professional industry's dogged determination to maintain the ordered hierarchy that defines what 'success' looks like. This cascades down from organisations to individual artists, and for an industry that spends its time asking others to listen, it could perhaps do more to reflect and listen to those who work for it. That said, it was heartening to read within this chapter emerging challenges to the status quo already taking place, for example, Jonathan Cole referencing composers moving away from the traditional reliance on publishers towards having a more self-managed model of working, where ownership and Intellectual Property (IP) are retained by the individual composer.

From my personal interaction with students at the RCM, I am constantly reminded of the creative potential these young, fresh, and creative minds have for informing the future evolution of our industry. I use the word 'evolution' deliberately, since this is not about dispensing with tradition, artistic excellence, or ambition, all of these characteristics referenced by this chapter's contributors. It is, rather, about finding ways of making more relevant these vital ingredients, in order to play a meaningful role for audiences and wider society. Often when I speak to young musicians about their hopes and fears for the future, this commitment and desire to 'make a difference' through their music-making shines through. The delineation between 'core work' and 'added value programmes' remains blurred in a young musician's mind while studying at a conservatoire, and yet this often becomes ossified once entering the profession, where traditional hierarchies persist. The same could be said for many staff, who have wide-ranging experience within the industry as professional performers, composers, and practitioners, often freelancing for multiple organisations, which gives them a unique perspective and outlook on the wider sector.

The demands placed on publicly funded organisations to address recruitment practices to widen access and inclusion create a disruption to the traditional practice of 'networks', which several contributors mention as a gateway into the profession. A better understanding of unconscious bias has led performing arts organisations to run more transparent recruitment practices, including anonymised CVs and screened auditions. There is clearly a need for the profession and conservatoires to work closer together to better prepare students for this new audition process, with initiatives such as the RCM's Centre for Performance Science perfectly placed to contribute towards this. The higher education institution (HEI) culture of encouraging students to speak up when they do encounter barriers or discrimination while establishing a career in the music industry will help change our sector and let it emerge from the challenges it currently faces in confronting this area.[3]

Chapter 3 highlights for me the gulf that exists between the safe environment of a conservatoire and the often challenging and at times volatile professional world facing emerging musicians. Neither music colleges nor the profession have the bandwidth to manage and support adequately these fledgling professionals, which suggests that a partnership approach with external organisations such as UK Music and Help Musicians UK could provide a viable and much-needed infrastructure to offer additional support to these graduates. Acquiring data from recent graduates would help both the industry and conservatoires identify the most pressing needs and gaps and therefore better target resources to equip students and organisations with the skills and mechanisms to support young musicians meaningfully and identify where the barriers lie. This is particularly valuable for solo artists and composers, whose careers can be particularly challenging to grow without the framework and support of a larger organisation such as an orchestra or opera house. There is also a need to keep nurturing and growing these young professionals to provide a continuous feedback loop into the profession, providing a reminder that learning does not finish upon graduation, and emphasising the value that a mentor can continue to contribute to a young artist's development.

Janis Kelly's pursuit of the 'elite' without 'elitism' in music is laudable, and artistic integrity must continue to sit at the heart of the symbiotic relationship between conservatoires and the profession. However, the tram tracks of 'Western classical music' are too often narrowly defined, with the meeting point for partnerships between conservatoire and the music industry almost exclusively focusing on the traditional highest-profile performance opportunities. I would like to see in the future each industry/conservatoire partnership to include at least one deviation from the traditional model, exploring new territories and even extending beyond the art form of music to incorporate wider performing arts organisations specialising in dance, drama, and theatre. There is much to learn from both sides about education and audience engagement by stepping beyond the confines of the music industry.

Moreover, David Hockings makes an interesting point in his explanation for how he recruits the future pipeline of RCM percussion students from secondary schools, via his RCM students participating in demonstrations and school workshops. The multi-layer benefits of this approach provide a snapshot of what can be achieved for a wide range of stakeholders and which could be replicated wider beyond the confines of more traditional education models.

Summary

There undoubtedly will continue to be challenges to the music sector in the years to come and likely a further reduction in the number of orchestras, venues, and festivals that will engage and commission tomorrow's performers and composers. That said, the convening powers music has to bring communities together, unlock the creative potential of individuals, and contribute positively to a healthier and happier society are overwhelmingly evidenced, and it is through these lenses that we need to focus our resources for developing and supporting the next generation of young musicians.

It is notable that there was minimal discussion in the chapter about 'risk', or about how our appetite to embrace and accept risk will be essential to drive forward innovation. Conservatoires can do more to encourage within the profession a culture of learning, where failure feeds innovation and imperfection drives further ambition. Finding the sweet spot that does not compromise artistic ambition will be challenging, but find it we must. The profession and conservatoires must jointly do more to facilitate a feedback loop for recent graduates so that we can learn where the industry barriers persist and how we can cultivate a sector that supports creative expression and growth.

The chapter's summary of tomorrow's musicians being 'curators and creators' is pertinent. 'Art for art's sake' is no longer a strong enough rationale to feed and sustain the classical music industry. It must harness and realise the creative talents of each and every emerging musician who can in turn support, shape, inform, and make relevant the art form to an ever more diverse and changing society. The responsibility for unlocking this potential lies squarely with both the conservatoires and the profession, and the need for greater partnership has never felt more urgent or more vital.

Chapter and Perspective Notes

1 Daykin et al., 'What works for wellbeing?'.
2 Examples of industry organisations promoting change include Keychange (www.keychange.eu/ themovement), Black Lives in Music (https://blim.org.uk/), and the League of American Orchestras (https://americanorchestras.org/catalyst-guide-audience-diversification/).
3 See www.ism.org/images/files/ISM-Dignity-2-report.pdf, which highlights the extent of the challenges still facing the sector.

4

REASSESSING MUSICAL EXCELLENCE

Miranda Francis, Vanessa Latarche, and Aaron Williamon

Introduction

An expert, it is said, is someone who comes to know more and more about less and less.[1] While true perhaps in many fields, this is certainly not so in music. For today's professional musician, an expert is one who must know more and more about . . . more and more. We expect musicians to be ready to perform, at a moment's notice, an ever-growing body of repertoire, across a widening range of genres, with people and in environments that, sometimes, they have never before encountered. To be in a position to 'know more' – or better yet, to be in a position to *act* on what they know – musicians have to command an impressive array of skills and know-how that we may readily associate with experts in other domains: the prowess of an athlete, the acumen of a surgeon, the inventiveness of an entrepreneur, the communicative skills of a diplomat, and so on.

How, then, can a conservatoire approach the task of preparing aspiring professional musicians to acquire and deploy the multifaceted skills needed to succeed in the music profession? Achieving musical excellence is neither a singular nor a fixed path for every person, but rather, one with opportunities and challenges that are as many and varied as there are individual musicians. To reflect this, we highlight three case studies of musical excellence: one capturing the distinctive learning environment of the Royal College of Music Junior Department (RCMJD) and two drawn from among students in the RCM's Keyboard Faculty. These are case studies that necessitate a reassessment of what may be considered a 'conventional' view of musical excellence: away from one that sees excellence only in terms of uniform and fixed standards, that prioritises a narrow set of musical specialisms, such as performance and composition in the Western classical tradition, and that arises from and is signalled by a small cluster of musical skills. To move beyond this view, we conclude by describing seven broad areas of skill and knowledge development that, when explicitly addressed through musical training, can provide a foundation upon which music students can pursue musical excellence, as they would define it for themselves.

DOI: 10.4324/9781003281573-8

Example 1: RCM Junior Department

The aim of the UK's 2022 *National Plan for Music Education* (NPME) is 'to enable all children and young people to learn to sing, play an instrument and create music together, and have the opportunity to progress their musical interests and talents, including professionally'.[2] Conservatoires have a significant role to play in the 'wider music education ecology'[3] and should take the 'lead on change within classical music education and the profession'.[4] We have a responsibility to address some of the inequalities that exist in music education and the music profession today and to develop new ways of working that support the young musicians we encounter to fulfil their individual musical potential.

The RCMJD offers musical training to young people between the ages of 5 and 18 years. Since its inception in 1926, the RCMJD (or 'JD' as it is affectionately known) has evolved to meet the musical needs of our students and has adapted to a changing educational and musical landscape. We provide a weekly programme designed to prepare young musicians for musical life in the twenty-first century, working to make them happy, successful, healthy, and entrepreneurial young musicians who can meet the ever-changing demands of the classical music profession. To do this effectively, our junior conservatoire programme is constantly evolving to meet the needs of our students, particularly as definitions of artistry are changing, and research suggests that our students are moving away from 'seeing themselves as a violinist, for example, and towards someone who describes themselves as a creative, an artist, and a musician'.[5] Perhaps most crucially, attending a junior conservatoire enables able young musicians to share musical experiences, to have fun, and to develop their musical skills with others. We foster a sense of musical community at the RCMJD, where everyone – young musicians, parents, teachers, and partner organisations – plays a crucial role in supporting music-making.

Young musicians travel to the RCM each Saturday from all over the UK for an individually tailored programme of instrumental, vocal, or composition lesson; chamber music, orchestral, and choral training; and a wide range of stimulating and challenging musicianship classes. Our students enjoy the opportunity to work alongside outstanding teachers who are also active professional musicians, gaining real-world expertise, reflecting how 'we depend on one another, on communities of practice, as we move along our own path to becoming an expert'.[6] We encourage our students to develop, in consultation with their teachers, the effective and efficient practice strategies necessary to progress towards excellence: to 'develop concentration, to set and meet personal goals, to self-evaluate, to be flexible' and to see 'the big picture'.[7] In addition to the classical musical training we provide, we support our students to widen their musical horizons and to 'create and play music across genres'.[8] For example, our students can learn to perform or improvise in a free, jazz, classical, or folk style. They compose for each other in a wide variety of genres: for film, for string quartet, for choir, as a live solo musician with electronics, or for professional groups. We offer students the opportunity to gain experience of performing in a variety of groups and contexts ranging from the informal, such as our weekly Performance Platform where individuals or groups receive supportive and constructive feedback, to formal opportunities such as our regular Late Night Jazz gig at the Royal Albert Hall or our major orchestral concerts at Cadogan Hall.

Rather than encouraging our students to strive towards a fixed notion of 'excellence', we aim to empower young musicians on our programme to realise their individual musical potential: a 'malleable and ever-changing'[9] concept and a dimension of human experience that takes many forms and occurs at many different levels. However, our annual auditions reveal huge disparities in the quality and quantity of musical opportunities that young people have enjoyed and the extent to which their musical potential has been nurtured prior to audition. Some have enjoyed private tuition for many years, while others have had limited access to music lessons and have little or no experience of ensemble music-making. Our audition panels seek to evaluate motivation and potential, rather than relying purely on musical standard attained, and we carefully consider the individual needs of each student. Once a student secures a place at a junior conservatoire, they can access means-tested bursary support from a variety of sources, and between 35 and 40% of RCMJD students receive some financial support each year. However, the challenge for any young musician lies in getting to the audition in the first place. Local education authorities no longer provide free peripatetic music teaching in schools, and this severely limits access to music provision for groups under-represented in higher education generally (as well as at the RCM specifically). As a result, only small numbers of students from under-represented groups have an opportunity during their formative years to study a musical instrument to a level sufficient to be likely to be offered a place to study at the RCM or RCMJD.

Music education in general has been 'underfunded and sidelined' in state schools over several years,[10] and a recent report found that barriers to accessing music education have altered little in the past 20 years.[11] There is no doubt that the COVID-19 pandemic also had a significant impact on music in UK schools,[12] heightening issues relating to the equality of access to music education.[13] As McPherson and Hallam state, 'all children are inherently musical and deserve access to the types of informal and formal experiences that will maximize their own, individual musical potential'.[14] We have, therefore, developed several new access pathways to the RCMJD, so that young musicians can access the tuition they need in order to develop their confidence and musical skills. For example, Associate members attend one musical class (such as orchestra or musicianship classes) to complement their local musical studies, and our Pathways programme (run in association with Future Talent) offers intensive individual lessons and ensemble tuition for one year as preparation for RCMJD auditions. New 'pipeline' projects that support students to progress and to navigate the current musical landscape are crucial. As the authors of *The Power of Music* state:

> Supporting talent development and progression is complex, as is the landscape of opportunities and pathways. Both the identification of individual talent, and the building and sustaining of equitable talent pipelines are key. There is no single model for progression through music. Identification and support for individual talented young musicians should be tailored to the young person's need.[15]

There is no doubt that junior conservatoire programmes can provide an effective progression pathway for young musicians from compulsory education through higher education to the profession. While studying at the RCMJD, our young musicians are signposted to explore any and all musical opportunities both inside and outside the conservatoire, and they dominate the orchestral lists of all major youth orchestras such as the UK's National Children's Orchestra, the National Youth Orchestra, and Chineke! Juniors. Crucially, attending a junior conservatoire programme enables young musicians to transition to higher education. For example, at the RCMJD, all of our students go on to higher education study, with

64% studying music at either university or conservatoire and with 25% continuing their musical studies at the RCM as undergraduates.

Junior conservatoires have a significant role to play in supporting and nurturing the musical potential of the next generation of music students from a diverse range of backgrounds. Increasing the number of students from groups currently under-represented in the classical music industry is a strategic priority for the RCM as a whole. As Henley so clearly states, 'if we want diversity in music, then we need diversity in music education provision'.[16] Approximately 40% of RCMJD students are from the global majority, and we believe that it is vital that our young musicians see themselves and their lived experience reflected in the professional musicians they work with as teachers and adjudicators and the music that they perform. We continue to transform and expand our artistic programme and curriculum to include works by under-represented composers and to incorporate student voice. RCMJD students, for example, were recently encouraged to suggest pieces that they would like to perform by under-represented composers. We received a large number of responses to this call-out, and as a direct result of this initiative, a student rehearsed and directed a performance of Coleridge-Taylor Perkinson's Sinfonietta 1 which was subsequently broadcast on the RCM's YouTube channel.

The RCMJD strives to be truly inclusive and to be an agent of meaningful change. We aim to foster talent pipelines by reaching out to and working alongside musical organisations in geographical 'cold spots' on joint musical projects involving students from both senior and junior programmes. Our *Sparks Juniors* programme offers first-access musical tuition for local young musicians aged five to eight from under-represented groups, supported by senior RCM student mentors (see also Chapter 14). The RCMJD also works closely with Nucleo, a local 'music for social action project', signposting students from our RCM *Sparks Juniors* programme to Nucleo's successful immersive weekday classes while facilitating pathways of progression for Nucleo students into the RCMJD and beyond. By fostering a number of 'dynamic partnerships'[17] of this nature, based on musical respect and shared musical goals, we aim to create meaningful 'mechanisms for transition'[18] between stages of learning and facilitating progression from compulsory school to conservatoire.

Junior conservatoire programmes should guard against simply 'widening access to excellence' but should aim to redefine musical excellence in the junior conservatoire context.[19] What does being 'excellent' mean for a young musician? Is it the quality of being outstanding, of standing out? Moving forward, we must embrace and celebrate notions of excellence that recognise different dimensions of achievement, from initial steps on a musical instrument, through developing tone, expression, technique, and gaining confidence in music-making with others, to developing a sense of personal musical authority and expertise in public performance, whatever be the genre or setting.

Example 2: RCM Keyboard Faculty

Case study: Gabriella

Gabriella[20] showed signs of a passion for music, most especially piano music, and a flair for performance as a child prodigy. Almost uncontrollable in her zest for playing to the public at every opportunity, in unconventional venues as well as traditional settings, Gabriella built a name for herself from a young age. She came to the attention of the wider musical community when she began to perform at major competitions as a teenager, winning prizes around the world. Occasionally students start at the RCM earlier than usual, and Gabriella was one such student, beginning her undergraduate studies early in order to have some direction to her studies and pursue an undergraduate degree. In some circles, she was already hailed as an excellent musician.

As an ambitious young pianist, all Gabriella really wanted to do was to play and be expressive, and even at this tender age, she exhibited excellence in technical skills. Her piano sound was, however, very raw and undisciplined, and she wanted to show how much she loved a phrase, usually with excessive over-phrasing. When teaching this kind of passionate young person, the last thing one wants is to diminish those natural feelings and temperaments, but one has to work with her to realise what might be considered as 'good taste', stylish, and, most of all, faithful to the composer's intentions.

Gabriella had tackled some of the major works in the piano repertoire before being accepted into the RCM, and she had already achieved much academically, so for her to attend a Bachelor's course at the conservatoire at a younger age than most others in her cohort meant that in some areas she was ahead, but in others there was some fast catching up to do. Living at home during her studies meant that she was not always able to socialise with her friends in the same way as she might have done if she had lived in student accommodation. Some would argue that this was detrimental to her development as a person, but for Gabriella, at this age, parental guidance over her social life as an underage student was paramount to her success in her studies from the outset. As Gabriella developed more musical as well as personal independence, there was a fine line between keeping her parents informed while allowing Gabriella to have private musical space in her lessons, which only she and her teacher occupied. This fine balance was necessary in order to earn Gabriella's trust, and as the years went on, she deepened intellectually.

Trust in any relationship is of paramount importance for the meeting of minds to function in tandem. That does not necessarily mean that the student has to agree with every detail that is imparted by the teacher, but that at least they are open to trying out the suggestion. If it then does not work, the professor can appreciate and accept that the student has a different viewpoint. Without trust and belief that a teacher has a student's interests at heart, there can be a psychological barrier that is difficult to overcome. The musical development of a student who cannot put their trust in their teacher can become stilted, and may become impossible to continue, with the inevitable parting of the ways between the two. Likewise, when a professor senses a lack of trust from a student, the tension in the relationship is hard to sustain, and usually a breakdown can occur. If trust is maintained throughout the studies and beyond, after the student has graduated, the artist can always ask for opinions, bounce off ideas, and be sure to gain some honest advice from their former teacher, all of which is invaluable for ongoing professional excellence and development.

Case study: Yu

Yu[21] auditioned for the RCM from her home country of China. She was rather shy and timid, but she was someone who had spent time learning the complete Chopin Etudes from an early age and could play them fluently. There is something to be said for the hours and hours of coaching in childhood to enable fluency and ability to play at speed and with clarity. But what is the impact of this? While it can be thrilling on one level, especially to see a young person getting around a keyboard so quickly, what about musical and artistic understanding?

On arrival to the RCM, Yu settled into her studies and defaulted to the intensive work ethic for practising her instrument that she had adopted from an early age. Her social interactions were limited, and her teacher suggested taking time out to go to concerts (of all types of music), visit art galleries, walk in nature, and so on. This advice was met with some suspicion at first, but eventually it was taken on board. As her observations of these other aspects of life broadened, and with the benefit of supporting academic study to inform her keyboard skills, a deeper and more refined level of musicality was found in her playing. Yu became curious, and gaining knowledge caused her curiosity to grow at each stage.

The realisation of where, as a student, you sit within the musical world is one step to finding your own path for your career. That process does not come easily to some, with many having unrealistic opinions of their own ability, often leading to many disappointments. Some would argue that learning to deal with disappointment is a life skill, perhaps even more so in the highly competitive music profession, but it can also be destructive to the self-belief of a vulnerable young musician. That sense of satisfaction when you know you have found your own path, have achieved perhaps over and above what you expected of yourself, is life-affirming.

Yu felt she had had a life-changing experience at the conservatoire. Yes, it was a competitive atmosphere, but for Yu to be able to understand a late Beethoven Piano Sonata, play it well, and share that experience with others was her form of musical excellence.

Supporting the development of musical excellence

As illustrated in these case studies, musical excellence is clearly multifaceted. The careers of musicians today comprise roles not only as a performer but also working as a teacher, impresario, facilitator, business owner, manager, and much more (see also Chapter 12). There is no doubt that the meaning of excellence is nuanced and personal for every musician at each stage in their musical development. Striving for excellence is a journey, and there is no fixed point of arrival. Excellence in the conservatoire lies in signposting and enabling students to find and follow progression pathways.

What are the broad areas of skill and know-how that facilitate progression? The literature on music performance education and, in particular, research on performance evaluation and assessment provide a starting point. Certain criteria for performance success have been articulated and employed worldwide for decades. Reviews by Thompson and Williamon (2003)[22] and McPherson and Schubert (2004)[23] have shown that performance evaluation systems in music can be reduced to four main dimensions, all of which inform grades in performance examinations and rankings in music competitions: Artistic, Technical, Ensemble, and Presentation.

Artistic (or musical) skills and knowledge refer to insight and ability to interpret and express music in ways that are sensitive to the music's character and mood, including the 'perceptive choice of tempo, phrase shaping, dynamic shadings, sense of line, and understanding of overall structure'.[24] *Technical* (or instrumental) skills and knowledge encompass the physical and instrumental command over elements of performance, including for example sound production and quality, pitch range and intonation, breathing, posture, and stamina. *Ensemble* skills and knowledge are the coordination of performers working together, covering both artistic and technical dimensions, as well as the capacity for members of the team to listen, lead, and follow where necessary.[25] *Presentation* (or stage) skills and knowledge refer to the ability to hold an audience's attention, maintain a sense of direction, create a sense of occasion, and deliver an entire performance convincingly.[26]

Research in performance science provides insight into three further dimensions that inform musical development. *Learning* (or practice) skills and knowledge refer to self-regulation processes whereby individuals assume responsibility for and control of their progress.[27] The self-regulated processes of forethought, performance/volition control, and self-reflection have been shown as central to effective learning in music and beyond, especially in terms of promoting effective monitoring of skill acquisition, identifying and correcting mistakes, and enhancing feelings of self-efficacy.[28]

Career skills and knowledge encompass those qualities and behaviours needed to enter into and engage fully in professional work in the arts.[29] Given the largely self-employed, portfolio careers that artists pursue, the performers' working conditions can be both complex and precarious (e.g. 'you're only as good as your last performance'), and deliberate attention to career development can be essential to functioning in such a high-pressure, competitive landscape. Importantly, different elements of musical excellence are likely to be required in different professional contexts. Recent research with musicians working in hospital contexts, for example, highlighted the need for musical and communicative versatility and the ability to connect and empathise through music: all forms of excellence that are specific to the setting and that the musicians reported were different from those they utilised in other aspects of their work.[30]

Finally, *Life* skills and knowledge are performance-related aspects of health and well-being that inform how musicians achieve degrees of self-fulfilment, positive attitudes towards learning and work, and long and productive careers. The physical and mental health of musicians has been shown to differ significantly from that of general population samples, both positively and negatively, to the extent that researchers and health professionals are now calling for better health education and promotion initiatives within music education settings.[31]

The first four dimensions, as well as Learning skills and knowledge, are integral to how musical performances are delivered, evaluated, ranked, and reviewed;[32] and they form the mainstay of music performance education today. Nonetheless, there are no standardised curricula stating how they should be taught or acquired, nor when and in what depth, through direct instruction.[33] Explicit advice and guidance on how to interweave Career and Life skills and knowledge into training are even more variable, although there are some notable exceptions.[34]

The seven areas of skill and knowledge that we outline here are broad and, perhaps, not exhaustive. When viewed as a whole, they are meant to stimulate thinking, and eventually action, towards developing and pursuing programmes of performance enhancement, both for individual musicians and for those who support, train, and employ them. In practice, music students should identify, together with teachers and mentors, specific skills and knowledge in each dimension that they consider essential for success. Then, for instance, they can develop multiple, bespoke performance profiles to identify aspirations, enhance goal-directed thinking, and target specific strengths and weaknesses.[35]

Summary

Musical excellence is fostered by sharing with students the tools to discover their creative identity and to fulfil their musical potential. Importantly, it is not the amount of training that matters here. Rather, fostering an awareness and supporting the development of Artistic, Technical, Ensemble, Learning, Presentation, Career, and Life skills and knowledge, as well as offering opportunities to think deliberately about these skills with teachers and peers, offer a framework for music education that recognises multiple artistic identities and diverse pathways to musical excellence. In a conservatoire context, excellence represents empowerment, and a conservatoire's global reach is enhanced by a community which is constantly evolving.

- Key take-away 1: the meaning of musical excellence is varied, nuanced, and personal for every musician at each stage in their musical development.
- Key take-away 2: striving for excellence is a journey, and there is no fixed point of arrival. Excellence lies in signposting and enabling students to find and follow their own progression pathways.
- Key take-away 3: supporting students in developing, maintaining, and enhancing their Artistic, Technical, Ensemble, Learning, Presentation, Career, and Life skills and knowledge can provide a foundation upon which students can pursue musical excellence, as they would define it for themselves.

Further information and reading

Kneebone, Roger. *Expert: Understanding the Path to Mastery*. London: Penguin, 2020.
McPherson, Gary. *The Child as Musician: A Handbook of Musical Development*. 2nd ed. Oxford: Oxford University Press, 2016.
Rink, John, Helena Gaunt, and Aaron Williamon. *Musicians in the Making: Pathways to Creative Performance*. Oxford: Oxford University Press, 2017.
Williamon, Aaron. *Musical Excellence: Strategies and Techniques to Enhance Performance*. Oxford: Oxford University Press, 2004.

Bibliography

ABRSM. *Learning, Playing and Teaching in the UK in 2021*. London: Associated Board of the Royal Schools of Music (ABRSM), 2021. https://gb.abrsm.org/media/66373/web_abrsm-making-music-uk-21.pdf.
Alessandri, Elena, Victoria J. Williamson, Hubert Eiholzer, and Aaron Williamon. 'Beethoven recordings reviewed: A systematic method for mapping the content of music performance criticism'. *Frontiers in Psychology* 6, no. 57 (2015): 1–14. https://doi.org/10.3389/fpsyg.2015.00057.
Araújo, Liliana, David Wasley, Rosie Perkins, Louise Atkins, Emma Redding, Jane Ginsborg, and Aaron Williamon. 'Fit to perform: An investigation of higher education music students' perceptions, attitudes, and behaviors toward health'. *Frontiers in Psychology* 8 (2017): 1–19. https://doi.org/10.3389/fpsyg.2017.01558.
Bull, Anna. *Class, Control, and Classical Music*. Oxford: Oxford University Press, 2019.
Cartwright, Phillip A., Mats B. Küssner, and Aaron Williamon. 'Key performance dimensions of the "well-tempered musician": A framework for artist management'. *International Journal of Arts Management* 23, no. 2 (2021): 18–29.
Chaffin, Roger, and Anthony Lemieux. 'General perspectives on achieving musical excellence'. In *Musical Excellence: Strategies and Techniques to Enhance Performance*, edited by Aaron Williamon, 19–39. Oxford: Oxford University Press, 2004.
Daubney, Alison, and Martin Fautley. 'U-turns in the fog: The unfolding story of the impact of COVID-19 on music education in England and the UK'. *British Journal of Music Education* 38, no. 1 (2021): 3–12. https://doi.org/10.1017/S0265051721000048.
DfE. *The Power of Music to Change Lives: A National Plan for Music Education (NPME)*. London: Department for Education (DfE), 2022. www.gov.uk/government/publications/the-power-of-music-to-change-lives-a-national-plan-for-music-education.

Fautley, Martin. 'Editorial: Music-making continues during the pandemic'. *British Journal of Music Education* 37, no. 3 (2020): 193–95. https://doi.org/10.1017/S0265051720000273.

Henley, Jennie. 'Music: Naturally inclusive, potentially exclusive?' In *Inclusive Pedagogy Across the Curriculum*, edited by Joanne M. Deppeler, Tim Loreman, Ron Smith, and Lani Florian, 161–86. Bingley, UK: Emerald, 2015.

Henley, Jennie, and D. Barton. 'Time for change? Recurrent barriers to music education'. *British Journal of Music Education* 39, no. 2 (2022): 203–17. https://doi.org/10.1017/S026505172200016X.

Kneebone, Roger. *Expert: Understanding the Path to Mastery*. London: Penguin, 2020.

McPherson, Gary E., and Susan Hallam. 'Musical potential'. In *Oxford Handbook of Music Psychology*. 2nd ed., edited by Susan Hallam, Ian Cross, and Michael Thaut, 433–48. Oxford: Oxford University Press, 2016.

McPherson, Gary E., and Emery Schubert. 'Measuring performance enhancement in music'. In *Musical Excellence: Strategies and Techniques to Enhance Performance*, edited by Aaron Williamon, 61–82. Oxford: Oxford University Press, 2004.

Myles Beeching, Angela. *Beyond Talent: Creating a Successful Career in Music*. Oxford: Oxford University Press, 2010.

Ritchie, Laura, and Aaron Williamon. 'Measuring musical self-regulation: Linking processes, skills, and beliefs'. *Journal of Education and Training Studies* 1, no. 1 (2013): 106–17. https://doi.org/10.11114/jets.v1i1.81.

Shaughnessy, C., A. Hall, and R. Perkins. 'Becoming the right musician for the job: Versatility, connectedness, and professional identities during personalised, online music-making in hospital maternity wards'. *Musicae Scientiae* (2023). https://journals.sagepub.com/doi/10.1177/10298649231165028.

Thompson, Sam, and Aaron Williamon. 'Evaluating evaluation: Musical performance assessment as a research tool'. *Music Perception* 21, no. 1 (2003), 21–41. https://doi.org/10.1525/mp.2003.21.1.21.

Thompson, Sam, Aaron Williamon, and Elizabeth Valentine. 'Time-dependent characteristics of performance evaluation'. *Music Perception* 25, no. 1 (2007): 13–29. https://doi.org/10.1525/mp.2007.25.1.13.

Underhill, Jodie. *The Heart of the School is Missing: Music Education in the COVID-19 Crisis*. London: Incorporated Society of Musicians (ISM), 2020. www.ism.org/images/files/ISM_UK-Music-Teachers-survey-report_Dec-2020_A4_ONLINE-2.pdf.

Waddell, George, and Aaron Williamon. 'Eye of the beholder: Stage entrance behavior and facial expression affect continuous quality ratings in music performance'. *Frontiers in Psychology* 8 (2017): 1–14. https://doi.org/10.3389/fpsyg.2017.00513.

Williamon, Aaron. 'Implications for education'. In *Expressiveness in Music Performance: Empirical Approaches Across Styles and Cultures*, edited by Dorottya Fabian, Renee Timmers, and Emery Schubert, 348–51. Oxford: Oxford University Press, 2014.

Williamon, Aaron, Terry Clark, and Mats B. Küssner. 'Learning in the spotlight: Approaches to self-regulating and profiling performance'. In *Musicians in the Making: Pathways to Creative Performance*, edited by John Rink, Helena Gaunt, and Aaron Williamon, 206–21. Oxford: Oxford University Press, 2017.

Williamon, Aaron, and Jane W. Davidson. 'Exploring co-performer communication'. *Musicae Scientiae* 6, no. 1 (2002): 53–72. https://doi.org/10.1177/102986490200600103.

Williamon, Aaron, and Sam Thompson. 'Awareness and incidence of health problems among conservatoire students'. *Psychology of Music* 34 (2006): 411–30. https://doi.org/10.1177/0305735606067150.

Zimmerman, Barry J. 'Self- regulated learning and academic achievement: An overview'. *Educational Psychologist* 25, no. 1 (1990): 3–17. https://doi.org/10.1207/s15326985ep2501_2.

PERSPECTIVE: CHAPTER 4

Afa Sadykhly Dworkin

Introduction

I am a violinist by training. I grew up in Baku, Azerbaijan, having been born in Moscow, Russia, and received my higher education training at the University of Michigan School of Music, Theatre & Dance. More than 30 years ago, my passion for music led me in a different direction: I launched my journey with a budding non-profit in the United States (US) called the Sphinx Organization, whose mission is to transform lives through the power of diversity in the arts. I fell in love with an idea, an ethos that resonated with what I came to recognise as a sense of belonging. While my parents were not musicians, they created an environment where I pursued my studies as a young artist and flourished as an individual in a sphere unfamiliar to them but organic and necessary for me. Because most of my friends, without regard to skin tone, cultural background, or postal code, sang and played instruments, as well, we shared that special sense of belonging. Access to musical studies and artistic expression is an essential right for every young person, and I wanted to be a part of something that makes that right attainable, even though it would eventually mean that I would move away from professional performance into the sphere of education and non-profit leadership. Today, I serve as President and Artistic Director for Sphinx, having built our educational and creative youth development programmes, as well as helping to launch and grow our professional touring ensembles and now nurturing dozens of administrators of colour who are leading the way in our industry. We reach 10,000 young people and 60 million in audiences through our annual programmes. I consider my station in life to be a deep privilege and an honour to uphold.

Perspectives

First, I appreciated the very opening of the chapter, illuminating how knowledge in music is uniquely subject to an expanded view, and the tendency to broaden how we define skill sets has a deeper and more augmented implication than many other fields. An expert in music is truly someone who needs to learn more about more. Art for art's sake is no longer

DOI: 10.4324/9781003281573-9

sufficient: art for the sake of our society and the betterment of the quality of life, with more consequential implications on the social–emotional subtext of our young people, is something that we have been observing in music education over the last couple of decades. Even more fascinating is the question of artist or musician citizenship. Increasingly, our music institutions are being called upon to serve our communities, our students, our supporters, patrons, and audiences. We are reimagining our institutions of higher learning as musical collectives of today and tomorrow and as agents of enrichment and service. I found the element discussing excellence to be interesting, as it explores a broadening and ever-changing direction for the concept that was once revered and regarded as rather fixed.

Today, in addition to agreeing with that definition, I am also drawn to thinking about the flip side of such an evolved concept: the benefit to the art form itself. From the limitation of the tonal structures that we have taught and studied for centuries as the mainstream within the construct of Western-only theoretical concepts to the very notion of what, in fact, constitutes the classical music canon, we have limited our art form to a more narrow, less informed, and therefore, one might argue, a less excellent version of itself. While that alone is unfortunate, even more detrimental is the diminishing or inconsistent relevance that classical music has had for our greater society. With the diversity prevalent in many large cities where conservatoires are often based, the reciprocity between their primary beneficiaries (students) and the institutions themselves is in question. If our students of diverse backgrounds are yearning to find a sense of relevance, belonging, and empowerment, then the art form, as with any evolving discipline, should strive to be more inclusive in response to that need. If we are to nurture the next generation of artists, we will look at the young artists, much like the described youngsters in the chapter, as future leaders who can achieve impact and bring about positive results as artists, but only if they develop that sense of connection and belonging. Music has a way of fostering a sense of empowerment and helping young people reach their full potential not just as artists but also as thinkers, leaders, community servants, and, truly, ambassadors for the art form. In order to truly thrive, that art form needs empowered individuals of all backgrounds, and, therefore, the very notion of excellence is not just broader but more vital and evolved today than it may have been two decades ago.

For centuries, certain voices from non-Western communities were simply excluded from the canon, from our textbooks, and from the repertoire imagined to be 'classical'. Musicians were also judged by their fluency in their primary instrument within the literature that was known, studied, and accepted as deserving. Our pedagogues were versed in helping us develop our instrumental fitness and enough mental agility to explore the relationship between ourselves and a one-dimensional sense of the classical repertoire. Today, our teaching artists are being called upon to expand their own competency, which involves not merely studying and teaching new repertoire but also partnering with their students in challenging some of the limiting concepts and including/expanding their training through citizenship, community engagement, and entrepreneurial skills that are so vital today. In relevance to the chapter, we are more excellent as a field/sector if we are more inclusive. We are more excellent if we are more relevant. We are more likely to succeed from the standpoint of impact and longevity for our art form if we develop innovative, broadly informed, agile, and skilled citizen artists who share their art form as leaders on and off stage. To paraphrase Aristotle, 'We are what we repeatedly do . . . therefore excellence is not an act, but a habit'. Our institutions of higher learning are on an exciting journey of transforming the potential of classical music to empower and to regain its relevance to broader communities. We must habitually strive to do so on a system level, beyond any one effort or initiative.

Summary

In summary, classical music education should foster excellence in all of its facets while equipping and empowering the student to see themselves as a portfolio career master. In today's age, excellence on the instrument alone is no longer sufficient. As music educators, we must continue to advocate for mastery and commitment to artistic excellence. In the words of Chimamanda Adichie, 'The single story creates stereotypes, and the problem with stereotypes is not that they are untrue, but that they are incomplete'.[36] For an extended period of time, in classical music education, we have been listening to and telling incomplete stories, but the time has come for us to complete the narratives not only for ourselves and our students but also for a more vibrant future for the art form itself.

Bibliography

Adichie, Chimamanda Ngozi. 'The danger of a single story'. Ted Talk, 2009. https://www.ted.com/talks/chimamanda_ngozi_adichie_the_danger_of_a_single_story?subtitle=en

Chapter and Perspective Notes

1 Attributed to Nicholas Butler Murray – philosopher, diplomat, and educator (1862–1947).
2 DfE, *The Power of Music*, 5.
3 DfE, *The Power of Music*, 66.
4 Bull, *Class, Control, and Classical Music*, 188.
5 ABRSM, *Learning, Playing and Teaching*, 58.
6 Kneebone, *Expert*, 305.
7 Chaffin and Lemieux, 'General perspectives', 33.
8 Bull, *Class, Control, and Classical Music*, 191.
9 McPherson and Hallam, 'Musical potential', 443.
10 Bull, *Class, Control, and Classical Music*, 191.
11 Henley and Barton, 'Time for change?'.
12 Underhill, *The Heart of the School*; Fautley, *Editorial*.
13 Daubney and Fautley, 'U-turns in the fog'.
14 McPherson and Hallam, 'Musical potential', 443.
15 DfE, *The Power of Music*, 62.
16 Henley, 'Music: Naturally inclusive', 23.
17 DfE, *The Power of Music*, 6.
18 Henley and Barton, 'Time for change?'.
19 Bull, *Class, Control, and Classical Music*, 185.
20 No real names have been used in this section, and the case studies reflect generalised and/or aggregated examples.
21 No real names have been used in this section, and the case studies reflect generalised and/or aggregated examples.
22 Thompson and Williamon, 'Evaluating evaluation'.
23 McPherson and Schubert, 'Measuring performance enhancement'.
24 McPherson and Schubert, 'Measuring performance enhancement', 64.
25 Williamon and Davidson, 'Exploring co-performer communication'.
26 Waddell and Williamon, 'Eye of the beholder'.
27 Zimmerman, 'Self- regulated learning'.
28 Ritchie and Williamon, 'Measuring musical self-regulation'.
29 Myles Beeching, *Beyond Talent*; see also Ch. 12.
30 Shaughnessy et al., 'Becoming the right musician'.
31 Araújo et al., 'Fit to perform'; see also Ch. 11.
32 Alessandri et al., 'Beethoven recordings reviewed'.
33 Williamon, 'Implications for education'.
34 For example, see Thompson and Williamon, 'Awareness and incidence of health problems among conservatoire students' and Myles Beeching, *Beyond Talent*.
35 For further discussion and suggestions for application, see Williamon et al., 'Learning in the spotlight', and Cartwright et al., 'Key performance dimensions'.
36 Adichie, 'The danger of a single story'.

5

PHILANTHROPY AT THE ROYAL COLLEGE OF MUSIC

Shaping the future of music education

Lily Harriss and Rachel Harris

Introduction

Funding is one of the most pressing strategic priorities for leaders of conservatoires that are not state-owned, and philanthropy is a vital and significant part of this. There are two strands to this philanthropy: giving to individual *students* and giving to support the *institution* directly to deliver its mission. Both strands are likely to be essential to the modern conservatoire. Why is there need? Conservatoire training is expensive because of the focus on individual tuition. It was then, as it is now, not realistic to charge fee payers the total cost of their education for the fear of pricing it beyond market feasibility. Undergraduates from the UK pay a standard regulated fee which currently only covers around one third of the full cost of their rich education; furthermore, the standard fee has not increased (at the time of writing) since 2017, without allowance for inflation. Nevertheless, this can still be unaffordable for students, particularly those who do not receive loans or scholarships and considering the increasing cost of living in cities like London.

For conservatoires in England that are judged to be 'World-leading specialist providers', the Office for Students (OfS) provides top-up funding, but there is still a shortfall. The criteria and amount of this funding are decided through a new process every five years, creating significant risk for conservatoires as the priorities of the regulator can change. At the time of writing, other top-up funding for arts subjects has been completely eroded, and capital funding is sporadic and only for small projects, meaning that this World-leading specialist funding is critical to survival. Overseas students are also hugely important to the financial sustainability of the UK Conservatoire, as they pay fees at a market rate, but often they can only afford to be admitted if they can access scholarship funding. The global COVID-19 pandemic also brought philanthropic need into sharper focus. Many cultural charities in the UK were devastated, with an estimated approximately £10 billion shortfall in income.[1] The performing arts faced the most significant crisis in living memory, profoundly affecting professionals in the field and creating an unprecedented requirement for funding to replace lost income streams. Thus, philanthropy makes a crucial contribution for higher education institutions such as the Royal College of Music (RCM).

DOI: 10.4324/9781003281573-10

What do we mean by philanthropy? Modern philanthropy can be defined as the wish to support the welfare of others, conveyed specifically by the generous donation of money to charitable causes.[2] Philanthropy focuses on quality of life for the interest of others (prosocial), in contrast to business initiatives, which are for the personal interest and focus on material gain, and government initiatives which are for the public good, such as the provision of services. Those who partake in philanthropy are philanthropists or donors. At English conservatoires, energy is spent on maximising other sources of funds, such as income from external hires, partnerships, and ticket sales. However, the amounts are modest, and philanthropy remains essential to deliver the rich educational experience on offer. Specifically at the RCM, donations, together with the investment income generated by the philanthropically funded endowment, are the second largest source of income after tuition fees. Accordingly, we can argue that those who work, teach, and perform in conservatoires must ensure that they cultivate, steward, and strengthen our community, including the mechanisms of philanthropic support. We can examine the usual quantitative means for measuring the impact of donated income and the activities to keep and grow this support channel. Yet, that should be combined with a greater understanding of our donors' (philanthropists') beliefs, thoughts, and feelings to support conservatoires with this endeavour.

Philanthropy at the Royal College of Music – A brief overview

The RCM has a long history of philanthropic support. It was founded in 1883 on the principle that world-class music education should be available to talented musicians regardless of financial means or societal position.[3,4] Philanthropy at the RCM has also had a significant impact on financial health and stability, particularly over the past decade with the most ambitious campaign in the College's history – More Music: Reimagining the Royal College of Music (2012–2022).

RCM originally emerged from the economic success of the 1851 Great Exhibition. The College is built on land bought out of the profits of the Exhibition in this area, sometimes referred to as Albertopolis. It was first named as the National Training School of Musicians (which ran from 1876 from 1882), which was insufficient to meet the vision and demand. A particularly determined interest was shown by the then Prince of Wales and his circle in making a success of the new College, and a meeting in 1882 was attended by national figures such as William Gladstone, the Prime Minister, and the Archbishop of Canterbury, at which the Prince officially launched the RCM. Everything hinged on a public appeal for raising the capital required to endow sufficient RCM scholarships – a priority which continues in conservatoires, including the RCM. From the beginning, the RCM Director had philanthropic investment as a critical priority, and the success that was achieved came on the back of the first Director, George Grove, and the philosophical and educational vision for the College. Grove secured donations because he was able to explain that the College would be vital for the future of the nation's musical life. He delivered 44 fundraising speeches across the country,[5] his persuasiveness resting on a compelling case for support. In fact, during its first 60 years, the RCM had only two substantial sources of income – student fees and interest generated from the scholarship capital from donations.

This social liberalism – fostering musical talent regardless of origin or status – had been integral to the College's original purpose as it was founded on philanthropy. The Prince of

Wales (the RCM's President) explicitly referred to this when he opened the RCM. The institution faced critical financial viability issues and workable accommodation in its first two decades. Both had to be resolved, and both needed philanthropic investment. Financially, everything depended on raising enough capital to fund a practical number of scholars and sufficient income to secure the first running costs. With the philanthropic aid of Samson Fox (1839–1903), they were able to make their vision possible. Mr Fox was a self-made Yorkshireman who patented corrugated boiler furnaces and pioneered water gas that was cheaper than coal gas. Notably, his love of music brought him to the RCM.

One of the benefits of having the RCM presented as a national enterprise by the Prince of Wales was that it helped professional music training to be recognised as a socially legitimate form of education and thus worthy of support. It was indicative of the College's perceived status and significance that substantial legacies came from people previously unconnected with it, and the RCM also received precious donations of instruments and musical materials from donors such as George Donaldson. It is also important to note that as well as donations to the building, the College also received significant funding towards establishing an endowment called the 'Patron's Fund', in honour of the College's Patron, King Edward VII,[6] and to encourage native composers and artists with the income from the fund. Ernest Palmer (1858–1948) was the benefactor, and the source of his substantial fortune was Huntley and Palmer biscuits.[7] This gift was an addition to his support of the scholarship programme and the 'Berkshire Scholarship'. This narrative of donors increasing and diversifying their giving to the RCM – to building appeals, scholarship programmes, and to core costs – continues, as explained later.

A much later critical phase of RCM philanthropy was the 1982–1983 Centenary Appeal under Director Sir David Willcocks. The appeal and events (which enjoyed prominent Royal family support) affirmed the RCM's national standing. Straightforward in its aims and strategically well-conceived, the appeal's success positioned the College for a centenary revitalised by an attractive purpose-built opera theatre and an adequately integrated library service with improved social space. The Centenary Appeal was launched a hundred years to the day that the Prince of Wales announced his idea of a Royal College of Music at St James's Palace, and it ended with a Centenary Concert at the Royal Albert Hall on 23 May 1983 to mark the date of the RCM's Royal Charter. The Centenary was structured around three high-profile gala events at the Royal Albert Hall. The second of these in January 1983 was attended by the Prince and Princess of Wales and was supported by internationally known musicians (such as Daniel Barenboim and Itzhak Perlman). The Britten Theatre development was especially significant, surpassed only by the More Music Campaign, mentioned above.

In comparison, *The Musical Times* reported that the RCM's founding Appeal had raised approximately £110,000 by April 1883; based on today's retail price index, it would be approximately £10.5 million – sufficient, then, to raise 50 full scholarships and to set the College underway. However, the difference with today is not just in the size of the sums needed but that the institutional standing was insufficient to ensure success. Still, active and consistent relationships and community building were cultivated and grown with an increase in supporters and a deepening of engagement whereby supporters who may have started their philanthropy at the College with a named scholarship also made a gift for the building development.

More Music: reimagining the Royal College of Music campaign

The More Music Campaign, completed in 2022, set out as a transformational endeavour not only to strengthen facilities through an ambitious building development but also to support talent by recruiting and retaining outstanding teachers and researchers; to ensure students and faculty had the equipment and instruments they need; and to provide financial assistance through scholarships, bursaries, and hardship funds, in order to attract students with outstanding potential from diverse backgrounds. The Campaign also promoted innovation which included providing performance opportunities, the development of digital platforms, and establishing a research hub. Finally, the Campaign also sought to help the College widen access to music education to diverse communities and to children from all backgrounds, as well as develop outreach and audience engagement and make its collections available online to all audiences.

The More Music Campaign exceeded its fundraising targets in all strands, apart from the building development, where the target was practically achieved. Approximately £42.5 million was raised against the around £40 million campaign target. Of that target, the full £25 million needed for the building development was secured. Targets in all other areas were exceeded, raising a total of approximately £11 million for endowed scholarships and student support, approximately £4.3 million for academic initiatives, and approximately £2.2 million for outreach activities over the course of the Campaign. Importantly, a further £14 million was raised during the Campaign period for annual revenue scholarships. The Campaign also delivered a new performance hall and performance studio, each with broadcast and integrated digital infrastructure; new visitor facilities and public spaces; increased provision for over 100 multi-purpose teaching, rehearsal, and practice rooms; additional recording capability, enabling increased access for global audiences; a major new museum, offering a permanent and interactive space for its internationally significant collections; and a rebuilt entrance hall, welcoming the public to performances and events. None of this would have been possible without philanthropic support.

In reviewing the seven years from 2016 to 2022, one observes that just over one fifth of the College's income, equating to ~£6.5 million each year, came from donations and endowments, highlighting how crucial this has become for the College – particularly in a period when much of the College's core fees and funding streams have been declining in real terms. This points again to the argument made earlier, whereby voluntary, donated income is a crucial factor in financial health and sustainability of charitable organisations. However, we should acknowledge the debate around philanthropic giving which centres around gift acceptance and reputational risk with private funding. More recently, there has been what can be described as 'hypercriticism', and generalised attacks on philanthropy have reached new heights in terms of scale and volume. These critiques and debates can undermine the drivers of philanthropic giving which, as will be discussed later, include social and psychological benefits.[8]

It is important to remember that charity law in the UK forbids any substantive benefits for donors, so fundraisers must rely on the power of intangible motivations, and organisations such as the RCM have only recognition and thanks to give their supporters. That said, it is important also to note that all the donations received in Campaign were cultivated and secured following robust due diligence policies and reviews by Council and with clear gift acceptance protocols to protect the College from any reputational risk. Still, and with all of this in the background, through the tremendous generosity of living donors and legacies, the College's permanent endowment fund now stands at around approximately £45 million and generates income each year to fund scholarships and other awards – enough income to cover one tenth of the overall annual tuition fees payable by students. Put together with annual fundraising, this helps the College to award over ~£4 million of scholarships annually, and as a result over half of the College's students receive financial support during their studies. Other donations are used to fund other aspects of the College's activities that would otherwise be unaffordable, including performances, the museum, and outreach activities.

This record illustrates how philanthropy is an essential element of the future of music education. Thus, for those who work in a conservatoire setting, and not for the development professionals alone, a deeper understanding of donors' (philanthropists') beliefs, thoughts, and feelings can help us keep and grow the community of support – to find the 'sweet spot' where their affinity, propensity, and ability intersect to support music education. Rather than focus primarily on income as a measure of the impact of philanthropy, we need to explore more fully the broader societal and personal benefits – to the donor as well as to us, the institution.

Impact of philanthropy at conservatoires – beyond income

Can giving be good for you? John Nickson, a successful fundraiser, philanthropist, and trustee of several organisations, including a Member of the Council at the RCM, attempted to answer this question in his book *Giving is Good for You: Why Britain Should Be Bothered and Give More*.[9] Drawing on interviews with more than 75 philanthropists, asking them their views on giving, he determined that at least 90% of the philanthropists were driven by a desire and determination to do good for others rather than for themselves. While examining the well-being of conservatoires, the 'healthy conservatoire', and the ability to continue to achieve excellence in music education during challenging times, we should also look at what this means to the support base, which has become even more critical. How can individuals and organisations that support music education relate their well-being with their engagement with the conservatoire, and what factors make this possible? This aspect of the relationship will allow us to understand another essential part of relationship-building that will help ensure consistent engagement and support.

We know that giving to others can be linked with well-being. Many people worldwide, especially in countries with a higher GDP per capita, have more material wealth than their parents, but one study found that the percentage of these populations claiming to be happy has not increased, and depression and anxiety rates are rising dramatically.[10] However, in responding to the UK Department of Health's mental health strategy *No Health Without Mental Health* (2011), the New Economics Foundation proposed in their *Five Ways to Wellbeing* that giving to others and the community is one factor for maintaining well-being. Indeed, philanthropy, or so-called 'prosocial spending', has been linked with well-being in domains outside of music.[11] Nevertheless, considering the scant research on the connections between philanthropic giving to conservatoires and well-being, an appreciation of this phenomenon could help understand the characteristics and motivations behind giving. It will also help conservatoires better understand how to engage their supporters and their community of support.

To explore this, we need to gain an understanding of the reported connections between philanthropy and well-being in a conservatoire setting. In a study undertaken by one of the authors at the RCM's Centre for Performance Science, data on this topic were collected via the *Philanthropy and Wellbeing in Conservatoires Survey*. This was an anonymous and exploratory cross-sectional survey to capture philanthropic giving in conservatoires in the UK and to explore its correlations and associations, if any, with well-being. The survey consisted of three main sections: demographic information; philanthropic involvement (including the level of giving, motivation, characteristics, and development); and the impact of music and giving on well-being. Validated scales were used to collect quantitative, numerical data on well-being, measured using the seven-item Short Warwick–Edinburgh Mental Wellbeing Scale (SWEMWBS). Respondents were asked about their feelings and thoughts, including being optimistic about the future, feeling useful, feeling relaxed, dealing with problems well, thinking clearly, feeling close to other people, and being able to make up their minds about things on a five-point scale from 1 (none of the time) to 5 (all the time).[12] Close relationships also drive outcomes related to well-being.[13] Relationships and connectedness were measured using the Inclusion of Other in Self (IOS) Scale,[14] a single-item pictorial measure of perceived emotional closeness for both their relationship with the conservatoire(s) they support and their relationship with the recipient(s). Respondents were also asked open questions about their experiences of giving to conservatoires and their perceptions of whether and how this links with their well-being.

Sixty-four adults responded to the survey (46.9% female), with over 42% between the ages of 55 and 64 years and almost 44% being 65 years or over (range = 25–65+), with levels of education from master's and above (43.2%), bachelor's degree (34.4%), university-level (10.9%), secondary education (9.4%), and no formal education (3.1%). Ethical approval for the study, including consenting procedures, was granted by the Conservatoires UK Research Ethics Committee (CUK REC), following the guidelines of the British Psychological Society. Of the 64 respondents, complete datasets were recorded for 63. This sample provided us with feedback that we have not collected before about how donors feel in their giving, allowing useful insight into something which can be considered intangible.

The study indicated associations between well-being and philanthropy in the conservatoire setting in the UK. Indeed, when using the SWEMWBS as a measure of well-being, these respondents demonstrated higher well-being than the national UK average.[15] Similarly, respondents reported a strong relationship with the conservatoire and their support beneficiaries.[16] These results support the existing literature connecting well-being and philanthropy[17] as well as well-being and music-making[18] and listening to music and well-being.[19] However, the data are not causal in that we cannot know that philanthropists' well-being is higher because they give – it could be the other way around or influenced by other factors, such as financial security. Still, there is scarcely any written work that examines the associations between philanthropy and well-being in the arts and music education. The available studies on music and well-being tend to focus on those who listen to or make music and/or participate in music therapy. There is a large gap for those who engage with music in other ways, specifically philanthropic support. We must look at this as part of the whole, whereby we expand our meaning of the impact of philanthropy from what it means to the conservatoire to reference in addition the well-being of the individual supporter.

When we explore responses to the open questions, the respondents detail additional connections between their involvement and giving to conservatoires and their well-being.

One way of understanding these responses is through Seligman's theory that the building blocks of well-being are based on the positive psychological concepts of Positive Emotion, Engagement, Relationships, Meaning, and Accomplishment (PERMA).[20] This way of thinking includes both hedonic and eudemonic well-being. The hedonic approach emphasises happiness, defining well-being in terms of pleasure attainment and pain avoidance, and can be described as subjective well-being, which is made up of personal evaluations of life satisfaction and the prevalence of positive rather than negative emotions. On the other hand, the eudemonic approach emphasises meaning and self-realisation, where well-being is understood as the entire functioning of a person; more precisely, resources, strengths, purpose, and meaning of life.[21] In the responses, the role of positive emotions stands out, with accounts of philanthropy at the conservatoire facilitating interest, joy, compassion, pride, amusement, and gratitude. Respondents referenced engaging with the music and young talent, which brought forth these feelings. This is consistent with other research on active music participation in communities, which has been reported to provide emotional release and facilitate relaxation and uplifting emotions.[22] It contrasts, though, with evidence that positive emotions are the least reported well-being component among professional musicians.[23] This may reflect a difference between those who make and perform the music professionally and those who listen, benefit from, and support it in other ways.

Another finding worth noting is the connection drawn by respondents between giving to music education and feeling accomplished. Respondents noted success in supporting talent and the future of music and accomplishment when seeing their generosity's effects on the institution and the students they support. Linked with this sense of accomplishment in supporting the future of music and talent, the results suggest that philanthropists' support of music education gave them a sense of meaning and belonging. The respondents reported that their philanthropy provided a means of contribution and 'giving back' to something they loved and were enthusiastic about – music and music education. Finally, reports from the respondents also point to the connection between their philanthropy to conservatoires and the enhanced involvement and focus on music in their lives. In line with this, their generosity also helped facilitate and enhance social interactions and the opportunity to meet people from the institutions; the staff, the students, and fellow music lovers and supporters were perceived as a clear benefit and something they valued. For example, respondents reported a 'powerful' relationship with the conservatoire they support and a 'strong' relationship with the recipients they support. This link between music participation and the provision of opportunities for connections with other people and enriched societal functioning is also reported elsewhere.[24]

Thus, we see evidence for the well-being effects of philanthropy and supporting music education, with benefits stemming from engagement with music education, music performance, and enhanced relationship-building through various interactions with the institution and beneficiaries. These findings contribute to research on music's role in well-being; engagement in the arts and culture is known to support health and well-being.[25] Future studies could explore the similarities or differences between the impact of studying or participating in music versus engaging as a philanthropic supporter, recognising that philanthropists may also be engaging in their support as listeners or engagers in music alongside their financial support.

There were benefits and challenges brought to the study by the dual role of the researcher, who was also the Director of Development at the RCM. For example, as a philanthropy professional, she understood concepts such as 'engagement' and 'developing meaning' as drivers for supporting the performing arts and music education. Thus, she was able to interpret the results based on not only experience but also previous education. However, her experience also required some mitigation of bias, and thus a quantitative, numerical and a qualitative, words-based analysis was applied to the findings to provide multiple interpretations of the data. This research provides a new way of looking at measures of impact and success for philanthropic engagement in conservatoires. For example, rather than just focusing on standard metrics such as donation levels, professionals in the field may highlight activities that create positive emotions and meaning, and the success of those activities and the perceived well-being of their supporters can also be measures for success. The study highlighted the area of knowledge overlapping philanthropy and well-being, which will aid philanthropy professionals working at conservatoires in understanding the critical building blocks and activities that are most conducive to creating a flourishing ecosystem for supporters, which in turn allows for more significant funding for the institutions they are involved with and importantly to build on that much-needed community of support which will help ensure the future and sustainability of specialist education.

There are implications here for developing donor engagement and stewardship programmes. These programmes may include activities focusing on relationship-building with the institution and the beneficiary. These activities should first focus on creating positive emotions, meaning and engagement, relationships, and accomplishment. Finally, a well-being framework can help trigger new philanthropic programmes based on deepened community building when applied to supporter activities in conservatoires. Philanthropic activity at a conservatoire may facilitate multiple forms of connectivity and promote well-being, and further research is required to understand associations with age, philanthropy, and well-being and how younger philanthropists to conservatoires might experience well-being from their involvement. This will allow conservatoires to develop giving programmes for the sustainability of future support. Future studies with larger datasets are also required to explore the associations further.

Consequently, we can help ensure the future success of conservatoires delivering the highest quality music education by strengthening the connection to the community of supporters and by cultivating the concept of philanthropy, so that it is understood to be more than merely a means of income and a way to strengthen our community and our mission to provide access to music and music education. We can do this with a greater understanding of our donors' (philanthropists') beliefs, thoughts and feelings, their well-being, and the power of engagement with music as an essential element of this important relationship.

Summary

In conclusion, philanthropy has been at the heart of the RCM's life and its finances since it was founded. It is crucial to the financial sustainability of the College itself, and, through the scholarship programme, to its commitment to be accessible to the best students from around the world regardless of their background. Returning to the initial observation that there are two strands to the philanthropy that is so important to the modern conservatoire, the first being for financial support to students and the second to support the institution directly to deliver its mission, for the RCM, it is the second strand that is increasingly important. While the first remains central to our core values of access and inclusivity and is often the type of philanthropy that brings the most satisfaction to our regular donors, the second strand of raising funds to support the RCM to deliver its mission is essential to enable it to invest in the facilities, technology, and capabilities to support its innovative and global strategy.

- Key take-away 1: philanthropic funding is a vital strategic priority for the modern conservatoire.
- Key take-away 2: research suggests that there could be important well-being and social benefits to conservatoire donors.
- Key take-away 3: conservatoires can use this insight to develop sustainable and mutually beneficial relationships with their donors.

Further information and reading

Breeze, Beth. *In Defence of Philanthropy*. Newcastle upon Tyne: Agenda Publishing, 2021.
Fancourt, Daisy, and Saoirse Finn. *What is the Evidence on the Role of the Arts in Improving Health and Well-Being? A Scoping Review*. World Health Organization, 2019. https://apps.who.int/iris/handle/10665/329834.
Nickson, John. *Giving is Good for You: Why Britain Should be Bothered*. London: Biteback Publishing, 2013.
Perkins, Rosie, Adele Mason-Bertrand, Daisy Fancourt, Louise Baxter, and Aaron Williamon. 'How participatory music engagement supports mental well-being: A meta-ethnography'. *Qualitative Health Research* 30, no. 12 (October 2020): 1924–40. https://doi.org/10.1177/10497323209 44142.

Bibliography

Aron, Arthur, Elaine N. Aron, and Danny Smollan. 'Inclusion of other in the self scale and the structure of interpersonal closeness'. *Journal of Personality and Social Psychology* 63, no. 4 (1992): 596–612. https://doi.org/10.1037/0022-3514.63.4.596.
Aron, Arthur, Elaine N. Aron, Michael Tudor, and Greg Nelson. 'Close relationships as including other in the self'. *Journal of Personality and Social Psychology* 60, no. 2 (1991): 241–53. https://doi.org/10.1037/0022-3514.60.2.241.
Ascenso, Sara, Rosie Perkins, and Aaron Williamon. 'Resounding Meaning: A PERMA profile of classical musicians'. *Frontiers in Psychology* 9 (2018). https://doi.org/10.3389/fpsyg.2018.01895
Breeze, Beth. *In Defense of Philanthropy*. Newcastle upon Tyne: Agenda Publishing, 2021.
Cohen, Annabel, Betty Bailey, and Thomy Nilsson. 'The importance of music to seniors'. *Psychomusicology: A Journal of Research in Music Cognition* 18, no. 1–2 (2002): 89–102. https://doi.org/10.1037/h0094049.
Corley, Thomas Anthony Buchanan. *Quaker Enterprise in Biscuits: Huntley and Palmers of Reading, 1822–1972*. London: Hutchinson, 1972.
Dunn, Elizabeth W., Lara B. Aknin, and Michael I. Norton. 'Spending money on others promotes happiness'. *Science* 319, no. 5870 (2008): 1687–88. https://doi.org/10.1126/science.1150952.
Easterbrook, Gregg. *The Progress Paradox: How Life Gets Better While People Feel Worse*. Random House Incorporated, 2003.
Fancourt, Daisy, and Saoirse Finn. *What is the Evidence on the Role of the Arts in Improving Health and Well-Being? A Scoping Review*. World Health Organization, 2019. https://apps.who.int/iris/handle/10665/329834
Hays, Terrence. 'Well-being in later life through music'. *Australasian Journal on Ageing* 24, no. 1 (March 2005): 28–32. https://doi.org/10.1111/j.1741-6612.2005.00059.x.
Laukka, Petri. 'Uses of music and psychological well-being among the elderly'. *Journal of Happiness Studies* 8, no. 2 (May 1, 2007): 215–41. https://doi.org/10.1007/s10902-006-9024-3.

Nickson, John. *Giving is Good for You: Why Britain Should Be Bothered*. London: Biteback Publishing, 2013.

Perkins, Rosie, Adele Mason-Bertrand, Daisy Fancourt, Louise Baxter, and Aaron Williamon. 'How participatory music engagement supports mental well-being: A meta-ethnography'. *Qualitative Health Research* 30, no. 12 (October 1, 2020): 1924–40. https://doi.org/10.1177/1049732320944142.

Perkins, Rosie, Adele Mason-Bertrand, Urszula Tymoszuk, Neta Spiro, Kate Gee, and Aaron Williamon. 'Arts engagement supports social connectedness in adulthood: Findings from the HEartS Survey'. *BMC Public Health* 21, no. 1 (June 24, 2021): 1208. https://doi.org/10.1186/s12889-021-11233-6.

Perkins, Rosie, and Aaron Williamon. 'Learning to make music in older adulthood: A mixed-methods exploration of impacts on wellbeing'. *Psychology of Music* 42, no. 4 (2014): 550–67. https://doi.org/10.1177/0305735613483668.

Ryan, Richard M., and Edward L. Deci. 'On happiness and human potentials: A review of research on hedonic and eudaimonic well-being'. *Annual Review of Psychology* 52 (2001): 141–166. https://doi.org/10.1146/annurev.psych.52.1.141.

Seligman, Martin. 'PERMA and the building blocks of well-being'. *Journal of Positive Psychology* 13, no. 4 (July 4, 2018): 333–35. https://doi.org/10.1080/17439760.2018.1437466.

Sulek, Marty. 'On the modern meaning of philanthropy'. *Nonprofit and Voluntary Sector Quarterly* 39, no. 2 (April 11, 2010): 193–212. https://doi.org/10.1177/0899764009333052.

Tennant, Ruth, Louise Hiller, Ruth Fishwick, Stephen Platt, Stephen Joseph, Scott Weich, Jane Parkinson, Jenny Secker, and Sarah Stewart-Brown. 'The Warwick-Dinburgh mental well-being scale (WEMWBS): Development and UK validation'. *Health and Quality of Life Outcomes* 5 (November 27, 2007). https://doi.org/10.1186/1477-7525-5-63.

University of Kent. *Coutts Million Pound Donor Report*. 2017. https://online.Coutts.com.

Wright, David C. H. *The Royal College of Music and Its Contexts: An Artistic and Social History*. Cambridge: Cambridge University Press, 2020.

PERSPECTIVE: CHAPTER 5

Susan Madden

Introduction

Since 2018, I have served as Manhattan School of Music (MSM)'s Vice President for Philanthropy and have overseen a significant increase in contributed income and helped expand the School's donor base and profile on New York City's philanthropic landscape. My successes include a 57% increase in the annual fund, a tripling of foundation giving, and the launch of new donor groups and high-profile donor stewardship events. I have created compelling new development materials, including a biennial report; worked with the President and trustees to secure more than $17 million for the endowment and $7 million in planned gifts; raised support for a new student lounge and other campus improvements; and significantly increased special-events' revenue. MSM's six highest-netting annual galas have occurred under my leadership.

Previously, I spent nearly a decade as Vice President of Development and then Senior Vice President for External Affairs at the Museum of the City of New York, where I helped raise $97 million for a capital campaign and $17 million to create *New York at Its Core*, a multimedia exhibition on New York's 400-year history. Before joining the Museum, I led a $7 million annual fundraising effort for Bette Midler's New York Restoration Project, including securing major gifts from Target, Goldman Sachs, and the Tiffany & Co. Foundation, among others, to renew community gardens citywide. I have also held senior development posts at the New York Philharmonic, Paley Center for Media, and Solomon R. Guggenheim Museum.

Perspectives

The specialised, in-depth training that MSM provides, including weekly private lessons with distinguished teaching artists for each of our musicians, is costly. Student services, distance learning and technology, healthcare, competitive salaries, and benefits for faculty and staff, plant and equipment, and logistical support all come at considerable expense and necessitate the nurturing and development of ongoing philanthropic support. Indeed,

DOI: 10.4324/9781003281573-11

philanthropy is vital, enabling the School to provide immensely talented students with a music education of the highest quality.

Since our founding in 1918, gifts from visionary individuals like our founder Janet Daniels Schenck, alumna Noémi K. Neidorff (BM '70, MM '72, Hon DMA '17), and her late husband Michael, whose centennial leadership gift made possible a magnificent renovation of our mainstage, have transformed the School. With the generosity and support of individual philanthropists, MSM has grown from a neighbourhood music school to become one of the world's premier conservatories and a vital cultural resource for New York City.

Contributions from individuals and foundations and, to a much lesser extent, state and federal government grants bolster the School's long-term stability, strengthen its financial health, and ensure that MSM will have a bright future, educating gifted musicians for generations to come. An average of $7 million has been raised in philanthropic support for the School for each of the past six fiscal years. As with most non-profits in the United States, the majority of charitable contributions to the School come from individuals.

While tuition is the School's largest source of revenue – annual tuition for the 2024–25 academic year is $55,750, with a discount rate of 41.8% – it does not fully cover annual operating costs. About 35% of MSM's annual budget comes from sources other than college tuition, including the residence hall, precollege and youth programmes, and contributed income.

In addition to securing support to deliver MSM's mission, raising funds for scholarships is an equal institutional priority and one of the primary goals of a recently launched endowment campaign. A vibrant scholarship programme enables the School to attract and retain students of the best technical and artistic ability in a highly crowded enrolment landscape. Scholarships support nearly 90% of our students and are especially important for international students, who are not eligible for federal loan programmes and who comprise roughly 50% of MSM's student body.

Philanthropy not only directly benefits MSM and its students, providing scholarships for aspiring musicians with financial need, making capital improvements to our historic campus, and growing our endowment; it also provides our donors with deeply meaningful ways to engage with the life of the School. These include attending superlative concerts and performances, meeting students and world-renowned faculty and guest artists at donor stewardship and cultivation events, and connecting with others who share a belief in the transformative power of music, including by serving as trustees and advisory board members. Contributing to scholarships and to conservatory learning can give donors enormous satisfaction and feelings of well-being and agency generated by giving back. Donors at every level continually report to the School how meaningful it is to know that their contributions are helping to ensure that promising artists whose financial means do not equal their exceptional musical gifts receive exemplary training. Ensuring the continued vitality of the performing arts by supporting the education of aspiring musicians is another motivating factor for donors.

As Lily Harriss and Rachel Harris note in their chapter, many scientific studies have shown links between charitable giving and an increase in donors' well-being. They write that a greater understanding of our donors' beliefs, thoughts, and feelings will help conservatories grow philanthropic support. I concur that this is a valid focus, because, as previously noted, most charitable donations in the United States are made by individuals. Foundation giving is also an important source of support, which too can be grown through thoughtful donor stewardship and engagement. Relationship-building with staff at non-profit foundations and those with family foundations is as critical as it is with individual donors. In point of fact, all giving may be considered 'individual giving'.

Over the past five years, MSM's annual fund has grown by about 57%, concurrent with the launch of new donor groups and a greater emphasis on donor stewardship, including offering more regularly scheduled, well-planned cultivation events. These include the launch of the Virtuoso Society, a giving programme for individuals contributing $1,250+ annually, and the President's Circle, a by-invitation-only group for donors of $10,000+. Members of these giving programmes as well as prospective donors are invited to special events throughout the year, about every month, including intimate pre-and post-concert receptions in the Peter Jay Sharp President's Residence, which give them opportunities to connect with students, staff, and distinguished alumni and faculty. An especially well-received event is an annual scholarship and planned-giving donor luncheon hosted by the President in his residence, featuring scholarship student performances. Additionally, scholarship students are encouraged to express their gratitude to donors in personalised thank you letters and videos facilitated by the Philanthropy Office.

At MSM, creating regular opportunities for donors to interact with talented music students and hear them perform and inviting them to stewardship events in which they may engage with other like-minded donors have helped lead to a marked increase in contributed income. The positive social benefits of giving are many, and the impact of supporting music education on well-being is worthy of further research and exploration, particularly given that individual donors make up such a large part of the donor base of music schools, including alumni, parents, and music lovers in the community.

With their dynamic student bodies of supremely talented young artists and their vibrant and inspiring performing arts programming, conservatories have many opportunities to engage donors and to demonstrate the value of what their support helps make possible. They would do well to consider how 'donors' beliefs, thoughts, and feelings' can impact philanthropy. Gaining a greater understanding of the ways in which giving to music education is particularly meaningful and satisfying to donors could benefit conservatories and other performing arts institutions worldwide.

Summary

I concur with the chapter's emphasis on the importance to the conservatory of cultivating and building philanthropic support, particularly from individuals. As philanthropy is essential to the 'healthy conservatory', and as most charitable giving in the United States comes from individuals, understanding what motivates donors to provide support and considering the effect of giving on well-being are therefore worth additional study. As the costs of providing high-level musical training continue to rise, creating an institutional culture that recognises the importance of philanthropy and that provides development offices with the necessary tools to nurture and build support from individuals by providing opportunities for donors to engage with talented students and with each other will continue to be important.

Bibliography

Association for Psychological Science (APS). 'The joy of giving lasts longer than the joy of getting'. *Editorial*, December 20, 2018.

Macmillan, Amanda. 'Being generous really does make you happier'. *Time Magazine (New York)*, 2017.

National Philanthropic Trust. *Charitable Giving Statistics*. www.nptrust.org/philanthropic-resources/charitable-giving-statistics.

Chapter Notes

 1 University of Kent, *Coutts Million Pound Donor Report.*
 2 Sulek, 'On the modern meaning of philanthropy'.
 3 Wright, *The Royal College of Music.*
 4 Wright, *The Royal College of Music*, 3.
 5 Wright, *The Royal College of Music*, 8.
 6 The original 1903 endowment was for £20,000 and with a further £7,000 added in 1906.
 7 Corley, *Quaker Enterprise in Biscuits.*
 8 Breeze, *In Defense of Philanthropy,* 8.
 9 Nickson, *Giving is Good for You*, 113.
10 Easterbrook, *The Progress Paradox*, 4–10.
11 Dunn et al., 'Spending money on others'.
12 Tennant et al., 'The Warwick–Edinburgh mental well-being scale'.
13 Aron et al., 'Close relationships'.
14 Aron et al., 'Inclusion of other'.
15 A one-sample t-test revealed a significant difference between the SWEMWBS scores collected for this study and the mean score reported for the national average, with a significant medium effect ($t(61) = 5.1$, $p < 0.001$, $d = 0.65$), such that the respondents' wellbeing scores on SWEMWBS scale were higher ($M = 26.7$, SD 4.74) than for the national average ($M = 23.6$). Data are available via the first author upon reasonable request.
16 Measured using Inclusion of Self and Other scales (IOS). A Pearson correlation coefficient was run to assess the connections between wellbeing and the strength of the relationships with the conservatoires and recipients. There was a moderate, positive correlation between SWEMWBS and IOS – C ($r = 0.24$, $p = 0.05$) and a stronger but moderate, positive correlation between SWEMWBS and IOS – R ($r = 0.29$, $p = 0.01$).
17 Cohen et al., 'The importance of music'.
18 Perkins et al., 'How participatory music engagement supports mental well-being'.
19 Laukka, 'Uses of music'.
20 Seligman, 'PERMA and the building blocks'.
21 Ryan and Deci, 'On happiness and human potentials'.
22 For example, Perkins and Williamon, 'Learning to make music'.
23 Ascenso et al., 'Resounding meaning'.
24 Perkins et al., 'Arts engagement supports social connectedness'.
25 Fancourt, 'What is the evidence'.

6

INTEGRATING REGULATION AND CREATIVITY

Kevin Porter

Introduction

Set against a climate of increasing accountability, compliance, and regulation, this chapter explores the role of governance, management, and leadership in conservatoires. At first glance such bureaucratic domains seem at odds with the creative ethos of a performing arts institution, but this chapter uncovers how conservatoires can demonstrate agility and creativity when responding to administrative constraints. It will look at this mostly from an English perspective (Scotland and Wales have their own national funding and regulatory arrangements, which are similar but distinct; the chapter will refer to the United Kingdom (UK) more widely where the similarities make that feel appropriate), but it will also make observations about the systems of governance and oversight internationally, by way of contrast.

Most of the English framework applies equally to all English universities and colleges, currently regulated by the Office for Students (OfS), whose registration process and regulatory framework determine whether a university or college can operate and charge tuition fees. OfS also acts on behalf of government to distribute institutional teaching funding and to push the latest government's political enthusiasm. While this means that some of the points this chapter will make will be relevant regardless of higher education (HE) institutional type, such as the effect of tuition fee regulation, it will aim to draw out the impacts and implications most relevant for small specialist institutions and especially for conservatoires. The rhetoric from the OfS and government is that they favour light-touch regulation and that institutions are gold-plating their own approach to compliance, but to what extent is this the case and what is the real direction of travel for the regulatory environment?

This chapter is not just about national oversight and regulation or the expectations placed on governing bodies/structures. It will also advocate for approaches to strategic management and governance that go beyond the diktats of such national systems towards a manifesto for institutional success. The extent to which this can be followed will depend upon the flexibility that national funding and regulatory systems permit and the resources available in the countries and cities in which conservatoires are located. Much will also

DOI: 10.4324/9781003281573-12

depend on the level of institutional ambition (or self-satisfaction) – what motivates the institution and how and can this be changed, if it needs to be and if the will is there. Finally, the chapter will draw the threads, in a UK context, on the state of health of conservatoires.

What is good governance in a modern conservatoire, and how is this affected by oversight and accountability?

It is self-evident that governance should support the business of any organisation. In a conservatoire context, this will mean supporting the core business objectives: a high-quality student experience and the myriad other activities and environment that contribute to that. Conservatoires are first and foremost teaching institutions, whose priority will be the quality of the student experience. They may have many other interests – research, community engagement, museums and archives, as performing arts centres – but education and training performing artists are their primary function. Conservatoires have a complex ecology and set of relationships, which are particular to their institutional contexts. For the Royal College of Music, London (RCM), a core aim is to replicate professional life – reflecting the standards and demands of a largely freelance profession (see also Chapters 4 and 12).

A key feature of conservatoires is that they must attract a roster of internationally renowned musicians as professors to deliver one-to-one lessons, to give masterclasses, and to conduct its ensembles and operas. Access to world–class musicians is fundamental to setting and delivering standards that are credible when compared with the best international competition. Conservatoires also need intimate relationships with orchestras, opera companies, and other ensembles to provide further professional exposure, such as opportunities for side-by-side experiences and collaborative artistic projects. Relationships with such musicians and ensembles are made possible by the inclusion on a conservatoire's staff of active musicians/arts managers with their own international reputations who have access to, and count among their peers, such world-class figures. This rich environment, while important to establish a conservatoire's credentials and ensure a high-quality student experience, is not straightforward to foster or maintain. Collaborations and partnerships of many types are crucial to this, though they are inherently time-intensive and complex and often require a whole-institution approach to succeed. This touches functions well beyond the academic or artistically creative – such as fundraising to provide the finance to make them work (see also Chapter 5); marketing to showcase and maximise the benefits of such relationships (and advise on reputational risk); and managers to conduct due diligence, manage risk, establish appropriate agreements, and facilitate relationships. This enables the best collaborations to extend beyond one-off contacts, as well as to ensure relationships and collaborations sit within a strategic framework that works for the conservatoire as well as for the partners.

At the same time, sometimes an effective strategic approach is to decline 'opportunities' that, in fact, benefit the collaborative partner more than the conservatoire itself or extend beyond what can be sustained. The most successful conservatoires will receive repeated, sometimes persistent, approaches from other institutions, individuals, and organisations on a scale that could not possibly be sustained, even despite oft promised but subsequently elusive extra resources. While it is, arguably, a marker of success to attract this attention, the art of a diplomatic rejection can be crucial. Ultimately, conservatoires are small institutions, when set alongside the average university, and taking on too many initiatives will overstretch the senior team (and the governance needed to oversee such initiatives), to the extent that failure risks becoming the outcome.

These matters are the preserve and under the full control of conservatoires. Sitting alongside this, there are those things that are outside their control. In England, conservatoires are subject to the same regulatory, accountability, and compliance regime as universities. This constitutes a significant burden, as well as some opportunities. The burden comes from a variety of directions – government; the law; and regulatory and other bodies. Increasingly, there is also, community pressure from students, staff, or the wider public on topics that occupy the public interest such as diversity, mental health, or sexual harassment to mention just those issues currently generating such interest. Whereas once conservatoires could afford to sit aside from such public debates and conclude these were not directly related to the education of students,[1] in the era of social media, conservatoires are drawn into them as readily as any other public organisation and expected to have a response. This is likely to generate an unfunded extra administrative load to support initiatives and report on progress, however worthy the cause. Statistics bodies alone seek an ever-increasing amount of data on all manner of aspects of the institution, from applicant and student data, financial, estates, and staff data. The Higher Education Statistics Agency (HESA) currently requires institutions to collect circa 220 individual items of data on each student.

The OfS became the regulator for English higher education in 2018, replacing the Higher Education Funding Council for England (HEFCE), which, along with its predecessors, had a very different role. Where HEFCE had been more arm's length from government, with a role to support the stability of the HE sector, and thereby institutions, the Office for Students, as the name suggests, is a regulator with its first priority to champion students, with no remit to support institutions themselves. Institutional failure is only of interest to the OfS in so far as it would adversely affect students. Universities and colleges are required to submit 'Student Protection Plans' to set out how they would deal with course or institutional closure. The OfS strategy[2] and business plan[3] set out these priorities. What does this mean for universities and colleges and especially conservatoires?

As was said in the Introduction section, the rhetoric from the OfS and government is that they say they favour light-touch regulation and that institutions are gold-plating their own approach to compliance. As the incoming interim Chief Executive Officer of the OfS, Susan Lapworth, said at – as she put it – her 'first public outing' in the role in May 2022: 'We will challenge institutions to take purposeful steps to dismantle internal bureaucracy that has accreted over time and is not needed to comply with our regulatory requirements'.[4] She went on to say:

> Institutions tend to have a well-developed system for moving documents from one committee to the next. Often the same people congregate as a different committee and consider the same documents all over again. And then those documents find their way to the governing body. . . . If we enquire about an issue relating to, for example, consumer law, an institution will tell us that all is fine and point to this mountain of documentation and process as evidence of that. But then when we look in detail at the primary evidence – the decisions the institution has made about the information it publishes when it recruits students, or the terms and conditions in its student contract – we start to see issues that suggest non-compliance. The assurance mechanisms have focused on process and not on substantive compliance.

While Lapworth makes some good points here, she is, arguably, also being somewhat naïve. An institution that does not do everything it could reasonably do for whatever process or other compliance task is opening itself to risk, whether from internal audit criticism, a student or staff complaint when things go wrong, or even an over-zealous governing body that thinks more could be done and therefore should be done. It is always easier to do more rather than less. HE administrators are often their own worst enemies – always thinking of what extra they could do that would, from their perspective, improve a process or provide extra information or simply reduce risk, without necessarily thinking about whether this actually adds value or is necessary and regardless of the accompanying workload. As with collaborative 'opportunities', it is often just as important to know when to say 'no'. Having a hard focus on who benefits from extra compliance, how much risk to take, and whether an administrative process or initiative fits with an institution's mission or strategy is important in ensuring that the outcome is not to be institutional overload. A ruthless top-down focus to assess which processes or initiatives can be culled completely, which addressed solely from a basic compliance perspective, and those that truly benefit the institution and deserve a full-blooded and enthusiastic approach will help to manage what is an ever-increasing load. And there are always new forms of compliance invented that require new processes. Usually these are accompanied by consultations, which generate their own load – it is not unusual for half a dozen consultations and surveys a day to drop into an inbox, together with reminders when one does not respond.

What is the conservatoire angle on this? A university is partly insulated by its size – whole teams are often responsible for a particular area, enabling the load to be spread widely. These are the 'layers' and committees to which Lapworth refers. Conservatoires can have these too, but there is less excuse for them – with a small staff there should be less reason for the same topic to go to multiple committees. The most obvious issue for conservatoires is the overhead that comes with compliance. A small senior leadership team, supported by a relatively small and probably already overworked managerial team and administrative staffing structure, will be responsible for multiple areas and will need to be focused on the core business of running and advancing the institution rather than becoming bogged down in compliance. At best, compliance will be a distraction. The only approach to avoiding becoming overwhelmed that the author has found is to ruthlessly triage what comes into the inbox – to respond to or even read only those consultations that are self-evidently of importance to the institution rather than being just interesting and to ceaselessly question the extent of any response required by a regulator or any other body to a new initiative. It would be easy for an institution to find that it is doing a brilliant job of compliance, only for the core business to be slowly declining. High-effort compliance rarely improves a conservatoire's league table rankings, helps to recruit high-quality students, or improves the student experience or artistic programme.

Governing bodies can help with this – they too need to be equally focused on discouraging too much enthusiasm for compliance, while taking an interest in ensuring that sufficient compliance is being undertaken (a significant volume of compliance cannot be avoided, and, indeed, some of it is helpful in supporting governance by providing a framework for good practice and generating data that provides information about institutional success and benchmarking). A governing body will not necessarily easily recognise when the right balance on compliance is being struck – it is natural to ask for more rather than less. It is part of the senior leadership team's job to guide the governing body. They are the gatekeepers to what is presented to it and must educate the governing body, while also being open to being interrogated in turn. It is through such interrogation that governing bodies can judge whether the correct balance is being struck – undertaken in the spirit of critical friend and with, hopefully, well-justified mutual trust.

Conservatoire freedoms and funding

Despite the onerous compliance regime, UK conservatoires probably have more functional independence than those in almost any other country. Looked at in its widest and most positive sense, the compliance regime sets high standards for governance and management that at their best assist in ensuring a level playing field between institutions and provides a framework to support governance in a way that, left to their own devices, would be difficult for small specialist institutions to replicate. Over the years, the UK quality assurance regime, for example, has evolved from a constraining one-size-fits-all overbearing framework into a more risk-based system overseen by the Quality Assurance Agency for Higher Education (QAA), albeit one that might soon rely too much on crude quantitative measures (as reflected by the OfS registration condition B3[5] that sets out minimum baselines for student outcomes, with regulatory action to be taken where too many students drop out or do not go on to professional employment or further study after graduation – two steps forward, one step back, perhaps). One-size-fits-all approaches to regulation rarely sit well with institutional types outside the conventional large university model. A conservatoire-relevant example would be graduate outcomes (progression to employment). Few performing arts graduates move into salaried full-time employment – their destinations are more commonly into freelance portfolio careers (see Chapter 12) that do not fit neatly into the categories applied by surveys, and even the most successful graduates can appear 'career failures' in the data that results.

To look to the positives, the English model does favour institutional autonomy. Individual higher education institutions have legal independence that comes from their constitutional arrangements, which can range from a conventional limited company through to a royal charter that can only be varied by the Privy Council. This makes it difficult to interfere in governance to the extent of directing a closure or merger, for example.

The rigours of securing registration with the OfS provide a high bar to new entrants. This not only assures quality for students but also provides safeguards for existing higher education institutions, as the level playing field means market entry requires significant investment and a willingness to adopt a strong governance regime and oversight. The OfS operates as a threshold standard regulator, so that as long as institutions successfully maintain registration, once achieved, no further impositions apply, and they have freedom to operate.

In many European contexts, conservatoires are directly under the control of a government department (Education or Culture), such that the principal's most important relationship is often with the minister, at whose whim they are in office. The Association Européenne des Conservatoires, Académies de Musique et Musikhochschulen (AEC), which describes itself as 'a voluntary coalition representing Higher Music Education Institutions (HMEIs) in Europe and beyond'[6] has a useful webpage that provides a glimpse into European national higher education systems.[7] In many European contexts, the teaching staff are not even directly employed by the institution but are on civil service contracts with the ministry that limits the numbers of hours they can teach and makes them almost impossible to fire. In such contexts, institutions have very constrained flexibility. The absence of more than nominal tuition fees across Europe means that all funding is by the state, and while this carries benefits, such as large capital funding for new facilities, if the minister can be persuaded, it also generates its own constraints – the inability to set fees means that institutions are limited by the level of funding the state is prepared to expend. This can have the effect of removing the freedom to decide where to innovate or develop. While colleagues in European conservatoires may feel otherwise, the regulatory burden to which they are subjected is much lighter than in the UK. For example, they are not required to submit the volume of statistical returns that are obligatory in the UK. That said, like everywhere in the world, they now encounter more oversight and direction than would historically have been the case.

A good example of this has been the European Union's Bologna Process, which established a common qualification framework for European higher education, centred around three 'cycles' and an associated European Credit Transfer and Accumulation System (ECTS).[8] A key motivation was to make European qualifications more attractive internationally by aligning them with the Bachelor's, Master's, and doctoral degrees offered in the rest of the world. The Bologna declaration was signed by EU education ministers in 1999, and there then followed a long process of agonising and, ultimately, implementation. The AEC was the key organisation supporting European conservatoires as they wrestled with how to approach this, against a backdrop where in many European institutions, historically, it did not matter how many decades it took to be educated in a context where there were no fee or funding concerns. The AEC now has a well-developed system of 'counselling visits' to support conservatoires in areas such as quality assurance and credit frameworks.[9]

In the United States, while conservatoires can largely charge what they wish and have the highest headline tuition fees in the world, they need to match these with generous scholarships to attract the best students. Many of the most successful US conservatoires have enviable levels of scholarship funds to entice students, and some are fully tuition-fee free as a result of generous donations. But this can confer its own constraints. Those institutions that are tuition-fee free are also dependent on investment returns and, without further fundraising, can lack the discretion or the motivation to invest in innovation. A heavy reliance on philanthropy also sucks up significant senior team energy expended on fundraising, and it can be hard to resist the distorting effects of a donor's personal preferences (see Chapter 5 for more on philanthropy in the conservatoire).

In the UK, the funding regime is a mix of state funding and tuition fees. UK undergraduate student fees are tightly controlled and are supported by tuition fee and living cost loans. Postgraduate and international student fees are unregulated other than by what the market can bear. UK conservatoires do not have scholarship funds that compare to those of many US conservatoires, nor do they have the advantages of the largely fee-free model of European conservatoires, but, in the UK, the ability to charge fees does confer freedoms and discretion over how and on what to spend and invest. Further, UK conservatoires are supported by still significant state funding. As the UK higher education funding system has evolved and the reliance on tuition fees has increased, fewer government teaching funding streams have survived, but in each of the nations of the UK, there is some form of dedicated funding for those small specialist institutions with the highest standing, and it still amounts to several million pounds a year. In England, the OfS – and HEFCE before it – have regularly undertaken assessment exercises to decide which small specialist institutions are judged worthy of this funding, with criteria most focused on judgements of whether they are world-leading. Institutions that meet this test enjoy a funding stream designed to make up the difference between an assessment of full teaching costs and regulated undergraduate tuition fees. While the resulting funding only partially bridges this gap, it provides essential underpinning to enable UK conservatoires to compete internationally. Having governing body members with government connections can be particularly useful when presenting the case to the government for the national value of conservatoire education and the importance of funding streams dedicated to meeting its necessarily high costs.

The benefits of size and focus

Conservatoire independence can be fragile, and its benefits are not valued everywhere. Small specialist institutions carry high management overheads for many of the reasons set out in this chapter, not least in an increasingly regulated world that demands accountability in an ever-increasing range of areas. There is also a risk of shallow expertise with few staff, often a single member of staff, with skills in a particular functional area. Such institutions will also have less scope than a university to easily restructure, again a function of size. However, they benefit from a single-minded focus. While conservatoires are increasingly diversifying and innovating in fields such as research, entrepreneurship, community engagement, multi- and cognate disciplinary subjects, material culture, collaboration, and partnership (as amply set out in the other chapters of this book), they maintain a single-minded focus on education in their art form and producing the next generation of professional performers. The entire staff understand this focus and daily demonstrate their commitment and dedication, matching that of their students. This makes human resource (HR) management in a conservatoire relatively easy – everyone knows why they are there, can see (and hear) the hard work of students, and seek to support it and replicate it in their own efforts. All financial resources, all fundraising, all governance do likewise.

A complement to the single-minded focus of the staff is that, to be truly effective, they should also be supported and have a commitment to professional development and networking in professional organisations, including those within the wider higher education sector. It may be the case that the conservatoire sector is distinctive, but it is still part of the wider HE world, and positive engagement with it, rather than insisting on asserting difference at every opportunity, will only provide benefits.

Some conservatoires have been embedded within universities. There was a period internationally in the 1980s and 1990s when this became a trend. In Australia, there was a government policy to absorb all conservatoires into universities, with decidedly mixed results. The policy was included within the controversial Dawkins reforms of the late 1980s,[10] named after the minister who reformed Australian higher education, introducing tuition fees and loans, alongside mergers of small institutions into universities. The travails of Sydney Conservatorium over quite a period (as part of the University of Sydney) and the painful and extended exercise to merge the performing arts institutions in Melbourne, both dramatically played out in the local press, provide evidence of this. A glance at the websites for conservatoires that have been merged into a university shows they are hard to find or understand. While part of the rationale for mergers internationally and in the UK has generally been to cut costs by reducing the overhead for stand-alone back-office functions such as HR or quality assurance, they come with the costs of losing some of those staff who would have identified with the single-minded focus on excellence that comes with being part of a stand-alone conservatoire. Performing arts as a discipline is rarely understood by others in the university and, unless it is supported by an enthusiastic Vice Chancellor, may struggle in a bid for resources. A usual part of the rationale for such mergers is that the high costs of conservatoire education (such as one-to-one teaching and professional-level performance spaces) can be supported by cross-subsidies, but inevitably those subject areas expected to do the cross-subsidising will resent it.

To thrive, conservatoires need to be independent and prepared to fight and lobby for that independence and funding by constantly renewing the case for their existence and the value they provide to society.

What does institutional success look like?

There are dangers and traps for conservatoires when they judge their own success and standing. Some of these flow from being small specialist institutions – at worst, they run the risk of becoming insular, and they lack the voices outside the discipline that might provide a point of comparison or context. It can be easy for conservatoires to bask in historic success and become complacent, while other institutions quietly innovate, improve facilities, and attract the best students with a turbo-charged scholarship programme. Suddenly a once-leading conservatoire might find that its mantle has faded.

Governing bodies and senior teams will advance their conservatoire if they are continuously interrogating institutional success. This will need to start by having a clear-sighted regard to what success looks like in their context. The strategic plan should reflect this, but so should policies and documents the institution produces from the financial forecasts to the HR plan. Conservatoires need to take a realistic and objective view of their place in the market, and their mission should extend from this – who are they trying to benefit? What value can they provide to society? This will require an understanding of their local, national, and international competition. A conservatoire that might once have aspired to world-class status might re-evaluate its role and conclude that it can provide more benefit to society and the arts by positioning itself to serve a more local community or by producing graduates for different sectors of the performing arts professions and achieve great and sustainable success in doing so.

Once an institution has decided what it would like its place in the world to be, it needs a plan to get there. This may involve significant change and buy-in across the institution. There is a mature academic literature on change management that institutions can draw on to determine an approach that works for them and their institutional ecology.[11] The author would observe that conservatoires, perhaps in part as a function of their small size, usually have a delicate ecology that comes from their history and their relationship with their professors, many of whom will see the conservatoire as a small part of their careers, the larger part being as an orchestral or opera musician, composer, or among the wealth of other performing arts professions – which makes them less susceptible to managerial direction. Professors will generally feel that their allegiance is first to their students and only second to the conservatoire employing them. At least in the UK, most will be working at much lower hourly rates than they will enjoy in the rest of their careers, and they teach, at least in part, in order to give back to the music profession rather than for the money. Attempts to engage them outside the lesson in curriculum development or even to subject them to quality control, for example through appraisal systems (if they can be devised), let alone institutional strategy, can be fraught and difficult. More positively, the challenges of the COVID-19 pandemic that compelled professors to engage with online teaching had the by-product of bringing them more closely into the conservatoire community in ways that are likely to have a lasting effect. It remains that upheaval from a new strategy can only follow a campaign to persuade the conservatoire community that it stacks up and ideally incorporating them into the decision-making. Otherwise, failure may be the outcome of a top-down diktat.

Measures of success need to be tailored to the mission and objectives of the institution. Conservatoires need to look outside the institution to judge comparative performance, and this can be difficult, as there are few objective quantitative measures to act as reliable reference points. League tables and individual student and graduate successes (such as orchestral and opera house positions and international competition successes, where these are factors relevant to institutional mission) provide only a partial and potentially distorting lens. Nevertheless, well-crafted key performance indicators (KPIs) across a range of areas (such as financial sustainability, student feedback, research grant successes, fundraising, student recruitment), linked to the conservatoire's strategic plan and objectives and, wherever they exist, benchmarked against other conservatoires or comparable institutions, can provide perspective for a senior team and the governing body. KPIs alone will only ever tell part of the story, and conservatoires need multiple ways to satisfy themselves that their strategic objectives are being met. This should be a continuous self-critical process that engages the entire conservatoire community, while not being deflected by small pockets of dissent (no strategy will have full buy-in from absolutely everyone, and often students will be the most conservative of all constituencies, unable to see beyond their individual experience to a wider vision). The single-minded focus of the entire conservatoire community on its one main discipline can be both an advantage and a struggle. If the whole institution is behind the strategy, success will be easier to achieve and recognise when it happens. Conversely, if the community is not fully behind the plan, it has a greater chance of running into the sand.

Summary

This chapter has set out a wide range of challenges and obstacles for conservatoires, while, hopefully, championing their unique features and value to society.

In the UK, at least, conservatoire education could be seen to have a bright outlook. While the decline of school music education in the UK challenges the pipeline for UK undergraduates[12,13] (and there will be equivalent challenges in other performing arts fields), conservatoires are now recognised as an important part of the UK higher education landscape. The successive assessment exercises by OfS and HEFCE referred to earlier (and the equivalent exercises in Wales and Scotland) and the political lobbying that has accompanied them have solidified the view in government and the higher education establishments that conservatoires add lustre to UK higher education as a whole and incur justifiably high cost. This is demonstrated by former Minister for Higher and Further Education, Michelle Donelan, on 20 October 2021, who, in an OfS press release launching the most recent review of specialist provider funding, said:

> This country is home to some of the world's best universities who teach, support, and develop not only our future scientists, doctors, and engineers but also those that add so

much to our culture – the artists, dancers, and musicians. To ensure we are supporting our world-leading specialist institutions the OfS has set out proposals to allocate funding . . . recognising the importance of these providers.[14]

This was reinforced in the same press release by Nolan Smith, director of resources and finance at the OfS, who said:

There is a clear case for additional funding for world-leading specialist providers. These providers are often small, and teach subjects which are expensive to deliver. Their graduates go on to make enormous contributions to the economic and cultural well-being of society. We believe that these proposals will help the OfS to allocate funding in a fair way, recognising the significant importance of these providers to the diversity of English higher education.

The case for such institutions as independent, appropriately funded flag-carriers for UK higher education is quite an achievement, and long may it continue.

- Key take-away 1: conservatoires cannot succeed without good governance and management.
- Key take-away 2: to thrive, conservatoires need to be independent and prepared to fight and lobby for that independence and funding by constantly renewing the case for their existence and the value they bring to society.
- Key take-away 3: compliance with the accountability demands of regulators and others needs to be proportionate. Those aspects of compliance that can bring benefits to the institution deserve a full-blooded response, but, otherwise, a low burden response is more appropriate.

Bibliography

Association Européenne des Conservatoires, Académies de Musique et Musikhochschulen. *AEC Vision & Mission*. Accessed August 10, 2022. https://aec-music.eu/about-aec/aec-vision-and-mission/.

Association Européenne des Conservatoires, Académies de Musique et Musikhochschulen. *Counselling Visits*. Accessed August 10, 2022. https://aec-music.eu/services/counselling-visits/.

Association Européenne des Conservatoires, Académies de Musique et Musikhochschulen. *Institutions National Overviews*. Accessed August 10, 2022. https://aec-music.eu/members/national-overviews/.

Australian Federal Register of Legislation. *Higher Education Funding Act 1988*, No. 2, 1989. www.legislation.gov.au/Details/C2016C00171/.

Cohen, Michael D., and James G. March. *Leadership and Ambiguity: The American College President*. New York: McGraw-Hill, 1974.

European Commission. *The Bologna Process and the European Higher Education Area*. Accessed August 10, 2022. https://education.ec.europa.eu/education-levels/higher-education/inclusive-and-connected-higher-education/bologna-process.

Lapworth, Susan. 'Reducing burden makes for good governance'. *WonkHE*, May 23, 2022. https://wonkhe.com/blogs/reducing-burden-makes-for-good-governance/.

Middlehurst, Robin. *Leading Academics*. Bristol, PA: Society for Research into Higher Education; Open University Press, 1993.

Office for Students. *OfS Sets Out Funding Proposals for World-Leading Specialist Providers*. October 20, 2021. www.officeforstudents.org.uk/news-blog-and-events/press-and-media/ofs-sets-out-funding-proposals-for-world-leading-specialist-providers/.

Office for Students. *Our Strategy*. March 23, 2022. www.officeforstudents.org.uk/about/our-strategy/.

Office for Students. *Office for Students' Business Plan: 2022–23*. May 26, 2022. www.officeforstudents.org.uk/publications/business-plan-2022-23/.

Office for Students. *Office for Students to Implement New Approach to Regulating Student Outcomes*. July 26, 2022. www.officeforstudents.org.uk/news-blog-and-events/press-and-media/office-for-students-to-implement-new-approach-to-regulating-student-outcomes/?utm_source=OfS+alerts&utm_campaign=88926a61cd-EMAIL_CAMPAIGN_2022_07_insight_brief_14_COPY_01&utm_medium=email&utm_term=0_83cc2ff0b1–88926a61cd-117045697.

Porter, Kevin. 'Management in the conservatoire of the future: Administering or leading'. *Studies in Higher Education* 23, no. 1 (January 1998): 7–16. https://doi.org/10.1080/03075079812331380452.

Whittaker, Adam, and Martin Fautley. *A-Level Music Decline and Disadvantage Attainment Gaps*. Birmingham City: Royal Birmingham Conservatoire, July 2021. https://bcuassets.blob.core.windows.net/docs/a-level-report-290621-pdf-132695100641559063.pdf.

Whittaker, Adam, V. Kinsella, and M. Fautley. 'Geographical and social demographic trends of a-level music students'. In *Report*. London: Royal College of Music, May 20, 2019. https://researchonline.rcm.ac.uk/id/eprint/502/.

Wright, David C. H. *The Royal College of Music and Its Contexts: An Artistic and Social History*. Cambridge: Cambridge University Press, 2020.

PERSPECTIVE: CHAPTER 6

Martin Prchal

Introduction

The views described in this Perspective are based on a long-term involvement in the higher music education sector from both an international and national perspective. Following a position as the first chief executive of the European Association of Conservatoires (AEC) for more than 10 years, I moved to a senior management position at the Royal Conservatoire in The Hague, where I had to deal with many of the issues described in Kevin Porter's chapter. These include finding a balance between existing rules for compliance and the continuous need for enhancement, the positioning of institutions as stand-alone conservatoires or as faculties in larger educational entities defining their position within higher education more broadly, developing an artistically-driven institution into a community of professionals that primarily act in the interest of students instead of the interests of the institution or of individuals working there, and seeing and assessing ourselves as 'world-leading' institutions.

Many of the perspectives described by Kevin Porter will resonate with conservatoire leaders around the world, even if some of the perspectives are strongly connected to the UK context. Kevin gives a very complete and interesting overview of issues on governance and positioning of music conservatoires, and how external factors can strongly impact these. His ideas on institutional success demonstrate his long-term experience in the sector and provide valid proposals on how this institutional success can be achieved and measured.

I would like to address some of the issues raised within the chapter by advocating for the need to develop a 'quality culture' in conservatoires, which will also strengthen their potential as 'learning institutions' and enhance their value on the whole.

Perspectives

Conservatoires as 'learning institutions'

As higher music education institutions, we should always ask ourselves how to enhance the learning experience of our students. But are they the only ones who should be learning?

DOI: 10.4324/9781003281573-13

How about the learning capacity of our institutions? Surely, if we as institutions want to continuously develop the student learning experience, we must seek, test, and implement new approaches of teaching and learning and, in doing so, undergo a process of learning ourselves. And what are the preconditions for institutions to be able to take this route?

There are three perspectives that I should like to address in this context: how we deal with our teaching staff, how we see our position as internationally oriented institutions, and how we deal with quality issues. As we will see, these issues are strongly interconnected.

About power relations, expectation management, and continuing professional development

In his chapter, Kevin Porter clearly describes how in the conservatoire context, it is sometimes challenging to involve teaching staff in institutional change processes. Teaching staff are often performing musicians with small contracts and busy careers outside of the institution. They may have been appointed on the basis of their artistic qualities rather than on proven didactic or academic skills. It is important to emphasise that, in a context in which many of the lessons are in one-to-one format, the influence of teachers on students can be significant. We are all aware that the one-to-one teaching model, when executed well, can lead to excellent results with regards to the artistic and instrumental development of students. At the same time, it can lead to unwanted power relations that can have negative effects on students both from a personal and educational point of view.

It could be maintained that one of the main challenges of conservatoires is expectation management. If the institutional culture is one that is mainly focused on narrow standards of musical excellence set by competitions and the top end of the performance industry, it could very well be that quite a few students will develop feelings of anxiety or even failure during their studies. Therefore, the discourse on excellence (a term frequently used by conservatoires) should be nuanced and multifaceted, simply because there cannot be any conservatoire in the world that will be able to demonstrate that all of its graduates are successful as top performers or composers in the traditional narrow understanding of musical excellence. At the same time, we also know that, in performance studies, mastering one's instrument or voice at a high artistic level is still an essential career skill for having a successful future in music, in addition to the many other skills such as musicianship, entrepreneurship, and academic skills, all of which have witnessed a stronger profile in conservatoires during recent decades.

Teachers play a vital role in this discourse and are a key part of an institutional effort to develop a quality culture that will not only pursue high artistic standards but also will be able to contextualise these in relation to the individual situations and capabilities of students. How to ensure that they will do so? In the ARTEMIS project of the European Association of Conservatoires (AEC), a new continuing professional development course for conservatoire teachers entitled 'The Artist as Teacher' was launched recently to address this need. Based on the 'The Artist as Teacher' course for conservatoire teachers developed by the Royal Conservatoire in The Hague and the international 'Innovative Conservatoire' (ICON) network, it addresses many different topics ranging from didactic skills to research-based education and social safety issues. Teachers embark upon a course of nine sessions of three hours each, while between sessions, they engage in an 'intervision' process to observe each others' teaching. Through this process, we learnt how important it is to support teachers by setting up a course in a way that addresses them as artist-teachers through a disciplinary, context-specific language to which they can relate. Too often, musicians teaching in conservatoires see teams of pedagogical experts without any knowledge of the context descend upon music academies for pedagogical trainings, only to face all kinds of misunderstandings and a strong resistance as a result.

About internationalisation

Another aspect that can be hugely beneficial for institutional learning and the development of a strong quality culture is internationalisation. It is interesting to see how internationalisation in higher education has developed over the years. It started with a heavy emphasis on the development of the individual through physical mobility and, somewhat later and based on the concept of internationalisation at home, the acquisition of international competences for those who could not travel. The next step was to give internationalisation a role in institutional development: institutions would work together at transnational level and, in doing so, engage in a learning and development process. The most recent step in internationalisation in higher education focusses on the role of internationalisation within the society, that is how internationalisation can contribute to the local and regional contexts of the institutions and to larger societal themes. If institutions agree that internationalisation is a tool for learning, they will have to formulate internationalisation strategies that do not focus solely on internationalisation as a purpose in itself or as an instrument for the recruitment for international fee-paying students, but on how internationalisation can inform all developments taking place in an institution to improve its quality, ranging from curriculum development to issues regarding diversity, inclusion, and staff development. Furthermore, it is the author's opinion that any institutional claims for a 'world-leading' status can only be based on the use of internationally recognised review and benchmarking mechanisms, such as those proposed by *MusiQuE* – Music Quality Enhancement or the deployment of international external examiners and 'critical friend' reviewers, rather than on nationally based criteria and review systems.

About enhancement and compliance

In his chapter, Kevin Porter makes some valid remarks about striking the balance between ensuring compliance to rules set by regulatory bodies on the one hand and the creativity needed in conservatoires to stay dynamic and relevant from an artistic and educational point of view on the other. In quality assurance, a developmental approach can already be seen in the move from quality assurance to quality enhancement and the emphasis on the presence of an institutional quality culture. Still, also in this context, one might place an even stronger emphasis on quality assurance as a tool for learning rather than on technocratic compliance with criteria and indicators. This may require instruments that ensure a shift from quantitative to qualitative quality assurance approaches, such as student focus groups and teacher panels, and the deployment of discipline-specific 'critical friends', for the discussion of curriculum and other relevant issues in a safe and informal environment, but within a clear and continuous structure of planning and follow-up and always with a clear understanding of the discipline and its artistic and educational content. It is essential that these instruments are then focused on enhancement and not just on compliance. With such a focus on enhancement, compliance will be almost automatically addressed through improvement measures, whereas when the focus is mainly on compliance, there could very well be very little enhancement. This will also assist conservatoires to become 'learning institutions' and continuously work on their quality culture.

Summary

All these considerations can only be addressed and implemented if the following conditions are met and which are admirably described by Kevin Porter: clear and visionary leadership, as well as the autonomy for institutions to make their own decisions. Whether or not this is done as an independent institution will depend on the context. While I take Kevin Porter's point that independence is important in the UK situation, there are also examples of institutions in other countries that are part of larger arts or comprehensive universities, which in some cases give them greater financial stability and support through specialised expertise in the field of (e.g.) human resources, regulatory processes, and fundraising. The need for autonomy will then depend on the regulatory and legal frameworks of the country where the institution is based: if these are heavy on accountability, requiring institutions to spend much of their resources on being compliant with rules and regulations, the development of these institutions (and this is especially the case for small institutes such as conservatoires) may be severely impacted. I agree with Kevin Porter that it is up to the sector itself to be prepared to fight and lobby to renew their case for their existence and for the value they provide to society.

Chapter Notes

1 Wright, *The Royal College of Music*.
2 Office for Students, *Our Strategy*.
3 Office for Students, *Business Plan 2022–23*.
4 Lapworth, 'Reducing burden'.
5 Office for Students, *Office for Students to Implement New Approach*.
6 Association Européenne des Conservatoires, 'AEC vision & mission'.
7 Association Européenne des Conservatoires, 'Institutions national overviews'.
8 European Commission, *The Bologna Process*.
9 'Association Européenne des Conservatoires, 'Counselling visits'.
10 Australian Federal Register of Legislation, *Higher Education Funding Act*.
11 See, for example: Cohen and March, *Leadership and Ambiguity*; Middlehurst, *Leading Academics*; and Porter, 'Management in the conservatoire'.
12 Whittaker et al., 'Geographical and social demographic trends'.
13 Whittaker and Fautley, *A-Level Music Decline*.
14 Office for Students, *OfS Sets Out Funding Proposals*.

PART II

Evolving the teaching and learning of music in a conservatoire

7

REIMAGINING THE ONE-TO-ONE STUDIO

Christina Guillaumier, Gabrielle Lester, and Diana Salazar

The centrality of the one-to-one studio

Although higher education pedagogies have evolved significantly since the growth of the French conservatoire model in the nineteenth century, one-to-one teaching in performance or composition continues to be core in the music conservatoire today. In a typical week at the Royal College of Music (RCM), over 1,000 hours of one-to-one lessons are delivered. This comes at a cost; high tuition fees reflect the extensive contact time and high staff-to-student ratio, with the majority of the College's teaching budget dedicated to providing each student with 30–45 hours of one-to-one tuition each year. The one-to-one lesson is considered by many musicians and students as a sign of quality, the implication being that the more contact time a student receives with a highly regarded professor, the better the student's prospects of success in the profession. Despite the apparent simplicity of the arrangement – in historical terms, a 'master' professor, using their specialist expertise and lived professional experience to teach an 'apprentice' student – lesson and teaching quality are challenging to define and measure. Learning and teaching practices inside one-to-one lessons can be elusive, unknown, or concealed, even to those inside the conservatoire.

Part of this elusiveness might stem from the wide variety of teaching approaches and student needs in the one-to-one space.[1] At conservatoire level, the responsibility of professors to support many facets of students' artistic, technical, personal, and professional development is complex and challenging. Lesson content is shaped according to individual students and may change in the moment to reflect their immediate needs. To facilitate this highly responsive dynamic, the one-to-one relationship between professor and student requires a sustained and protected space where mutual understanding and trust can develop. This space needs to be flexible and uninhibited, allowing individuals to be their authentic selves. It must also accommodate the nuances of advanced musical performance craft and interpretation on specific instruments.

At its best, the one-to-one situation provides a platform for this type of specialised focus and awareness of individual students' needs and aspirations,[2] maintaining the flexibility for student–teacher roles to shift dynamically in the lesson according to the learning aims. In

DOI: 10.4324/9781003281573-15

this way, a professor has the freedom and autonomy to explore a continuum of roles which might range from being an instructor-demonstrator to a musical role-model, professional mentor, personal advisor, or artistic collaborator. The need for versatility in the one-to-one teaching studio has long been understood: Glezarova reflects that the teaching methods of the renowned violin teacher Yuri Yankelevich 'were flexible and varied. The only thing that remained consistent was his unflinching dedication to his goal . . . The essential goal is to uncover and maximise the use of the student's inner resources.'[3]

Control and influence

The flexibility and personalisation afforded by one-to-one tuition appear ideally suited to the aspiring professional musician on a unique personal trajectory. But in recent decades, research has delved into the lived experiences of conservatoire students and staff, subjecting the model and, by association, the conservatoire to increased scrutiny.[4] Many of these studies have problematised the power relations inherent in the master–apprentice model, noting that the intimacy of the one-to-one teaching environment combined with a 'culture of concealment'[5] can also lead to vulnerabilities for both students and teachers.[6] At its worst, the one-to-one music lesson has become a site for serious abuses of power, as seen in the cases of child sexual abuse at specialist music schools in the UK, where the actions of some music teachers devastated the lives of their students.[7] In recent years, similar concerns have been raised about the conduct of teaching staff at conservatoires in the UK and internationally. Despite institutions' efforts to develop robust policies and reporting mechanisms, incidents still occur, and it is clear that abuses of power in conservatoires have not yet been eradicated.

We saw in Chapter 3 that synergies with the profession are a distinguishing feature of the conservatoire experience, providing conservatoire students with a remarkable support network for professional training and opportunities. However, this close relationship with the profession can charge the conservatoire learning environment with authority and influence untypical of a university setting. The weight of this professional hierarchy isn't limited to the relationship between a student and their one-to-one professor. Other conservatoire-specific factors, such as the way in which life-changing decisions about scholarships or external performances are delegated to specific gatekeepers, serve to amplify the power (or at least the perceived power) of key individuals. Furthermore, there are contributing factors external to the conservatoire. Many young musicians will have grown up accustomed to musical environments characterised by 'restraint and control'[8] where it is taboo to challenge leadership. Arguably, traditional settings like youth orchestras, music exams, and competitions play a role in reinforcing a culture of subservience to master musicians. The historic tendency for traditional classical music experiences to condition young musicians to comply is now recognised, and organisations like the National Youth Orchestra of Great Britain are now developing radically new approaches to empower young musicians. However, one of the most pressing challenges for conservatoires is to provide an environment where *all* students feel empowered to speak up and challenge behaviours without fear of the potential impact on their career prospects. How do we equip students, individually and collectively, to initiate courageous conversations about behaviours? And how do we equip teaching staff to enable and respond to these conversations?

The one-to-one teaching space is a single example in the conservatoire's complex ecology of power relations. It is susceptible to many types of mismanagement or abuse, with 'the potential for power to operate invisibly' leading to negative consequences for students' artistic, personal, and professional outcomes.[9] Examples might include manipulation, favouritism, microaggressions, unconscious biases, gatekeeping of opportunities, or rejection of students' interests. Due to the power imbalance between professor (the recognised musician as professional) and student (the unknown musician as aspiring professional), students may not feel empowered to challenge certain behaviours or request a change of professor. Equally, they might also idealise the professor's position, authority, and influence.[10]

Conservatoire training is a time for students to develop their unique artistic identity. For some students at the start of this journey, there may be a temptation to grow into the mould of the master teacher, who is viewed as *the* model of success. While it is inevitable that teachers will project aspects of their own worldview onto their students, there is a risk that the teacher's voice, opinions, and musical values may dominate to an unhealthy level, as highlighted by Creech in her study of student and teacher talk during lessons.[11] It is essential that professors create space for differentiated thinking and original ideas, some of which might deviate in uncomfortable ways from the professor's own musical experiences and ideals. This situation needs to be balanced to avoid unnecessary conflict.

It is equally important to recognise that power imbalances are not always the professor's fault, and in some cases negative impacts may not be immediately perceptible to both the professor and/or the student. Furthermore, while power may be subject to abuse, it can also be a positive enabler. As Burwell points out, 'without power as energy, efficacy, the ability to affect change – learning cannot take place'.[12] For music students, the powerful influence of professional artist-teachers can inspire and motivate.[13] And the professional standing of a teacher can, rightly or wrongly, open doors to professional opportunities. Indeed, it is this influence, a by-product of professional standing and reputation, that often attracts prospective students to study with a particular professor.

Nonetheless, historic abuses of power in one-to-one teaching have tainted the world of classical music education. This is further exacerbated by mainstream portrayals of abuse in popular media, such as *Whiplash* (2014) and *Tár* (2022). These characterisations can perpetuate the myth that abuses of power in one-to-one teaching are a common and necessary rite of passage that musicians must endure to reach their professional goals. Conservatoires like the RCM therefore find themselves in a position wherein the continued use of one-to-one lessons as their primary mode of teaching can appear to the wider world as outdated and, at worst, damaging to students. In defending the conservatoire's position, we must be cautious of an uncritical approach that assumes that the one-to-one model is better due to tradition, perceived value, and a focus on utopian one-to-one teaching conditions that rarely reflect the complex realities of today's students. Appeals to experience such as 'it's a tried and tested method' or 'if it ain't broke, don't fix it' are insufficient. How can we tell if one-to-one teaching is beneficial? Traditionally, the student's end-of-year recital might have been considered the measure of success, but this is only one fleeting measure, and it is not the only outcome of teaching.[14] And when seeking student evaluation of teaching, students may feel inhibited from discussing their honest experiences of lessons due to the noted power dynamics. As bastions of one-to-one teaching, conservatoires should lead in the search for answers about the efficacy of one-to-one teaching in higher education. Driven by a duty of care to our students, conservatoires have a responsibility to understand and evidence quality in one-to-one pedagogy, to share this understanding more widely, and to promote evidence-informed innovation.

Building communities of practice

A recurring observation in the scholarship on one-to-one conservatoire teaching is the isolation of the student–teacher dyad. Creech and Gaunt highlight the 'peripheral membership' of instrumental teachers in their institutional communities of practice.[15] This is explored further by Burwell et al., who suggest that the physical and social isolation of one-to-one professors can limit pedagogical innovation, arguing that professors are 'often obliged to develop their work in relative isolation, relying on reference points that are limited to their personal histories and accumulating experience'.[16] The absence of robust induction training, peer observation, and regular appraisal systems for hourly teachers in many conservatoires can exacerbate this risk, as highlighted by a recent EU-funded project, PRIhME (Power Relations in Higher Music Education).[17]

We argue that metaphors like the 'secret garden' and master–student 'apprenticeship' can send an imprecise message about the kind of teaching and learning that take place in the studio, as well as the broader ethos of the one-to-one model today. Such metaphors, graphic and powerful, can prioritise negative and exclusionary aspects over the freedom that privacy brings to exploration and experimentation. Isolation from distraction can be conducive to learning; in a safe space, the student is free to explore and try new approaches without fear of being observed – other than by the teacher, who functions as a guide and sounding board. Here, the teacher can amplify what the student is doing or deconstruct to provide alternatives or simply agree and appreciate the innovation and experimentation. The aim is for learning to happen as part of a constructive and dialogic process, with both members actively learning in this one-to-one space. As part of a balanced and varied curriculum, the opportunity for a student to learn one-to-one in a safe space can and should be an enabling and freeing experience.

Over the past decade, accelerated during the COVID-19 era, there has been a move to support conservatoire professors through novel training and professional opportunities.[18] Devising such activities requires creative thinking to recognise the time constraints of busy professionals as well as the resource challenges of renumerating part-time hourly professors for activity outside their teaching. One example at the RCM is the growing practice of students working on a one-to-one basis with two or even three professors. This co-delivery of teaching is becoming standard practice in many faculties, with the student experiencing two or more expert voices. These two perspectives might align or contradict, illuminating different approaches while diluting the noted risks of unhealthy teacher dominance and singular role models. The structure also embeds a peer support mechanism that emerges naturally from teaching. In its most effective form, the two or more professors connect regularly to share information on the student's needs and their progress. These moments of dialogue can arise naturally, promoting reflective practice and collaborative problem-solving about pedagogical challenges.

The RCM has also launched *Teacher Cafés*, to create a supportive online peer sharing space for professors to share their teaching experiences with others. Prompted by the COVID-19 lockdown, these facilitated online fora were designed to bring teachers together to reflect on the transformation that the one-to-one teaching experience was undergoing through the digital pivot. These reflective spaces were well-received, and attendance was high, with participation from all faculties. The ability to connect remotely via Zoom or Teams has been invaluable in bringing together part-time teachers to discuss methods and approaches, to share experiences about problem-solving, and to learn more about the broad range of challenges that both teachers and students face. The range of discussion topics underlined the multifaceted role of professors today, with recurring themes including student mental health, general lesson structuring, technical troubleshooting in the online lesson, resources to support more diverse programming, and support for neurodiverse students, all areas that transcend the boundaries of instrumental or vocal specialisms. Our experience at RCM suggests that there is a need post-pandemic to expand the opportunities for professors to connect with one another, to help them recognise their multifaceted impact on student development, and to engage *all* professors in this process, not only those who self-select to do so.

Exploring new models

To maintain excellence, the traditional apprenticeship model must evolve to recognise the multifaceted needs of students today, and there are encouraging signs that this evolution is already underway. In 2012, Creech and Gaunt called for a shift of emphasis from the apprentice model towards transformative learning – an approach that 'suggests a focus on student reflection autonomy, and motivated, self-directed learning'.[19] Today, conservatoire students are exposed to many ways of learning; while the one-to-one approach remains at the core, a further goal is to position one-to-one lessons as complementary to and porous with all areas of conservatoire study. One potential outcome of a more reflective, if still isolated, one-to-one space is to nurture connections between the principal study and the wider curriculum. As such, the one-to-one lesson can invite pause for thought, providing facilitated time for students to synthesise and identify how outcomes from the one-to-one lesson can be applied in myriad professional settings. However, to facilitate this level of meaningful connectivity, there is a need for more effective communication with professors, documentation of best practices, and robust evaluation of student outcomes.

It is important to remind ourselves of the increased expectations placed on one-to-one professors in the conservatoire today. Teaching in this context is demanding work, and the burden of responsibility to support all aspects of students' artistic, technical, personal, and professional development is growing. Two external pressures are at play: a rapidly changing music profession and students in higher education who require significant additional support.[20] To meet the needs of this landscape, the conservatoire must be open to change. We note that scholarship in one-to-one teaching tends to problematise the one-to-one teaching scenario without necessarily engaging in constructive dialogue with teachers themselves to formulate solutions. Too often, teachers are treated only as *subjects* in research, rather than true participants or co-researchers, risking the alienation of conservatoire professors and stagnation of learning and teaching. Greater understanding of and meaningful collaboration with these teachers will be essential to evolve practices in ways that meet the needs not just of students but also of the instructors themselves and of the wider music profession. This should be informed by an understanding of how teachers' professional and peer learning experiences outside the conservatoire mediate their work with students.

Having problematised the strengths and challenges of the one-to-one teaching studio, we now consider how long-standing, ingrained approaches in this teaching space might be disrupted. The digital pivot during the COVID-19 pandemic prompted a radical change to learning and teaching in the conservatoire that might not otherwise have happened. We can look to this period for evidence that change is possible and for inspiration about the form this could take. The second part of this chapter explores some of the ways in which the pandemic moved one-to-one performance and composition teaching forward, and how those alternative ways of working might be springboards for future evolution. We draw upon data collection and analysis from an RCM research project funded by the UK Society for Research in Higher Education.

Technology as mediator?

To uncover the lived experiences and pedagogies experienced by students and staff during the pandemic, the RCM conducted research to investigate experiences of technologically mediated lessons in the one-to-one studio. In this project, RCM teachers and students were invited to reflect in interviews on their experience of online instrumental teaching during the COVID-19 pandemic. The insights that emerged from this study naturally reflected unstructured adaptation during a time of uncertainty, but the findings can also inform future approaches to one-to-one teaching and learning more broadly. It is vital that any learnings from this period are not forgotten. The research was designed around the following questions:

- In what ways can digital learning in music performance at a higher education level complement and enhance the traditional master–apprentice model of teaching?
- How do the interactions between student and teacher change in a hybrid learning environment, and what is the impact of this on learning?
- How might digital pedagogies provide a more open, inclusive, and reflexive pedagogical framework for both staff and students?
- How could a conceptual framework mapping practice-led learner engagement with digital learning inform curriculum development in a future where online and other non-traditional performance modes will be increasingly prevalent?

The project included thematic analysis of the interviews, alongside a comprehensive literature review, thereby setting out a framework that could underpin a future blended approach to instrumental teaching in higher music education.[21] This chapter focusses on only the interviews; the full literature review can be accessed in the project report.[22]

Research methodology

In total, eight RCM students and eight RCM teachers participated in individual interviews of approximately 45 minutes, conducted over Microsoft Teams by Samuel Mallia, the project research assistant and then a PhD student in Music Education at the RCM. Since the principal investigator and co-investigator are both curriculum managers,[23] the use of a research assistant ensured that participants were less likely to associate the interviews with any kind of performance review or assessment. It was felt that this would put participants more at ease and willing to share both positive and negative experiences. Ethical approval was granted by the Royal College of Music Research Ethics Committee.

Each instrumental family has its own culture and conventions of instrumental teaching;[24] to recognise the range of practices across the conservatoire, we sought to work with participants from a variety of instrumental groups. Eight students were selected from an open call for participation, including one or more undergraduate students representing brass, keyboard, percussion, strings, voice, and woodwind. For staff, we sought to engage with a range of instrumental families, while also spanning 'digital inhibitors', 'reluctant adopters', and 'digital innovators'.[25] To identify an appropriate mix of participants, we requested nominations from line managers across the conservatoire, based on observations of engagement with technology during COVID-19. Since identifying and sharing innovative practice were key aims, there was a slight bias towards reluctant adopters and digital innovators – a leaning which we accepted due to the potential for richer findings. Staff participants represented the faculties of keyboard, strings, brass, and percussion. The teachers who were able to draw the most from the experience of using digital interventions to support their teaching can be characterised as 'transformative-style teachers'.[26] The interview questions were the same for both student and teacher interviewees, focusing on previous experience and confidence using technology, initial impressions of online teaching, exploration of changes to lesson structure/content that were necessary in the new digital context, and changes to established practices. The interviews were audio-recorded and transcribed before undergoing thematic analysis and cross-referencing with the findings of the literature survey.

We recognise that the small sample size (eight teaching staff and eight students) for this research provided only a snapshot of the teaching practices developed during this period of online teaching and at one specific, UK-based conservatoire. Therefore, the findings that follow are shaped by the RCM's specific learning and teaching culture and policies and may exhibit a UK-centric bias. Nonetheless, the project literature review illuminated common themes in this mode of teaching globally, indicating that there would be applicability beyond the UK.

The role of artistic independence

Perhaps unsurprisingly, since the interviews were conducted during the COVID-19 pandemic, one of the key points identified by staff was a renewed understanding of student independence and, more critically, the pivotal role of the teacher in enabling that independence. Most of the teachers observed the extent to which students relied on their feedback and endorsement on a weekly basis. The forced physical separation from the instrumental teacher during lockdown revealed to the teachers some of the disadvantages of the one-to-one method of teaching and served to challenge their assumptions about how students were structuring their time in between their contact hours, for example. Several teachers reflected on how students appear to rely on mimicry, even within a remote learning context. This was seen as problematic because of the technology but, critically, also illuminated the degree to which students, even at this advanced stage of their artist trajectories, continued to depend on the teacher to demonstrate an aspect of technique and/or interpretation so that they could imitate it. This approach took some of the teachers by surprise because it was more prevalent than they expected. Our participants repeatedly observed how dependent their students seemed to be on demonstration: so much so, that even when the teachers were trying to explain and narrate, this was perceived as being 'talked at' and less valuable for maintaining engagement and sustaining learning.

This tendency for modelling through teacher exemplars has been critiqued by Burwell for placing the student in a passive role.[27] One of the teachers noted that 'we got a lot more out of the sessions if they didn't play that much' with the focus remaining on conversation. Perhaps the role of dialogue within the one-to-one lesson can acquire new meaning and become less about demonstrating and more about encouraging deep listening, critical reflection, and independence, opening possibilities for repertoire coaching, career advice, and structuring practice. During the COVID-19 lockdown, teachers spoke of their attempts to encourage students to trust their instincts and to rely more on their own critical listening. In encouraging and empowering students to move away from such dependency, the student and teacher were able to co-create a space for collaborative input. This recognition of the need to foster an independent artistic vision was a significant finding in our interviews with teachers.

Revisiting old skills and learning new ones

Following on from the recognition that a more independent approach to the one-to-one context needed to be embraced, teachers also focused on the skills necessary to achieve that independence successfully. Apart from the need for upskilling in technology, and in the use of remote teaching platforms, teachers found that they were looking at the music lesson from all angles. This was in the literal sense of not only asking students to place the camera at different angles to view themselves as performers but also pedagogically looking at the ways in which they could creatively capture a student's imagination.

Once the technological challenges were surpassed, and both students and teachers were able to communicate reasonably well verbally and by using their instruments, another unexpected insufficiency came to light: critical reflection and active listening were mentioned as tools that teachers assumed students have already acquired and rely on by the time they are in a conservatoire. It appears however that in the perception of students, these terms have yet to be humanised and contextualised and remained ambiguous for most.[28] For example, Teacher M noted 'what we haven't done and what we haven't encouraged the students to do enough of is to listen to themselves more critically'.

Not all students understood what critical listening to a recording meant to their own performance of that same work. Critical listening, with or without the guidance of a teacher, should enable the student to look beyond simply reproducing the performance that they hear, instead thinking about the parameters that they need to focus on to bring their own artistic interpretation of a work to life. Herein lies the need for artistic independence, which is unlikely to materialise if it is not consistently encouraged.

Reflection is also a key part of learning enhancement, but unless this is practised regularly, opportunities for artistic and intellectual growth are not maximised. Some students were taken aback by the difference they observed in what they thought what they were playing as opposed to what they were playing in reality:

> I was very shocked that I found myself intrigued, because I thought I was doing exactly what he [the teacher] told me to do. But no, it was just my perception of it, because I was perceiving the sound differently from in the recording. And it's very, very interesting, because it's like an exercise that you're recording yourself, and then you're listening to

yourself, and you will see that it doesn't sound as the way you played it. And especially for a teacher, that's his job to give me feedback and help me to develop myself, especially coming from him, this was extremely important to really understand not only the way I hear myself, but how people can hear my performances too.

(Student F)

Going forward, might recording and critical listening be integrated as part of a student's practice from the outset rather than depending on the teacher's preference?

Furthermore, an accomplished reflective practice leads to critical listening and self-evaluation. In this context, technology offers enormous potential. Teachers observed that using apps to scan and annotate music was helpful in encouraging deeper engagement with the musical score. This renewed focus on students' deep listening as well as analytical skills even within the one-to-one sessions. The increased focus on recording their playing at various instances encouraged a more nuanced understanding of what a recording truly captures – simply a moment in time. The use of recording technology for learning purposes enabled students to develop an increased confidence in their artistic voices *in development*. In this sense, addressing recording technology, its uses, benefits, and disadvantages in the individual lesson helped address a critical issue that causes anxiety among students – rather than attempting to achieve a perfect recording, which is ephemeral, recording is defamiliarised and subsequently reconnected with as being simply another tool at musicians' disposal. One participant suggested that, going forwards, teachers could:

[I]ntroduce just five minutes of recording, and then ask me to reflect on those five minutes. . . . You can already see a lot of problems or good stuff within that short time. . . . I'm definitely continuing with that, and whether I'll be successful, I'm not sure, but I'll try.

(Student B)

Students also made observations about their own recording practice:

Really have to make sure that I could record it smoothly. In like one take two, three takes, because in the beginning, it would take me two days to record three pieces just because I would have so many mistakes, I wasn't happy with. And I would have to stop and re-take. And it made me change how I practice to make sure that I could not stop and just do really easy smooth recordings . . . just be responsible of your own progress.

(Student E)

Filming performances was another discussion point that offers insights into how students might reap benefits as they make the leap from the practice room into the performance space:

So I think one of the strategies that I learned regarding videos is not to be afraid to just film yourself as often as you can, because at some point it will be good. . . . If you do it so much, it becomes such a routine that you already don't care about all the bad ones, all the bad takes. And you also get less nervous about it.

(Student G)

Familiarising oneself with being externally observed seemed initially to shock students, but it was clearly a topic they considered necessary for enhancement.

Our analysis also brought to the fore innovative methods of lesson documentation such as using online diaries on a learning management system and a renewed focus on encouraging active and deep listening. In their comments, teachers observed that, due to the challenges of real-time performance and feedback in the online space, they needed to deploy very different kinds of teaching strategies to be effective. So, for example, teachers noticed that skills such as deep score-reading, active listening, and critical reflection needed to be brought back to the forefront of the lesson. These skills, which teachers often assume students already have, were spotlighted in the restricted learning and teaching contexts of the pandemic. As a result, any insufficiencies that the students had in these areas needed to be addressed before maximum benefit could be obtained from this transformed teaching context.

Prioritising a learner-focussed approach

Initially, online teaching began as a synchronous practice, where the teacher and student attempted to replicate the qualities of their usual in-person lesson hour over Zoom or Teams. Over time, however, teachers deviated from this model and began to consider the possibilities of asynchronous teaching. This led to an increased reflection about what kind of learning was happening, or could happen, outside the defined weekly contact time with their students. This is a critical insight for the development of one-to-one teaching in the twenty-first century. Contemporary lifestyles, learning modes, and artistic models whereby students are encouraged to join the music sector and take the performance opportunities as they come require them to be far more flexible in organising learning and practice time outside their studio time with their teacher. Recent definitions of artistic citizenship and the concept of 'musicians as makers'[29] empower, and indeed almost insist on, students taking the ownership of their artistic lives far sooner than conservatoire students of earlier generations. In our view, it is the role of the contemporary conservatoire to provide models for independent and focused study outside of the teaching time. This time can be curated more effectively with the assistance of technology. Practice videos, or guided technique videos created by teachers for their students, provide one example of this.

Through this research, we found that many one-to-one teachers saw a transformation in their role, from a normalised (and comfortable) position traditionally dominated by demonstration and direction to one of increased dialogue and facilitation. This shift of relations, during and around the one-to-one lesson, enabled a re-envisioning of the student–teacher relationship in the one-to-one context. For a one-to-one teaching context, this might be viewed as a paradigmatic shift where the traditional emphasis on the teacher's view and opinion is replaced by a co-learning approach to teaching. Within this new context, multimodal ways of teaching and learning need to be acknowledged and would determine the effectiveness of this approach.

Underpinning these new approaches to the changing shape of the one-to-one lesson is communication. All teachers recognised the importance of communicating their expectations in advance of each lesson clearly to the students, rather than just responding in the moment to what happens in real-time performance. As one of our participants put it, an online situation is a:

> [M]uch more concentrated and intense experience . . . because to get through what you want to say to the student, you need to explain it at least three times more clearly than you would need to explain it in a room.
>
> *(Teacher N)*

Furthermore, clear communication helped eliminate anxiety on both the part of the students and the teacher. It set a clear framework for the lesson time and ensured that even if there were any technical disruptions, the lesson could still proceed to achieving some, if not all, of its objectives.

The transformational and disruptive nature of technological interventions within the one-to-one space requires that new techniques come into focus. Teachers collectively identified helpful tools that included deeper score-analysis, discussion of previously recorded work submitted in advance of the lesson, and both demonstration and narrative. As one teacher characterises it,

> [E]ven though I suppose you do an awful lot of talking, because that's how I felt that the lessons were worked best when we were analysing their playing from the recordings . . . that used the time much better.
>
> *(Teacher M)*

A challenge in integrating these components is pacing and timing, assuming the reliability of the internet connection. Storytelling and narrative were always important tools in a music teacher's toolkit, but our project demonstrated that the necessity of such tools is amplified through digital platforms, which completely defamiliarise the normal setting. Several of our participants noted this strong emphasis on the role of description, where telling, or a reflective version of it, comes to the forefront of their teaching method. When this critical evaluation of process and product is embedded into the lesson, the discourse for evaluating self-knowledge and progress encourages independent learning. Psychological challenges included what one teacher called 'the need to calibrate our feelings, our tempo, our perception of the sound, or the amount of the sound that we deliver, of the style, of the voicing' (Teacher J).

As students are exposed to more performances, recordings, masterclasses on various online platforms, they may be overwhelmed by the content and lack the means to evaluate it. While the volume of information is not within the teacher's control, the means to provide the evaluative, reflective, and critical edge to all that the student sees and hears is crucial. Our findings from the pilot project show that the twenty-first-century musician needs to be equipped to constantly evaluate and critique musical performances, materials, and processes almost as quickly as they are made available to them.

Conclusions

During this research project, we observed that the online experience of students and staff during the COVID-19 pandemic led them to view the one-to-one environment, relationships, and communication from new perspectives. For students, the emphasis on self-directed recording led to unexpected changes in the organisation of their practice and a normalisation of digital recording practices for self-evaluation. For staff, disruption to the established format of modelling and demonstration in lessons may have initially led to not only the intensification of their workload but also the exploration of new models of teaching, drawing upon listening, dialogue, and musical analysis. Our analysis of student and staff responses brings to light new and divergent approaches in the one-to-one teaching space. It is these affordances that the conservatoire of the twenty-first century should aspire to integrate into normalised practice. To do so effectively, conservatoires should recognise the multiple roles and responsibilities of the principal study teacher today and use these to shape a collective understanding of healthy and balanced one-to-one relationships. The pandemic demonstrated that teachers could be much more agile than expected, but this was an extreme situation that generated considerable strain on individuals. For lasting change in the one-to-one studio, we require a flexible model of staff development that values reflective and progressive teaching at the same level as musical expertise.

- Key take-away 1: imaginative use of digital technology, both online and offline, can provoke pedagogical reflection, in turn disrupting traditional models of one-to-one teaching in the conservatoire in productive ways.
- Key take-away 2: recognising the multifaceted responsibilities of one-to-one teachers today, conservatoires have a duty to support the development of artist-teachers as expert pedagogues through more robust peer observation and staff development initiatives.
- Key take-away 3: for scholarly research to produce meaningful change in the one-to-one lesson, there needs to be a greater dialogue with professors as co-researchers and/or collaborators, as well as the recognition of how professional power dynamics can mediate the teacher–student dyad.

Bibliography

Bull, Anna. *Class, Control, and Classical Music*. New York, NY: Oxford University Press, 2019.
Bull, Anna. 'Power relations and hierarchies in higher music education institutions'. In *Research Report*. PRiHME (Power Relations in Higher Music Education) Network; Association of European Conservatoires, September 2021. https://eprints.whiterose.ac.uk/178369/1/AEC_Power_relations_expert_paper_Anna_Bull.pdf.
Burwell, Kim. 'Authoritative discourse in advanced studio lessons'. *Musicae Scientiae* 25, no. 4 (December 2021): 465–79. https://doi.org/10.1177/1029864919896085.
Burwell, Kim. 'Power relations in the music teaching studio'. *British Journal of Music Education* (July 13, 2023): 1–11. https://doi.org/10.1017/S0265051723000220.
Burwell, Kim, Gemma Carey, and Dawn Bennett. 'Isolation in studio music teaching: The secret garden'. *Arts and Humanities in Higher Education* 18, no. 4 (October 2019): 372–94. https://doi.org/10.1177/1474022217736581.
Carey, Gemma, and Catherine Grant. 'Teacher and student perspectives on one-to-one pedagogy: Practices and possibilities'. *British Journal of Music Education* 32, no. 1 (March 2015): 5–22. https://doi.org/10.1017/S0265051714000084.
Carey, Gemma Marian, Ruth Bridgstock, Peter Taylor, Erica McWilliam, and Catherine Grant. 'Characterising one-to-one conservatoire teaching: Some implications of a quantitative analysis'. *Music Education Research* 15, no. 3 (September 2013): 357–68. https://doi.org/10.1080/14613808.2013.824954.
Carey, Gemma, Catherine Grant, Erica McWilliam, and Peter Taylor. 'One-to-one pedagogy: Developing a protocol for illuminating the nature of teaching in the conservatoire'. *International Journal of Music Education* 31, no. 2 (May 2013): 148–59. https://doi.org/10.1177/0255761413483077.

Creech, Andrea. 'Interpersonal behaviour in one-to-one instrumental lessons: An observational analysis'. *British Journal of Music Education* 29, no. 3 (November 2012): 387–407. https://doi.org/10.1017/S026505171200006X.

Creech, Andrea, and Helena Gaunt. 'The changing face of individual instrumental tuition: Value, purpose, and potential'. In *The Oxford Handbook of Music Education*. Vol. 1, edited by Gary E. McPherson and Graham F. Welch, 693–711. Oxford University Press, 2012. https://doi.org/10.1093/oxfordhb/9780199730810.013.0042.

Dammers, Richard J. 'Utilizing internet-based videoconferencing for instrumental music lessons'. *Update: Applications of Research in Music Education* 28, no. 1 (November 2009): 17–24, https://doi.org/10.1177/8755123309344159

Duffy, Celia. 'ICON: Radical professional development in the conservatoire'. *Arts and Humanities in Higher Education* 15, no. 3–4 (July 2016): 376–85. https://doi.org/10.1177/1474022216647385.

Garrett, Bethan. 'Touching the infinite': Inspiring Individuality in a Conservatoire Environment'. In *Teaching Music Differently: Case Studies of Inspiring Pedagogies*, edited by Tim Cain and Joanna Cursley, 145–61. Abingdon, Oxon: Routledge, 2017.

Gaunt, Helena. 'One-to-one tuition in a conservatoire: The perceptions of instrumental and vocal teachers'. *Psychology of Music* 36, no. 2 (April 2008): 215–45. https://doi.org/10.1177/0305735607080827.

Gaunt, Helena. 'Apprenticeship and empowerment: The role of one-to-one lessons'. In *Musicians in the Making: Pathways to Creative Performance*, edited by John Rink, Helena Gaunt, and Aaron Williamon, 28–55. New York, NY: Oxford University Press, 2017.

Gaunt, Helena, Celia Duffy, Ana Coric, Isabel R. González Delgado, Linda Messas, Oleksandr Pryimenko, and Henrik Sveidahl. 'Musicians as 'makers in society': A conceptual foundation for contemporary professional higher music education'. *Frontiers in Psychology* 12 (August 3, 2021): 713648. https://doi.org/10.3389/fpsyg.2021.713648.

Gaunt, Helena, Guadalupe López-Íñiguez, and Andrea Creech. 'Musical engagement in one-to-one contexts'. In *Routledge International Handbook of Music Psychology in Education and the Community*. 1st ed., edited by Andrea Creech, Donald A. Hodges, and Susan Hallam. Routledge, 2021. https://doi.org/10.4324/9780429295362.

Glezarova, Maria. 'Aspects of Yankelevich's teaching methods'. In *The Russian Violin School: The Legacy of Yuri Yankelevich*, edited by Masha Lankovsky, 162–76. Oxford University Press, 2016. https://doi.org/10.1093/acprof:oso/9780199917600.001.0001.

Guillaumier, Christina. 'Reflection as creative process: Perspectives, challenges and practice'. *Arts and Humanities in Higher Education* 15, no. 3–4 (July 2016): 353–63. https://doi.org/10.1177/1474022216647381.

Guillaumier, Christina, and Diana Salazar. *Transforming Performance Pedagogies: Interactions between New Technology and Traditional Methods*. Society for Research in Higher Education, 2023. https://srhe.ac.uk/wp-content/uploads/2023/02/Guillaumier-Salazar-Report.pdf.

Haddon, Elizabeth. 'Hidden instrumental and vocal learning in undergraduate university music education'. In *Advanced Musical Performance: Investigations in Higher Education Learning*, SEMPRE Studies in the Psychology of Music, edited by Ioulia Papageorgi and Graham Welch, 247–64. Farnham, Surrey; Burlington, VT: Ashgate, 2014.

Haddon, Elizabeth. 'Continuing professional development for the musician as teacher in a university context'. In *Developing the Musician: Contemporary Perspectives on Teaching and Learning*, edited by Mary Stakelum, 191–206. London: Routledge, 2016.

Jay, Alexis, Malcolm Evans, Ivor Frank, and Drusilla Sharpling. *The Report of the Independent Inquiry into Child Sexual Abuse*, October 2022. www.iicsa.org.uk/reports-recommendations/publications/inquiry/final-report.html.

Lebler, Don. 'Student-as-master? Reflections on a learning innovation in popular music pedagogy'. *International Journal of Music Education* 25, no. 3 (December 2007): 205–21. https://doi.org/10.1177/0255761407083575.

Palmer, Tim, and David Baker. 'Classical soloists' life histories and the music conservatoire'. *International Journal of Music Education* 39, no. 2 (May 2021): 167–86. https://doi.org/10.1177/0255761421991154.

Perkins, Rosie. 'Learning cultures and the conservatoire: An ethnographically-informed case study'. *Music Education Research* 15, no. 2 (June 2013): 196–213. https://doi.org/10.1080/14613808.2012.759551.

Pike, Pamela D., and Isabelle Shoemaker. 'Online piano lessons: A teacher's journey into an emerging 21st-century virtual teaching environment'. In *American Music Teacher*. Gale Academic One-File, 2015.

Presland, Carole. 'Conservatoire student and instrumental professor: The student perspective on a complex relationship'. *British Journal of Music Education* 22, no. 3 (November 2005): 237–48. https://doi.org/10.1017/S0265051705006558.

Watty, Kim, Jade McKay, and Leanne Ngo. 'Innovators or inhibitors? Accounting faculty resistance to new educational technologies in higher education'. *Journal of Accounting Education* 36, (September 2016): 1–15. https://doi.org/10.1016/j.jaccedu.2016.03.003.

Wickström, David-Emil. 'Inside looking in. Strategies to counteract misconduct in artistic teaching within higher music education'. In *Voices for Change in the Classical Music Profession: New Ideas for Tackling Inequalities and Exclusions*, edited by Anna Bull, Christina Scharff, and Laudan Nooshin, 54–68. New York: Oxford University Press, 2023. https://doi.org/10.1093/oso/9780197601211.001.0001.

PERSPECTIVE: CHAPTER 7

Helena Gaunt

Introduction

Though it is rare these days for me to be in an oboe lesson, my own journey with the one-to-one environment as a student musician, teacher, researcher, and now conservatoire leader continues to be a central reference point in my practice. Its transformational potential is clear to me, as are its challenges.

As a young oboe player, I was privileged to have lessons from some of Europe's best oboists. I held them in awe, trusted their expertise, and wanted to be improved by them. I took the power dynamics of the interactions for granted, hardly reflecting on the part I might be playing in them. I had little conscious awareness of what it might mean to learn or to teach.

It was a few years after starting to teach at the Guildhall School of Music & Drama in my late twenties that I started to wonder more about the nature of the one-to-one environment. Intrigued and at times confused about how and why learning did or didn't materialise with different students, I started what then became a lifelong search. With my horizons expanding as a novice researcher in the field, I began to understand the impacts of relational aspects of one-to-one teaching on students' learning and teachers' perspectives. Almost inevitably a Pandora's box of questions (more than answers) opened up, and the value of collaborative exploration, coaching techniques, and 'critical response' forms of feedback alongside more directive teaching approaches became apparent.[30]

Now, as the Principal of the Royal Welsh College of Music & Drama in the UK, the potential of one-to-one as a fundamental and holistic part of students' development remains, to my mind, incontrovertible. Yet, it is also vital to acknowledge that there are considerable challenges for this teaching environment in a contemporary context of radical change in the arts industries, alongside change in student mindsets and needs, the obligations of safeguarding, and inclusive practice. Those teaching may often experience more stable, clearly defined career paths than their students ever will, added to which they must embrace students' increasingly diverse learning styles and navigate mental health challenges and the power dynamics of this environment with nuanced professionalism.

DOI: 10.4324/9781003281573-16

What then are the critical issues now for shaping one-to-one provision within a conservatoire?

Perspectives

Reflection in the context of paradigm shifts in society and the music industry

As highlighted by the authors of this chapter, much research and the ongoing development of one-to-one teaching have pointed towards the value of reflection, for both teachers and students, through reflective diaries, learning biographies, communities of practice, and so on.

Much of this confirms that one-to-one teaching and learning have been evolving. There are, however, important questions about the frame of reference for such reflection. To what extent has it been supporting incremental development without, however, addressing fundamental questions about purpose and context? Is the frame of reference for this reflection sufficient now for preparing students for a rapidly changing professional world and positioning of the arts in society?

I would argue that the depth and speed of contemporary change call for a more radical reflective shift that opens up the mental models underpinning the one-to-one environment, its purpose and practice, and challenges habits of understanding in relation, for example, to appropriate repertoires, the social structures of music-making, and issues of quality. In other words, I would argue for 'paradigm reflection' alongside 'professional reflection', to use Sloboda's terminology.[31] Such a shift in the underpinning for one-to-one could draw on frameworks such as 'musicians as makers in society',[32] bringing musical craft and artistic skills into much closer dialogue with the wider aspects of 'making' music and situated musical experience. This would mean that the one-to-one environment might, for example, focus on programming, places for music-making, and engagement with audiences, alongside the core of playing/singing. Equally, it would call for more creative elements to be embedded within a student's instrumental/vocal development such as improvisation, arranging, and composing.

In this chapter, the authors beautifully illustrate how the disruption of the COVID-19 pandemic elicited paradigm reflection and possibilities to reframe the one-to-one environment through online technologies. COVID-19 brought into sharp relief some of the habits and expectations (both positive and negative) of existing practices, holding up a reflective mirror that catalysed self-awareness and change in a way that would not have happened in the ordinary course of things. Opportunities opened up for asynchronous feedback, greater self-determination, and perhaps deeper, more multi-layered reflection for musicians on their purpose and identity. The chapter, however, also raises questions about how collective learning from this experience can be taken forward rather than being allowed to dissipate.

Contemporary learning partnerships

The authors also point out significant shifts (amplified by the COVID-19 pandemic) in students' and young professionals' mental health, personal resilience, and expectations of work and work–life balance. Furthermore, it has been widely acknowledged that as increasingly diverse young people access professional training – a huge gift in itself – greater understanding of and support for different cultural experiences, learning styles, and needs are required. As the complexity, and at times fragility, of the relational aspects of learning partnerships in one-to-one teaching become ever clearer, so the imperative then grows to strengthen the framework of professionalism around this work, including the development of research, training, and support and articulation of quality thresholds, in order to fulfil the duty of care as education providers to both students and staff.

The authors rightly call for greater professional development for one-to-one teachers, where teachers can be centrally involved in concerted efforts to evolve practice to meet contemporary and future demands. Significant questions remain, however, about how to enable this. Here again, I suspect paradigm shift is needed. Diverse attempts have and are being made within different institutions and sector organisations to implement professional development schemes: for example supporting to submit for Advance HE Fellowships, participating in teaching observations, or engaging in international workshops and online courses. While all of these demonstrate positive outcomes, to date, they have largely been optional for teaching staff, generally appealing to those already oriented to critical reflection and innovation. A systematic approach engaging all teachers with a view to embedding cultural change and assuring consistently safe and high-quality curation of learning partnerships is yet to be established.

Summary and implications: curating reflective space

Professional contexts involving sustained one-to-one interactions these days almost invariably require forms of specific qualification, supervision and/or regulation, and ongoing professional development, whether in the field of medicine, executive coaching, or for example financial advice. The one-to-one environment in music is unusual in having little of this in place, although there is perhaps a clear need for it.

An immediate stumbling block, however, lies in the fact that in the UK at least, a high proportion of one-to-one teachers in conservatoires are employed on an hourly basis and to teach rather than engage in wider activity. There are good reasons for this – they almost all work as creative practitioners within the industry, and teaching is a relatively small part of their portfolio. But the situation also creates a problematic disconnect between the central importance of the teaching they do and the marginal contractual arrangement they have with the institution. This makes initiating any more formal training and development framework almost impossible, and as things stand now, engagement in teaching qualification or professional development opportunities relies on teachers volunteering their time or being paid additionally ad hoc.

If a significant shift is to be made with this agenda, revisions are likely to be needed at a contractual level. This will almost certainly be challenging to achieve, but it might have multiple benefits, given the impact these teachers can have on conservatoires, and the growing issues of duty of care for conservatoires towards their students and staff. Whatever the practical ways forward, balanced approaches to ongoing professional and paradigm reflection, both within the teaching space itself, and in structuring one-to-one within the overall curriculum and student experience, are much needed. Without these, it seems hard to imagine how conservatoires will continue to deliver the signature pedagogy of one-to-one teaching in ways that effectively navigate its challenging complexities in fast-changing contemporary contexts. Investing in such reflection may be essential to future-proofing conservatoire practice. It could also make an important contribution to the wider transformation of higher education through developing greater awareness and understanding of this signature pedagogy.

Bibliography

Gaunt, Helena, Celia Duffy, Ana Coric, Isabel González Delgado, Linda Messas, Oleksandr Pryimenko, and Henrik Sveidahl. 'Musicians as "makers in society": A conceptual foundation for contemporary professional higher music education'. *Frontiers in Psychology* 12 (2021): 1–20. https://doi.org/10.3389/fpsyg.2021.713648.

Lerman, Liz, and John Borstel. *Critique is Creative*. Middletown, CT: Wesleyan University Press, 2022.

Sloboda, John. 'Challenges facing the contemporary conservatoire: A psychologist's perspective'. *ISM Music Journal* (September/October 2011): 13–15.

Chapter and Perspective Notes

1 Carey and Grant, 'Teacher and student perspectives'.
2 Creech and Gaunt, 'The changing face of individual instrumental tuition'; Carey and Grant, 'Teacher and student perspectives'.
3 Glezarova, 'Aspects of Yankelevich's teaching methods', 167.
4 See Presland, 'Conservatoire student and instrumental professor'; Gaunt, 'One-to-one tuition'; Carey and Grant, 'Teacher and student perspectives'; and Lebler, 'Student-as-master?'.
5 Carey et al., 'Characterising one-to-one conservatoire teaching', 359.
6 Burwell, 'Authoritative discourse in advanced studio lessons'; Bull, 'Power relations and hierarchies'; Burwell, 'Power relations in the music teaching studio'.
7 Jay et al., *The Report of the Independent Inquiry into Child Sexual Abuse.*
8 Bull. *Class, Control, and Classical Music,* 95.
9 Gaunt, 'Apprenticeship and Empowerment', 43.
10 Gaunt, 'Apprenticeship and Empowerment', 43.
11 Creech, 'Interpersonal behaviour in one-to-one instrumental lessons'.
12 Burwell, 'Power relations in the music teaching studio', 2.
13 Presland, 'Conservatoire student and instrumental professor'.
14 Haddon, 'Hidden instrumental and vocal learning in undergraduate university music education'.
15 Creech and Gaunt, 'The changing face of individual instrumental tuition', 703.
16 Burwell et al., 'Isolation in studio music teaching', 373.
17 See Wickström, 'Inside looking in', 54–68.
18 Examples include the Healthy Conservatoires Network resources and events, supported by Conservatoires UK (see https://healthyconservatoires.org/) and the 'Artist as Teacher' seminar series delivered by the European Association of Conservatoires (AEC), in collaboration with the Royal Conservatoire The Hague (see https://aec-music.eu/).
19 Creech and Gaunt, 'The changing face of individual instrumental tuition', 704.
20 Research indicates that mental health conditions reported by students are nearly seven times as high as a decade ago (see https://researchbriefings.files.parliament.uk/documents/CBP-8593/CBP-8593.pdf), and the cost-of-living crisis is having a negative impact on students' studies (see HEPI/Advance HE 2023 Student Academic Experience Survey at: www.hepi.ac.uk/2023/06/22/student-experience-academic-survey-2023/).
21 Guillaumier and Salazar, *Transforming Performance Pedagogies.*
22 Guillaumier and Salazar, *Transforming Performance Pedagogies.* Data are held by the first author.
23 Dr Christina Guillaumier, at the time Head of Undergraduate Programmes, and Dr Diana Salazar, Director of Programmes.
24 Dammers, 'Utilizing internet-based videoconferencing for instrumental music lessons', 17–24; Pike and Shoemaker, 'Online piano lessons'.
25 Watty et al.,'Innovators or Inhibitors?'.
26 Carey et al. 'Characterising one-to-one conservatoire teaching'.
27 Burwell et al., 'Isolation in studio music teaching'.

28 For an exploration of reflection's embedding in UK conservatoire curricula, see Guillaumier, 'Reflections as creative process'.
29 Gaunt et al., 'Musicians as "makers in society"'.
30 Lerman and Borstel, *Critique is Creative*.
31 Sloboda, 'Challenges facing the contemporary conservatoire'.
32 Gaunt et al., 'Musicians as "makers in society"'.

8

THE MUSICIAN IN THE DIGITAL AGE

Technology in the conservatoire

Thom Gilbert and Diana Salazar

Introduction: technology in the conservatoire

For hundreds of years, musicians' lives have been shaped by numerous technologies, from the printing press, to the development of musical instrument design and materials, to advances in concert hall acoustics. But the digital era marks a new pace and intensity of technological change. Technology is now ubiquitous in the world today. It influences our behaviour and evolves practice in ways that can challenge, surprise, and inspire. The arts are no exception, and whether one chooses to apply technology for reasons of creativity or convenience, effectiveness or efficiency, its significance in mediating musical relationships has increased exponentially.

Often critiqued for their insularity, music conservatoires are more likely to be perceived as traditional rather than innovative and the rapid growth of digitisation can sit uneasily with these traditional values.[1] Learning and teaching practices tend towards intense and embodied experiences that focus on person to person interaction, where real-time collaborative activity is central to the success of the music-making and learning.[2] Technology in classical music contexts is often viewed as a distraction from the vital essence of practical instrumental, vocal, or composition teaching, and there can be suspicion about the ability of digital means to transmit or enhance the nuances of a live and embodied experience. Such tensions have been explored by authors such as Stanley Godlovich, Garry Crawford et al., Julian Johnson, Mark Katz, and particularly Amy Blier-Carruthers, who notes that:[3]

> [M]any of the issues that disturbed earlier recording artists are true for performers today – distrust of the technology, dislike of the process, doubts about the captured performance, disillusionment with editing, disagreement with the level of perfection expected for the recording[,] and discomfort about the concept of a disembodied performance existing at all.[4]

Despite these issues, a modern and future-looking programme of study in any genre of music, including Western classical performance or composition, must acknowledge and

DOI: 10.4324/9781003281573-17

embrace the realities and affordances of the digital world. Brian Kavanagh recognises the imperative for classical music organisations to adapt:

> [A]lthough the digital space may seem antithetical to traditional classical music culture, orchestras and opera companies must adopt digital technology in response to shifts in the logics that define their industry[;] otherwise they risk being (further) marginalised in an increasingly techno-literate society.[5]

This chapter explores some of the ways in which today's conservatoire musicians can engage with digital technologies in and through their practice. Through discussion of case studies from the Royal College of Music (RCM), we propose an integrated approach to digital artistry in the conservatoire. We argue that an informed and progressive approach to the integration of technology in music-making offers practical benefits and new artistic possibilities for conservatoire students today. Indeed, failing to engage with the digital challenge risks impairing the professional viability of our students in finding success in increasingly self-directed, diverse, and technologically enabled careers.[6]

The digital world and musicians' employability

The last twenty years have seen a dramatic shift in how recorded music is made and consumed, leading to fundamental changes in the relationships between musicians, their audiences, and the supporting industries. The recording industry has become a vital component of the wider classical music ecology, expanding into the audiovisual domain through cinema and television broadcasting. More recently, on-demand streaming has become the dominant format for the consumption of recorded music and video content. This shift towards online consumption was undoubtedly accelerated by the COVID-19 pandemic, when for both musicians and audiences, online music was the only readily available experience.[7] As musicians and ensembles across the world innovated at speed to remain connected with their audiences, those who had already begun to explore the possibilities of digital performance had a head start.[8] Musicians who had established a model for distributing their work independently online found themselves empowered and agile in a market that is now unlikely to return entirely to pre-pandemic norms.[9] Post-pandemic there are signs of further expansion, as evidenced by high-profile launches such as The Met: Live at Home and Apple Music Classical.[10]

Effective artistic communication on camera requires a different performance approach and aesthetic, and video editing decisions can radically alter musical expression.[11] Representing one's playing and sound accurately in recordings requires knowing enough about the technology to do so. Just as a musician in a live performance setting would consider elements of stagecraft, balance, projection, and their sound in the acoustic space, the digital domain brings its own performance considerations and digital knowledge, and technical skills are now essential for artists-in-training. Many conservatoire graduates go on to establish portfolio careers which depend on flexible modes of working and adaptability for industry demands (see Chapter 12). With increased access to technologies today, musicians can now take control of the complete process from recording to publication. In this culture of DIY content creation and self-publishing, it is no longer appropriate for musicians to rely on being 'serviced' by specialist technicians, engineers, and producers. The 'service' model of recording and production is evolving into an era of self-sufficiency.[12]

In a world where we are now surrounded by digital media in all areas of our lives, it is easy to forget that the ability to capture and transmit one's music has transformational consequences for musicians and their practice. Beyond recording and streaming, technologies such as online communication, social media, new interactive sound technologies, and virtual reality are reinventing the artistic identities and possibilities for musicians.[13] The rapid pace at which these technologies emerge and evolve can appear daunting, but their impact and potential are clear, and there is a risk of conservatoires being left behind.

Modes of engagement with digital technology

It is challenging to define what technology in the conservatoire is when the term spans such a wide variety of tools and contexts; from sound recording, to virtual performance spaces, to digital scores for performance, a wide spectrum of technology in live performance (from amplification to immersive and interactive electronics), and social media for artist promotion and entrepreneurship. In this chapter, we focus on the applications of technology for *performing classical musicians*, who make up the majority of students at the RCM. Until the pandemic, the role of digital technology in performing classical musicians' lives and livelihoods was generally overlooked. For classical musicians, technology has generally been viewed as a tool for reproduction rather than expression.[14] This relationship is quite different to that of popular and jazz musicians, whose entire musical histories have been shaped by the development of recording technologies.[15] For classical musicians, digital technologies are more often associated with composition practice, for instance technologies for scoring, sound creation, or developing extended sounds in performance.[16] There is scant scholarship that explores the role of creative technologies for classical *performers*, beyond that which examines audience experiences of streamed classical music performances.[17] While there is literature that touches on the benefits of self-recording for learning, this has generally focused on methods of online instrumental teaching rather than students' own skills development and creative practice.[18] Mindful of this gap in the scholarship, this chapter homes in on technologies that support the development of performance skills and artistic identity.

We propose that engagement with performance-related digital technologies can progress through multiple stages. This can be mapped as a taxonomy of engagement (see Figure 8.1), drawing upon a staged model similar to Bloom's taxonomy of learning in combination with elements of Puentedura's 'Substitution, Augmentation, Modification, and Redefinition' (SAMR) model of technology integration.[19] The levels of engagement in this model are designed to promote deeper investigation of technology in performance. Commencing with superficial exposure to technological mediation, at the model's peak students demonstrate technological fluency that can reimagine our discipline.

1. **Observation:** in this initial encounter, students have the opportunity to observe digitally informed practices in action. This might include listening to and watching recorded performances with attention paid to the mediation of performance via technologies, or observing technology in action through examples of works that involve multimedia or digital interaction. This step assists with normalisation and acclimatisation to the digital in performance. While this initial 'entry' level to the taxonomy is highly accessible

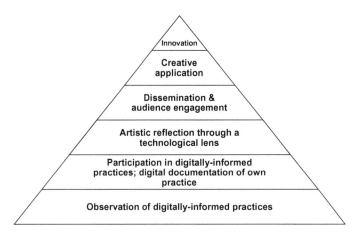

FIGURE 8.1   A taxonomy of conservatoire musicians' engagement with digital music technology.

(a form of 'substitution' in Puentedura's SAMR model), students might perceive work that engages with the digital as particularly new, radical, or beyond their reach. Conservatoires can mitigate this by embracing digitally informed practices in their curriculum and artistic programme at an earlier stage in students' studies, moving digital practices such as streamed concerts, operas, or work with electronics from the periphery to the core of their work.

2. **Participation and documentation**: recording one's own performances, even via a consumer device like a smartphone, is a significant first step to develop active engagement with technology. Furthermore, participation in recording sessions or broadcasts, even if these are managed entirely by specialist staff, exposes students to a new model of performance, where the deconstruction of works through recorded 'takes' provides an entry point into discovering the potential of technology. In addition, performance alongside the technological apparatus of microphones, cameras, and lighting becomes normalised. The elements of involvement and adaptation characterising this step are most aligned with Puentedura's dimension of technology as 'augmentation'.[20]

3. **Artistic reflection through a technological lens**: this step introduces a feedback loop whereby students use technology to discover ways for them to learn and improve. Self-recording can illuminate many aspects of sound, posture, and technique; however, Waddell and Williamon observe that musicians tend to record themselves more than they listen to those same recordings.[21] With a structured approach to reflection, self-recording (whether audio or audiovisual) can become a powerful tool for self-development. The element of feedback (and feedforward) here characterises entry into the 'modification' domain of SAMR.

4. **Dissemination and engagement**: all steps of the taxonomy thus far have focused on the individual performer's experience. At Step 4, this extends to an external listener or audience. Here, students reflect on the way in which their performances can communicate with audiences via technology, and how they as a performer are heard, seen, and perceived through this mediation. This focus on technology for artistic communication invites students to reflect more deeply on their programming, artistic, and technical decisions.

5. Reflecting on the outcomes of Step 4 can instigate the **creative application of technologies in practice**, enabling students to take ownership over direction, sound, editing, and many more aspects. Crucially in Stages 5 and 6, students move beyond content creation, applying their understanding from levels 1 through 4 to apply technology towards the shaping of their artistic persona.

6. Peak engagement combines all aspects of the taxonomy to explore the new and unknown as a form of **innovation**, aligned with Puentedura's 'redefinition' category, where 'technology allows for the creation of new tasks, previously inconceivable'.[22] Here, students move beyond imitation and into experimentation, where new ideas reimagine their practice and even the discipline. At this level of engagement, students reach a high level of digital fluency that enables them to not just use or understand technologies in their practice but also apply technologies towards the creation of *new* practices. In doing so, students can construct an artistic identity where digital technologies move beyond the extension or enhancement of 'traditional' practice and become a defining characteristic of who they are as artists. Composer Leah Kardos suggests that this kind of 'fluency in digital literacies is promoted through practice-led enquiry and adopting the mindset of the "curious musician."'[23]

The above framework uses sound recording as a vehicle for developing performers' aesthetic awareness and practical skills in technology. But it is important to recognise the practical challenges of implementation. Student engagement with performance technologies requires institutional support, and meaningful engagement via the student's principal study requires regular exposure to technological listening, exemplars, and role models. Given the focus on principal study development in the conservatoire, positive reinforcement from instrumental and vocal professors is key. Embedding technology in the one-to-one lesson can be a steep learning curve for professors, leading to feelings of vulnerability compared with their confidence and expertise in more traditional areas and 'reference points that are limited to their personal histories'.[24] Too often, technology becomes viewed as an optional 'extra' or something to be 'bolted on' in an already crowded curriculum. An integrated approach is more likely to succeed, where technology is embedded as a natural extension of existing practices.

Having outlined this framework, we move to some examples from the RCM that unpack these considerations in more depth.

Supporting performance practice online: the Virtual Learning Environment in the conservatoire

In 2016, the RCM launched its first Virtual Learning Environment (VLE), 'Learn.rcm', hosted on the emerging platform Canvas. While being an established technology in universities, online support for the highly practical and individual learning at a conservatoire is relatively recent and represents a fundamental challenge to established models of tuition. As expected, the VLE quickly found a home in supporting students' academic courses at the RCM. The principal challenge involved its role in supporting performance practice and the one-to-one tuition model. The displacement of learning to an online platform may feel especially disruptive in this practice-led environment.[25] This situation posed two key questions:

- How can a VLE meaningfully support a practice-led instrumental or vocal programme that is very different to the formats typical of academic subjects?

- How can it be used at scale, equitably, to support hundreds of students and their teachers when working relationships are individual and programmes of study largely bespoke?

Our initial response was to provide each professor with their own 'course' to collect and curate resources, share recordings, provide feedback, plan practice, and build community between students in their studio. Engagement with this platform via video recordings and feedback would stimulate engagement on the first three levels of the framework above: technologically mediated observation, documentation, and reflection on practice. A successful application to the Higher Education Funding Council for England (HEFCE) provided funding to pilot this adoption of blended learning techniques among a group of six professors in the Strings, Keyboard, Percussion, Brass, and Vocal faculties. The focus of the project was to explore how the VLE could support students not only in their weekly one-to-one lessons but also, and perhaps more importantly, in the hours of isolated practice in between to develop the self-regulation and routines to maximise the benefits of their face-to-face tuition.

Feedback from the pilot project revealed benefits for professors and students ranging from practical improvements, like reducing photocopying and improving the lesson booking process, to more fundamental changes to learning and teaching practices. Professors found that providing comments on video performances, for example, facilitated reflections deeper than in-the-moment reactions and that the platform provided a space for following up overlooked or displaced issues in the face-to-face hour. Students echoed these benefits, commenting that online feedback prompted deeper processing and reinforcement of in-person comments. Students also found benefits for their broader digital skills and confidence in recording, production, and online interactions.

Another welcome outcome of the project was that the involvement brought professors closer to the College as a community, providing a better understanding of the relationship between their work and students' broader programmes of study. This helped professors, all of whom were hourly paid freelancers, to feel better connected to their students, their peers, and the wider conservatoire community. While online learning is itself often perceived as isolating, in this instance it helped to break down the isolation of the one-to-one teaching studio.

Following the project's conclusion, an unresolved question was how these benefits could be realised at scale. The aspiration of providing an online space for every professor presented significant obstacles as VLEs are optimised to support large groups of students pursuing the same learning objectives simultaneously. Even with willingness and enthusiasm from staff, the realities of upskilling and providing support for hundreds of discrete online spaces would be impractical to deliver.

Faculty-based support with the VLE

To address this and to confront some of the emerging digital challenges in the one-to-one teaching space, the next step was to explore if online support could be provided at a faculty (instrumental family) level rather than studio level, and if this might provide an alternative, more sustainable model.

The RCM's Digital Learning Team collaborated with the Percussion staff to develop one combined 'course' for the entire faculty. The emphasis was to provide support and foster a community between students and staff without professors needing to maintain individual spaces. A model was developed to provide access to relevant resources, information, and support to all students in the faculty while using the administration functions in Canvas to channel other communications and resources by instrument group or teacher. This allowed for enough bespoke interaction while bringing the faculty together to share practice. A suite of videos was produced with a focus on the core technique and repertoire, common to all students to support them during practice, focusing initially on year one undergraduates in the early months of their study.

While this model sacrifices the level of individual support proposed in the HEFCE project, it provided meaningful online support and enabled community building and sharing of practice. Individual professors could contribute without the responsibility of an individual space, and all students could benefit equally. The model also addressed issues around privacy and the personal nature of the one-to-one relationship, providing a workable alternative that supplemented rather than directly challenged established practices.

While the VLE offers many possibilities for managing digital media and developing students' (and teachers') digital fluency, it also highlights factors that constrain its growth in the conservatoire. Digital tools are ideal for sharing content, but the one-to-one lesson, particularly in the UK, is characterised by a private and protected relationship between teacher and student. Moving towards a more open culture of digital documentation and content sharing can leave professors feeling exposed and vulnerable, threatening their ownership of their teaching space. However, doing so can disrupt the established master–apprentice model in ways that promote more democratic relationships and dialogue between performance teachers and their students. As Burwell notes, 'institutions should take responsibility for opening the spaces needed for teachers to optimise their own participation in its communities of practice', and it is possible that digital spaces are the key to this.[26]

The musician in the digital age

'Musician in the Digital Age' is a ten-credit (5 ECTS) undergraduate elective module that exposes students to contemporary and emerging practices in digital performance. The module challenges students to consider the role of technology in their artistic practice, how this might impact on their career ambitions, and to develop the critical skills to examine creative affordances and limitations in today's technologies. Through practical workshops and lectures, the students consider the role of technology in three broad areas that align with the engagement framework above:

1. As a tool for reaching and developing an audience through content creation (level 4)
2. Collaborating online musically, whether as a performer, student, or teacher (level 5)
3. The transformation of musical performance and learning through technology (level 6)

Classes introduce students to the practical and theoretical underpinnings of how recorded music is made, consumed, and monetised. Students develop the technical skills and confidence to make high-quality audio and video recordings of themselves using modest recording equipment and mobile devices such as smartphones and tablets. A major aim of the module is to dispel the widespread perception among performing students that recording is exclusively the domain of highly skilled engineers with professional quality equipment.

The module also considers issues of dissemination and connectivity, including distanced performance. Students explore the possibilities of remote musical collaboration and reflect on the creative potential and technical challenges of communicating effectively, either verbally or through performance, over a network connection. From basic videoconferencing software to advanced low latency technologies, students experience performing together over a network and are encouraged to explore the potential benefits of remote collaboration for their work as artists, students, and teachers.

Lastly, the module explores research-led applications of technology in musical performance and learning today. This extends to simulation, data capture and analysis, and virtual reality as tools for research and performance enhancement. In collaboration with the College's Centre for Performance Science (CPS), students experience the CPS' Performance Simulator and consider how data mapping and tracking can enhance musical performance.

The module provides students with a learning experience that combines practical skills with new research and cutting-edge professional practice. The curriculum is updated annually to ensure that content is current and reflects emergent thinking. The combination of current theory and practice ensures that students look beyond the functional aspects of software or hardware tools and instead engage with digital possibilities on a more critical level, seeking out the creative affordances of applying, combining, adapting, or even subverting technologies. This enquiry-led approach acknowledges and embraces the unknowns of our digital future, emphasising to students that technology isn't a simple 'fix' for problems; instead, it is framed as an evolving network of possibilities. This appreciation of the dynamic nature of digital technology in our lives is an important springboard for students to develop problem-solving, resilience, and agility in preparation for their professional careers.

The module assessment reflects these values by using a student-devised project model. Students are tasked to devise a project which explores an aspect of the integration of technology in their artistic practice. They are encouraged to consider which of the technologies and concepts covered in the course most closely relate to their personal development and aspirations and to explore these technologies in the context of their own practice. This could be learning the technical skills to create professionally viable recordings to support their performing career, exploring the use of digital technologies to become a more effective teacher, or developing an in-depth understanding of the potential and challenges of collaborating online. In linking the exploration of these technologies to a personal perspective on artistic and professional development, students prioritise and commit significant time and energy to a project that feels intrinsically valuable to them.

By necessity, during the COVID-19 pandemic, this assessment was modified to be presented digitally rather than as an in-person demonstration. Students were free to present their project in whatever way best suited them. This resulted in a wide array of digital presentation formats being used and enabled further learning in video and audio editing and web design as students decided how best to document and present their efforts for an audience. These digital presentations invited media-rich documentation of creative process rather than summative descriptions. Students explored many corners of their project research and process to collect and share audio, video, data, and photographic evidence of their project development. The active mining of this digital evidence base has prompted deeper self-reflection, evaluation, and critique from students and, post-pandemic, is now the standard mode of submission.

The digital in performance

One of the most pressing questions for conservatoires today is how the traditional, analogue craft of classical performance training at the core of the curriculum should evolve without compromising the richness of traditional performance models. At the RCM, we propose that this need not be a binary opposition of analogue versus digital.

For many years, livestreaming has been an important component of the performance programme at the RCM. Each year, many of the College's public performances are broadcast live using professional real-time audio and camera-mixing techniques, coordinated by a team of engineers. The professionally edited films are published on the RCM's YouTube channel, reaching many thousands of listeners across the world.[27] Providing professional broadcast support for student performances is becoming increasingly important for exposing students to current broadcasting practices and providing a global platform for their work. However, we recognise that students are often passive participants in this context. Students *observe* digital professionals at work around them but don't necessarily have structured opportunities to *understand* the digital relationships and mediation at play in this context.

However, there are many ways in which RCM students can become more actively involved in the digital space. Studio recording projects, even if they are supported by professional engineers, provide an opportunity for dialogue, critical reflection, and decision-making about one's sound and expression in recorded media. Slater suggests that the process of recording is a 'poetic moment' and highlights the 'importance of understanding the inextricably entwined nature of technical, musical, and social understanding in the moment of performing for a recording'.[28] Conservatoire curricula today can play an important role in illuminating these relationships by recognising recorded performances as equal and complementary to live performances. There are good reasons to do so as video recordings become common requirements for competitions and first-round orchestral auditions.

Assessment can be an important vehicle for students to develop fluency with the recording process by anchoring digital skills to their principal study. Furthermore, this type of assessment may provide a more inclusive performance format for students who struggle with performance anxiety. Work is already underway at the College to explore this, and selected technical assessments are now conducted as video submissions. However, this represents only one small step towards the acceptance of technologically mediated assessment as a standard (rather than emergency) format. The leap to professional performance for camera as an accepted assessment that is complementary (rather than in opposition) to the traditional recital represents a paradigm shift that requires the winning of heart and minds across the institution.

In addition, there are many ways for students to explore more experimental approaches to technology in performance. The RCM's termly electronic music concert series provides a platform for students to perform repertoire with electronics, including backing tracks, click tracks, interactive scores, live sound processing, surround sound, and interactive media. These elements can feel unfamiliar and daunting compared to piano accompaniment, but a supportive environment with guided preparation and technical rehearsal of the works can help to demystify repertoire with electronics, promoting a culture of experimentation and risk-taking. In a similar way, strong collaborations between student composers and performers can open up the creative process of developing new works with electronics and produce two-way benefits.

In addition to content creation and real-time performance, there is a scope to mobilise digital communication technologies for performance and remote collaboration. At the RCM, we have seen this work in practice through the Global Audition Training Programme, where students received a wealth of feedback on their mock orchestral auditions, presented via distance learning technology to panellists around the globe.[29] As Roger Mills has explored, distance performance using low latency systems like LoLa can also promote new understandings of collaborative process in ensembles.[30] Performers must accept the affordances and limitations of the technology, and, in doing so, their approaches to communication, listening, and collaboration become more adaptable. Encouraging chamber groups to rehearse even occasionally via LoLa can prompt a deeper exploration of effective communication at a distance. But to facilitate the normalisation of distance collaboration, technologies need to become more transparent and user-friendly for staff and students alike. Without this, the complexity of set-ups, as well as disruptive 'failings' of technology in rehearsal, diverts attention away from key performance considerations and becomes a psychological barrier for effective integration.

Finally, in a digitally informed curriculum, we recognise that many of our students may be more expert than professors. The RCM's Digital Learning Ambassador scheme promotes peer-to-peer learning, where students who are passionate about digital performance share their knowledge and experience with fellow students and staff. Providing students with the agency to share skills, design their own projects, and co-create new types of digitally informed performance is essential for embedding meaningful digital engagement.

Where next? The digital musician as today's musician

Today's digital technologies offer myriad possibilities for classical musicians to reimagine musical performances. Digital opportunities that were once out of reach for most musicians are now readily available in consumer smartphones. At the professional side of the spectrum, motion capture and virtual reality are expected to revolutionise immersive musical experiences.[31] And at the time of writing, we are only just beginning to understand the implications of artificial intelligence for creative practice. This complex and dynamic network of digital possibilities can be challenging for students to navigate and can be more challenging still for professors. In a conservatoire environment that privileges the tradition of live, acoustic performance, there is a risk that digital technologies are confined to special projects, experienced only by limited numbers of staff and students with the existing skills and confidence to engage. But the omnipresence of digital technologies across the arts means that conservatoire students require digital fluency to thrive. Representing oneself as a professional performer is no longer limited to the concert hall or even a live performance. The performance 'space' of the digital age is malleable, porous, illusive, and sometimes invisible. This demands a changed narrative in the conservatoire – a narrative that positions digital technology not as a threat, or as a gimmick, or even as a tool, but as an enabler: of deeper student learning; of expanded access to classical music; and of the creation of new and engaging musical experiences. In this way, conservatoires can equip their students 'to avoid nostalgia for norms without falling into the fetish of the new, or newly mediated'.[32] Today's generation of students are those who can unlock the potential of digital technologies for classical music with attention paid to personal authenticity and the integrity of the classical music art form. But they will only feel empowered to do so if we as conservatoires are brave enough to adapt our performance, curriculum, and assessment structures in support of this.

Summary

- Key take-away 1: to prepare students for a digital world, today's conservatoire curricula should normalise a wide range of professional practices that use technology (e.g., digital performances and audiences, video auditioning, self-promotion, online collaboration, etc.), with opportunities for student progression and specialisation.
- Key take-away 2: investment in staff development is critical to support these ambitions, reduce anxieties around technology, and enable a culture of peer-to-peer support and collaboration.
- Key take-away 3: authentic assessments that combine performance with technology can be effective vehicles for students to develop their technological fluency without compromising core learning objectives.
- Key take-away 4: conservatoires are uniquely placed to promote technology for artistic innovation, experimentation, and the evolution of music as an art form.

Acknowledgements

We thank Stephen Johns, RCM Artistic Director (2010–2024), for his feedback and suggestions on this chapter.

Further information and reading

Slater, Mark. 'Performing in the studio'. In *The Oxford Handbook of Music Performance*. Vol. 1, edited by Gary E. McPherson, 509–27. Oxford University Press, 2022. https://doi.org/10.1093/oxfordhb/9780190056285.013.31.
Waddell, George, and Aaron Williamon. 'Technology use and attitudes in music learning'. *Frontiers in ICT* 6 (May 31, 2019): 11. https://doi.org/10.3389/fict.2019.00011.

Bibliography

Bayle, Laurent, and Catherine Provenzano. '11. The Interface between Classical Music and Technology'. In *Classical Music*, edited by Michael Beckerman and Paul Boghossian, 103–18. Open Book Publishers, 2021. https://doi.org/10.11647/obp.0242.11.
Beckerman, Michael, and Paul Boghossian, eds. *Classical Music: Contemporary Perspectives and Challenges*. Open Book Publishers, 2021. https://doi.org/10.11647/obp.0242.
Bennett, Dawn. *Understanding the Classical Music Profession: The Past, the Present and Strategies for the Future*. London: Routledge, 2016.
Blier-Carruthers, Amy. 'The Influence of Recording on Performance: Classical Perspectives'. In *The Bloomsbury Handbook of Music Production*, edited by Andrew Bourbon and Simon Zagorski-Thomas, 205–20. New York: Bloomsbury Academic, 2020.
Bloom, Benjamin Samuel. *Taxonomy of Educational Objectives: The Classification of Educational Goals. Vol. Handbook I: Cognitive Domain*. New York: McKay, 1956.
Bourbon, Andrew, and Simon Zagorski-Thomas, eds. *The Bloomsbury Handbook of Music Production*. New York: Bloomsbury Academic, 2020.
Burland, Karen, and Stephanie Pitts, eds. *Coughing and Clapping: Investigating Audience Experience. SEMPRE Studies in the Psychology of Music*. Farnham, Surrey; Burlington, VT: Ashgate, 2014.

Burnard, Pamela. 'Reframing creativity and technology: Promoting pedagogic change in music education'. *Journal of Music, Technology & Education* 1, no. 1 (November 16, 2007): 37–55. https://doi.org/10.1386/jmte.1.1.37_1.

Burwell, Kim, Gemma Carey, and Dawn Bennett. 'Isolation in studio music teaching: The secret garden'. *Arts and Humanities in Higher Education* 18, no. 4 (October 2019): 372–94. https://doi.org/10.1177/1474022217736581.

Charron, Jean-Philippe. 'Music audiences 3.0: Concert-goers' psychological motivations at the dawn of virtual reality'. *Frontiers in Psychology* 8 (May 23, 2017): 800. https://doi.org/10.3389/fpsyg.2017.00800.

Cohen, Susanna, and Jane Ginsborg. 'The experiences of mid-career and seasoned orchestral musicians in the UK during the first COVID-19 lockdown'. *Frontiers in Psychology* 12 (April 9, 2021): 645967. https://doi.org/10.3389/fpsyg.2021.645967.

Cohen, Thomas F. *Playing to the Camera: Musicians and Musical Performance in Documentary Cinema*. Nonfictions. London; New York: Wallflower, 2012.

Colotti, Clara. 'A review of contemporary practices incorporating digital technologies with live classical Music'. In *Innovation in Music: Future Opportunities*, edited by Russ Hepworth-Sawyer, Justin Paterson, and Rob Toulson. Perspectives on Music Production. New York: Routledge, 2021.

Crawford, Garry, Victoria Gosling, Gaynor Bagnall, and Ben Light. 'An orchestral audience: Classical music and continued patterns of distinction'. *Cultural Sociology* 8, no. 4 (December 2014): 483–500. https://doi.org/10.1177/1749975514541862.

Denk, Janis, Alexa Burmester, Michael Kandziora, and Michel Clement. 'The impact of COVID-19 on music consumption and music spending'. Edited by Joshua L. Rosenbloom. *PLoS One* 17, no. 5 (May 13, 2022): e0267640. https://doi.org/10.1371/journal.pone.0267640.

Dromey, Christopher, and Julia Haferkorn. *The Classical Music Industry. First Issued in Paperback. Routledge Research in Creative and Cultural Industries Management*. New York; London: Routledge, Taylor & Francis Group, 2020.

Duffy, Sam, and Patrick G. T. Healey. 'Music, speech and interaction in an instrumental music lesson: An ethnographic study of one-to-one music tuition'. In *Language, Music and Interaction*, edited by Martin Orwin, Christine Howes, and Ruth Margaret Kempson, 231–80. College Publications, 2013.

Godlovitch, Stanley. *Musical Performance: A Philosophical Study*. London; New York: Routledge, 1998.

Haferkorn, Julia, Sam Leak, and Brian Kavanagh. *Livestreaming Music in the UK – Report for Musicians*, 2021, 3890959 Bytes. https://doi.org/10.22023/MDX.14974092.V1.

Hepworth-Sawyer, Russ, Justin Paterson, and Rob Toulson, eds. *Innovation in Music: Future Opportunities. Perspectives on Music Production*. New York: Routledge, 2021.

Hugill, Andrew. *The Digital Musician*. New York: Routledge, 2008.

Johnson, Julian. *Who Needs Classical Music? Cultural Choice and Musical Value*. New York: Oxford University Press, 2011.

Kardos, Leah. 'The curious musician'. In *The Oxford Handbook of Technology and Music Education*, edited by Alex Ruthmann and Roger Mantie, 317–22. Oxford Handbooks. New York, NY: Oxford University Press, 2017.

Katz, Mark. *Capturing Sound: How Technology Has Changed Music*. Berkeley: University of California Press, 2004.

Kavanagh, Brian. 'Reimagining classical music performing organisations for the digital age'. In *The Classical Music Industry, Routledge Research in Creative and Cultural Industries Management*, edited by Christopher Dromey and Julia Haferkorn, 126–38. New York, NY: Routledge, 2018.

Klein, Eve. 'Performing nostalgia on record: How virtual orchestras and YouTube ensembles have problematised classical music'. *Journal on the Art of Record Production* 9 (2015): 1–13.

MacFarlane, T. et al. *Culture in Crisis: Recommendations for Policy Makers*. London: Culture Commons Ltd, 2022. https://www.culturalvalue.org.uk/wp-content/uploads/2022/05/Culture-In-Crisis-Digital-Recommendations-to-Policy-Makers-May-2022-FINAL.pdf.

Mills, Roger. 'Telematics, art and the evolution of networked music performance'. In *Tele-Improvisation: Intercultural Interaction in the Online Global Music Jam Session. Springer Series on Cultural Computing*, 21–57. Cham: Springer International Publishing, 2019. https://doi.org/10.1007/978-3-319-71039-6_2.

Minors, Helen Julia, Pamela Burnard, Charles Wiffen, Zaina Shihabi, and J. Simon Van Der Walt. 'Mapping trends and framing issues in higher music education: Changing minds/changing practices'. *London Review of Education* 15, no. 3 (2017). https://doi.org/10.18546/LRE.15.3.09.

Nowak, Raphaël. *Consuming Music in the Digital Age: Technologies, Roles and Everyday Life.* Houndmills, Basingstoke, Hampshire: Palgrave Macmillan, 2016.

Orwin, Martin, Christine Howes, and Ruth M. Kempson. *Language, Music and Interaction.* London: College Publications, 2013.

Otondo, Felipe. 'Music technology, composition teaching and employability skills'. *Journal of Music, Technology & Education* 9, no. 3 (December 1, 2016): 229–40. https://doi.org/10.1386/jmte.9.3.229_1.

Puentedura, Ruben R. *Learning, Technology, and the SAMR Model: Goals, Processes, and Practice*, 2014. www.hippasus.com/rrpweblog/archives/2014/06/29/LearningTechnologySAMRModel.pdf.

Ruthmann, S. Alex, and Roger Mantie, eds. *The Oxford Handbook of Technology and Music Education.* 1st ed. Oxford University Press, 2017. https://doi.org/10.1093/oxfordhb/9780199372133.001.0001.

Simones, Lilian, Franziska Schroeder, and Matthew Rodger. 'Categorizations of physical gesture in piano teaching: A preliminary enquiry'. *Psychology of Music* 43, no. 1 (January 2015): 103–21. https://doi.org/10.1177/0305735613498918.

Slater, Mark. 'Performing in the studio'. In *The Oxford Handbook of Music Performance.* Vol. 1, edited by Gary E. McPherson, 509–27. Oxford University Press, 2022. https://doi.org/10.1093/oxfordhb/9780190056285.013.31.

Stepniak, Michael, and Peter Sirotin. *Beyond the Conservatory Model Reimagining Classical Music Performance Training in Higher Education.* London: Routledge, 2021.

Waddell, George, and Aaron Williamon. 'Technology use and attitudes in music learning'. *Frontiers in ICT* 6 (May 31, 2019): 11. https://doi.org/10.3389/fict.2019.00011.

Walmsley, Ben, Abigail Gilmore, Dave O'Brien, Anne Torreggiani, and Alice Nightingale. *Impacts of Covid-10 on the UK Cultural Sector and Where We Go from Here.* Centre for Cultural Value, n.d. www.culturehive.co.uk/wp-content/uploads/2022/01/Culture_in_Crisis.pdf.

Zhukov, Katie. 'Exploring the role of technology in instrumental skill development of Australian higher education music students'. *Australian Journal of Music Education*, no. 2 (July 1, 2015): 66–78.

PERSPECTIVE: CHAPTER 8

Peter Maniura

Introduction

My response to Gilbert and Salazar's excellent and insightful chapter is framed by my professional practice as a multi-camera music director, a curator of innovative digital services (The Space, BBC Arts Online), and increasingly as a lecturer on digital creativity and transformation in the performing arts. I propose to set a broader context in which to place the challenges the authors so accurately outline in tackling the digital deficit in the conservatoire environment and to reflect on the key issues they identify.

For the past ten years, I've been the Director of the IMZ Academy – the training and research and development arm of the Vienna-based IMZ International Music and Media Centre, which is an international business network dedicated to the promotion of the performing arts through audiovisual media. Back in 2013, we realised that there was a growing skills deficit in music and arts television, because public service television companies worldwide were no longer providing the specific training in performing arts programme-making (multi-camera directing of concerts, opera and dance, the visualisation of musical scores, film and audio editing with music) which the generation of programme makers and creatives now in their 50s had been able to take for granted.

We initially set up the IMZ Academy to run training courses for today's young media professionals but very quickly realised that we had to expand our activities to encompass training for performing arts organisations and their employees, as so many of them were beginning to invest in digital capture, often with very little knowledge and guidance. We began in 2015 with a course on digital for opera houses, followed by dance, and in 2017 our first engagement with the orchestral sector: 'Reimagining the orchestra for the digital age'. Initially, we aimed at decision-makers and creative leaders to help them understand what 'good' looked like in a digital context and what digital options and creative potential existed.

Perspectives

During this work, I became very familiar with the attitudes, perspectives, and prejudices with regard to both technology and digital which are so clearly set out in the opening

DOI: 10.4324/9781003281573-18

sections of Gilbert and Salazar's chapter. These have been prevalent not only in conservatoires but also in my experience throughout the music and performing arts industries from top to bottom, among both individuals and institutions with, of course, some notable exceptions, of which the Royal College of Music (RCM) is one.

It is fascinating to compare the RCM's digital evolution with the IMZ Academy's approach to the subject which, although approaching the topic and challenge from different perspectives (in the IMZ's case from that of broadcast media), demonstrates a remarkable degree of convergence in identifying the problems and in positing or developing potential solutions. Over the past decade, the IMZ Academy has tackled the issue of digital transformation at three levels: first, by helping broadcasters and independent producers understand and engage creatively with the subject; second (as outlined above), by running courses for performing arts institutions to offer expert advice and guidance on how to develop their creative digital strategies; and, third, by engaging with the formation of future young musicians at the conservatoire level. From all our work over the last decade, it has become abundantly clear that a major change was required in the mindset of the leaders of Europe's conservatoire sector towards digital and its implications for and impact on the careers of the musicians they were training and that concomitant shifts were needed, both in terms of pedagogical approach and the curriculum itself.

Therefore, during 2019, with some trepidation as we are not educationalists, we began a dialogue with Stefan Gies, the CEO of the European Association of Conservatoires (AEC) and his team. It was based on the conviction that the broadcast media industry, with its international networks, professional and technical expertise and with the IMZ as its representative, might have a contribution to make to the skills gap relating to the provision of training and hands-on experience in digital at the conservatoire level. The outcome was an experimental workshop which we ran in partnership with the AEC and the University of Music and Performing Arts (MDW) in Vienna in October 2019. It was entitled 'The complete performer of the future – embracing media skills in music education' and was aimed at decision-makers in the European conservatoire sector. The methodology of IMZ Academy is to offer highly focused workshops to relatively small numbers of participants, with an emphasis on discussion and practical exercises. The participants in Vienna were some 20 rectors, department heads, professors, and alumni from across the European conservatoire landscape. The key messages which emerged from the workshop were that the main obstacles to providing training in digitals skills and creativity were lack of specific expertise within institutions (both editorial and technical); lack of money, resistance, or incomprehension from teaching staff; and already full curricula and timetables. This result fully bears out Gilbert and Salazar's above observation that:

> Too often technology becomes viewed as an optional 'extra' or something to be 'bolted on' in an already crowded curriculum. An integrated approach is more likely to succeed, where technology is embedded as a natural extension of existing practices.

The guiding principle in the IMZ workshops is always to identify digital transformation as first and foremost a *creative* opportunity, not as something which is just a technical issue and thus to tackle directly the binary thinking that counterpoints 'artists' and 'technicians'.

Gilbert and Salazar rightly indicate that an integrated approach to digital is the best way to counter this, but in Vienna in October 2019, for many institutions, this seemed but a distant glimmer.

Then came COVID-19. By the time we organised our second workshop for conservatoires in December 2020, this time online, the world had changed and so had attitudes. I was particularly struck by a comment made by Deborah Kelleher, Director of the Royal Irish Academy of Music, in an online symposium I attended. She suggested that 'Digital competencies are now top of the list in the toolkit of what music students require'.

The shift in attitudes created a space for thinking to progress from merely reactive – 'we're doing this because we have to', to proactive – 'we're doing this because we need to plan for the future of our students and of the industry'.

Both Diana Salazar and Matt Parkin, who had just moved on from his position as Head of Digital at the RCM, were lecturers at this workshop and gave a compelling joint presentation based on their experience and strategy at the RCM (in some ways a forerunner of the approach and case studies offered in the foregoing chapter) which addressed head-on the key aims of the course, namely:

1. To help conservatoires define and develop their digital strategy for the benefit of their students.
2. To explore the role that digital skills can play in the development of a complete classical musician in the twenty-first century.
3. To share best practices in digital courses for music students as part of the undergraduate and postgraduate experience.

There is no doubt that these courses provided a forum for discussion and development around digital, which had previously been lacking in the conservatoire sector, and that partnership working by the IMZ and AEC resulted in a much broader range of expertise and experience being available to participating conservatoires. For the future, these cross-disciplinary partnerships and exchanges seem to offer a vital means of broadening the conversation around digital and giving the conservatoire sector access to perspectives and expertise beyond the everyday.

But big challenges remain. The enlightened approach to digital taken by the RCM is still the exception and not the rule across the sector, although internationally there are pioneers too – the Royal Conservatoire of the Hague and the New World Symphony in Miami are just two that come to mind. However, for many smaller, more isolated, or less richly endowed institutions, an integrated digital curriculum is still beyond reach.

Summary

Gilbert and Salazar present a coherent and well-evidenced vision for the future, but in a post-pandemic world, there is a real danger of what I would call 'digital backsliding', as old prejudices re-emerge, and institutions and individuals start to think 'well, we had to do all that digital stuff during the pandemic, and now we can get back to what really matters'. This manifests in a shift of spending, resources, and people away from digital; this is already happening in some performing arts organisations, both in the UK and internationally, because everyone is under enormous financial pressure. In these circumstances, it is incredibly important that hard-won ground and resources are maintained, because, as the authors note: 'failing to engage with the digital challenge risks the professional viability of our students in finding success in increasingly self-directed, diverse, and technologically enabled careers.'

I would argue that partnership and collaboration between higher education music institutions and audiovisual media producers dedicated to classical music are some of the ways to combat this tendency by broadening the horizon of what a creative digital strategy can mean for both institutions and students and by putting the emphasis firmly on the creative opportunities they open up.

Above all, we all need to learn to trust the geniuses in the room, by which I mean both current students and alumni. As the authors astutely observe, 'in a digitally informed curriculum we recognise that many of our students may be more expert than professors.' In all the courses I have run, the greatest impact is always made, and most practical outcomes achieved, when students hear from their peers or from inspirational alumni who have developed creative digital practices, which are a part of their music-making and of their identity and development as creative artists.

Now, more than ever, is the time to reaffirm that digital innovation and creativity are not a 'nice-to-have' but rather a necessity in our conservatoires; a crucial component in the formation of diverse and versatile artists; a vital link to audiences new and old; and a key to the future health, relevance, and vitality of our world of music.

Chapter Notes

1 Stepniak and Sirotin, *Beyond the Conservatory Model*; Johnson, *Who Needs Classical Music?*
2 Duffy and Healey, 'Music, speech and interaction'; Simones et al., 'Categorizations of physical gesture'.
3 Godlovitch, *Musical Performance*; Crawford et al., 'An orchestral audience'; Mark Katz, *Capturing Sound*.
4 Blier-Carruthers, 'The influence of recording'.
5 Kavanagh, 'Reimagining classical music performing organisations', 135.
6 Bennett, *Understanding the Classical Music Profession*; Minors et al., 'Mapping trends and framing'.
7 Denk et al., 'The impact of COVID-19'.
8 Cohen and Ginsborg, 'The experiences of mid-career'.
9 MacFarlane, T. et al., 'Culture in crisis'.
10 For instance the Metropolitan Opera's new streaming platform, 'The Met: Live at Home', launched in October 2022. Accessed October 7, 2022. www.metopera.org/about/press-releases/the-met-announces-launch-of-new-streaming-platform-making-live-simulcasts-available-for-home-audiences/. At the time of writing, Apple is also expected to launch a dedicated classical music streaming app. Accessed October 24, 2022. www.digitaltveurope.com/2022/09/29/apple-set-to-launch-classical-music-streaming-app/. See also Haferkorn et al., *Livestreaming Music in the UK*.
11 Katz, *Capturing Sound*; Cohen, *Playing to the Camera*.
12 Bennett, *Understanding the Classical Music Profession*; Minors et al., 'Mapping trends and framing issues'.
13 Charron, 'Music audiences 3.0'; Crawford et al., 'An orchestral audience'; Nowak, *Consuming Music*.
14 Klein, 'Performing nostalgia on record'.
15 Katz, *Capturing Sound*.
16 Otondo, 'Music technology, composition teaching'; Burnard, 'Reframing creativity and technology'; Kardos, 'The Curious Musician', in Ruthmann and Mantie, *The Oxford Handbook of Technology and Music Education*; Hugill, *The Digital Musician*.
17 Burland and Pitts, *Coughing and Clapping*.
18 Waddell and Williamon, 'Technology use and attitudes'; Zhukov, 'Exploring the role of technology'.
19 Bloom, *Taxonomy of Educational Objectives*; Puentedura, 'Learning, technology'.
20 Puentedura, Learning, Technology.

21 Waddell and Williamon, 'Technology use and attitudes'.
22 Puentedura, *Learning, Technology*, 2.
23 Kardos, 'The curious musician'.
24 Burwell et al., 'Isolation in studio music teaching', 373.
25 Kardos, 'The curious musician'.
26 Burwell et al., 'Isolation in studio music teaching', 388.
27 See: www.youtube.com/@RCMLondon.
28 Slater, 'Performing in the studio', 524.
29 See www.dkdm.dk/en/news/global-audition-training for more information about the Global Audition Training Programme.
30 Mills, 'Telematics, art'.
31 Colotti, 'A Review of Contemporary Practices'.
32 Bayle and Provenzano, 'The interface', 114.

9

DIALOGUES WITH MUSICAL HISTORIES

Learning from the past

Ingrid Pearson

The history of the RCM collections

The acquisition and use of collection materials in the education and training of musical practitioners at the Royal College of Music (RCM) were founding principles of the College, having characterised similar institutions established in continental Europe earlier in the nineteenth century.[1] The agenda pursued by the RCM's first Director Sir George Grove embodied the recognition of the value of such materials. Most well-known in artistic circles is his work as a lexicographer, which began in the 1860s and culminated in *A Dictionary of Music and Musicians (1450–1880)*, published from 1879. Edited by Grove, this was the first English-language encyclopædia of music. Through its subsequent editions and transformations, what became *The New Grove Dictionary* continues to be an authoritative, comprehensive, and essential reference work. Among other achievements reflecting Grove's respect for and understanding of the value of collection materials are his instigation of Breitkopf & Härtel's 1891 publication of facsimiles of the autograph manuscripts of the symphonies of Beethoven, and his pioneering work with manuscript sources of the symphonies of Schubert.[2]

The nature of the RCM collections was also profoundly shaped by gifts from important early benefactors including Sir George Donaldson and the Maharajah Sourindro Mohun Tagore, together with holdings from the libraries of the Concerts of Antient [sic] Music and the Sacred Harmonic Society. To this day, collection materials have their home in two main physical spaces: the Library and the Museum. While the presence of a library within an institution like the RCM can be taken for granted, museums of musical instruments have, in fact, been part of conservatoire learning and teaching since the 1860s. By the late 1880s, collections of instruments and related materials, often acquired by association with a particular individual, had formally been configured into museums in conservatoires in Paris, Florence, Brussels, and Berlin. The RCM's own Museum was the first to be established in a British conservatoire. Following the opening of Sir Arthur Blomfield's red-brick Victorian building in May 1894, items were housed in the Donaldson Museum, a space which now serves as the reading and reference room of the Library.

DOI: 10.4324/9781003281573-19

Since the formative years of Grove and his successors Sir Hubert Parry and Sir Hugh Allen, RCM collection materials have played a fundamental role in the College's curricula. The current centrality of these items, as David Wright observes, reflects the institution's 'wider cultural shift' and its recognition of the importance of an understanding of context.[3] Among the values of collection materials the College currently recognises are their role in the delivery of a 'transformative, holistic education' through creating and disseminating explicit and tacit knowledge, across practice as well as theory.[4] These items facilitate and embody an 'enquiry-based approach to learning' which in turn helps cultivate 'artistic innovation'.[5] The presence and ongoing acquisition of such treasures deliver a strong institutional statement about the importance of cultural heritage in music education.[6] Furthermore, the Library and Museum serve as national and international resource, attracting musicians and scholars from around the globe. The associated Wolfson Centre in Music & Material Culture provides easy access to aspects of the collections that are not on display, for the purposes of research and conservation.

One of the iconic Museum holdings is the South German clavicytherium, an upright single-strung harpsichord, which dates from c.1480. This is the earliest surviving stringed keyboard instrument in the world, and its keyboard has recently been the subject of a reversible restoration. One of the treasures in the Library is the autograph score of Mozart's Piano Concerto no. 24 in C minor, K. 491. There is much to be learnt from this manuscript: the orchestra parts are clearly set out, whereas the solo part is sometimes sketchy and incomplete, suggesting that it was at least partly improvised during the composer's own performances.[7]

Teaching through the collections

Visitors and members of the RCM community, both staff and students, are exposed to collection materials on a day-to-day basis, within the College's campus in South Kensington. Upon entering the Blomfield Building, one is greeted by statues, busts, and portraits, recognising royal patrons as well as prominent musicians. Among recent enhancements to the estate, the café in the Cotes-Burgan Atrium juxtaposes photographs of the current generation of College musicians in action with a portrait of Lady Mary Dering *née* Harvey, probably the first woman named as a composer within English printed music.[8] As we descend to the lower level, we see the Library and Museum, facing each other, positioned to reflect their centrality and importance. Flanking the Museum is the Lavery Gallery, where a selection of Milein Cosman's pen and ink drawings of musicians is currently on display.[9] Both the Library and Museum facilitate further interaction between visitors and the RCM community. As well as housing their collections, the Library and Museum profoundly shape learning and teaching. For example concerts in the Museum feature repertoire contemporary with its historical instruments, as well as newly composed works utilising their timbres and the acoustics of the space. This platform enables RCM students to share their music-making with a broad cross-section of audiences. In a separate bespoke Museum space, designed for small groups, RCM students can demonstrate and hone their skills as educators, facilitators, and cultural mediators, while opening a window on the world of the professional musician. On the concert platform, at the RCM and beyond, as well in the recording studio, musical scores from the collections regularly come to life. These activities also embody the RCM's role as a public arts institution, serving the society through facilitating study, education, and the enjoyment of tangible and intangible evidence concerning music through acquisition, conservation, research, knowledge exchange, exhibition, and enactment.[10]

Complementing these physical encounters are those of a more intimate nature, embedded in the College's undergraduate and postgraduate degree programmes. Early experiences, particularly during undergraduate study, manifest primarily descriptive knowledge; but as knowledge, familiarity, and confidence increase, students progress through object-oriented knowledge to strategic and conditional knowledge, allied to individual expertise and interests.[11] While we might expect collection materials most obviously to support historical studies, they impact other areas of the curriculum, including applied skills (musicianship, aural, and stylistic studies) and music leadership (learning and participation, teaching skills, and techniques). In-depth study of collection materials takes place at all levels of study. Both the process and product of a student's investigation into collection materials are often disseminated by means of a lecture-recital or dissertation. Students are also able to present work through the medium of a special exhibition, either in the physical space of the Museum or in digital format.[12] Additionally, collection materials mediate student learning, catering for different learning styles as well as levels of expertise and experience.

Collection materials also enhance and complement the bespoke one-to-one tuition which lies at the heart of the College's teaching. This important element has been a constant throughout the RCM's history, as discussed in other chapters of this book. As such, this core element of practical instrumental, vocal, and compositional learning embodies musical knowledge as a transformative product of action, which, in this case, is the individual student's artistic practice. In delivering this, conservatoire teachers are themselves custodians of tacit knowledge and facilitate a type of action or experiential learning.[13] Instrumentalists, i.e. those whose musical activities are mediated through an external item, such as a piano, violin, or clarinet, have always undertaken what is now termed object-based learning. As those who learn in action, fusing tactile, kinaesthetic, aural, and visual means, RCM students are ideally equipped to benefit from interactions with collection materials.

The scholarly context

Encounters with collection materials are also particularly valuable and transformative for RCM students, integrating the following aspects: learning in and through action, the connections they make as practitioners with their existing embodied knowledge, and the process of exchange which takes place between them and a particular item. The late 1960s heralded an increasing recognition of the importance of action learning, particularly through the work of Jerome Bruner and Jean Piaget. Building on John Dewey's acknowledgement of the symbiosis of observation and knowledge,[14] Bruner articulated learning as an active process, grounded in social and cultural aspects. This aspect is clearly demonstrated by the way RCM students interact with collection materials, and in so doing build on their current knowledge and skills.[15] While these social and cultural milieux are most obviously replicated in the College's rich programme of artistic events, working with collection materials encompasses a range of practical activities. These mirror the ways in which both undergraduate and postgraduate programmes of study foreground musical practice, including rehearsing, performing, speaking, writing, and recording. Piaget's regard for knowledge as a transformative product of action is regularly demonstrated by RCM students across both practice and theory.[16] By the 1990s, Mihaly Csikszentmihalyi and Rick Robinson had identified the 'informed experience' which occurs through exposure to works of art. Viewed as art objects, RCM collection materials have the power to transform the nature of each student's exploration.[17] The resultant connection between the information and the encounter demonstrates a 'reflective intelligence' of the kind articulated by David Perkins.[18]

Musical learning also involves the acquisition of tacit knowledge. First described by Michael Polanyi and developed in the work of Donald Schön and Henk Borgdorff, this type of expertise and skills is peculiar to practitioners, encompassing both abstract and corporeal understandings.[19] One of the values of collection materials lies in the ways they enable students to elicit and articulate this tacit knowledge especially through haptic (i.e. hands-on) interactions with individual items. These experiences further develop students' artistic identities, both individually and collectively.[20] The value of objects as tools to facilitate learning has been recognised since the nineteenth century, particularly through the work of John Ruskin.[21] During the twentieth century, there was a growing awareness of connections between engaging with materials and understanding them.[22] Through what is now termed object-based learning, we recognise the distinctive vocabularies through which objects communicate, as well as how we use these when we interrogate what the object reveals about the society and culture from which it originated. We can also begin to understand and articulate how an object might preserve, perpetuate, or challenge a particular discourse.[23]

Two particular characteristics define the RCM's approach to collection materials. The first involves the deliberate selection and juxtaposition of different types of items united by a shared feature. For example materials may have originated from the same geographical location, or from the same era in history, or be associated with or have been owned by a particular individual or institution. In this way, broader narratives can be shaped through understanding and articulating the contexts that led to their creation, use, dissemination, and collection. In this respect, RCM students directly benefit from the relatively recent transformation of the identity of museums, where the focus has shifted from the objects themselves to the people who interact with them. A second characteristic of the RCM's approach concerns the use of actual collection materials in real-world musical situations, demonstrating a belief in history as enacted and re-enacted. In certain respects, this practical engagement exhibits elements of Lev Vygotsky's 'play-based learning' as well as what Etienne Wenger and Jean Lave term 'situated learning'.[24] Engagement with RCM collection materials allows students to personalise their knowledge and, in so doing, to acquire bespoke knowledge through a tailor-made experience. They gain knowledge at the RCM through its cultural context and the community of practice into which they are integrated.[25] The resulting synergy from such a blend of play-based and inquiry-oriented approaches is most effective and powerful because it replicates many aspects of musical learning as well as providing an immersive sensory encounter.[26]

Case study: London in the late eighteenth century

Taking four portraits by Thomas Hardy (1757–1804) as the starting point, we embark on a voyage which begins in the late eighteenth century. Commissioned by the music publisher, seller, and instrument dealer John Bland, these portraits connect his commercial activities with their subjects Joseph Haydn, Johann Peter Salomon, William Shield, and Samuel Arnold.[27] Through viewing the images, students are invited to consider the contrasting reception of these important musicians. Furthermore, recognising the variety of activities of such musicians helps us to question prevailing composer-centric accounts of musical history. As well as selling the engravings of Hardy's portraits, Bland used these images to promote the music he was selling. These activities demonstrate to students the importance of print culture within Georgian society; today, we are still pre-occupied with the power of the image, as modern musicians utilise visual merchandising in promoting themselves and their activities.

Among music published by Bland are the six string quartets in Haydn's op. 64. By corroborating the RCM's autograph of the C major quartet op. 64/1 with early printed editions, students have the opportunity to reappraise the textual fidelity which often characterises approaches to music of the past. While Bland's edition corresponds with Haydn's autograph, both differ from contemporary editions printed in Vienna by Kozeluch, and in Paris by Sieber. Furthermore, Haydn's arrival at Dover on New Year's Day 1791 suggests that he had prepared the text for the Vienna edition before his departure for London. This material presents students with two slightly different versions of the C major quartet, both of which emanate from Haydn, compelling them to reconsider the status of a manuscript, particularly an autograph, within the genesis and dissemination of a work. For composers active during the eighteenth and early nineteenth centuries, rather than marking the end of the evolution of a work, an autograph manuscript was a step in a process which often now appears equally fascinating and frustrating.[28] In corroborating different versions of a work, such as an autograph manuscript and subsequent early printed editions, students glimpse something of the fluid and often collaborative process of the creation of a piece of music, embracing its commission, composition, and initial publication, as well as corrections for rehearsals and performance, and subsequent revisions. Interactions with these materials also reveal something of the intricate and complicated relationship between manuscript (i.e. handwritten), printed (i.e. commercially produced) and annotated materials, and the differing levels of authority between these sources. Students can then understand performance practices as lived relationships between people and objects. They also recognise the value of devising a score that reflects their individual artistic choices and balances their own priorities against any need to service the composer's intentions.

We might recall that England's relative political stability during the late eighteenth century fostered an economy in which the emerging middle classes were able to avail themselves of artistic offerings. In London this included high-quality musical instruments that were made locally. Amongst Bland's contemporaries in the musical instrument trade, the Broadwood firm enjoyed an international reputation as makers of keyboard instruments. Students are able to practise and perform on the RCM's Broadwood grand piano, which shares features of the instrument Haydn saw at their London workshop in 1791.[29] Similarly revelatory are practical encounters with the clavichord made in 1794 by the Viennese maker Johann Bohák. This is the only surviving keyboard instrument thought to have belonged to Haydn.[30]

Of particular value are the aural and tactile insights this instrument offers into Haydn's last three sonatas (in C, D, and E-flat, Hob. XVI/50–52), particularly in relation to his dynamic and articulation markings. In the light of evidence suggesting that Haydn composed at the piano, this instrument also takes students closer to his compositional working practices.[31] Instruments contemporary with the Broadwood include a one-keyed flute by Thomas Cahusac and an instrument by Astor & Co. with four keys, confirming the rapidity of developments in woodwind instrument making.[32] Other instruments by Cahusac include an oboe with two keys as well as five- and six-keyed clarinets in C and in B-flat, which reflect the popularity of these designs in Britain as well as on the continent.[33] A treble recorder by John Preston demonstrates to students that the demand for this type of wind instrument continued despite the popularity of the transverse flute.[34]

While Haydn continues to enjoy a reputation as a representative figure of eighteenth-century music, his association with Salomon has assured the latter his own prominent place in music history. In contrast, the activities and artistic output of their English-born contemporaries Shield and Arnold have been overlooked. Shield and Arnold held positions in important but rival London establishments: Shield at Covent Garden and Arnold at the Little Theatre in the Haymarket, at a time when pasticcio was the most prevalent form of stage work. A genre which flourished in the cosmopolitan environment of London, pasticcio was a truly collaborative art form, embracing singers, the in-house composer, and director of music, as well as the theatre manager. It was underpinned by a set of values with less emphasis on originality and the authority of a single creator. London at this time was also a major European centre of engraving, although the majority of stage works published appear as vocal-score anthologies. These publications include some but not all of the musical numbers likely to have been performed on stage, thereby demonstrating to students the challenges of understanding the work in its entirety. These anthologies present infrequent indications of an individual musical number's complete instrumentation choosing instead to prioritise the names of singers and, less often, composers. They serve as a reminder that the reception of these works rested almost entirely on the reputation of the performers, in direct contrast to the reverence now routinely accorded to composers. Furthermore, in comparison to works premiered in locations such as Naples, Vienna, and Paris, only a handful of manuscript full scores and sets of orchestral parts pertaining to London repertoire are extant. Therefore, our knowledge of details of orchestration in London stage works relies heavily on detecting cues in these vocal scores, again impairing an understanding of specifics of the composer's craft, particularly in comparison with continental contemporaries like Haydn.

The authorial fluidity prevalent at this time may be seen in the propensity for borrowing music written by other composers, for example through the score of Shield's pasticcio comic opera *Robin Hood*, premiered at Covent Garden in 1784.[35] This work incorporates music by Pasquale Anfossi, Samuel Baumgarten, Ferdinando Bertoni, Tomaso Giordani, Henry Harington, Garret Wesley [First Earl of Mornington], and Charles Smith, as well as Irish and Scottish folk music. Working with these materials reveals to students how the prominence of pasticcio and other collaborative works in the output of both Shield and Arnold has exacerbated their neglect.

In understanding something of an era before the advent of social media, students learn how stage works were important mechanisms to raise questions and promote debate, thus demonstrating the power of music and the theatre to promote an agenda of social reform.[36] We celebrate Arnold for his opposition to slavery, manifest in his comic dialogue opera *Inkle and Yarico*, first staged in August 1787 at London's Little Theatre in the Haymarket. Set in the West Indies, the work is typical of its era in functioning as a vehicle actively to reflect societal concerns, in this case the growing abolitionist movement.[37] Contemporary with this work is Arnold's 1787–1797 edition of the works of George Frideric Handel. The popularity of Handel's music is confirmed by the prevalence of performances of his music in the Register of Programmes of the Concerts of Antient Music. While not an exhaustive set,

Arnold's pioneering achievement made authoritative versions of many of Handel's works available and, in so doing, anticipated the musical/textual anthologies of canonical composers compiled in the nineteenth century.

Case study: the Sylvan Trio as musicians in the interwar years

In addition to providing high-level musical training and education, the College has always played an important role as a facilitator of musical connections. This is nicely illustrated through the activities of the Sylvan Trio, an ensemble formed by three contemporaries: flautist John Francis (1908–1992), oboist Sylvia Spencer (1909–1979), and pianist Millicent Silver (1905–1986).[38] By the late 1920s all three were undergraduate students at the RCM, which, under the leadership of Sir Hugh Allen, gave 'pioneering support to British composers and performers'.[39] Undeterred by a lack of chamber music for flute, oboe, and piano, the three friends 'brought into notice many uncommon works for wind instruments' as *The Musical Times* noted in December 1929.[40] Coached by Dame Ethel Smyth, among others, the Trio's debut concert took place at College on 5 November 1928.[41] Something of their effect on fellow RCM students is captured by oboist Natalie Caine's remark that she took up her instrument, following a performance by the Trio at College in 1929.[42] By 1930 the Sylvan Trio was broadcasting for the BBC, and by 1934 they were managed by the illustrious firm of Ibbs and Tillett. Encompassing a breadth truly indicative of the lives of working musicians in the pre-war years, collection materials pertaining to the Sylvan Trio include autograph and copyist manuscripts, letters, contracts of engagement, printed concert programmes, and photographs. These items help students to recognise how, in contrast to composers, performers' artistic by-products are evanescent and intangible, particularly as regards those who were active before the advent of digital recording in the 1970s. In placing performers at the centre of the narrative, these items also reveal to students how many of the challenges faced by the Sylvan Trio, whether individually or collectively, continue to challenge musicians in the twenty-first century.

These materials demonstrate the development of new repertoire for a non-canonic ensemble, both within the Trio and for the players as individuals. The Sylvan Trio actively created new repertoire through transcription and arrangement, including music by J.C. Fischer and William Shield, as well as by commissioning trios from a number of their contemporaries, including Lennox Berkeley, Walter Leigh, Alec Rowley, and Alec Templeton. Berkeley's response to Spencer's 1934 letter requesting a trio for the ensemble indicates his willingness to rise to the challenge presented by 'rather an odd combination', adding that 'I have no doubt that it can be made to sound well, and I think that a composer who knows his job ought to be able to write for any combination of instruments.'[43] Berkeley completed the work in 1935, and its first BBC broadcast was given by the Sylvan Trio on the British Empire Broadcasting Service in March 1936. Documents attesting to the importance of Spencer's role in liaising with composers include her 1935 letter to her friend Benjamin Britten requesting a work for oboe and piano to perform at the Trio's concerts for young children. While Britten eventually obliged with 'The Grasshopper' and 'The Wasp', his correspondence with Spencer presents students with first-hand accounts of a composer/performer collaboration and a rare example of a composer discussing performance practices associated with their music.[44] 'The Grasshopper' was premiered at the Children's Day Concert on 2 May 1935 as part of the Leith Hill Musical Festival, along with John Francis's performance of 'The Flight of the Bumble Bee' by Nikolai Rimsky-Korsakov and Millicent

Silver's performance of Gordon Jacob's 'The Bluebottle'.[45] In the post-war years Britten drew on his fortuitous association with the Sylvan Trio, working with John Francis at the Aldeburgh Festival of Music and the Arts and in the English Opera Group.

Other items of correspondence include exchanges of letters with Thomas Beecham, Léon Goossens, Imogen Holst, Malcolm Sargent, and Grace Williams, offering evidence of the calibre of musicians with whom the Trio were associated. Concert programmes testify to the Trio's unstinting efforts to build their profile. They performed in various venues across the UK: in public and private schools, for local music clubs, as well as for various organisations including the Society of Women Musicians, at the National Gallery during World War II, and for the British Broadcasting Corporation. Their BBC activities also included broadcasts which enabled them to reach a wider audience, helping to establish this instrumental combination as one worthy of attention. The Sylvan Trio's concert-giving activities embraced a range of audiences, live and through the medium of radio broadcasts. Their commitment to younger audiences prefigures opportunities enjoyed by current RCM students through the College's learning and participation programme known as Sparks, as well as the relationship with the Tri-borough Music hub.[46]

Conclusion

Today's students enjoy significant and valuable encounters with a breadth of collection materials. These interactions enhance each student's musical skills and knowledge, hone valuable observational and transferable skills, and assist in their practical application.[47] Musical instruments, manuscripts, printed scores, concert programmes, portraits, and other works of visual art, as well as letters and other documents help to facilitate meaningful and lifelong links between students as musical practitioners and external cultural, social, historical, and political spheres.[48] Collection materials also position students in direct contact with narratives addressing, for example, the role of women in music history, colonial and post-colonial debates, social equality, and endangered materials and sustainable alternatives for music-making, encouraging them to reflect on the power of music and its relevance to society at large. Displays of and discussions pertaining to objects from non-European or popular contexts have the potential to strengthen students' sense of community, regardless of their social, cultural, and economic backgrounds.

On an individual level, these experiences also enhance a student's well-being, motivation, and physical movement, as well as the cognitive, affective, and conative parts of the mind.[49] Learning with and through collection materials embodies the multidimensional nature of music and strengthens artistic advocacy on an individual as well as collaborative level.[50] Exposure to these items enables students to connect the past with the present and, in so doing, to learn valuable lessons for the future, proving that encounters with these items are of immense value to society at large. Collection materials enhance the RCM's delivery of transformative musical education and training through developing, enhancing, and strengthening skills and knowledge. Their power also to regenerate and redefine beliefs and values are absolutely essential in the twenty-first century as we face some of humanity's greatest challenges.[51]

- Key take-away 1: a breadth of items housed in the RCM's collections manifest the institution's rich cultural heritage.

- Key take-away 2: the portfolio of skills enjoyed by practical musicians ensures that encounters with such materials are equally revelatory and rewarding.
- Key take-away 3: the resultant synergy between objects and individuals is a powerful force which further nourishes artistic citizenship on both individual and collective levels.

Acknowledgements

With thanks to Mr Peter Linnitt, RCM Librarian, and Professor Gabriele Rossi Rognoni, Curator of the RCM Museum, for their contributions towards this chapter.

Bibliography

Borgdorff, Henk. 'The debate on research on the arts'. *Dutch Journal of Music Theory* 12, no. 1 (2007): 1–17.

Bruner, Jerome S. *Toward a Theory of Instruction*. Cambridge, MA: Harvard University Press, 1966.

Burnett, Richard. *Company of Pianos*. Goudhurst: Finchcocks Press, 2004.

Caird, George. 'Benjamin Britten's temporal variations: An enigma explored'. *The Double Reed* 42, no. 3 (2019): 66–97.

Chatterjee, Helen. 'Object-based learning in higher education: The pedagogical power of museums'. *University Museums and Collections Journal* 3 (2010): 179–81. https://doi.org/10.18452/8697

Chatterjee, Helen. 'Staying essential: Articulating the value of object based learning'. *University Museums and Collections Journal*. Accessed November 14, 2023. http://umac.icom.museum/2007/Chatterjee_07.pdf.

Cosman Keller Trust: Works in Public Collections. Accessed November 14, 2023. www.cosmankellertrust.org/milein-cosman/works-in-public-institutions/.

Csikszentmihalyi, Mihaly, and Rick Robinson. *The Art of Seeing: An Interpretation of the Aesthetic Encounter*. Malibu, CA: J. Paul Getty Museum, Getty Center for Education in the Arts, 1990.

De Jong, Tim, Marcus Specht, and Rob Koper. 'Contextualised media for learning: Context-aware and ubiquitous learning'. *Journal of Educational Technology & Society* 11, no. 2 (April 2008): 41–53.

Dewey, John. *The Quest for Certainty*. New York: Minton, Balch & Company, 1929.

Dudley, Sandra, ed. *Museum Objects: Experiencing the Power of Things*. London: Routledge, 2012.

Fitton, Judith. 'Obituaries: John Francis'. *Pan: The Journal of the British Flute Society* 9, no. 3 (September 1992): 25.

Francis, Sarah. 'Obituary: Natalie Caine'. *The Guardian*, February 17, 2009. Accessed November 14, 2023. www.theguardian.com/music/2009/feb/17/obituary-natalie-caine.

Google Arts and Culture. Accessed November 14, 2023. https://artsandculture.google.com/partner/royal-college-of-music.

Gotwals, Vernon. *Two Contemporary Haydn Portraits*. Madison, WI: University of Wisconsin Press, 1968.

Graves, Charles L., and Percy M. Young. 'Grove, Sir George'. In *Grove Music Online*. Oxford University Press. Accessed November 14, 2023. www.oxfordmusiconline.com/grovemusic/view/10.1093/gmo/9781561592630.001.0001/omo-9781561592630-e-0000011847.

Hodges, Henry. *Artifacts: An Introduction to Early Materials and Technology*. London: John Baker, 1964.

Hollis, Helen Rice. *The Musical Instruments of Joseph Haydn – An Introduction. Smithsonian Studies in History and Technology Number 38*. Washington: Smithsonian Institution Press, 1977.

Hooper-Greenhill, Eilean et al. *Measuring the Outcomes and Impact of Learning in Museums, Archives and Libraries*. Leicester: Research Centre for Museums and Galleries, University of Leicester, 2003.

International Council of Museums (ICOM). Accessed November 14, 2023. https://icom.museum/en/resources/standards-guidelines/museum-definition/.

Jahreie, Cecilie F., Hans Christian Arnseth, Ingeborg Krange, Ole Smørdal, and Anders Kluge. 'Designing for play-based learning of scientific concepts: Digital tools for bridging school and science museum concepts'. *Children, Youth and Environments* 21, no. 2 (2011): 236–55. https://doi.org/10.1353/cye.2011.0010

Jamieson, Andrew. 'Object-based learning: A new way of teaching in Arts West'. *University of Melbourne Collections* 20 (June 2017): 12–14.

Kerr, Jessica M. 'Mary Harvey – the Lady Dering'. *Music & Letters* 25, no. 1 (1944): 23–33.

Korda, Andrea. 'Object lessons in Victorian education: Text, object, image'. *Journal of Victorian Culture* 25, no. 2 (2020): 200–222. https://doi.org/10.1093/jvcult/vcz064

Lawes, Henry. *The Second Book of Ayres, and Dialogues, for One, Two, and Three Voyces*. London: T. H. for Jo. Playford, 1655.

Lawson, Colin et al. *Director's Choice, Royal College of Music Museum and Library Collections*. London: Scala Arts and Heritage Publications, 2015.

Lelkes, Jenny. 'How inclusive is object-based learning'. *Spark: UAL Creative Teaching and Learning Journal* 4, no. 1 (2019): 76–82.

Levin, Robert, ed. *Wolfgang Amadeus Mozart Piano Concerto in C Minor K 491 Autograph Facsimile*. Kassel: Bärenreiter, 2014.

Nonaka, Ikujiro, and Hirotaka Takeuchi. *The Knowledge Creating Companion*. New York: Oxford University Press, 1995.

'Objects of the Royal College of Music' outlined in the College's founding charter, granted by Queen Victoria on 23 May 1883, *The Times*, issue 30800. Saturday April 21, 1883, col. E, 6.

O'Quinn, Daniel. 'Mercantile deformities: George Colman's "Inkle and Yarico" and the racialization of class relations'. *Theatre Journal* 54, no. 3 (2002): 389–409.

Perkins, David. *The Intelligent Eye; Learning to Think by Looking at Art*. Santa Monica CA: The J. P. Getty Trust, 1994.

Piaget, Jean. *Science of Education and the Psychology of the Child*. Translated by Derek Coltman. New York: Orion Press, 1970.

Polanyi, Michael. *The Tacit Dimension*. Garden City, NY: Doubleday & Company, 1966.

Rosow, Lois. 'Lallemand and Durand: Two eighteenth-century music copyists at the Paris Opéra'. *Journal of the American Musicological Society* 33, no. 1 (1980): 142–63. https://doi.org/10.2307/831205

'Royal College of Music'. *The Musical Times and Singing Class Circular* 70, no. 1042 (December 1929): 1121–22.

Royal College of Music Sparks. Accessed November 14, 2023. www.rcm.ac.uk/sparks/.

Royal College of Music Strategic Plan 2017–2027. Accessed November 14, 2023. www.rcm.ac.uk/media/RCM%20Strategic%20Plan.pdf.

Schön, Donald A. *The Reflective Practitioner: How Professionals Think in Action*. London: Temple Smith; Aldershot: Ashgate, 1983 (2/1991).

Shield, William. *Robin Hood, or, Sherwood Forest: A Comic Opera, as Performed with Universal Applause . . . Selected & Composed by William Shield*. London: John Bland, 1785.

Tri-borough Music Hub. Accessed November 14, 2023. www.triboroughmusichub.org/.

Vartianen, Henriikka, and Jorma Enkenberg. 'Learning from and with museum objects: Design perspectives, environment, and emerging learning systems'. *Education Technology Research and Development* 61 (2013): 841–62. https://doi.org/10.1007/s11423-013-9311-8

Vygotsky, Lev. *Mind in Society: The Development of Higher Psychological Processes*. Cambridge, MA: Harvard University Press, 1978.

Wenger, Etienne, and Jean Lave. *Situated Learning: Legitimate Peripheral Participation*. Cambridge: Cambridge University Press, 1991.

Wolf, R. Peter. 'Rameau's "Les Paladins": From autograph to production'. *Early Music* 11, no. 4 (1983): 497–504. https://doi.org/10.1093/earlyj/11.4.497

Woodall, Alexandra. 'Sensory engagements with objects in art galleries: Material interpretation and theological metaphor'. unpublished PhD thesis, University of Leicester, 2016.

Wright, David C. H. *The Royal College of Music and Its Contexts: An Artistic and Social History*. Cambridge: Cambridge University Press, 2020.

PERSPECTIVE: CHAPTER 9

Lisa Colton and Ruth K. Minton

Introduction

The University of Liverpool supports a wide range of performance activity, including classical, popular, and jazz repertory; as a university environment, all practical work is embedded into a core curriculum of wider historical, theoretical, creative, and technological topics. As joint authors of this Perspective, we bring two sets of experience to our reflections. Head of Department, Lisa Colton, brings experience in teaching medieval and renaissance music to a team whose main focus lies in repertoire of the last 300 years; her expertise in archival work and cultural history informs her commitment to fostering a curriculum that draws on primary sources (from manuscript fragments to material objects) and reflects diverse musical histories. Professional pianist and musicologist Ruth K. Minton's scholarship is based on nineteenth-century keyboard music and its performance on historical instruments, especially as pertaining to the role of the piano in the compositions of Franz Schubert. Minton's conservatoire training at the Royal Welsh College of Music and Drama, alongside her academic studies at the University of Oxford – coupled with experiences teaching from primary to higher education, including at the Royal Birmingham Conservatoire and now the University of Liverpool – demonstrates her commitment to championing educational and performance opportunities for learners.

Perspectives

Understanding the past is a key component of hope for the future. Ingrid Pearson's chapter explores dialogues with music histories through the collections held at the Royal College of Music (RCM) and highlights the importance of the objects to RCM students, with a mention of outreach in relation to the Tri-borough Music hub. Supporting musical education is a core part of higher education institutions' mission to promote the arts, particularly in the climate of funding cuts. The collections and objects held at the RCM are a vital resource for wider engagement. Pedagogical practices show that varying modes of delivery engage students and that hands-on experience brings historical practices into the present day.[52] Supporting these forms of education enhances the potential enjoyment of studying historical

DOI: 10.4324/9781003281573-20

music and objects in a practical manner for everyone, regardless of previous experience. From a performance perspective, as well as from a scholarly one, playing on historical instruments provides students with a knowledge of the sound-world in which composers lived; early instruments also offer musicians different aspects of technical awareness to feed into their performance. Pianists, for instance, gain a greater appreciation for the pedals as 'special' effects, because pedals were historically not standardised. Pianists can further understand the importance of finger dexterity when playing late eighteenth-century repertoire, because early piano keys were narrower and shallower, with actions much lighter and more responsive overall, particularly on Viennese keyboard instruments at the turn of the nineteenth century.[53] The training needs of performers to think for themselves and interpret a score are assisted by a knowledge of objects from history, particularly instruments; as Janet Ritterman notes: 'stylistic integrity demands this [imagination, to taste, and to personal responsibility] wholeness of approach, in which composers' ideas are complemented by performers' understanding'.[54] A consideration of teaching methods and areas of study that incorporate historical collections can only promote music and wider engagement for all, from primary to higher education and beyond.

Pearson foregrounds the importance of accessing historical objects – paintings, scores, library materials, early instruments – to learners at the RCM, though the principles echo work undertaken more widely. The 'hands-on' experience of the musical past can be a radical intervention for musicians, and at the RCM, this follows the spirit of George Grove, Hubert Parry, and Hugh Allen. Comparable collections housed at other UK locations associated with higher education are equally remarkable for their similarly bold pedagogical approach within curricula, but the specific interests of donors have led to the unique scholarly contribution of each place: St Cecilia's Hall – Concert Room and Music Museum (University of Edinburgh) draws its 500-piece exhibition from around 6,000 instruments, which are regularly used in practical engagement activities and to inform replicas, while the Bate Collection (Faculty of Music, Oxford University) was developed from the donation of early woodwind instruments by Philip Bate in 1963, with Bate's explicit instruction that those instruments should be used and played. There is little doubt that the early music revival of the twentieth century was influenced by the availability of historical instruments to students and staff at the Universities of Cambridge and Oxford, whether through research-based organological enquiry or through tactile encounters on early or reproduction instruments. David Munrow, arguably the most significant influence on professional and amateur participation in early music during the 1960s/1970s, was himself a collector of instruments, especially those that looked similar to images in early iconography; while teaching in Lima, the year before his studies at Cambridge, Munrow built a substantial personal collection of Peruvian folk instruments, using them to interpret European repertoire in recordings that varied from being touchingly lyrical to showing the virtuosity of his showstopping 'Turkish nightclub piece'.[55] The incorporation of non-Western instruments and playing styles into the modern performance of medieval music was further influenced by figures associated with mainland Europe (especially Basel) and with the United States of America.[56]

Nonetheless, the accumulation of such instrumental 'treasures', to use a word from the chapter, is not in itself benign, and the nature of collections has been influenced by complex social and political dynamics: the impact of colonialism on travel, trade, and intellectual exchange; the wealthy northern European youths whose privileged lives led them to encounter (and take home) souvenirs of a 'grand tour' around the Mediterranean; and the potential for exoticism in the curation of non-Western musical objects in educational settings, all give pause for thought. The historical lack of women and non-white composers and performers from many such UK classrooms and their practical curricula creates an urgency for academics to situate instrument collections in nuanced contexts, to move the focus (as Pearson explains) from objects to people. It is partly to this end that students can engage with complex musical pasts through working with collections of instruments donated to the RCM by Bengali musicologist Maharajah Sourindro Mohun Tagore (1840–1914). Using those instruments to explore his several arrangements of *God Save the Queen*, for example, undermines any simple narrative of West/East, privileged/marginalised, classical/vernacular and serves to show students some of the complex cross-cultural imperatives in composition, orchestration, musical style, and the history of performance. Active, object-based and enquiry-focused learning environments – such as those described by Pearson – fruitfully challenge historical assumptions about music and its pasts. The RCM's involvement of its students in the curation and presentation of those collections is a powerful opportunity to forge new narratives in our pedagogy and wider practice. It will be instructive to trace active learning environments such as those described in 'Dialogues with musical histories' through public performances and the publication of research. The impetus to invest in material histories of music is currently strong, and the collections of the RCM could serve as powerful routes to the creation of new knowledge.[57]

Summary

The RCM collections are, without question, an invaluable resource to the College's students, who often progress to careers in which their specialist musical knowledge can be shared with diverse communities and new generations of learners. In a society where music education is fighting for every opportunity, it is vital that the collections are made accessible to as many as possible. The reach of public engagement activities, common to many museums and galleries, can now be extended through developments in digitisation and the ability to stream sounds and performances on early instruments. Beyond the specific musical properties and expressive affordances of historical instruments that can be gleaned through their use in practice and performance, access to collections can ultimately feed into a deeper understanding of music's role in history and heritage, illustrating that repertoire is not merely a soundtrack of or from the past but rather is representative of a vibrant and embodied culture of arts over the centuries which can also inform our future.[58]

Bibliography

Bilson, Malcolm. 'The Viennese fortepiano of the late 18th century'. *Early Music* 8, no. 2 (1980): 158–62. https://doi.org/10.1093/earlyj/8.2.158

Borghetti, Vincenzo, and Tim Shephard, eds. *The Museum of Renaissance Music: A History in 100 Exhibits*. Turnhout: Brepols, 2023.

Breen, Edward. 'David Munrow's "Turkish nightclub piece"'. In *Recomposing the Past: Representations of Early Music on Stage and Screen*, edited by James Cook, Alexander Kolassa, and Adam Whittaker. Abington: Routledge, 2018.

Brooks, Jeanice, Matthew Stephens, and Wiebke Thormählen, eds. *Sound Heritage: Making Music Matter in Historic Houses*. Abingdon: Routledge, 2022.

Cole, Michael. *The Pianoforte in the Classical Era*. Oxford: Oxford University Press, 1998.

Entwistle, Noel J. *Styles of Learning and Teaching: An Integrated Outline of Educational Psychology for Students, Teachers, and Lecturers*. London: David Fulton Publishers, 2016.

Gravells, Ann. *Preparing to Teach in the Lifelong Learning Sector*. 5th ed. London: SAGE Publications.

Haines, John. 'The Arabic Style of Performing Medieval Music'. *Early Music* 29, no. 3 (2001): 369–80. https://doi.org/10.1093/earlyj/XXIX.3.369.

Ritterman, Janet. 'On teaching performance'. In *Musical Performance: A Guide to Understanding*, edited by John Rink. Cambridge: Cambridge University Press, 2002.

Rowland, David. 'Pianos and pianists c. 1770–c. 1825'. In *The Cambridge Companion to the Piano*, edited by David Rowland. Cambridge: Cambridge University Press, 1998.

Chapter and Perspective Notes

1 Namely, the Paris Conservatoire and the Conservatoire Royal de Musique in Brussels.
2 Charles Graves and Percy Young describe how Grove 'examined details that previous scholars would have ignored, and he set new standards in meticulous analysis'; see Graves and Young, 'Grove, Sir George'.
3 Wright, *The Royal College of Music*, 337.
4 *Royal College of Music Strategic Plan,* 7.
5 *Royal College of Music Strategic Plan,* 8.
6 Quality photographs and expert insights bringing the College's treasures to life can be found in Lawson et al., *Director's Choice*.
7 See Levin ed., *Wolfgang Amadeus Mozart Piano Concerto in C minor*.
8 Hawker, portrait of Lady Dering, oil-on-canvas, 1683, GB.L.cm 2021.1. Three songs by Dering appear in Lawes, *The Second Book of Ayres* . . . . See also Kerr, 'Mary Harvey – the Lady Dering'.
9 Emilie (Milein) Cosman (1921–2017) fled Germany in 1938, settling in England in 1939. Her collection of over 1,300 pen and ink drawings and prints were bequeathed to the RCM in 2017; see www.cosmankellertrust.org/milein-cosman/works-in-public-institutions/.
10 Adapted from the current ICOM definition of a museum; see https://icom.museum/en/resources/standards-guidelines/museum-definition/.
11 These three levels have also been identified elsewhere; see Vartianen and Enkenberg, 'Learning from and with museum objects'.
12 Digital exhibitions are currently available through the Google Arts and Culture platform; see https://artsandculture.google.com/partner/royal-college-of-music.
13 These musicians are selected on the basis of their professional standing, teaching experience, and rank among the leading soloists, orchestral musicians, composers, and academics from the UK and Europe.
14 First articulated during his Gifford Lectures, presented at the University of Edinburgh during the 1928–1929 academic year, John Dewey's ideas were subsequently published as *The Quest for Certainty*; see Chapter VIII, 'The Naturalization of Intelligence'.
15 Bruner, *Toward a Theory of Instruction*.
16 Piaget, *Science of Education*, 29.
17 Csikszentmihalyi and Robinson, *The Art of Seeing*, 152.
18 Perkins, *The Intelligent Eye*, 15.
19 See Polanyi, *The Tacit Dimension*, 4; Schön, *The Reflective Practitioner*, 307–25; and Borgdorff, 'The debate on research', 11–12 and 14.
20 Eliciting tacit knowledge through contextualisation and decontextualization is discussed in Nonaka and Takeuchi, *The Knowledge Creating Companion*. For a discussion of the value of haptic engagement with objects, see Dudley, *Museum Objects*.
21 See Korda, 'Object lessons in Victorian education'.
22 Hodges, *Artifacts: An Introduction*.
23 See Jamieson, 'Object-based learning', and Lelkes, 'How inclusive is object-based learning', 78–80.
24 Vygotsky, *Mind in Society*. See also Jahreie et al., 'Designing for play-based learning'; and Wenger and Lave, *Situated Learning*.
25 See Wenger and Lave, *Situated Learning*, and de Jong et al., 'Contextualised media for learning'.
26 The importance of sensory engagement is discussed in Woodall, 'Sensory engagements with objects'.

27 The portraits of Haydn, GB.L.cm PPHC000001, and Salomon, GB.L.cm PPHC000297, were gifted in 1933 by Arthur F. Hill, at that time honorary curator of the Donaldson Museum. In 1936 Edward Rimbault Dibdin, a descendent of the Dibdins active in eighteenth-century musical life, gifted the portrait of Shield, GB.L.cm PPHC000277. The portrait of Arnold, GB.L.cm 2021.3. was acquired in 2021 with the assistance of the Art Fund, the V&A Purchase Fund, and a contribution from the then RCM Director, Professor Colin Lawson.

28 For a stimulating discussion of this in relation to earlier eighteenth-century Parisian practices, see Rosow, 'Lallemand and Durand', and Wolf, 'Rameau's "Les Paladins"'.

29 Grand piano by John Broadwood & Son, 1799, GB.L.cm 338. Richard Burnett notes that during this London visit Haydn came into contact with several English piano makers and subsequently returned to Vienna with a Grand by Longman & Broderip; see Burnett, *Company of Pianos*, 179.

30 Clavichord by Johann Bohák, 1794, GB.L.cm 177; see Hollis, *The Musical Instruments of Joseph Haydn*, 10.

31 See Gotwals, *Two Contemporary Haydn Portraits*, 61.

32 Cahusac flute in boxwood, late eighteenth-century, GB.L.cm 0326FL4, and Astor flute in ebony, late eighteenth-century, GB.L.cm 0775.

33 Oboe in boxwood, c. 1790, GB.L.cm 0435; five-keyed clarinet in C, late eighteenth-century, GB.L.cm 0326C26, and six-keyed clarinet in Bb, c.1790, GB.L.cm 0450.

34 Treble recorder dating from 1774 to 1789, GB.L.cm 0402.

35 The work was premiered at London's Theatre Royal in Covent Garden Theatre on 17 April 1784, and a selection of music was published in short score by John Bland the following year; see Bland, *Robin Hood, or, Sherwood Forest*, see GB-Lcm H 162/4.

36 This initiative was also taken up in print culture of the day, for example, James Gilray's etching *Wouski*, published in London by Hannah Humphrey in 1788.

37 See O'Quinn, 'Mercantile deformities'.

38 At the RCM, Francis studied with Robert Murchie. He was a member of the RCM professoriate from 1954 until 1980. Among his former pupils are Sir James Galway and RCM professor Susan Milan. Spencer began RCM studies in 1923 in the Junior Department. As a scholar and pupil of Léon Goossens, she was awarded the ARCM in oboe performance in April 1930. Silver studied both piano and violin at the RCM. She married Francis in 1932. After WWII, Silver established a considerable reputation as a harpsichordist, particularly with the London Harpsichord Ensemble which she co-founded in 1945. While a member of the RCM professoriate, her pupils included Trevor Pinnock, Melvyn Tan, and Christopher Kite. Silver's daughter Sarah (b. 1938) studied oboe at the RCM and was a member of the professoriate from 1974 until about 2006. Following her parents' example, Sarah worked closely to expand the repertoire for her instrument, particularly in collaborations with Gordon Crosse, Stephen Dodgson, Gordon Jacob, and William Matthias.

39 Wright, *The Royal College of Music*, 142.

40 'Royal College of Music', 1122.

41 Fitton, 'Obituaries: John Francis', 25.

42 Francis, 'Obituary: Natalie Caine'.

43 Francis, notes for the Chester Music 2013 publication of the score.

44 GB-Lcm MS 13190 and 13191; the works were later published by Faber in 1980.

45 Caird, 'Benjamin Britten's temporal variations', 68.

46 See www.rcm.ac.uk/sparks/. Overseeing the delivery of music education in the Royal Borough of Kensington and Chelsea, the London Borough of Hammersmith & Fulham, and the city of Westminster, the Tri-borough Music Hub is funded by Arts Council England; see www.triborough musichub.org/.

47 See Chatterjee, 'Staying essential', and Chatterjee, 'Object-based Learning'.

48 Lelkes, 'How inclusive is object-based learning'.

49 Hooper-Greenhill et al., *Measuring the Outcomes*.

50 Jamieson, 'Object-based learning'.

51 Hooper-Greenhill et al., *Measuring the Outcomes*.

52 See Gravells, *Preparing to Teach*; Entwistle, *Styles of Learning and Teaching*.

53 See Bilson, 'The Viennese fortepiano'; Rowland, 'Pianos and pianists c.1770–c.1825', 22–26; Cole, *The Pianoforte in the Classical Era*, 306–7.

54 Ritterman, 'On teaching performance', 84.

55 Breen, 'David Munrow's "Turkish nightclub piece"', 124–38.

56 Haines, 'The Arabic style of performing medieval music'.
57 See, for example, Borghetti and Shephard, *The Museum of Renaissance Music*, whose chosen 'exhibited' objects include instruments, scores, stained glass, furniture, bedding, woodcuts, cutlery, and paintings from across the world.
58 See the arguments made by the various contributors to Brooks et al., *Sound Heritage*.

10

CULTIVATING RESEARCH CULTURES

Richard Wistreich and Rosie Perkins

Introduction

Research is now firmly embedded in the ecosystems of most advanced conservatoires. It is nevertheless fair to say that the full potential of the symbiosis of research with learning and teaching has yet to be realised. One of the major challenges over the last 50 years has been to transform music conservatoires from being training schools for musicians into fully fledged institutions of higher education. In this chapter, we set out to show how the idea and practice of research (broadly understood as critical enquiry) can provide the catalyst to help effect and sustain this transition. We begin by setting out some of the tensions for an institution that must combine and balance the development of professional musicians' artisanal skills with its aspiration to educate critical and creative thinkers. Through three examples, drawn from recent activities at the Royal College of Music (RCM), London, we aim to demonstrate the unique advantages of doing research specifically within a conservatoire. We conclude by reflecting on the potential that research has for mobilising culture change, both within the conservatoire and music research more generally.

Research in the music conservatoire

The business of music conservatoire education might be summed up as 'the creation and critical investigation of music'.[1] In terms of conservatoires' core pedagogical work, however, the main priority is widely understood to be preparing students to become music professionals.[2] Many conservatoires share the RCM's claim that it aims to support its students 'to take creative responsibility for their own learning . . . characterised by the integration of practical musical experience with reflective critical thinking, based on enquiry-led learning through doing'.[3] Enabling students to become 'creative, independent, and critically engaged artists'[4] presupposes their having both the knowledge and the agency to generate and shape their own artistic and associated practices. However, many of the skills considered necessary to becoming a music professional have conventionally been taught in conservatoires through the so-called 'master-apprentice' model, by which experienced practitioners pass

DOI: 10.4324/9781003281573-21

on their expertise to their students through a teacher-directed process of demonstration and emulation ('knowledge transfer'). The pedigree of this model can be justified (and often is, if only tacitly) on account of its efficiency and success in reproducing and maintaining traditional modes of musical practice. But in terms of 'creation and critical investigation', it has an obvious inherent paradox, which can even form an intransigent impediment to fostering the ideal of learning based on independent enquiry and discovery – the 'student as researcher'.

In fact, the one-way direction of the 'master–apprentice' teaching system has, for some time now, been considerably diluted in conservatoire pedagogy (if not by any means replaced altogether) in favour of a more heuristic model. The enquiry-led approach is predicated on 'ensuring that . . . students acquire their knowledge by means of a process of active learning . . . driven by [their] own decisions about appropriate ways in which an issue or scenario might be approached.'[5] It is relatively straightforward to imagine how such an approach fits with conventional university music learning, focused on thinking about, talking about, writing about, and critiquing aspects of music. However, fully adopting such an obviously empowering learner-directed model in a music conservatoire remains wholly conditional on the potentially conflicting need to acquire, develop, and maintain the sophisticated technical skills indispensable for expert musical practice (the (in)famous '10,000 hours').[6] This kind of musical learning is often assumed to require close regulation and intervention by teachers coupled with intensive periods – usually alone – of iterative exercises in embodiment of what are often minutiae of physical nuance ('practising'). At its best, 'practising' can indeed involve critical investigation and creative reflection. Teaching students to do so both effectively and autonomously, however, is typically nebulous and fragmentary compared to the more typical modes of directed 'knowledge transfer' in conservatoires. Thus, however much student artists may wish to exercise their agency and power to be reflective and innovative practitioners ('creative artists'), in the ideology that underpins the inherent rationale for conservatoire education (and, indeed, for professional music practice in general), professional preparation tends to focus on the acquisition of skills appropriate to the reproduction of the dominant musical order.

The tensions inherent in conservatoire education very briefly outlined in this sketch can, like any stresses, not only be limiting but also conducive to constructive exploitation. This is one important entry point for an exploration of the role of research within a music conservatoire setting. In this chapter, we focus attention on three recent examples of research projects undertaken at the RCM.[7] Each example demonstrates how its value as research has in various ways been enhanced by virtue of its being located within the conservatoire. All three not only feed directly back into the RCM's overall strategy of enabling students to combine practical musical experience with self-directed, reflective critical thinking,[8] but they also each exemplify challenges to more widely established paradigms of music research methodology and suggest possible alternative approaches.

Music practice as research

There has been much vigorous debate in recent decades about the question of whether and, if so, under what conditions any kind of artistic practice qualifies as research. Here is not the place to rehearse either the general arguments or even the particular issues that are raised by the performance of pre-existing musical works. At its most basic, this comes down to whether performers are to be understood as essentially just 'executants' of other people's compositions, or if their interpretations in fact constitute fresh layers of originality (or at least, produce 'new insights'). Nevertheless, there is now an established dogma regulating how creative practice in general can be accountable as research, which is modelled more-or-less directly on the structures that govern the scientific research method.[9] In brief, 'research-based practice' entails particular forms of 'reflection' and begins with the identification of a problem or question and defines a methodology for investigating it. Presentation of the outcomes and any new insights arising from the process of investigation must be demonstrated through reflective observation, which is reported in the form of a comprehensive account or commentary (almost always written).[10] This is not, of course, how most performing musicians would ever think of 'explaining' their activities, nor are they likely to structure their typical working methods according to such a model. So, as things currently stand, unless performers are prepared to accept this re-structuring of their processes (e.g. in order to justify their activities within institutions of higher education), their particular forms of practice – however experimental or methodologically well-founded – will not currently count as 'research'.[11]

Preparation for performance: practising as research

Most musicians (including professionals and conservatoire students) spend a lot of time *preparing* to perform. This entails a complex blend of intellectual and embodied processes, many of which have been learnt and internalised, often from an early age. This nexus of foundational knowledge is combined with actions and decisions particular to the challenges of the music in hand, and even the most experienced performers would probably be hard-pressed to disentangle the generic from the specific. Unless the performance is going to be entirely improvised, the preparation of works in Western art music practice is typically focused on compositions by someone else that are represented to the performer as notation; there is also a strong likelihood that a large proportion of what conservatoire-trained musicians work on has been performed many times before by many others. Nevertheless, it is common wisdom that – subject to certain technical and stylistic parameters tacitly agreed on by the dominant community of players, listeners, and critics – each performer is not only aiming at, but also is expected to present an individual, a fresh interpretation of the work, however canonical and well-known. A key question for the professional musicians who work in conservatoires, as well as for their students, is whether the process of preparation and resulting performance of such 'standards' meets the threshold for 'research' according to the definition set out in shorthand form by those who officially evaluate and fund higher education research: 'a process of investigation leading to new insights effectively shared.'[12]

Danny Driver, a leading professional pianist and professor of piano at the RCM, is clear that it does, as long as 'new insights' include 'new experiences' for performers and listeners in which case, he says, 'as a performer I share that new experience and impart new knowledge – it's not just for me, it's also for the audience'. However, he is more sceptical about whether 'it can generate "new knowledge" in a standard scientific way' (Driver earlier trained as a natural scientist).[13] This conundrum is more than just an abstract question about whether new performances of well-known musical works are capable of producing 'new insights' (most people would agree that they can – indeed, this is often the implicit test of a successful interpretation). In fact, it cuts to the heart of debates about the conditions under which musical performance (as opposed to the creation of new works) can be classified as 'research'.

Danny Driver's recent project to perform and record what are arguably among the most challenging solo piano works of the twentieth century, György Ligeti's *Études* for piano, provides an excellent case study for thinking about how performers of others' musical works might understand their own work as 'research'. Even as consummate a pianist as Driver found himself having to develop new and occasionally counter-intuitive technical competencies in order simply to be able to play Ligeti's fiendishly difficult notation, a process he describes as 'an exhilarating and exhausting venture'.[14] His preparation to perform included mastering 'pianistic challenges . . . progressively over years by devising, modifying, and refining specific practice methods to drive hand independence, aural independence, and polyrhythmic awareness to levels exceeding that required by traditional pianistic practice'.[15] Driver is clear that while 'preparing performance is not the same thing as scientific process', a hypothesis or question can emerge in the process and in the course of working it out; for example, 'working a piece into your body and making it yours is a kind of experimental process.'

Analysis of the process of preparing to perform in such terms may not necessarily feature in the everyday interchanges between conservatoire students and their teachers, nor when students work alone in the practice room. Yet, this kind of conceptual approach challenges the student player to consider all aspects of their practice as fundamentally a process of investigation that both builds upon their accumulating aggregation of technical and intellectual knowledge and is directed towards the practical realisation of individual musical works in performances. Nevertheless, musicians do not normally begin by sitting down to set out their research questions and subsequently writing an account of the process either as they go along or after the event. Rather, they *demonstrate* all this in the moment of performance, and almost certainly also in one way and another when they tackle new works in the future and draw on the embodied and mentally internalised experiences that they have accumulated. The question is, however, whether either such processes or their kinds of 'outputs' make performance-based conservatoire students 'researchers'. We believe they can.

Researching music history through performance

Although an important part of conservatoire activity involves the creation of new music (composing and improvising), most of the music that students typically prepare for performance was created by others in the distant or recent past. Hence, engaging with 'music as history' and the often-contested concepts that shape music historiography is important to the education of reflective, critically thinking musicians. Meanwhile, many staff researchers at the RCM identify primarily as music historians. Most of them work within more or less conventional historiographical models, such as studying musical works and their performance practices, investigating institutions or musicians' biographies, or exploring broader impacts of music on societies and cultures in different eras and places. Their research outputs tend to be in the form of books, articles, and other word-based formats. Through their teaching, this expertise feeds directly into enabling students to develop their own research skills, so they can acquire control over how they understand in historical terms the music they perform or compose. Perspectives might range from specific matters of historically contingent styles, techniques, or genres to much broader questions of social, cultural, and ideological context. However, it is one thing to form an essentially abstract historical perspective on the material a musician happens to be learning and performing. It is entirely another to approach this music from the other side and to experience rehearsal and performance not so much as activities in which students are simply exercising their practical skills as musicians but rather as practising historians – 'doing history through music-making'. It is precisely within the conservatoire setting that the conditions for research that involves such a practice-centred approach are particularly propitious.

It is this approach that was tested out over the four years' duration of 'Music, Migration and Mobility', a major Arts and Humanities Research Council-funded research project that investigated the history and legacy of migrant musicians from Nazi-occupied Europe in Britain in the middle years of the last century.[16] The project involved documentary research in archives and libraries to recover details of biographies, which was complemented by a series of oral testimonies from the few still-living musicians and some of those who had studied with them. This was coupled with geographical research that framed the experiences and trajectories of the migrants in terms of their 'mobilities', producing a richly layered historical narrative. A third, and important strand of the project was the recovery of a large quantity of more-or-less forgotten compositions by the musicians featured in the study. Some of these works were then selected for closer attention and put into practice in a series of rehearsals, workshops, and both live and recorded performances by a group of students and mentors, who worked together over many months and, in so doing, became members of the research team. As well as playing and discussing the works, some students also kept diaries of their developing thoughts about their experiences. Although almost all the music was unfamiliar to them, because of their high-level performing skills, they usually had little trouble in sight-reading the scores and even producing serviceable renditions, as professional musicians are trained to do.

However, without further context, they were limited in knowing how much further they could progress towards understanding this music. An important part of the process of developing their performances thus involved the students also immersing themselves in obtaining additional information about the music, its composers, and their stories of migration and mobility, as it was being produced elsewhere on the project. The students reported that this not only provided them with historical context but also a much deeper connection and hence investment in the material than performers usually have the chance to develop. Meanwhile, their intensive engagement with the music produced invaluable insights for the historians, ranging from specific information arising from the process of realising written scores as sound, to making connections between the composers' stories and particular stylistic features of their works. This produced a unique circular feedback loop between the student musician-researchers and the historians. Unlike the typical model of historical music research involving performers in which the musicians often play a relatively passive role in exploring the researcher's aims or hypotheses, this project entailed a very different way of doing history through music-making. Here, the musicians did not only use contextual historical background somehow to inform their performances (something that is always distinctly opaque and highly subjective, derived as it is from extra-musical, word-based information); rather, their experiences of actually preparing and playing the music together (something that they are particularly skilled at doing) also directly informed the historians' and geographers' decisions about how to develop and shape their own work. In the words of Norbert Meyn, the project's Principal Investigator and leader of this performance strand, 'we put them in conversation with each other, and I would say that there is a kind of equal balance in both directions.'[17]

Researching music and well-being

Alongside matters of performance preparation or music history, conservatoires are a unique environment for considering the role of music, and indeed of musicians, beyond the purely cultural field. In an environment that increasingly prioritises health and well-being – whether in government policy or educational settings – research exploring if, how, and why music can support well-being is now a core part of the RCM's research environment. Over the last decade or so, projects led by the Centre for Performance Science have generated insights into how music can enhance well-being as well as support people to overcome challenges such as mental illness or loneliness.[18,19,20,21] This research is situated within a much wider arts-and-health corpus,[22] much of which emanates from universities and uses methods from the social or medical sciences. Why, then, engage in this type of research in a conservatoire? The initial motivation did not come from a health-driven agenda to provide evidence for whether music can meet health needs. Rather, it was music-driven, informed by previous research (now widely corroborated) suggesting that conservatoire students could benefit from opportunities to develop flexible and broad experiences of music-making, preparing them for sustainable and fulfilling careers (see also Chapter 12).[23] Fifteen years ago, opportunities for professional musicians were rapidly expanding in health and care settings but were not reflected in many conservatoire programmes. By entering this field of research, we hoped to understand what it might mean to students – as well as to those with whom they were making music – to work in health-related settings.

Our research showed that such work can support both students' artistic and overall professional development. For example, RCM students were trained and supported to work on a project exploring how learning a musical instrument in older adulthood can support well-being. Those students who took part in the research reported a reformulation of how they thought about and taught older adult learners, as well as developing teaching skills relevant to a range of educational contexts.[24] Other musicians – both students and professionals – facilitated group singing workshops for women experiencing symptoms of postnatal depression. These musicians reported the development of both context-specific and more generic facilitation skills and described how the work also had the potential to enhance their own well-being.[25] Additionally, the research illuminated the challenges that musicians can encounter when working in some health-related settings, including emotional and social labour, that are distinct from those typically encountered in conservatoire training.[26]

In these examples, students were typically participating as *musicians* (e.g. teaching older adults or facilitating singing sessions) and/or as *research participants* (e.g. consenting to take part in interviews). If we are to 'critically investigate' music, though, should we not also be equipping conservatoire students with the skills to join such research as *researchers*? As noted earlier, there are many ways that students can investigate – research – their own musical processes. Indeed, in the above examples, the students were critically investigating their own roles as musicians, arguably acting as researchers as they did so. But they can also learn to investigate the musical processes of others or, indeed, the roles that music can play in health and well-being. The sorts of social scientific methods used in such investigations are now taught to students at the RCM, in particular in the MSc in Performance

Science programme (see also Chapter 14), and recently formed the basis for a textbook on *Performing Music Research*, written by four conservatoire-based academics.[27] Indeed, there is no reason why such methods could not also be further integrated at undergraduate level and for students taking practice-based postgraduate programmes at the RCM, much as they are in some other university music departments and conservatoires.[28] As we have seen, musician-researchers, including students, have a unique and central role to play in music research. In projects focusing on music and well-being, musicians bring an understanding of both the musical and artistic components of such work and, with the right training, can acquire the research skills needed to understand its impacts.

This touches on the wider imperative for conducting research on music and well-being in a conservatoire. As institutions training the music professionals of the future, we aspire to what Helena Gaunt and colleagues refer to as a 'broader civic mission'. As they argue, 'in revisiting purpose and vision for [Higher Music Education], questions cannot . . . be ignored about the ways in which musical practises are indeed of value in societies'.[29] One way of addressing such questions is to add to the evidence base, generating knowledge about the role of music in societies that can be translated into meaningful and sustainable action. For example, our research on singing and postnatal depression formed the basis for ongoing music programmes that now run across and beyond the UK (see also Chapter 14).[30] Such programmes benefit the parents who take part *and* the musicians for whom new professional – including research – opportunities have been opened. A second important way of addressing these questions and developing a 'civic mission' is through embedding research-informed approaches within conservatoires. If those studying and working in music take a critical, enquiry-led approach to reflecting on, developing, and refining their own views of how music is, and can be, of value, there is potential for a more radical and holistic reformulation of the purpose and vision of conservatoire education.

Summary

The examples showcased in this chapter highlight just some of the areas of research activity at the RCM, which also include, among others, the creation of new music (composition) and music education. Nonetheless, we have attempted through our critical reflections to shed light on some of the unique possibilities – as well as tensions – of practising research within a conservatoire. In this final section, we look to the future and focus on two areas of potential for establishing enquiry-led endeavour at its heart.

First, we have considered the challenges of turning the aspiration for a genuinely enquiry-led model of conservatoire teaching and learning into a reality. We suggest that for this to happen, we must validate the idea of the 'student as researcher' in everything the student does by challenging them to question the assumptions they bring with them about what music is and how it works in the world. This will involve including research skills in the curricula from the first year of study. This is not only about learning processes and methods of research, although some grounding in research ethics, definitions of knowledge, and critical reflection would be useful. More fundamentally, students would be challenged to question their assumptions about what becoming a professional musician entails and how this relates to their development as genuinely 'creative and critical practitioners'.[31] They would be supported to test out new ideas through creating their own small collaborative group research projects as early as the start of undergraduate study and would subsequently have access to pathways of progression that allow them to develop and refine research skills throughout their conservatoire education. Such pathways, as well as nurturing reflective and questioning musicians in and of themselves, would also support students as they enter the profession (see also Chapter 12). Dawn Bennett argues that 'the creative industries workforce has long engaged in protean careers, which necessitate the continual development of new opportunities and the attainment of the corresponding skills'. In other words, musicians graduating from conservatoires need to be ready and able to 'change form at will'.[32] Through embedding an enquiry-led approach throughout their learning, students should experience the sorts of questioning, experimentation, and innovation that will be required for navigating the professional world.

Alongside this, we are interested in the role of research in effecting a deeper change in institutional culture, such that everyone who teaches and works in conservatoires is also encouraged to think about their teaching and their practice as musicians as being essentially enquiry led. This can be achieved through involving them in the shaping and facilitation of a new kind of curriculum model, such as described above, which encompasses all aspects of learning and teaching. It also flows *from* the students: as they become more empowered to think critically about their practice, teachers and academic management alike will need to respond to demand and bring into being the ideal of genuinely student-led enquiry-based learning. Alongside this, professional musician-teachers will then be able to notice that the conservatoire has the power to influence the ways in which the wider music profession can develop, including through acquiring research skills. These would be provided across all the academic courses on offer in the institution, both in core provision and through specialist research-based programmes, open to staff as well as their students. As a result, conservatoires capitalise on their considerable strengths in interdisciplinarity, working to remove silos so that research, rather than standing apart, becomes fully integrated with all other aspects of their culture.

- Key take-away 1: research, broadly understood as critical enquiry, is now fully embedded in the ecosystems of most advanced conservatoires.
- Key take-away 2: the special possibilities afforded by undertaking research within the conservatoire environment can stimulate new methodological approaches for music research more generally.
- Key take-away 3: conservatoires should strive to embed the idea of 'student as researcher' in everything the student does. This includes equipping them to learn through questioning and experimentation, challenging assumptions about what being a professional musician entails, with appropriate study pathways running from first-year undergraduate through to research-led postgraduate programmes.
- Key take-away 4: conservatoires can gradually shift their institutional culture, so that all teachers (and management) are encouraged and empowered to think about their own practice and teaching as also being essentially enquiry led.

Acknowledgements

We are grateful to our colleagues, professors Danny Driver and Norbert Meyn, for agreeing to be interviewed for this chapter and giving permission to use their words. We also thank Professor Robert Adlington for his valued comments on a draft of this chapter.

Further information and reading

Hutchings, W. *Principles of Enquiry-Based Learning*, 2006. www.ceebl.manchester.ac.uk/resources/papers/ceeblgr002.pdf.

Nelson, R. *Practice as Research in the Arts: Principles, Protocols, Pedagogies, Resistance*. Basingstoke: Palgrave Macmillan, 2013 (rev. 2022).

Williamon, A., J. Ginsborg, R. Perkins, and G. Waddell. *Performing Music Research: Methods in Music Education, Psychology, and Performance Science*. Oxford University Press, 2021.

Bibliography

Bennett, Dawn. 'Academy and the real world: Developing realistic notions of career in the performing arts'. *Arts and Humanities in Higher Education* 8, no. 3 (October 2009): 309–27. https://doi.org/10.1177/1474022209339953.

Borgdorff, Henk. *The Conflict of the Faculties: Perspectives on Artistic Research and Academia*. Amsterdam: Leiden University Press, 2012.

Ericsson, K. Anders, Ralf T. Krampe, and Clemens Tesch-Römer. 'The role of deliberate practice in the acquisition of expert performance'. *Psychological Review* 100, no. 3 (July 1993): 363–406. https://doi.org/10.1037/0033-295X.100.3.363.

Fancourt, D., and S. Finn. *What Is the Evidence on the Role of the Arts in Improving Health and Well-Being? A Scoping Review*. World Health Organization; Regional Office for Europe, 2019. https://apps.who.int/iris/handle/10665/329834.

Fancourt, D., and R. Perkins. 'Effect of singing interventions on symptoms of postnatal depression: Three-arm randomised controlled trial'. *The British Journal of Psychiatry* 212, no. 2 (February 2018): 119–21. https://doi.org/10.1192/bjp.2017.29.

Fancourt, D., R. Perkins, S. Ascenso, L. A. Carvalho, A. Steptoe, and A. Williamon. 'Effects of group drumming interventions on anxiety, depression, social resilience and inflammatory immune response among mental health service users'. Edited by Terence J. Quinn. *PLoS One* 11, no. 3 (March 14, 2016): e0151136. https://doi.org/10.1371/journal.pone.0151136.

Gaunt, Helena, Celia Duffy, Ana Coric, Isabel R. González Delgado, Linda Messas, Oleksandr Pryimenko, and Henrik Sveidahl. 'Musicians as "makers in society": A conceptual foundation for contemporary professional higher music education'. *Frontiers in Psychology* 12 (August 3, 2021): 713648. https://doi.org/10.3389/fpsyg.2021.713648.

Gladwell, Malcolm. *Outliers: The Story of Success*. London: Penguin Books, 2009.

Haseman, Brad. 'A manifesto for performative research'. *Media International Australia* 118, no. 1 (February 2006): 98–106. https://doi.org/10.1177/1329878X0611800113.

Healey, Mick, and Alan Jenkins. 'Developing undergraduate research and inquiry'. *The Higher Education Academy*, June 2009. www.heacademy.ac.uk/knowledge-hub/developing-undergraduate-research-and-inquiry.

Hutchings, Bill. *Principles of Enquiry-Based Learning*. University of Manchester, 2006. www.ceebl.manchester.ac.uk/resources/papers/ceeblgr002.pdf.

Macnamara, Brooke N., and Megha Maitra. 'The role of deliberate practice in expert performance: Revisiting Ericsson, Krampe & Tesch-Römer (1993)'. *Royal Society Open Science* 6, no. 8 (August 2019): 190327. https://doi.org/10.1098/rsos.190327.

Nelson, Robin. *Practice as Research in the Arts: Principles, Protocols, Pedagogies, Resistances*. Basingstoke: Palgrave Macmillan, 2013.

Perkins, Rosie. 'Learning cultures and the conservatoire: An ethnographically-informed case study'. *Music Education Research* 15, no. 2 (June 2013): 196–213. https://doi.org/10.1080/14613808.2012.759551.

Perkins, Rosie, Lisa Aufegger, and Aaron Williamon. 'Learning through teaching: Exploring what conservatoire students learn from teaching beginner older adults'. *International Journal of Music Education* 33, no. 1 (February 2015): 80–90. https://doi.org/10.1177/0255761414531544.

Perkins, Rosie, Adele Mason-Bertrand, Urszula Tymoszuk, Neta Spiro, Kate Gee, and Aaron Williamon. 'Arts engagement supports social connectedness in adulthood: Findings from the hearts survey'. *BMC Public Health* 21, no. 1 (December 2021): 1208. https://doi.org/10.1186/s12889-021-11233-6.

Perkins, Rosie, Sarah Yorke, and Daisy Fancourt. 'Learning to facilitate arts-in-health programmes: A case study of musicians facilitating creative interventions for mothers with symptoms of post-natal depression'. *International Journal of Music Education* 36, no. 4 (2018): 644–58. http://discovery.ucl.ac.uk/10051617/1/IJME 2018 Fancourt.pdf.

'REF2021 Unit-Level Environment Template Statement'. *Research Excellence Framework*, 2021. https://results2021.ref.ac.uk/environment/statements/unit/406d6572-f6b6-4c63-8331-4716f6aa050c.

Royal College of Music. *Learning, Teaching, and Assessment Strategy*. Royal College of Music, 2021. www.rcm.ac.uk/media/RCM%20Learning%20Teaching%20and%20Assessment%20Strategy.pdf.

Shaughnessy, Caitlin, Andrew Hall, and Rosie Perkins. 'Becoming the right musician for the job: Versatility, connectedness, and professional identities during personalized, online music-making in hospital maternity wards'. *Musicae Scientiae*, April 29, 2023. https://doi.org/10.1177/10298649231165028.

Smith, Hazel, and Roger T. Dean, eds. *Practice-Led Research, Research-Led Practice in the Creative Arts. Research Methods for the Arts and Humanities*. Edinburgh: Edinburgh University Press, 2009.

Tymoszuk, Urszula, Neta Spiro, Rosie Perkins, Adele Mason-Bertrand, Kate Gee, and Aaron Williamon. 'Arts engagement trends in the United Kingdom and their mental and social wellbeing implications: Hearts survey'. Edited by Rainbow T. H. Ho. *PLoS One* 16, no. 3 (March 12, 2021): e0246078. https://doi.org/10.1371/journal.pone.0246078.

PERSPECTIVE: CHAPTER 10

Wendy Heller

Introduction

As a conservatory-trained singer who now teaches musicology in a liberal arts university, I have spent much of my career considering the role of research in these two very different environments. An undergraduate voice major at New England Conservatory (NEC), I received a Master of Music in Musicology at NEC and then completed my PhD at Brandeis University. Although I would go on to accept a position at Princeton University, where I have taught for 25 years (also serving as Department Chair from 2016 to 2022), my first teaching experiences were in the conservatoire: I taught undergraduate music history at NEC while completing my doctorate between 1986 and 1990 and also spent a semester teaching graduate seminars at the Boston Conservatory.

As passionate as I was about teaching musicians, I recognised that musicologists teaching in a conservatory environment faced fundamental, systemic problems. In my experience, the administration and the studio instructors tended to view music history as a distraction from students' central responsibilities; the superb music history teachers who trained me at NEC were not expected to do research, nor were their accomplishments recognised. Students who were interested in music history had little incentive to pursue their research interests. At Princeton, I faced a different problem: how to persuade the administration that applied music was a worthwhile endeavour that should count as more than an extracurricular activity.

Perspectives

Richard Wistreich and Rosie Perkins' chapter eloquently captures a fundamental problem that I witnessed both as a student and faculty member at an American conservatory in the late twentieth century. Should the master–teacher model be the primary mode of imparting knowledge about music from one generation to another? Is a conservatoire merely obliged to provide vocational training – an apprenticeship with a master – and is that adequate for musicians in the twenty-first century? Is there a way for the educational process to be less

DOI: 10.4324/9781003281573-22

'top-down' and generated more by student inquiry, without diluting the experience and leaving students with insufficient skills to compete?

My own experience as an undergraduate at NEC in the 1970s reflects the traditional conservatoire approach, albeit with some notable exceptions. Under the leadership of Gunther Schuller (1967–1977), NEC students were exposed to an expansive vision of music education, which included jazz, American music, ethnomusicology, early music and dance, and Third Stream.[33] As a result, my colleagues and I had the opportunity to engage in what would later be called practice-based research. It is telling, however, that most of this activity took place outside of canonic repertory. Two experiences come to mind. Long before American music garnered much attention among musicologists, the NEC Chorus, under the direction of Lorna Cooke de Varon, sang excerpts from Schuller's edition of Scott Joplin's *Treemonisha*.[34] Although I was but one singer in a larger chorus, I became aware of the fact that performing musicians could also be musical archaeologists; we could bring to light a previously unknown work that might be edited, orchestrated, and performed, which – as in this case – gave the performers and the audience insight into music and race in early twentieth-century America. How much more exciting it might have been had these issues been simultaneously addressed in a music history class or a collaborative research project! As a participant in NEC's Collegium Terpsichore, I saw first-hand how historical evidence could be used to reconstruct sixteenth- and seventeenth-century dances.[35] Although some of these programmes continued into the 1980s – the jazz and improvisation programmes remaining vibrant – NEC reverted into a more conventional conservatoire under the leadership of cellist Lawrence Lesser (1983–1996). Students still had the opportunity to take classes in medieval music, Turkish music, and American music – but the privileging of canonic repertory was nonetheless palpable, widening the split between performance and research.

How then might a conservatoire break this cycle and expand its curriculum to include more 'independent enquiry and discovery', to quote Wistreich and Perkins, and place more emphasis on critical thinking and active learning? Conservatoire students must necessarily devote a substantial amount of their energy to practice and rehearsal; a well-crafted research paper, based on exhaustive research in primary and secondary sources, requires students to make a substantial time investment, perhaps inviting criticism from their principal teacher. (Paradoxically, the problem at Princeton is just the opposite – thesis advisors might criticise a student for devoting too much time to their senior recital or non-credit performance activities.)

To address this problem, Wistreich and Perkins offer three case studies of research projects at the Royal College of Music (RCM) intended to provide the requisite balance between scholarship and performance. The first project, focusing on preparation for performance, involved using practice as research: an individual focusses on their own process of preparing and learning music. The second project involved a more collaborative process, where students participated in a large Arts and Humanities Research Council (AHRC) research project, dealing with the migration of musicians from Nazi Germany to Britain, taking on different pieces of the project. The third case study focused on the work that might be done by students in the realm of health and well-being.

Of the three case studies, the second one on 'Music, Migration and Mobility' is perhaps the most conventional. Student performers worked collaboratively with scholars, archivists, and one another on a large project, each taking on tasks that matched their skills. Such an undertaking has the advantage of allowing students to familiarise themselves with many different types of research questions and materials, while also having the opportunity to see the fruits of their labours in multiple contexts (performances, publications, exhibit) in a way that is rarely possible in a conventional research paper. This kind of project seems particularly valuable for music students who are used to working collaboratively in rehearsals and is also excellent hands-on-training for a student preparing to write a thesis. However, it also requires a robust infrastructure – funding, administrative oversight, and general agreement among the faculty that this is a worthwhile endeavour.

The third case study, dealing with health and wellness, is also a particularly exciting way for young musicians to look beyond the walls of their practice room and engage more broadly with the public. Helping others – in this instance, adult learners who wished to begin playing instruments or women suffering from postpartum depression – also improved the well-being of the students, who have the opportunity to use their skills as musicians to engage with others, think critically about the impact of music on listeners, and learn something about empirical research. My own conservatory experience offered nothing in the way of training in the social sciences, nor was wellness a priority; given the pressure we were under to compete and excel, it was all too easy to lose sight of the pleasures of music-making that had initially inspired us to pursue careers in music. Community service may be a pathway for professional music students to restore their relationship with music and recall the pleasures that might recede into the background after an injury or repeated disappointments, as Jonathan Coopersmith discusses in his study of music and flourishing at the Curtis Institute of Music.[36] It is also important for conservatoire students – who may find themselves teaching students in universities – to recognise the benefits of making music in non-professional contexts. My own preliminary study of music and flourishing at Princeton University, for instance, showed how high-achieving students relied upon musical activities – many of which were extracurricular – to relieve stress.[37] The fact that some of those students went on to conservatory or graduate school did not alter the fact that in college, at least, music provided a respite from academic pressures. It was not entirely clear from Wistreich and Perkins' chapter what the final product of such research might have been, or whether such a product is even necessary or desirable. Did the students write papers about their experiences or conduct studies to quantify the beneficial effects of music on the populations with whom they worked? Or might we assume that the activities themselves were sufficient to raise students' awareness of different methodologies?

But perhaps the most potentially controversial approach is the one involving preparation for performance, in this instance pianist Danny Driver's work on the Ligeti *Études*. For scholars used to conventional musicological methods, the notion that practising constitutes a form of research may seem insufficiently rigorous. There are certainly a number of exceedingly thoughtful and experienced musicians whose reflections on their own process could be truly illuminating, revealing aspects of a work's structure, its technical difficulties, and the knowledge one gains after a deep dive into a difficult work, providing insights that would not be gleaned from traditional historical or analytical approaches. The potential problems, however, concern the parameters that one might set for excellence, particularly for young students. To what extent might such a project be based primarily on subjective feelings at the expense of historical or analytical precision? For students with little experience in research or writing, there is a risk of creating something that might be deeply personal but insufficiently grounded, historically or methodologically. Given the relatively low standing of academics in many conservatories, the question remains whether there is sufficient commitment on the part of administrators to provide students undertaking such research with faculty mentors who are able to provide adequate guidance. Another problem is that scholars trained in historical musicology or ethnomusicology might not have the requisite experience in practice-based studies to mentor students properly or evaluate the work once it is completed.

Summary

The three case studies described by Wistreich and Perkins bode well for the future of music education in the conservatoire. They demonstrate a commitment on the part of the faculty and administration of the RCM to invest time, money, and energy in training musicians in a holistic fashion that will leave them better prepared to face the tough realities of the music business. As performing organisations and concert promoters seek to diversify their programming, performers must be prepared to look beyond the repertory that their teachers might have played. Collaborative projects, particularly ones that lead students and scholars to explore non-canonic repertory, can be particularly valuable; students who work on the wellness of others are also more apt to be kinder to themselves and withstand the special pressures of a career in music. Whereas my own conservatory education emphasised the humanities, musicians today can learn much from conducting empirical research. At Princeton, the addition of a programme in Music Cognition, under the direction of Elizabeth Margulis, has provided a new way for performers, scholars, and scientists to interact and learn from one another.[38]

Practice-based research offers an exciting path forward, whereby musicians can use their skills and experience to ask different kinds of research questions that may feel more urgent to many players and singers. Nonetheless, as noted above, these projects may be difficult to evaluate. At the heart of the matter is the difficulty of achieving a balance between academics and performance to arrive at a consensus of what constitutes excellence.

American PhD programmes, for instance, have yet to embrace the practice-based research conducted in many European institutions (the primary exception being those schools that offer PhDs in composition.) I am confident, for instance, that the Princeton University Graduate School would not approve many of the practice-based projects that have earned students advanced degrees in recent years in Europe and the UK. This suggests that there need to be many more conversations between universities and conservatoires on the international stage; otherwise, we run the risk of developing separate strands of music research that are not in conversation with one another, widening still further the gap between academics and performance. Nonetheless, it is apparent that the initiatives undertaken by the RCM provide an excellent basis for a fruitful dialogue.

Bibliography

Blake, Ran. 'Teaching third stream'. *Music Educators Journal* 6 (1976): 30–33. https://doi.org/10.2307/3395185.

Coopersmith, Jonathan. 'Music flourishes: Lessons from a conservatory'. In *Music and Human Flourishing*, edited by Anna Celenza. Oxford: Oxford University Press, 2023.

Heller, Wendy. 'They say: "Music should be seen and not heard": Performance and flourishing in the liberal arts university'. In *Music and Human Flourishing*, edited by Anna Celenza. Oxford: Oxford University Press, 2023.

Schuller, Gunther. *Gunther Schuller: A Life in Pursuit of Music and Beauty*. Rochester: University of Rochester Press, 2011.

Sparti, Barbara, and Nona Monahin. 'In memoriam: Julia Sutton'. *Dance Chronicle* 36 (2013): 285–90. https://doi.org/10.1080/01472526.2013.792318.

Chapter and Perspective Notes

1 Royal College of Music, 'REF2021 Unit-Level Environment Template Statement', 1.

2 We understand the term 'music professional' as including any professional practice that involves music. This includes not only performing or composing but also any other music-based careers, including (but not limited to) education, performance science, therapy, caring, research, curation, arts administration, and so on.

3 Royal College of Music, *Learning, Teaching, and Assessment Strategy*, 1–3.

4 Royal College of Music, *Learning, Teaching, and Assessment Strategy*, 1.

5 Hutchings, *Principles of Enquiry-Based Learning*, 2.

6 Gladwell, *Outliers*; Ericsson et al., 'The role of deliberate practice in the acquisition of expert performance'; Macnamara and Maitra, 'The role of deliberate practice in expert performance'.

7 Although similar kinds of work of course take place in other music conservatoires.

8 A key clause of the *RCM Teaching and Learning Strategy* states: 'We encourage and support students to take creative responsibility for their own learning, and understand each student's development as a process of risk-taking, evidence-informed critical reflection, and self-directed approaches to discovering and articulating knowledge.'

9 A comprehensive review of the debates is Nelson, *Practice as Research in the Arts*. See also Haseman, 'A manifesto for performative research'; Smith and Dean, *Practice-Led Research, Research-Led Practice in the Creative Arts*; Borgdorff, *The Conflict of the Faculties*.

10 Critical reflection on the research process, and documentation of it in discursive form, is also part of the research results. The researcher is obligated to the research community to situate each study in a broader research context and to elucidate both the process and the outcome in accordance with customary standards.

    Borgdorff, *The Conflict of the Faculties*, 26.

11 In *Practice as Research in the Arts*, Robin Nelson is candid that his 'project has aimed to valorize PaR such that it might be recognized as equivalent to other modes of research, achieving status and funding within the academy' (7).

12 *REF 2021 Guidance on Submissions*, Annex C, 90. Interestingly, in REF 2014, the statement read 'A process of investigation leading to new *knowledge*, effectively shared' (our emphasis); it is unclear whether this change denotes a different order of outcome or is merely rhetorical.

13 Driver, Interview.

14 Driver, liner notes for György Ligeti, *The 18 Études*.

15 Description accompanying the submission of the CD recording of György Ligeti, *The 18 Études* to Research Excellence Framework 2021.

16 See www.musicmigrationmobility.com.

17 Norbert Meyn, Interview.

18 Tymoszuk et al., 'Arts engagement trends in the United Kingdom and their mental and social well-being implications'.

19 Perkins et al., 'Arts engagement supports social connectedness in adulthood'.

20 Fancourt and Perkins, 'Effect of singing interventions on symptoms of postnatal depression'.

21 Fancourt et al., 'Effects of group drumming interventions on anxiety, depression, social resilience and inflammatory immune response among mental health service users'.

22 Fancourt and Finn, *What Is the Evidence on the Role of the Arts in Improving Health and Well-Being?*

23 Perkins, 'Learning cultures and the conservatoire'.

24 Perkins et al., 'Learning through teaching'.

25 Perkins et al., 'Learning to facilitate arts-in-health programmes'.

26 Shaughnessy et al., 'Becoming the right musician for the job'.

27 Williamon et al., *Performing Music Research*.

28 See, for example: University of Sheffield. www.sheffield.ac.uk/undergraduate/courses/2023/music-bmus; University of Leeds. https://ahc.leeds.ac.uk/courses/a004/music-ba.
29 Gaunt et al., 'Musicians as "makers in society"', 2–3.
30 Run by Breathe Arts Health Research. https://breatheahr.org/programmes/melodies-for-mums/.
31 Healey and Jenkins, 'Developing undergraduate research and inquiry'.
32 Bennett, 'Academy and the real world', 311.
33 Gunther Schuller was President of NEC from 1967–1977.
   The Third Stream programme, now called Contemporary Improvisation, was founded by Ran Blake and Gunther Schuller in the 1970s as a kind of fusion of jazz with Western and non-Western music traditions, emphasising improvisation and oral training. See Blake, 'Teaching third stream'; Schuller, *Gunther Schuller: A Life in Pursuit of Music and Beauty*, 437–98.
34 Schuller's edition of *Treemonisha* was performed at the Houston Grand Opera in 1976 and was recorded by Deutsche Grammophon. The Treemonisha choruses were performed by the NEC Chorus, directed by Lorna Cooke de Varon, on 29 March 1977, along with music by Monteverdi, Bach, Brahms, Schütz, Tomkins, and Irving Fine. Accessed May 8, 2023. http://endeavor.flo.org/vwebv/holdingsInfo?bibId=211902.
35 NEC's Collegium Musicum, led by Dan Pinkham and the Collegium Terpsichore, directed by Julia Sutton, were among the first such groups established at American conservatories. On Sutton's career, see Sparti and Monahin, 'In memoriam: Julia Sutton'.
36 Coopersmith, 'Music flourishes', 19–36.
37 Heller, 'They say', 113–36.
38 https://music.princeton.edu/music-cognition-lab/.

11

THE HEALTHY MUSICIAN

George Waddell, David Hockings, and Aaron Williamon

Introduction

Anyone who has experienced the act of music-making can attest to the powerful experiences that it can bring. The feelings of satisfaction and accomplishment from a skill patiently learnt. The joys of emotional expression and the creative process. The opportunities for social engagement and public praise. The benefits of honing one's memory, dexterity, coordination, and concentration. The ability to boost mood, lower stress, and maintain quality of life. Of course, with these myriad benefits can come challenges. Bouts of frustration driven by slow progress or seemingly insurmountable technical obstacles. Anxiety triggered by the act, or mere thought, of public performance. Discomfort and pain from tender fingers, untested muscles, strained voice, or joints unaccustomed to long periods of unfamiliar posture and unergonomic furniture. To make music across a lifetime, and to enjoy its benefits fully, is to find balance between these elements.

These opportunities and challenges find a home in the conservatoire. Indeed, the heightened environment only serves to amplify both, with musicians undertaking what may be the most intensive and potentially fulfilling study of their lives in the pursuit of their dream careers. And such considerations do not end when entering that profession. In addition to recognising the pride and thrill that can come with making music one's profession, the outside observer may be surprised to learn of the epidemics of pain, injury, anxiety, depression, and general ill health that have been found to pervade the members of professional orchestras and other practitioners in the performing arts. Upon learning this, one might rightfully wonder whether such negative experiences are an unavoidable element of musical performance. If so, how can a musician fully prepare for them? If not, how could these come to be, and how could they be prevented? Could musicians' training, practices, and perspectives be enhanced not only to combat ill health and injury but also to take advantage of the health-promoting aspects of music-making and actively promote their physical and mental well-being? And what role can, and should, conservatoires play in ensuring this evolution?

This is not a chapter on the intricacies of musicians' health, the physical mechanics of making music, or specific strategies for optimising the well-being of any one musician or

DOI: 10.4324/9781003281573-23

their students.[1] Instead, we focus on the multifaceted role of the modern conservatoire in establishing the importance of health and well-being among those learning and working in the music profession. First, we consider the realities faced by the professional musician for which the conservatoire must prepare them. Then, we examine curricular and extracurricular approaches taken in recent years by conservatoires, which place health and well-being at the centre of their training, considering their efficacy and practicality. Finally, we outline the role a conservatoire can play in the wider performance ecosystem through its research and its engagement with networks, policymakers, and experts across performance domains, not only to improve working conditions for professional artists but also to amplify the benefits of music-making for the well-being of our local and global communities.

Preparing for the profession

A case study in musicians' health: the young professional percussionist

While musicians may share some health experiences and challenges, many will also be specific to the instrument, genre, and professional settings in which they practice their art. Rather than attempt an impossibly exhaustive list, let us instead consider a hypothetical UK-based professional percussionist in her early years following conservatoire training. Our early-career percussionist has learnt an astonishing variety of individual instruments and musical genres, each studied in detail under the guidance of a range of specialist teachers. She must be able to perform on any one of these instruments at little notice and thus must maintain practice time on each to hone its individually complex and precise technique. Alongside this versatility and flexibility, she is expected to have a particular strength in a specialist area to stand out among a competitive environment, requiring even further hours of practice.

In her early years of study, she found the physical and varied nature of percussion performance to cause a considerable strain on her mind and body. Some drums are struck with bare hands, leading to blisters and bruises. The repeated contact points of sticks and mallets in her hands could cause pain and damage over time. For some instruments, she had to control many mallets at once, each held between the fingers, where the skin was particularly soft and easily blistered. Other instruments, such as the cymbals, were deceptively heavy, taking all her endurance and control to perform with precision. The sheer variety of instruments and techniques, sometimes sitting, standing, striking, suspending, or sprinting from one instrument to the next, left scant opportunity for her body to warm up for, or adapt to, any one technique. She is also acutely aware of the risks to her hearing, learning early on to wear hearing protection in practice and performance wherever possible. To meet these challenges, her years in the conservatoire were spent training the whole body to cope with the strain of any given day, developing her strength, endurance, and flexibility within and outside of the practice room. Crucial to this was her development of healthy lifestyle habits, practice strategies, and mental rehearsal techniques that allowed time for rest and recovery.

Mentally, her work comes with costs and benefits. Her job demands proficiency in IT skills, excellent spoken and written communication, and experience with community engagement. She was grateful that her conservatoire training provided this knowledge but still found it daunting to be able to maintain such a portfolio of professional skills on top of her musical practice. Landing a job with a professional orchestra shortly after graduating was a thrill and a significant confidence boost, but UK orchestras perform often with relatively few rehearsals, thus she must ensure she is fully prepared for each one in the demanding schedule. Underpreparing leaves many risks; a percussionist's part, and their responsibility for a mistake within the ensemble, is rarely hidden. The amount of repertoire covered by her orchestra, and speed with which they move through it, continues to amaze her. She is grateful that they covered the core works in her training and that her professors encouraged her to learn to teach herself as she now needs to be her own coach. On top of these responsibilities, she maintains a busy teaching schedule which, while providing personal fulfilment and a much-appreciated boost to her income (a source of constant worry in a precarious profession), requires maintaining yet another skill set that she developed within the conservatoire.

Despite these challenges, she loves what she does. She takes pride in the skills she has honed over decades of diligent work, setting and seeing through goals and ambitions she has held since childhood. The feeling of accomplishment from a performance well done makes up for those that could have gone better and drives her to hone her skills continually. She finds deep meaning in her work, having the opportunity to share her skills with audiences of all ages and helping to inspire the next generation of musicians through her performance and teaching. She is able to work and connect with fellow musicians who share her passion. And while her mental and physical health still faces the occasional challenge, her training has equipped her with the skills and habits to cope when things get difficult and bounce back quickly after to thrive in her work and personal life.

Musicians' health and well-being

One might imagine that a percussionist, due to the overtly physical nature of their craft, is an outlier among musicians in the challenges they face. But musicians of all kinds can grapple with their health. A landmark 1988 study surveyed 2,212 performers across 47 American orchestras, finding that 76% reported having at least one medical problem that severely affected their performance, including high incidence of pain in the neck, back, arms, and hands as well as high levels of stage fright, depression, and issues with sleep.[2] Health concerns for musicians have not dissipated over time[3] and are not isolated to professional practice, with a similar finding in 2017 of 80% of conservatoire students across the UK and Europe experiencing pain, especially of the neck, shoulders, back, and right arm.[4]

This is not to say that the health and well-being of student musicians are in a disastrous state. Fitness tests conducted within conservatoires have shown that students generally show age-appropriate levels of heart and lung health, strength of their grip (an indicator of overall health), and range of motion in the shoulder. Over three-quarters of musicians were found to exceed the minimum recommended amount of physical activity per week, though the amount of moderate and vigorous exercise conducted by musicians was on the low side, with core body strength (a protector against back pain) and lower body flexibility particularly lower than the age-appropriate average.[5]

Musicians' mental well-being is similarly complex. A common measure follows the *PERMA* model which considers the degree to which an individual regularly feels *Positive emotion*, is *Engaged* in their activities, perceives having strong *Relationships* with others, and finds *Meaning* and a sense of *Accomplishment* in their lives. Professional musicians have been found to score at least as well as the general population on all five measures and higher than average on *Positive emotion*, *Relationships*, and *Meaning*. This is perhaps unsurprising, given the collaborative nature of music-making and the opportunities it provides for engaging, meaningful, and fulfilling experiences.[6] Indeed, a wealth of recent research has demonstrated the benefits of engaging with and making music at all levels and the power it has to help individuals manage their emotions, to promote their self-development, to provide respite in challenging times, and to foster connections with others.[7] On the other hand, musicians can face significant mental strain resulting from their work; one in ten conservatoire students surveyed across the UK, Poland, and Australia were found to have symptoms of burnout.[8]

This picture is further complicated by music students' perceptions of their own health and their ensuing behaviours. While their levels of well-being and fatigue have been found to be generally better than comparable groups outside of music, they still perceive their own health to be worse, which can lead to lowered expectations of themselves and fewer health-promoting behaviours. This is borne out in lower reports of seeking out professional help, taking proactive steps to manage stress, and regularly undertaking physical activity, as well as low reports of sleep quality.[9]

Building a healthy conservatoire

The health challenges faced by student and professional musicians are myriad. When placed in the context of the complexities of training a musician within the modern conservatoire, designing and implementing an institutional approach to health and well-being are far from simple. The Health Promotion in Schools of Music (HPSM) project, resulting from a US-based collaboration of music educators and healthcare experts convened in 2004, highlighted the importance of recognising the risk of noise-induced hearing loss, of training music educators in health and well-being principles to influence future generations of young musicians, and that performance-related injuries are not inevitable and are indeed preventable through effective training and practice. Crucially, they recognised that music schools can set collective values and actions that influence student behaviours. They recommended that music schools (1) develop and offer a mandatory module targeting health concerns for all undergraduate music students, (2) target issues of hearing health, (3) help students engage with professional healthcare resources, and (4) adopt a clear health promotion framework that is implemented across the organisation.[10]

This section considers how these first three goals can and are being addressed within the conservatoire through curricular and extracurricular programmes. The section that follows then examines how the conservatoire can contribute to the development and implementation of frameworks that can reach across institutions and industry.

Designing curricula

The musician in training balances many pressures on their time and capacity, making daily decisions as to what activities and efforts must be prioritised. Such choices can emerge internally, driven by an individual's interests, aptitudes, and ambitions. And some are externally driven, influenced by mentors, instructors, peers, family, idols, and the educational institution itself. From a student's perspective, the core curriculum signals what topics and activities the institution believes should take priority, especially in the early years of under-graduate training when student choice is limited. Indeed, the transition into a conservatoire can weigh heavily on students' mental health, exacerbated by perceptions of significantly heightened expectations and workload and competitive atmospheres, and contending with negative feedback.[11] Striking the right curriculum balance in the early years is crucial. Con-flict may arise when an institution emphasises its commitment to, and the importance of, health in practice and performance in its messaging and extracurricular support, and yet the topic does not find a place in the academic calendar. The student may even feel that the expectations, pressures, and challenges of the intensive study required in musical training, exacerbated by a culture that may implicitly celebrate sacrificing one's health in the pur-suit of artistic achievement, are at odds with the goal of optimising mental and physical well-being.

A range of experts in musical training and musicians' health have joined the call of the HPSM in recommending dedicated, mandatory modules on musicians' health as early as possible in music students' training. One such effort set out a hypothetical instruction model focusing on basic anatomical knowledge, achieving physical fitness, consideration of com-mon issues and responses to pain and injuries, instrument ergonomics, the organisation of practice sessions, the protection of hearing, performance stress, nutrition and diet, and issues specific to the touring musician.[12] Another model emphasises healthy practice strate-gies through promoting warm-ups, breaks, appropriate pacing of activities across time, varying content, and mental rehearsal. This would then be taught alongside the knowl-edge of anatomy and awareness of body movement, posture, breathing, adapting the musi-cal instrument to the individual, stress management, and general exercise.[13] While such approaches may be rigorous in their consideration of the physical components of a musi-cal performance, they leave room for more balance to be placed on the important role of mental well-being in a musician's training, including the development of active coping and resilience strategies as discussed above.

The Royal College of Music has operated compulsory undergraduate instruction in musi-cians' health since 2003.[14] In its current iteration as 'Healthy Musician', redeveloped in 2020 in line with the recommendations discussed above, it covers the following topics with all first-year undergraduates in their first term of study with a focus on how to access pro-fessional support:

- *Physical health and lifestyle*: common issues faced by musicians; practical development of strength and stamina; responding to pain; diet and nutrition; sleep and lifestyle.
- *Mental health and well-being*: components of and strategies for mental well-being; rec-ognising how and where to seek support.
- *Hearing health*: the nature of musical noise and the hearing mechanism, legal regulations for and industry risks of sound exposure; symptoms and effects of noise-induced hearing loss; hearing protection strategies.
- *Healthy practice*: effective goal setting and time management; principles of self-regulated learning; mental rehearsal; effective warm-ups and rest periods.
- *Healthy careers*: strategies for career development to combat anxieties about future employment prospects; recognising and building healthy lifestyle and practice habits to maintain long and sustainable careers (see also Chapter 12).

- *Healthy strategies*: principles of positive adaptation, coping strategies, and resilience; building one's internal and external support structures; how to bounce back and learn from challenges.
- *Healthy performance*: the nature and management of anxiety and stage fright; pre-performance routines; simulation strategies to prepare for performance.[15]

This training is followed in their second term by instrument-specific health workshops organised within their faculties, and in their second year by a compulsory module targeting professional skills and career development. This is then supplemented by a range of extra-curricular support such as that discussed in the following section. The RCM offering has been joined by a growing body of health courses for musicians, developed and implemented within schools of music and conservatoires.[16] In several cases, the efficacy of such modules has been examined, such as modules offered at the University of Music Freiberg[17] and at the Royal Northern College of Music in Manchester.[18] These studies demonstrated the efficacy of such training as a preventative measure against ill health and a promoter of vitality, positive emotions, and increased feelings of well-being. They also highlighted the complexity of implementing such training, particularly in designing support systems that can address the specific and ongoing challenges of specific musicians across a varied cohort.

To implement such a programme is the aim of any conservatoire that wishes to support its students' optimal health and prepare them for the realities of a performance career, but this can be easier said than done. Carving space within a fixed budget and busy curriculum is no easy matter, requiring either additional burden on student workload or making room through content reductions elsewhere. And for a module to be fully successful, it must integrate with the wider portfolio of artistic, academic, and extracurricular programmes offered by the institution, ensuring that the knowledge, practical skills, and priorities are echoed and reinforced throughout a student's progression through the conservatoire.

Extracurricular provision

In line with practices across higher education, conservatoires regularly employ professional teams to support students across a range of musical and non-musical areas, many of which can impact upon their health. These departments (often supported by student-led student associations or unions) can provide guidance and support in areas such as finance, accommodation, chaplaincy, academic and language support, career support, and general advice on healthy lifestyle habits including sleep, diet, and exercise. Support can be provided for students with health issues, disabilities, and diverse learning needs, with teaching and assessment procedures reasonably adjusted to accommodate. Support offices also provide a route through which students can report instances of bullying, harassment, and abuse to be acted upon by the institution – experiences which can be devastating to well-being. As part of their team, some conservatoires employ in-house counsellors, massage therapists, physiotherapists, yoga or meditation practitioners, or similar experts in mental and physical well-being and practice or refer students on to external specialists.

Conservatoires will often offer group and individual coaching on awareness and use of the body, some of which have been specially adapted to musical settings. Two such examples commonly seen are the Feldenkrais Method and the Alexander Technique. Both approaches were developed outside of music and aim to help performers develop their self-awareness of their bodily movements, thoughts, and intentions during practice and performance though small-group or one-to-one instruction by specifically trained practitioners. While the body of rigorous evidence for their effectiveness compared with standard healthcare approaches is limited, decades of adaptation to musical challenges have led to their integration into the curricular and extracurricular activities of many conservatoires.[19]

Finally, a crucial factor in the conservatoire is the role of the one-to-one instructor who guides the day-to-day practice and development of each musician, and whose influence on their behaviours, expectations, and priorities is profound. Alongside their musical expertise, many will bring relevant knowledge of and a strong priority for health and well-being, perhaps arranging their own sessions and support systems for students across their teaching studio. But until a systematic approach to educator training is in place, their expertise will inevitably vary from instructor to instructor. Some students speak of the 'luck' of securing a teacher whose approach, personality, and knowledge align with their own aims and foster healthy and efficient development,[20] and conservatoires generally have procedures in place to monitor the efficacy of the pairings and to adjust as necessary. For these reasons, researchers have highlighted the importance of making health and well-being training available not only to students but also to the instrumental teaching staff,[21] the challenges of which mirror issues of carving out time and resources within a student diary and are exacerbated by even busier schedules of staff members, who often maintain full portfolios of musical work outside of the conservatoire. This raises a final crucial point in considering the health of all people in a conservatoire: while much of the research and discussion focusses on students, it is also vital for an institution to acknowledge and support the health of their staff for their own benefit so that they in turn are better placed to support the health of the students.

Shaping a healthy industry

Conservatoires do not exist in a vacuum, nor can their consideration of musicians' health and well-being be conducted in isolation. The educational, political, economic, and social factors within which a conservatoire operates affect the health of the students who enter it and the industry demands for which they are preparing. But a conservatoire need not be a passive entity; through research and interaction with external groups, it can help shape these trends.

Pioneering research

The impact of research in the conservatoire is discussed elsewhere in this volume (see Chapter 10), but it is worth briefly highlighting here the role it, and thereby the institution, can play in enhancing musicians' health. Much of the research discussed above stemmed from the *Musical Impact* project,[22] which was carried out as a collaboration of member institutions of Conservatoires UK. By surveying, monitoring, and speaking with over 1,500 students, teachers, and professionals, the researchers were able to build a picture of health and well-being practices within the modern conservatoire by studying them directly. Through such research, conservatoires can meet their responsibility to identify issues, design solutions, and evaluate their efficacy.

Substantial research has also been carried out by conservatoires examining the wider impact of engaging with and participating in music-making on society.[23] Music is increasingly being used in health and care settings, which provides a growing area of employment for conservatoire graduates. Conservatoire research has demonstrated that music students' own involvement in providing musically driven care can benefit their own well-being in the process (see also Chapter 10).[24] Research that enhances teaching and learning strategies or develops technologies and tools to make musical training more efficient can reduce the strain on a musician's mental and physical resources.[25]

Networks, policy, and knowledge exchange

The knowledge gained through experience and research benefits not only the members of any one conservatoire but also the wider conservatoire sector, the music industry, and the performance ecosystem. It is therefore vital that a healthy conservatoire actively joins and leads such activity to share best practices, shape policy, and learn from others.

For example, in 2015 the *Musical Impact* team constituted *Healthy Conservatoires*, a network that brings together stakeholders from across the wider performing arts community to assist in supporting health promotion and occupational well-being. At the time of writing, the network includes over 200 individual members from across the UK conservatoire and performing arts sector as well as over 100 international performing arts organisations. In addition to setting out an eight-dimension framework for performers' wellness,[26] it convenes regular meetings of members to share new knowledge and practice across performance disciplines and fosters new research on performers' health. This has included the *Healthy Performer* project, creating videos helping performers understand and access relevant healthcare specialists and learn from the latest research and guidance.[27] Another has been the *HEartS Professional* initiative, which has looked at how challenges felt across the performing arts were exacerbated by the COVID-19 pandemic.[28] Findings across the project were then filtered into policy recommendations for reformed funding models, greater integration of arts and health, and further opportunities for virtual and hybrid performance shared with relevant industry partners and government bodies.[29]

A range of industry bodies representing and advocating for musicians incorporate well-being concerns into their activities, if not as their core mission. Relevant bodies in the UK include the Musicians' Union,[30] Independent Society of Musicians,[31] and the British Association for Performing Arts Medicine (BAPAM).[32] BAPAM provides crucial links for UK conservatoires, giving them streamlined routes for musicians to access relevant healthcare specialists with musical expertise. Conservatoires can also collaborate directly with such bodies on issues of research, guidance, and policy. An example includes the *2020 BAPAM Hearing Conservation Guidelines for the Performing Arts* which were developed as a collaboration with the Healthy Conservatoires Network and constituent members and are being used to help inform institutional practices on the key issue of hearing protection and health.[33]

Summary

To be, and to train, a professional musician is a challenging and rewarding endeavour. Ill health need not and should not be a consequence of or barrier to this. New practices and research continue to demonstrate how carefully considered training, expert support, and a preventative and proactive ethos towards musicians' health can not only limit the challenges but also activate the benefits to well-being of engaging with music. Over recent decades, conservatoires have worked to develop their curricular and extracurricular programmes towards reaching this aim, though challenges persist and more work remains to be done. As centres of practice and research, conservatoires can engage with the wider sector in developing and implementing good practice. Doing so will help maximise the benefits and ensure the sustainability of the performing arts profession for generations to come.

- Key take-away 1: a healthy musician realises the importance of their mental and physical well-being, recognising and balancing challenges and enablers to their well-being.
- Key take-away 2: a healthy conservatoire provides an inclusive, health-supportive environment in which musicians can thrive, making musicians' health a clear priority through its curricular and extracurricular programmes.
- Key take-away 3: conservatoires have a responsibility and opportunity to engage with the wider sector to share good practice and help shape a healthy industry.

Further information and reading

Ascenso, Sara, Antolla Della Fave, Rosie Perkins, and Aaron Williamon. 'Fostering musicians' well-being'. In *The Oxford Handbook of Music Performance*. Vol. 2, edited by Gary E. McPherson, 574–59. Oxford University Press, 2022.
Ginsborg, Jane, Claudia Spahn, and Aaron Williamon. 'Health promotion in higher music education'. In *Music, Health, and Wellbeing*, edited by Raymond MacDonald, Gunter Kreutz, and Laura Mitchell, 357–66. Oxford University Press, 2012.
Healthy Conservatoires Network. www.HealthyConservatoires.org.

Bibliography

Ackermann, Bronwen J., Dianna T. Kenny, Ian O'Brien, and Tim R. Driscoll. 'Sound practice-improving occupational health and safety for professional orchestral musicians in Australia'. *Frontiers in Psychology* 5 (2014): 973. https://doi.org/10.3389/fpsyg.2014.00973.
Araújo, Liliana S., David Wasley, Rosie Perkins, Louise Atkins, Emma Redding, Jane Ginsborg, and Aaron Williamon. 'Fit to perform: An investigation of higher education music students' perceptions, attitudes, and behaviors toward health'. *Frontiers in Psychology* 8 (2017): 1558. https://doi.org/10.3389/fpsyg.2017.01558.
Araújo, Liliana S., David Wasley, Emma Redding, Louise Atkins, Rosie Perkins, Jane Ginsborg, and Aaron Williamon. 'Fit to perform: A profile of higher education music students' physical fitness'. *Frontiers in Psychology* 11 (2020): 298. https://doi.org/10.3389/fpsyg.2020.00298.
Ascenso, Sara, Rosie Perkins, and Aaron Williamon. 'Resounding meaning: A PERMA wellbeing profile of classical musicians'. *Frontiers in Psychology* 9 (2018). https://doi.org/10.3389/fpsyg.2018.01895.
Ascenso, Sara, Aaron Williamon, and Rosie Perkins. 'Understanding the wellbeing of professional musicians through the lens of positive psychology'. *Psychology of Music* 45, no. 1 (2017): 65–81. http://dx.doi.org/10.1177/0305735616646864.
Chesky, Kris S., William J. Dawson, and Ralph Manchester. 'Health promotion in schools of music: Initial recommendations for schools of music'. *Medical Problems of Performing Artists* 21, no. 3 (2006): 142–44. http://dx.doi.org/10.21091/mppa.2006.3027.
Cruder, Cinzia, Deborah Falla, Francesca Mangili, Laura Azzimonti, Liliana S. Araújo, Aaron Williamon, and Marco Barbero. 'Profiling the location and extent of musicians' pain using digital pain drawings'. *Pain Practice* 18, no. 1 (2018): 53–66. https://doi.org/10.1111/papr.12581.

Farruque, Sanchita, and Alan H. D. Watson. 'Developing expertise and professionalism: Health and well-being in performing musicians'. In *Advanced Musical Performance: Investigations in Higher Education Learning*, edited by Ioulia Papageorgi and Graham Welch, 319–31. New York: Routledge, 2016.

Fishbein, Martin, Susan E. Middlestadt, Victor Ottati, Susan Straus, and Alan Ellis. 'Medical problems among ICSOM musicians: Overview of a national survey'. *Medical Problems of Performing Artists* 3, no. 1 (1988): 1–8.

Jones, Rhian, and Lucy Heyman. *Sound Advice: The Ultimate Guide to a Healthy and Successful Career in Music*. Shoreditch Press, 2021.

Manchester, Ralph. 'Health promotion courses for music students: Part 1'. *Medical Problems of Performing Artists* 22, no. 1 (2007a): 26–29. http://dx.doi.org/10.21091/mppa.2007.1006.

Manchester, Ralph. 'Health promotion courses for music students: Part II'. *Medical Problems of Performing Artists* 22, no. 2 (2007b): 80–81. http://dx.doi.org/10.21091/mppa.2007.2017.

Manchester, Ralph. 'Health promotion courses for music students: Part III'. *Medical Problems of Performing Artists* 22, no. 3 (2007c): 116–19. http://dx.doi.org/10.21091/mppa.2007.3025.

Matei, Raluca, Stephen Broad, Juliet Goldbart, and Jane Ginsborg. 'Health education for musicians'. *Frontiers in Psychology* 9 (2018): 1137. https://doi.org/10.3389/fpsyg.2018.01137.

McPherson, Gary, ed. *Oxford Handbook of Music Performance*. Vols 1 and 2. Oxford University Press, 2022.

Paparo, Stephen A. 'The Feldenkrais method'. In *The Oxford Handbook of Music Performance*. Vol. 2, edited by Gary E. McPherson, 3–21. Oxford University Press, 2022.

Pecen, Ellis, David J. Collins, and Áine. Macnamara. '"It's your problem. Deal with it". Performers' experiences of psychological challenges in music'. *Frontiers in Psychology* 8 (2017): 2374. https://doi.org/10.3389/fpsyg.2017.02374.

Perkins, Rosie, Adele Mason-Bertrand, Daisy Fancourt, Louise Baxter, and Aaron Williamon. 'How participatory music engagement supports mental well-being: A meta-ethnography'. *Qualitative Health Research* 30, no. 12 (2020): 1924–40. https://doi.org/10.1177/1049732320944142.

Perkins, Rosie, Helen Reid, Liliana S. Araújo, Terry Clark, and Aaron Williamon. 'Perceived enablers and barriers to optimal health among music students: A qualitative study in the music conservatoire setting'. *Frontiers in Psychology* 8 (2017): 968. https://doi.org/10.3389/fpsyg.2017.00968.

Perkins, Rosie, Sarah Yorke, and Daisy Fancourt. 'Learning to facilitate arts-in-health programmes: A case study of musicians facilitating creative interventions for mothers with symptoms of postnatal depression'. *International Journal of Music Education* 36, no. 4 (2018): 644–58. https://doi.org/10.1177/0255761418771092.

Ramirez-Melendez, Rafael, and George Waddell. 'Technology-enhanced learning of performance'. In *The Oxford Handbook of Music Performance*. Vol. 2, edited by Gary McPherson, 527–52. Oxford University Press, 2022.

Rotter, Gabriele, Katharina Noeres, Isabel Fernholz, Stefan N. Willich, Alexander Schmidt, and Anne Berghöfer. 'Musculoskeletal disorders and complaints in professional musicians: A systematic review of prevalence, risk factors, and clinical treatment effects'. *International Archives of Occupational and Environmental Health* 93, no. 2 (2020): 149–87. https://doi.org/10.1007/s00420-019-01467-8.

Shepheard, Rob, Finola M. Ryan, Paul Checkley, and Claire Cordeaux. *Hearing Conservation for Performers: Best Practice Guidance 2020*. London: BAPAM, 2020.

Valentine, Elizabeth R., Judith Kleinman, and Peter Buckoke. 'The Alexander technique'. In *The Oxford Handbook of Music Performance*, Vol. 2, edited by Gary E. McPherson, 22–41. Oxford University Press, 2022.

Williamon, Aaron, Lisa Aufegger, and Hubert Eiholzer. 'Simulating and stimulating performance: Introducing distributed simulation to enhance musical learning and performance'. *Frontiers in Psychology* 5 (2014): 25. https://doi.org/10.3389/fpsyg.2014.00025.

Williamon, Aaron et al. *Policy Brief: Hearts Professional: The Health, Economic and Social Impact of COVID-19 on Professionals in the ARTs: Findings and Policy Implications for Cultural Recovery*, 2022. https://doi.org/10.24379/RCM.00002303.

Zabuska, Anna, Jane Ginsborg, and David Wasley. 'A preliminary comparison study of burnout and engagement in performance students in Australia, Poland and the UK'. *International Journal of Music Education* 36, no. 3 (2018): 366–79. https://doi.org/10.1177/0255761417751242.

Zander, Mark F., Edgar Voltmer, and Claudia Spahn. 'Health promotion and prevention in higher music education'. *Medical Problems of Performing Artists* 25 (2010): 54–65. https://doi.org/10.21091/mppa.2010.2012.

Zaza, Christine. 'Prevention of musicians' playing-related health problems: Rationale and recommendations for action'. *Medical Problems of Performing Artists* 8 (1993): 117.

Zaza, Christine. 'Research-based prevention for musicians'. *Medical Problems of Performing Artists* 9, no. 1 (1994): 3–6.

PERSPECTIVE: CHAPTER 11

Emma Redding

Introduction

The conservatoire has changed. Its responsibility in helping prepare the musician of tomorrow is now fundamentally different as is its obligation to wider society. The conservatoire is publicly spirited and globally connected, no longer positioned as the owner and conserver of knowledge but as the conduit through which learning takes place. It looks both outward and inward, with those leading and teaching within the conservatoire understanding that its purpose is to generate as much as it is to preserve. The conservatoire is, more than ever before, committed to supporting musicians' health and well-being.

I write this as Director of the Victorian College of the Arts (VCA) at the University of Melbourne, Australia. The VCA offers a range of degree programmes in visual arts, performing arts, and screen arts. Prior to this, I was Professor in Performance Science and Head of Dance Science at Trinity Laban Conservatoire of Music and Dance, London. I co-wrote the first ever master's degree in dance science and have since played a major role in developing dance science as a recognised field of study in higher education. In 2022, I was awarded an MBE in the Queen's New Year Honour's List for my services to Dance.

Perspectives

Not so long ago, music students and their professors believed that the more practice they do, the better their performance will become and that a certain level of suffering (e.g. fatigue, pain) was an accepted part of being an artist. The focus of music education and training was on technical practice, repetition, and, to a large extent, imitating the master teacher. It is true that music playing is a highly skilled activity, which requires years of concerted and high-quality practice. However, teaching practices passed down from generation to generation, based on anecdotal evidence and tradition rather than scientific knowledges or critical reflection, require review. This is where research into musicians' health is welcomed.

We are at an exciting point in time because of the relatively new but fast-growing area of research into musicians' injuries, health, well-being, and performance, which is the

DOI: 10.4324/9781003281573-24

investigation of performing artists through science. The high incidence of injuries among musicians and the potential for adopting teaching practices from sports and exercise science are finally being explored.

Other performing arts, such as dance, have for some time been integrating science into training, education, and support. Dance conservatoires are applying principles of periodisation to training schedules, and strength and conditioning fitness training is being built into a dancer's regimen.[34] Professional dance companies now provide specialist onsite physiotherapy, psychology, and nutrition support. Dance is an immensely physical and highly skilled art form, and, as such, injuries are common. Dancers almost expect to become injured at some point in their careers[35] and are now more likely to disclose that they have an injury and seek treatment than they did in the past and in comparison to musicians. The focus of research into musicians' health has been predominately, but not solely, on psychological preparation, and it is worth recognising the 40-plus years of dance science research that has investigated the physical and biomechanical demands of dance, the physiological capacities of dancers, and the need for fitter dancers, to consider whether these questions could be usefully applied to music.[36]

The somewhat new and much-needed research into performing arts medicine and science has led to the creation of national and international advocacy organisations, which bring together doctors, surgeons, teachers, academics, and performing artists to collaborate on developing guidelines and recommendations for improving musician and performing artist training.[37,38] In the UK and other parts of the world, the availability of specialist healthcare for performing artists has also improved. This chapter describes the significant relationship between health, well-being, and music performance. It advocates that health and well-being in the conservatoire are everyone's responsibility.

While injuries cannot be completely prevented, the risks can be reduced, and treatments and rehabilitation programmes improved, becoming more available. Healthy practice should be every teacher's goal, which means understanding how the body works biomechanically; how music is learnt and retained; and how warming up, regular exercise, and good nutrition can assist students' ability to sustain hours of daily practice and postpone the onset of fatigue. Examples of how the conservatoire must work with professional organisations, community, and industry to establish an accepted and embedded approach to musicians' health across the lifespan are proposed in this chapter. Recommendations apply not only to orchestras but also to arts funders, policymakers, and the commercial industry.

There are optimal ways in which to deliver health promotion education for musicians successfully, and ideally all teachers would share this responsibility since the ultimate goal is for all practice and performance to be healthy. Embedding health education into curricula as a standalone and/or elective subject is second-best, but better than nothing at all. Music health education should be compulsory for all students, scheduled during the day in the best room spaces and taught by health and music specialists – as opposed to at the end of the day in suboptimal room spaces. This is important to ensure good student compliance, engagement, and enjoyment.

This chapter proposes that if musicians engage in more healthful training, practices, and performance, they will more effectively address ill health and injury and actively promote their physical and mental well-being. Additionally, if future generations of healthier musicians advocate for healthy practice beyond the focus on the self, forming a healthier music industry, they may even shape a healthier society. Music, like other creative arts, can after all address the social determinants of health among other populations.[39]

The chapter proposes three key messages for the promotion of the healthy musician. The first is that the challenges and enablers to accessing mental and physical well-being should be addressed. The second is that the conservatoire must prioritise musicians' health if they are to succeed and enjoy sustained careers. The third message is that the conservatoire has a responsibility to help shape a healthier music industry. This chapter should be read by academic and professional staff of music conservatoires. It might also be appreciated by music school teachers, professional musicians, and those who employ and support them.

Summary

The healthy conservatoire should be a place in which musicians flourish. The view that the musician can be both artist and athlete; caring about their physical and mental health, maintaining a healthy work–life balance; and engaging in deliberate, purposeful, and healthy musical practice is one that is becoming the norm, rather than the exception. The conservatoire has changed for the better, and it is exciting to be a part of that change.

Bibliography

Angioi, Manuela, George S. Metsios, Yiannis Koutedakis, and Matthew Wyon. 'Fitness in contemporary dance: A systematic review'. *International Journal of Sports Medicine* 30, no. 7 (2009): 475–84. https://doi.org/10.1055/s-0029-1202821.

Gaunt, Helena. 'Introduction to special issue on the reflective conservatoire'. *Arts and Humanities in Higher Education* 15 (2006): 3–4. https://doi.org/10.1177/14740222166555.

Rodrigues-Krause, Josianne, Mauricio Krause, and Alvaro Reischak-Oliveira. 'Cardiorespiratory considerations in dance: From classes to performances'. *Journal of Dance Science and Medicine* 19, no. 3 (2015). https://doi.org/10.12678/1089-313x.19.3.91.

Sheppard, Alexa, and Mary C. Broughton. 'Promoting wellbeing and health through active participation in music and dance: A systematic review'. *International Journal of Qualitative Studies on Health and Wellbeing* 15, no. 1 (2020). https://doi.org/10.1080/17482631.2020.1732526.

Turner, Bryan S., and Steven P. Wainwright. 'Corps de Ballet: The case of the injured ballet dancer'. *Sociology of Health and Illness* 25, no. 4 (2003): 269–88. https://doi.org/10.1111/1467-9566.00347.

Vassallo, Amy J., Evangelos Pappas, Emmanuel Stamatakis, and Claire E. Hiller. 'Injury fear, stigma and reporting in professional dancers'. *Safety and Health at Work* 10, no. 3 (2019): 260–4. https://doi.org/10.1016/j.shaw.2019.03.001.

Wyon, Matthew. 'Preparing to perform: Periodisation and dance'. *Journal of Dance Medicine and Science* 14, no. 2 (2010): 67–72. https://doi.org/10.1177/1089313X1001400205.

Chapter and Perspective Notes

1 A wide range of texts are available on this subject, including Jones and Heyman, *Sound Advice* and McPherson, *Oxford Handbook of Music Performance*.
2 Fishbein et al., 'Medical problems among ICSOM musicians'. For a review of the physical injuries faced by musicians, see Rotter et al., 'Disorders and complaints in professional musicians'.
3 Ackermann et al., 'Sound practice'.
4 Cruder et al., 'Profiling the location and extent of musicians' pain'.
5 Araújo et al., 'Fit to perform'.
6 Ascenso et al., 'Resounding meaning'.
7 Perkins et al., 'How participatory music engagement supports mental well-being'.
8 Zabuska et al., 'A preliminary comparison study'.

9 Araújo et al., 'Fit to perform'.
10 Chesky et al., 'Health promotion in schools of music'.
11 Perkins et al., 'Perceived enablers and barriers'.
12 Farruque and Watson, 'Developing expertise and professionalism'.
13 Zaza, 'Prevention of musicians' playing-related health problems'; Zaza, 'Research-based prevention for musicians'.
14 Manchester, 'Health promotion courses for music students: Part III', 117–18.
15 For a summary of the RCM's use of performance simulation, see Williamon et al., 'Simulating and stimulating performance'.
16 Manchester, 'Health promotion courses for music students' documented such courses in 11 institutions.
17 Zander et al., 'Health promotion and prevention'.
18 Matei et al., 'Health education for musicians'.
19 See Paparo, 'The Feldenkrais method', and Valentine et al., 'The Alexander technique'.
20 Pecen et al., 'It's your problem'.
21 Farruque and Watson, 'Developing expertise and professionalism: Health and well-being in performing musicians', 327–28.
22 This includes Araújo et al. 2017 and 2020, Ascenso et al. 2017, Cruder et al. 2018, Perkins et al. 2017, and Matei et al. 2018. To learn more about the *Musical Impact* project, visit www.Healthy Conservatoires.org/musicalimpact.
23 See a range of such research at www.PerformanceScience.ac.uk/musichealth.
24 Perkins et al., 'Learning to facilitate arts-in-health programmes'.
25 See Ramirez-Melendez and Waddell, 'Technology-enhanced learning of performance'.
26 Comprising emotional, environmental, financial, intellectual, occupational, physical, social and spiritual wellbeing. See www.HealthyConservatoires.org/framework.
27 www.HealthyConservatoires.org/films/.
28 Examining the Health, Economic, and Social impact of COVID-19 on PROFESSIONALS in the ARTs; www.HealthyConservatoires.org/HEartSPro.
29 Williamon et al., *Policy brief: HEartS professional*.
30 https://musiciansunion.org.uk/health-safety-wellbeing/health-and-safety.
31 www.ism.org/advice-centre/health-wellbeing.
32 www.bapam.org.uk.
33 Shepheard et al., *Hearing Conservation for Performers*.
34 Wyon, 'Preparing to perform'.
35 Vassallo et al., 'Injury fear, stigma and reporting'; Turner and Wainwright, 'Corps de Ballet'.
36 Angioi et al., 'Fitness in contemporary dance'; Rodrigues-Krause et al., 'Cardiorespiratory considerations in dance'.
37 The National Institute for Dance Medicine and Science (NIDMS, www.nidms.co.uk/) works to provide the dance sector with access to high-quality, affordable, dance-specific healthcare and dance science support services in private practice and the NHS.
38 The International Association for Dance Medicine and Science (IADMS, https://iadms.org/) is a global community that provides evidence-based research, resources, and programming that can improve the health of dancers and the use of dance to improve health.
39 Sheppard and Broughton, 'Promoting wellbeing and health'.

12

LIFELONG CREATIVE CAREERS

Gary Ryan and Diana Roberts

Introduction

This chapter focuses on the role of conservatoires in preparing students for creative careers. It argues that careers in music have changed rapidly over the past decades, with entrepreneurship, technology, and the COVID-19 pandemic contributing to a quickly changing professional landscape. Against this backdrop, the chapter considers critically what world-leading career support looks like in the conservatoire setting, including introducing the Royal College of Music (RCM)'s Creative Careers Centre. Finally, the chapter outlines new RCM initiatives designed to facilitate entrepreneurship, audience development, and creativity.

New arrivals: starting at the RCM

September is an exciting time at the RCM, marking a new academic year and the arrival of a new cohort of talented young musicians from the UK and around the world. Over 100 of these enthusiastic new arrivals will be commencing their undergraduate studies on the Bachelor of Music (BMus) programme, a point at which many have made a conscious choice to pursue the possibility of a career in music. They and their families, however, often have legitimate concerns about how viable a musical career is and what shape it might take. They might also have wrestled with deciding between music and another degree subject that could be more widely perceived to lead to a 'proper job'. As most students now take on a substantial amount of debt to finance their studies, this decision is arguably even more significant than in the past.

Those entering a performance programme have been awarded a place based on a highly competitive audition process during which they performed live to a panel of instrumental specialists or submitted a video of their performance for consideration.[1] Although selected for their potential, within this group, there is still a wide range of musical ability, backgrounds, and experiences. A young musician's professional training has often been underway for many years up to this point, and many students arrive from specialist music

DOI: 10.4324/9781003281573-25

schools having had teaching of the highest calibre from a very young age. A select few might have achieved success in high-profile competitions (such as the BBC's Young Musician of the Year) and often have a fledgling career taking shape. In the UK, many have played in the National Youth Orchestra and/or attended the Junior Departments of the main conservatoires. Some have been nurtured by excellent local authority and county music hubs, but a significant number arrive from schools or areas where musical opportunities and high-quality instrumental teaching are increasingly hard to come by, especially following cumulative government funding cuts to music in schools in the UK and the variable provision of Music A-level at sixth form level.[2]

Simultaneously, many other students further along the path of their studies will be joining postgraduate programmes at the RCM after their undergraduate degree at another conservatoire or university, which may not necessarily have been in music. They might be studying for a postgraduate performing/composing qualification (such as the MMus, MPerf, or MComp) or choosing to study performance science, music education, starting a PhD, or pursuing an Artist Diploma. There are many different routes which can now be taken to study, not all of them requiring the same level of instrumental proficiency or relating to the music profession in the same way. Some postgraduate students will also be returning to study after having professional experience in a wide range of areas within and outside music. Of the total number of students currently at the RCM, over 50% come from outside the UK, many leaving their home countries for the first time. They have often learnt musical terminology in different languages and educational systems, and their knowledge of the English language will be variable. Entering the conservatoire can also be a very challenging time emotionally and financially. Just learning to live independently without immediate family support can be quite an adjustment even before getting around to the rigorous demands of practising and studying music.[3]

This wide range of nationalities, backgrounds, and experiences has implications for how a conservatoire needs to think about preparing students for what is now a global profession, not just a national one. We cannot know for sure what type of professional opportunities students will encounter post-graduation, or how their career aspirations may develop from those they bring into the conservatoire. Indeed, recent research conducted at the Royal Northern College of Music revealed that students' career intentions can change over the course of conservatoire study, tending away from aspirations for a performing career towards a portfolio, freelance career combining many professional activities.[4] Other scholars have written of the need for students' career expectations to be balanced against what Bennett and Bridgstock term 'graduate realities'.[5] Their findings illustrated a creative industry characterised by portfolio careers, but a student body focused largely on performance roles. What does this mean for conservatoires, which educate highly skilled performers? Certainly, there are challenges associated with incorporating curricula opportunities to support diverse career preparation while maintaining space for in-depth work on technique and artistry that are central to much of conservatoire education.[6] How do we continue to do this to the highest standards, while supporting and guiding the diverse student body towards portfolio careers that may span widely across different musical arenas?

Building portfolio careers

As new faces arrive in September, many other RCM students will be graduating and moving out into the profession full-time. This process has often been well underway during their studies, with many students already undertaking instrumental teaching and/or a variety of paid external performing and community engagements alongside their studies. For students on performance programmes, however, exceptional playing ability is not an automatic guarantee of employment success. In a rapidly changing professional landscape, there are increasingly many other skills that help to convert musical ability into a career. An aspiring musician should be encouraged to explore as many different musical areas relating to their specialism as possible to develop their musical versatility and employability.

It has been suggested that careers in the performing arts are a 'messy concept' that require graduates to be 'enforced entrepreneurs'.[7] Indeed, in future years, a new BMus violinist joining the RCM might go on to forge a career which involves playing solo recitals and concertos from time to time, performing as part of an established string quartet, deputising for players in major orchestras, playing for the occasional film session, and teaching violin in several schools. They may compose student repertoire, teach at summer schools, launch their own festival, act as an adjudicator or juror, or train as an examiner for organisations such as the Associated Board of the Royal Schools of Music (ABRSM). They could opt to pursue broader musical careers in education, publishing and editing, research, recording engineering, or in arts organisations. Alternatively, they may develop specific interests in the therapeutic properties of music and work in music therapy, community, or health contexts. Such breadth is also reflected in the range of graduate destinations, which include settings as diverse as orchestras, opera houses, arts organisations, educational institutions, and entrepreneurial start-ups.

Many of these paths may not be immediately apparent to students before joining the RCM, however, and can be introduced to them during their studies. How can a conservatoire help students become aware of the multitude of opportunities that complement and extend their core studies in performance or composition? RCM programmes are consequently structured in such a way as to develop and encourage intellectually curious, versatile, and imaginative musicians with an entrepreneurial mindset who can turn their hand to different activities, as well as emphasising 'professional capabilities'.[8] All undergraduate students, for example, study a core curriculum in the first two years alongside their instrumental lessons, including aural training, improvisation, history, and harmony, alongside topics such as health and well-being and a bespoke career preparation module which introduces the entrepreneurial skills and knowledge required to thrive in the profession.

As they enter their later years of study, students then gradually branch out into musical areas that particularly interest them via various options, many of which explore the topics mentioned above. To give a snapshot, these could be related to improvisation, orchestration and arranging, jazz harmony, accompaniment, chamber music, contemporary music, electronic music, sound recording, instrumental teaching, music history, musical care, performance psychology, conducting, business (including tax and legal matters), and enterprise. They can also try out related instrumental studies; a violinist might take up Baroque violin, for example, and a guitarist may study the lute or jazz guitar. Postgraduate students have similar flexibility, specialising in one main area (e.g., performance, composition, conducting, performance science, music education) while also accessing wider learning opportunities and career preparation across the College.

Every student who starts their education at the RCM is a unique musical individual. Our role as a conservatoire is to help these young musicians attain the highest level they possibly can by drawing out their particular talents and interests. To be an effective entrepreneur, you will need a good musical product to sell, and any instrumentalist will need to develop technical and musical skills of the very highest level to stand a realistic chance of sustaining a successful career involving performance. They will also need to have mastered a very wide range of solo, chamber, and (where applicable) orchestral repertoire for their instrument. Students electing to study performance at a conservatoire specialise in a main instrument (their Principal Study) and usually choose a specific teacher they wish to learn with. They often play several instruments to an excellent standard and may pursue a second study on another instrument. Then there are principal study composers, who are usually also proficient in at least one instrument. The emphasis for these students is very much on playing, performing, and composing music. This has always been the traditional perception of the conservatoire, in contrast to studying music at a university, where courses are often seen as being more academically weighted.[9] Students at the RCM receive regular one-to-one tuition from world-leading teachers and performers and enter a vibrant musical environment where an extraordinary array of musical knowledge and experience is gathered in one place. They can also learn a huge amount from one another, forming lifelong musical connections, partnerships, and ensembles with their peers that they carry into the profession.

The RCM curriculum is designed to mirror the professional world, with an extensive calendar of events throughout the year that features orchestral concerts and operatic productions with renowned international conductors alongside countless solo and chamber music performance opportunities, all of which help students gain the necessary performing experience they will need in the future. A select number of students will also be selected for side-by-side schemes with major orchestras and organisations such as the London Symphony Orchestra (LSO), English National Opera (ENO), and Royal Opera House (ROH), gaining invaluable experience working alongside regular members of the orchestra. In addition, the RCM Performance Laboratory (pictured on the front of this volume) enables students to improve their live performing skills and work at reducing performance anxiety by playing to different kinds of virtual audiences projected on to a screen in front of them.[10] Student initiative is also encouraged via the RCM's *Great Exhibitionists* series which is curated, devised, and performed entirely by students, often in collaboration with other artistic disciplines, including dance, poetry, art, and visual media.

The challenge in designing a curriculum to prepare students for the profession is that each instrumental discipline requires significantly different methods of training alongside the core academic components outlined above. A performance of a Baroque suite on any instrument for example can be improved by an understanding of the harmonic language, a stylistic awareness of each dance movement, and knowledge of its historical context. The practical skills required to become an opera singer or conductor however are very different from those of a harpist or lutenist. Within each instrumental discipline, there are also various specialisms. A violinist may focus on quartet playing as opposed to becoming an orchestral player or soloist. A keyboard player might be better suited to becoming an accompanist, harpsichordist, organist, or repetiteur. One composer could specialise in experimental electronic music and another in opera or writing for film and television. A conservatoire is therefore split into various faculties consisting of Brass, Composition, Keyboard, Historical Performance, Percussion, Strings, Vocal, and Woodwind. Students are then able to explore a wide variety of activities relating more specifically to the professional skills they need on their instrument through their Faculty Studies. Within orchestral training, for example, there will be orchestral sectionals and mock auditions specific to each instrument, alongside work developing a knowledge and mastery of the relevant orchestral extracts needed in the profession.

It is also essential for any performing musician to practise efficiently.[11] Many hours spent practising are not necessarily productive, unless a student has good analytical skills and manages their time well. Understanding physical demands, deciding what to focus on, and setting goals are essential. Many instrumentalists (brass players and singers for example) also have greater physical limits on how long they can practise for. A significant amount of teaching at the RCM therefore will involve an emphasis on helping students with these aspects so that the large amount of time they invest in practice is not only productive musically but also physically sustainable into the future.

There are also a host of other attributes required for sustainable, long-term careers in music. Good punctuality and a well-kept diary, together with regular attendance and prompt communication are vital skills. Musicians also need to be well organised and self-motivated to practise, especially if this aspect of their lives was timetabled or supervised before coming to the RCM. If a musician turns up late or underprepared for a rehearsal or concert, they are unlikely to be asked again, as there will be plenty of others chasing the same opportunity. Likewise, if a student is unprepared for lessons, then they are unlikely to fully benefit from the expertise their teacher can provide. Some students can find it hard to adjust when the onus is on them to decide what to play, when to practise, whether to fill out a concert application, or apply for a scholarship fund. Any freelance musician will also have to organise flights, book hotels, arrange visas and travel itineraries, and so on. They will also need to keep track of their income and expenses and learn how to manage their taxes.

The REACT report also highlights a range of professional competencies useful for an artistic career. These include many of the points highlighted above, covering aspects such as entrepreneurship, versatility, psychological wellness, improvisation, the capacity to rethink music in a rapidly changing society, and competencies to work in community settings (see also Chapter 14).[12] Carey and Coutts argue for 'a shift in focus from discipline-specific knowledge and skill acquisition only, to developing students' social responsibility, leadership, and entrepreneurial capabilities', suggesting that this 'requires the creation of extended learning opportunities that enhance, rather than dilute, students' performative music learning outcomes'.[13] Similarly, Gaunt and colleagues suggest that the preparation for a professional musical life requires both musical artistry as well as sustained experience of engaging with communities.[14] We are also reminded that lifelong creative careers require 'strategic, lifelong and self-regulated learning'.[15]

With all of these factors in mind, the RCM also continues to reflect on its place in wider society in the light of recent cultural debates (in relation to under-represented composers to cite just one more recent example). Reviews of the major academic programmes also take place every few years where changes are made to the course following recommendations from a panel of external advisors with connections to the wider music profession. In recent years, students entering the RCM may now also be working towards qualifications in non-performance-based specialisms, such as performance science or music education. This further extends RCM's offer and brings into focus specialisms centred around educational practice, research, and reflective critique of music and musical practices.

In summary, there is a creative tension in a modern conservatoire between balancing the traditional need to develop the necessary instrumental technique and all-round musical artistry required by a student with helping them to develop a wide range of other competencies and interpersonal skills which they will need to stand a realistic chance of establishing a long-term career in music. To further help students navigate this, RCM students and alumni are supported by the RCM's Creative Careers Centre.

RCM Creative Careers Centre (CCC)

The RCM Creative Careers Centre (CCC, formerly known as the Woodhouse Professional Development Centre) is the RCM's flagship careers department for early-career musicians, recognised internationally for its innovative and supportive approach.[16] The department was established in 1999 by then-Director, Dame Janet Ritterman, and the department's founding manager, Sue Sturrock, a progressive action for a British music conservatoire at that time. A legacy was bequeathed to the RCM from Paul Woodhouse to support musicians in their career development, via the benefactor Peter Willan. The core aim of the CCC is to support musicians in bridging the gap between student and professional life, while constantly adapting to the parameters of an increasingly competitive and complex music industry. Offering bespoke career advice, guidance, referrals, resources, and a broad spectrum of professional opportunities to both students and alumni for up to five years after graduation, the Centre's evolving services include weekly one-to-one career development sessions, student/graduate-aimed opportunity bulletins (lifelong provision for graduates), a graduate/student mentor scheme, and regular workshops/presentations led by both graduates and industry specialists (also lifelong provision).[17]

Support is offered on career planning and development, self-promotion, branding/identity, business and marketing, finances, and funding. Access is provided to a wide variety of resources, professional opportunities, and contacts – all of which are designed to aid preparation for a successful, lifelong career in music. The CCC sustains a bespoke approach to accommodate individual needs, interests, and skills – most crucially, at a time that is right for its users. It strives to develop professional and pioneering partnerships with leading industry specialists, reputable arts organisations, and local communities. These, in turn, deliver unique career-building opportunities and a direct route into the music industry.

The CCC's primary goal is to offer a broad range of support, resources, services, and professional connections, which will enable musicians to discover their strengths and identity; gain hands-on experience and new skills; develop an entrepreneurial mindset; and ultimately build a successful, fulfilling career. Although the core goals of the CCC have remained constant, there have been several landmark moments of change to fulfil its mission of remaining relevant and impactful. This section will emphasise the need for adaptability of support, entrepreneurship, agency, autonomy, and equity throughout.

Evolution of the CCC and entrepreneurship

Having originated within the Woodhouse Professional Development Centre, both the RCM's 'Marketing' and 'Learning and Participation' departments had become stand-alone entities by 2012. A departmental takeover[18] refocused purpose and vision – to provide a holistic career service that prioritised the uniquely individual needs and offerings of musicians. In 2015, the department was rebranded to RCM CCC, after which followed significant departmental advancements that embedded the development of entrepreneurship and related skills into the curriculum. This included new and ongoing undergraduate modules in which musicians focus on enterprise, innovation, and entrepreneurship and develop a business or creative idea to pitch to a panel and a postgraduate module which takes those ideas to execution. The rationale for introducing entrepreneurial activities at a curricular level was twofold: to offer musicians the opportunity to take risks in a safe and supportive environment and enable them to develop entrepreneurial and business skills – thereby creating viable career-forging and/or professional portfolio ideas.[19] Until this important juncture, the CCC was primarily viewed as a vehicle for extracurricular support and added institutional value. This significant moment of change incorporated more of what the department can offer at the curricular level and has led to the elevation of entrepreneurship.

Where once agents would attend final conservatoire recitals, selecting their preferred artists to nurture through lifelong career decisions, the modern musician survives largely by self-managing a unique, diverse portfolio of activities that typically sit outside of common employment structuring.[20] Such a career choice requires knowledge, experience, meaning, a diverse skill set, confidence, commitment, mental and physical support and resilience, a deep understanding of oneself, independence, support from others, and a network. Indicatively, this long list is by no means extensive. It is also crucial to recognise that no musician can build a freelance portfolio career alone, and no two professional portfolios will be identical. As such, at the heart of the CCC lies a focus on agency and equity cultivation. Within agency, we nurture independence, self-reliance, and resilience, which prepare the individual for an often structureless career path and the need to self-start. Within equity, we recognise each musician's unique skills, visions, and trajectories, thereby instilling self-belief and confidence.

Are we, as a conservatoire, best serving the needs of a modern musician in relation to agency and equity? The CCC's response to this is to engage in a deep analysis of the individual's unique strengths and qualities, as opposed to a checklist of generic professional information/skills, which is not appropriate in our context. As such, we work with musicians on a one-to-one basis, or in a supportive group setting, underpinning our efforts with coaching mindsets and approaches. This has taken on the form of a new module for postgraduate students, named Professional Musician. Each musician herein is provided with a dedicated qualified career coach, who assists in their self-exploration of, and reflection on, their strengths, identity, growth, vision, planning, and goal setting. This approach sets musicians up for a healthy, proactive, and sustainable career, offering a deeper understanding of artistic identity and areas for professional growth. This new module has become an intrinsic stepping stone for those wishing to pursue the aforementioned entrepreneurial-focused module.

The impact of the COVID-19 pandemic

The RCM and the CCC witnessed first-hand how the COVID-19 pandemic impacted and, in many cases, devastated the lives, livelihoods, and opportunities of arts workers.[21] New graduates who entered the profession at that time were among the hardest hit, and work opportunities via our Professional Portfolio Development schemes came to a halt. UK Music's 'This Is Music 2021 Report' stated that 69,000 jobs had ceased to exist as a result of COVID-19.[22]

In response, the CCC adapted its services considerably. In March 2021, we announced a new scheme, *RCM Accelerate*, to support graduating students with the launch of their careers. The scheme was designed to help kick-start a new creative project, social enterprise, or business idea or to develop an existing initiative. As a minimum requirement, the scheme supports the career development of one RCM musician (the applicant(s)) and at least two further arts freelancers. At the end of a rigorous application process, and within the crucial framework of a post-COVID-19 regeneration, successful applicants receive grant funding of up to £5,000 and benefit from ongoing mentoring and peer support to foster and encourage proactivity, creativity, connectivity, and an entrepreneurial mindset. Throughout the scheme, musicians are expected to consider and incorporate the prime values of equality, diversity, inclusion, and environmental concerns. The scheme is intended to reflect the RCM ideals of an inclusive, open, and just society, supporting students from diverse social, economic, and ethnic backgrounds and thus fulfilling the RCM's obligation as a positive, meaningful, cultural change-agent and a relevant, persuasive, and world-leading advocate for the future of music.

From the entrepreneurial and career coaching modules, to *RCM Accelerate*, the RCM's CCC offers students and graduates a supportive career pathway built on creativity, innovation, meaningful individual output, viability, sustainability and, ultimately – employability. From 2022 onwards, the winners of *RCM Accelerate* are announced on graduation day, thereby celebrating publicly the diverse skills, strengths, passions, and capabilities of the modern musician. The depth, breadth, and impact of *RCM Accelerate* projects are illustrated via two graduate reflections in Box 12.1. Overall, these developments have nurtured the agency, equity, collaborative power, and confidence of musicians to emerge into the industry with a viable segment of their professional portfolio already underway. COVID-19 further highlighted the need for musicians to be entrepreneurs: creatively adaptable, innovative, diverse in outlook, and technologically adept.[23]

BOX 12.1   GRADUATE REFLECTIONS ON RCM ACCELERATE

RCM Accelerate has massively helped me in launching my career, especially since I graduated at an uncertain time for the music industry in 2021 when COVID-19 restrictions were still in place. At a time of such uncertainty, RCM Accelerate allowed me to take my career into my own hands and launch my ensemble, 97 Ensemble. I am incredibly thankful for this, and it has opened many doors for me and taken me further into the world of equality, diversity, and inclusion in music which is something I am very passionate about.

I've massively benefited from many aspects of RCM Accelerate, even the application process! The Creative Careers Centre had provided many talks and information worksheets for potential applicants which were extremely useful to me as I had never filled out a project funding application before. I learnt a lot about budgeting, branding, and how to pitch an idea successfully. I am incredibly thankful for all this and have since gone on to be granted £5000 from the Marchus Trust and have much more confidence in filling out other applications.

If I had to summarise in one sentence the biggest benefit of RCM Accelerate to me it would be that it has allowed me to take control of my career path and for me to take the direction I want to take.

[Niki Moosavi, cellist, BMus graduate 2021]

At a time of graduating into the uncertainty of the post-pandemic world, the Accelerate scheme was a vital learning experience, giving me structure, motivation and the funding necessary to kick-start my schools opera project, OperaEd. With the mentorship of Diana Roberts, I was able to experiment with ideas, learn new skills (particularly in fundraising), and pay other creatives to collaborate with.

I would highly recommend the Accelerate Scheme application. The funding is linked to a recognised institution (RCM). You receive support and contacts from a team who celebrate you and your project, making you feel part of a cohort of other individuals/partnerships who have also started their journey at a similar stage. Most importantly, the scheme is designed to build confidence and allow your vision to become reality: in 2022, OperaEd successfully delivered a thirty-minute workshop and a thirty-minute performance to three schools and one inclusive theatre and performing arts company, in London, supporting the work of 21 professional freelancers.

[Helen Cooper, soprano, MPerf graduate 2021]

Embracing technology

A significant institutional development in 1999, the CCC remains the sole dedicated UK conservatoire music-careers department. As such, it represents a unique selling point and has been cited by prospective students as a primary reason to study at the RCM over other institutions. During the pandemic, the CCC adapted at every turn, pivoting to best serve musicians and supporting those changes through advancing use of technological innovation. To mark 20 years of the department and embrace the rapid developments in global communication technology, we devised and delivered a month-long series of daily online workshops, events, and one-to-one support for students and graduates, entitled 'The Modern Musician: Past, Present, and Future'. In total, 24 events were delivered, as well as 88 tailored one-to-one sessions. Fifty-seven global speakers were featured (industry specialists and graduates), and, across all events, there were 572 attendances – from first-year undergraduates, to graduates who left the RCM in 1983.

As outlined earlier in this chapter, the challenges we face include overcoming negative perceptions pertaining to employability in music. Recognising the value and importance of strong connections between students and recent graduates in this regard, in 2020, we launched an online graduate/student mentoring programme and a student/graduate online community space. Training was provided for students and graduates in the set-up of digital teaching and performing platforms; we established a new Online Teaching and Performance Service, attracting clients from Japan, Canada, Europe, and the United States. We embraced technology and encouraged our musicians to follow suit. While understandably not universally applicable across all student/graduate/audience bodies, our utilisation of technology and adaptation of existing services offered hope, encouragement, and sustained support through an otherwise devastating time for the arts.

A current digital project, Portfolio Career Pathways, is an online platform for musicians to explore available career options. For example if a student is interested in developing a segment of their portfolio as an orchestral musician, they can click through a supportive, educational series of digital resources (videos, factsheets, graduate interviews, links to opportunities and relevant industry organisations/bodies, where and how to access physical and mental health and well-being support, and so on), presented in the form of an engaging, accessible step-by-step guide. Our aim is to reflect as many pathways as possible, including options outside of music. This platform can be accessed and utilised by students, staff, and professors.

The CCC's future vision

Space for risk-taking, creativity, and meaningful output

Partnerships with many of London's most prestigious galleries – including our *"In Tune With . . .*' series collaboration with the Royal Academy (RA) of Arts – have provided students with experiences in creativity, agency, and audience development. In conjunction with the RA's education team, and arts philanthropist Dasha Shenkman OBE, we placed musicians' agency, education, and the cultivation of audiences centrally within our planning. Summer 2019 saw a repeat of the ever-popular '*In Tune With the Summer Exhibition*', which featured musician-curated pop-up style performances, inspired by artworks across eight gallery spaces. The year 2019 represented our most ambitious programming yet, including a student-created/led chamber orchestra performing a brand-new choreographed work. Through partnerships and collaborations such as these, the CCC aims to reignite a range of opportunities for RCM musicians, with creativity, agency, and audience-awareness at the centre of all future projects.

Audience and community

While technical ability and principal study skills lie at the heart of the RCM's emphases, the pandemic has demonstrated that long-term sustainability is as much dependent upon focused audience development as individual artistry. Core questions arise such as: Why do audiences and communities engage with our art form? Where do they find meaning, purpose, and, at music's full potential – transformation? How do we raise awareness of the need for audience understanding and development among our musicians and integrate that necessity into training? How will audiences engage in the future?

Addressing these questions successfully will inevitably demand the greater cultivation of entrepreneurship throughout the wider institutional community. Benefits of audience interaction can already be found within the works of RCM Sparks, Music Education, and the Centre for Performance Science (see also Chapter 14), which regularly demonstrate first-hand how music can transcend other forms of communication and create transformative impact. As such, the development of musicians' skill sets, in direct relation to audience and community engagement, requires the cultivation of bespoke projects at the degree level. The subsequent immersive experience will, in turn, maximise the individual awareness of potential impact and positively benefit and enhance the prospects of employment and sustainability. In the long term, the CCC aims to collaborate with the RCM's Centre for Performance Science on related, impactful research and development projects.

Institution/department deeper collaboration

Through a career development lens, we support musicians via our direct links with students, graduates, and industry bodies/professionals. The CCC aims to maximise the benefits of this standpoint in future – thereby addressing diversity, equality of opportunities, and the best preparation for musicians at multiple stages of a lifelong creative career development and with a broad spectrum of portfolio desires. The more conservatoires play a challenging role within the profession, the greater the scope of students' confidence, versatility, and originality, thereby emboldening the possibility of positive, industry-wide change. The goal is to equip RCM students with the confidence and versatility to create their own distinctive career paths and to enable them to play their own part in strengthening the music profession for an uncertain future.

Summary

This chapter has explored the foundations for long-term creative careers in music, focusing on the different skills, competencies, and knowledge required by professional musicians and on how conservatoires can support both students and graduates towards their professional potential. Responding to rapidly changing professional landscapes, it is also imperative that conservatoires address key issues of equality and diversity, as well as critically reflecting on the roles of conservatoire graduates today.[24] Key reflections moving forward include: needing to place a stronger emphasis on health and well-being (including financial, recognising the need for and provision of scholarships for all students), offering more student-led initiatives incorporating up-to-date digital technology, embedding tailored career coaching support and a general coaching and entrepreneurial ethos, and supporting a broader range of tangible career pathways – at curricula level and beyond. From the best vantage point, we need to create frequently open dialogues with the music profession to prepare and serve the talent pipeline and broader musical ecosystem. As Rineke Smilde puts it, 'the conservatoire needs to constantly fine tune and adjust itself to the needs of the profession, and vice versa',[25] requiring institutional adaptability, reflection, and agility to best support students for lifelong creative careers.

- Key take-away 1: most students embarking on a conservatoire education will be considering a career in music. This career is likely to be multifaceted, built on a diverse portfolio of musical activities.
- Key take-away 2: lifelong creative careers in music require a plethora of different knowledge, skills, and competencies in addition to musical ability. These include practice and preparation, organisation, self-motivation, entrepreneurship, financial and legal awareness, adaptability, agility, experience in different musical contexts including in the community, confidence, self-awareness, communication, presentation, digital and marketing know-how, and self-promotion.
- Key take-away 3: conservatoires need to respond with adaptable career support, reflecting critically on their values and cultures to embrace new career possibilities, new technologies, and new audiences/communities.

Acknowledgements

Thanks to Niki Moosavi and Helen Cooper for providing their feedback on RCM Accelerate.

Further information and reading

Beeching, Angela M. *Beyond Talent: Creating a Successful Career in Music.* New York: Oxford University Press, 2020.

Bennett, Dawn. *Understanding the Classical Music Profession: The Past, the Present, and Strategies for the Future.* London: Routledge, 2016.

RCM Creative Careers Centre. www.rcm.ac.uk/life/preparingforprofession/creativecareers/.

Bibliography

Bartleet, Brydie-Leigh, Christina Ballico, Dawn Bennett, Ruth Bridgstock, Paul Draper, Vanessa Tomlinson, and Scott Harrison. 'Building sustainable portfolio careers in music: Insights and implications for higher education'. *Music Education Research* 21, no. 3 (2019): 282–94. https://doi.org/10.1080/14613808.2019.1598348.

Bennett, Dawn. *Understanding the Classical Music Profession: The Past, the Present, and Strategies for the Future.* London: Routledge, 2016.

Bennett, Dawn, and Ruth Bridgstock. 'The urgent need for career preview: Student expectations and graduate realities in music and dance'. *International Journal of Music Education* 33, no. 3 (2015): 263–77. https://doi.org/10.1177/0255761414558653.

Burt, Rosie, and Janet Mills. 'Taking the plunge: The hopes and fears of students as they begin music college'. *British Journal of Music Education* 23 (2006): 51–73. https://doi.org/10.1017/S0265051705006741.

Carey, Gemma, and Leah Coutts. 'Fostering transformative professionalism through curriculum changes within a Bachelor of Music'. In *Expanding professionalism in music and higher music education: A changing game*, edited by Heidi Westerlund and Helena Gaunt, 42–58. Routledge, 2021.

Duffy, Celia. (2013). Negotiating with tradition: Curriculum reform and institutional transition in a conservatoire'. *Arts and Humanities in Higher Education* 12: 169–80. https://doi.org/10.1177/1474022212473527.

Gaunt, Helena, Celia Duffy, Ana Coric, Isabel R. González Delgado, Linda Messas, Oleksandr Pryimenko, and Henrik Sveidahl. 'Musicians as "makers in society": A conceptual foundation for contemporary professional higher music education'. *Frontiers in Psychology* 12 (2021): 3159. https://doi.org/10.3389/fpsyg.2021.713648.

Jørgensen, Harald. 'Western classical music studies in universities and conservatoires'. In *Advanced Musical Performance: Investigations in Higher Education Learning*, edited by Ioulia Papageorgi and Graham Welch. London: Routledge, 2014.

López-Íñiguez, Guadalupe, and Dawn Bennett. 'A lifespan perspective on multi-professional musicians: Does music education prepare classical musicians for their careers?' *Music Education Research* 22, no. 1 (2020): 1–14. https://doi.org/10.1080/14613808.2019.1703925.

López-Íñiguez, Guadalupe, and Dawn Bennett. 'Broadening student musicians' career horizons: The importance of being and becoming a learner in higher education'. *International Journal of Music Education* 39, no. 2 (2021): 134–50. https://doi.org/10.1177/0255761421989111.

Pennill, Nicola, Keith Phillips, and Michelle Phillips. 'Student experiences and entrepreneurship education in a specialist creative arts HEI: A longitudinal approach'. *Entrepreneurship Education* 5 (2022): 399–423. https://doi.org/10.1007/s41959-022-00085-9.

REACT – Rethinking Music Performance in European Higher Education Institutions. *Artistic Career in Music: Stakeholders Requirement Report.* UA Editora, 2021. https://doi.org/10.48528/wfq9-4560.

Shaughnessy, Caitlin, Rosie Perkins, Neta Spiro, George Waddell, Aifric Campbell, and Aaron Williamon. 'The future of the cultural workforce: Perspectives from early career arts professionals on the challenges and future of the cultural industries in the context of COVID-19'. *Social Sciences and Humanities Open* 6 (2022): 1–12. https://doi.org/10.1016/j.ssaho.2022.100296.

Smilde, Rineke. *Musicians as Lifelong Learners: Discovery through Biography*. Delft: Eburon Academic Publishers, 2009.

Spiro, Neta, Rosie Perkins, Sasha Kaye, Urszula Tymoszuk, Adele Mason-Bertrand, Isabelle Cossette, Solange Glasser, and Aaron Williamon. 'The effects of COVID-19 lockdown 1.0 on working patterns, income, and wellbeing among performing arts professionals in the United Kingdom (April–June 2020)'. *Frontiers in Psychology* 11 (2021): 1–17. https://doi.org/10.3389/fpsyg.2020.594086.

Williamon, Aaron, ed. *Musical Excellence: Strategies and Techniques to Enhance Performance*. Oxford University Press, 2004.

Williamon, Aaron, Lisa Aufegger, and Hubert Eiholzer. 'Simulating and stimulating performance: Introducing distributed simulation to enhance musical learning and performance'. *Frontiers in Psychology* 5, no. 25 (2014): 1–9. https://doi.org/10.3389/fpsyg.2014.00025.

PERSPECTIVE: CHAPTER 12

Michelle Phillips

Introduction

I am Head of Enterprise (Academic) and Senior Lecturer in Music Psychology at the Royal Northern College of Music (RNCM). Prior to embarking on a PhD in music psychology at the Centre for Music and Science at the University of Cambridge (under the supervision of Ian Cross), I trained as a chartered accountant. My research focusses on both music perception (including music and Parkinson's disease, perception of live and recorded music, music and time, and music and neuroscience) and on how to equip music conservatoire students with skills for their future careers as freelance (or self-employed) musicians. In 2020, I was awarded £900k from the Office for Students and Research England to lead a project with partners Royal Central School of Speech and Drama and University of the Arts London, which explored the most effective ways to equip specialist creative industries students with entrepreneurial skills. I have been invited to give keynote and invited talks on music and entrepreneurship at numerous conservatoires worldwide, have published multiple articles on this topic in peer-reviewed journals, and am part of the Impact Research Group – a group of international entrepreneurship academics. In 2021, I was awarded a Fellowship of Enterprise Educators UK and was also elected to the board of the Institute for Small Business and Entrepreneurship (ISBE). I am a saxophonist and play with the Equinox Saxophone Ensemble.

Perspectives

Twenty-four per cent of creative and performing arts graduates in the UK go on to self-employed careers within 18 months of completing their degrees.[26] Their self-employed or freelance careers require them to be adept in multiple entrepreneurial skills, for example, managing their finances, having knowledge of tax and tax returns, project management, quoting and invoicing for performances and compositions, generating ideas for new artistic work, networking, marketing their work, teamwork, and many other skills. It is therefore essential that specialist higher education arts institutions such as conservatoires prepare students for their careers in the industry by developing their skills in these areas. Moreover,

DOI: 10.4324/9781003281573-26

the need to prepare music conservatoire graduates for their futures is heightened, given existing and new research on the value of music in everyday life; musician graduates will likely go on not only to contribute significantly to the UK economy but also will generate social and cultural value for individuals, communities, audiences, and health and well-being value through, for example, work with people living with dementia or Parkinson's. Music is powerful, and is an essential part of human life, and conservatoires have a responsibility to equip graduates with skills which allow them to generate this value and have an impact with their art.

The entrepreneurship education community in the UK and worldwide is an active and passionate one, and engagement enables music conservatoires to hone and develop practice in how to equip music students with skills in this area. Not only do organisations such as Enterprise Educators UK and the Institute of Small Business and Entrepreneurship offer webinars, workshops, and annual conferences for members; models and best practice guidance have also been developed regarding how entrepreneurship might be embedded into higher education degree programmes. For example, the EntreComp framework[27] allows institutions and students themselves to reflect on which entrepreneurial skills they might need to develop and provides guidance on how to ensure students graduate with all relevant entrepreneurial experience and tools. The Advance HE framework[28] also underlines the three areas which institutions should think about when designing degree programmes: enterprise, entrepreneurship, and employability. Finally, the QAA (2018) Guidance on Entrepreneurship and Enterprise, developed under the leadership of Prof. Andy Penaluna (himself a fine arts graduate), presents a four-stage model of how students might journey through the learning of entrepreneurial skills from developing enterprise awareness, to an entrepreneurial mindset, to entrepreneurial capability, and finally entrepreneurial effectiveness.[29]

In 2023, the RNCM won the Times Higher Education award for 'Outstanding Entrepreneurial University' and was awarded third place in the international Triple E Awards for 'Young Entrepreneurial University of the Year'. We also launched 'RNCM Innovate', our platform for experimentation and discovery, enabling students and staff to push the boundaries of traditional music practices and drive the industry of tomorrow. Prior to this, in 2020, the RNCM was awarded £900k from the Office for Students and Research England to lead a two-year project which explored how specialist creative arts higher education institutions might best equip students with entrepreneurial mindsets and skills ('StART Entrepreneurship project').[30] The project was led by Dr Michelle Phillips (Principal Investigator), with partners (and Co-Investigators) at the Royal Central School of Speech and Drama and University of the Arts London. This project forefronted aspects of entrepreneurship education such as those discussed above – the rapidly changing music industry, the impact of the COVID-19 pandemic, the need to equip students for an international career, the importance of digital skills, and the value of mentoring – and asked how specialist arts institutions can best equip all graduates for the music industry of the future. Moreover, the StART Entrepreneurship Project sought not primarily to develop knowledge regarding how creative industries students might be trained to *slot into* the industry as it exists but to lead the industry of the future and to generate, make, and realise new ideas that would define how the industry looks in 10, 20, or 50 years' time.

The StART Entrepreneurship Project involved the testing and creation of new in-curriculum modules, drop-in clinics for development of ideas, global majority workshops, a two-day entrepreneurship bootcamp, and a series of 15 workshops with industry experts, alumni mentoring, and other activities. Key findings from the project include that the terminology used when engaging students in entrepreneurship training is important, and the term 'entrepreneurship' is not always relatable. Terms such as 'creative innovation' may be more appropriate; for example the RNCM Creative Innovators Award, which offers students the chance to pitch ideas and win industry-mentoring and financial support from the £5,000 prize fund, is not labelled an 'entrepreneurship' award. Second, degree programmes must cater for students' own beliefs, values, and attitudes, for the 'unique musical individual'. One useful tool here is the concept of 'effectuation',[31] which trains students in idea generation that begins with who they are as people and artists and helps them to turn their passion into a new idea or enterprise.[32] This allows students to develop skills in social entrepreneurship in areas which align with their identity, which may be, for example, belonging, diversity, equality and inclusivity, music in healthcare settings, or music and climate change. Risk-taking is also important, as mentioned in Chapter 12 – specialist music study should allow students to lead independent projects and try out experimental ideas (such as during the RNCM's 'Lab Week'), which may fail, and to reflect on and learn from the experience. Music conservatoires should therefore offer students the chance to develop self-reflection skills within the curriculum in order for them to continually evaluate, develop, and test their own entrepreneurial competencies. Other key findings from the project include that financial skills are key to equipping students for freelance careers, embedding finance classes into the curriculum from the first year of study is an impactful way to do this, and that enabling students to study alongside engaging with the music industry as part of their studies (e.g., through professional placements) is also important.

Summary

Specialist music graduates are outstanding entrepreneurs – the formation of a new quartet or band is the creation of a new enterprise, the verbal presentation of a programme to an audience requires finely honed presentation skills akin to a pitch, the setting up of workshops to support music education in schools might be registered as a charity, and the income from composition commissions qualifies a graduate as self-employed, in the same way as any freelance consultant. Entrepreneurship underpins all elements of music conservatoire training and professional careers in the music industry. It is not an add on or a set of skills which should be offered only, or chiefly, as optional (extracurricular) rather than embedded meaningfully into a curriculum. It is the responsibility of today's music conservatoires to prepare all of our highly skilled students not to join a conveyor belt into the current industry but to create new ideas, be creative and innovative, and to lead and shape the music industry of the future.

Bibliography

Advance HE. *Enterprise and Entrepreneurship Education: A Focus Framework Aligned to the Employability Framework*. UK Professional Standards Framework, 2019. www.advance-he.ac.uk/teaching-and-learning/employability-enterprise-and-entrepreneurship-higher-education.

Bacigalupo, Margherita, Panagiotis Kampylis, Yves Punie, and Godelieve Van den Brande. 'EntreComp: The entrepreneurship competence framework'. *Luxembourg: Publication Office of the European Union* 10 (2016): 593884.

Birdi, Kamal. 'Insights on impact from the development, delivery, and evaluation of the CLEAR IDEAS innovation training model'. *European Journal of Work and Organizational Psychology* 30, no. 3 (2021): 400–4. https://doi.org/10.1080/1359432X.2020.1770854.

Pennill, Nicola, Keith Phillips, and Michelle Phillips. 'Student experiences and entrepreneurship education in a specialist creative arts HEI: A longitudinal approach'. *Entrepreneurship Education* 9 (2022): 399–423. https://doi.org/10.1007/s41959-022-00085-9.

Phillips, Michelle, and Hannah McCabe. 'Socially distanced work experience in a music degree programme'. In *Advance HE, 3 Es for Wicked Problems: Employability, Enterprise, and Entrepreneurship: Solving Wicked Problems,* 2022. www.advance-he.ac.uk/knowledge-hub/3-es-wicked-problems-employability-enterprise-and-entrepreneurship-solving-wicked.

Phillips, Michelle, and Ava Podgorski. 'Best practice considerations for arts educators when developing intensive online courses for creative industries higher education students'. In *Progress in Entrepreneurship Education and Training, FGF Studies in Small Business, Entrepreneurship*, edited by Joern H. Block et al., Springer, 2023.

QAA. *Enterprise and Entrepreneurship Education: Guidance for UK Higher Education Providers.* Gloucester: The Quality Assurance Agency for Higher Education, 2018. https://www.qaa.ac.uk/docs/qaas/enhancement-and-development/enterprise-and-entrpreneurship-education-2018.pdf?sfvrsn=15f1f981_8

Sarasvathy, Saras D. 'Causation and effectuation: Toward a theoretical shift from economic inevitability to entrepreneurial contingency'. *Academy of Management Review* 26 (2001): 243–63. https://doi.org/10.5465/amr.2001.4378020.

Chapter and Perspective Notes

1 This was a particularly common occurrence during the COVID-19 pandemic and poses considerable challenges when trying to assess an applicant's true sound quality and technical ability.
2 See for example www.ism.org/images/images/ISM_Music-a-subject-of-peril_A4_March-2022_Online2.pdf; www.musicteachermagazine.co.uk/news/article/arts-funding-cuts-at-higher-education-levels-to-go-ahead-in-england. 'Sixth form' is educational provision for students typically aged 16-18.
3 Burt and Mills, 'Taking the plunge'.
4 Pennill et al., 'Student experiences and entrepreneurship'. See also Bennett, *Understanding the Classical Music Profession.*
5 Bennett and Bridgstock, 'The urgent need for career preview'.
6 See also Duffy, 'Negotiating with tradition'.
7 Bennett and Bridgstock, 'The urgent need for career preview'.
8 López-Íñiguez and Bennett, 'A lifespan perspective'.
9 Jørgensen, 'Western classical music studies'.
10 See www.rcm.ac.uk/research/projects/performancelaboratory/.
11 Williamon, *Musical Excellence.*
12 REACT – Rethinking Music Performance in European Higher Education Institutions.
13 Carey and Coutts, 'Fostering transformative professionalism', 54, 46.
14 Gaunt et al., 'Musicians as "makers in society"'.
15 López-Íñiguez and Bennett, 'Broadening student musicians' career horizons'.
16 See RCM's Annual Review. www.rcm.ac.uk/about/strategies-values/.
17 See www.rcm.ac.uk/life/preparingforprofession/creativecareers/.
18 Led by Diana Roberts, the co-author of this chapter.
19 'Enterprise and entrepreneurship' is also one of five key areas of importance that have been identified for higher music education institutions supporting their students for portfolio careers (along with mobility, digitisation, gender parity, and health and wellbeing).
20 Bennett and Bridgstock, 'The urgent need for career preview'.
21 Spiro et al., 'The effects of COVID-19 lockdown'.
22 See www.ukmusic.org/wp-content/uploads/2021/10/This-is-Music-2021-v2.pdf.
23 Shaughnessy et al., 'The future of the cultural workforce'.
24 Gaunt et al., 'Musicians as "makers in society"'.
25 Smilde, *Musicians as Lifelong Learners.*

26 Graduate Outcomes data for 2019 graduating cohort.

27 Bacigalupo et al., 'EntreComp: The entrepreneurship competence framework'.

28 Advance HE, 'UK professional standards framework (UKPSF) (online) enterprise and entrepreneurship education: A focus framework aligned to the employability framework'.

29 QAA, 'Enterprise and Entrepreneurship Education: Guidance for UK Higher Education Providers'.

30 See Phillips and McCabe, 'Socially distanced work experience in a music degree programme', Phillips and Podgorski, 'Best practice considerations for arts educators when developing intensive online courses for creative industries higher education students', Pennill et al., 'Student experiences and entrepreneurship education in a specialist creative arts HEI: A longitudinal approach'.

31 Sarasvathy, 'Causation and effectuation: Toward a theoretical shift from economic inevitability to entrepreneurial contingency'.

32 Useful also here is the CLEAR IDEAS model: Birdi, 'Insights on impact from the development, delivery, and evaluation of the CLEAR IDEAS innovation training model'.

PART III

Conservatoires of the future

13

THE PHYSICAL AND VIRTUAL SPACES OF THE CONSERVATOIRE

Colin Lawson and Talia Hull

Introduction

The personal experience of performing around the world suggests that both the acoustic and physical dimensions of a concert space can have a significant influence on the musical experience both of performers and audiences. For the performer, these factors often affect comfort level on stage, which may be enhanced or compromised varyingly by the ambience. In technical terms, a performance may need different degrees of projection and articulation in different circumstances. At the same time, audience engagement may well be affected by such factors as proximity to the stage and sight-lines. It remains true that there is no accounting for the particular mood of an audience on a given evening, an especially relevant observation for smaller venues. As one writer put it in 1800:

> For example, yesterday the cards were unfavourable for this lady [in the audience], this young gentleman has been jilted by his sweetheart, this official was passed over in advancement. . . . The banker has won only 99% [interest], the malicious denouncer has failed to catch his prey, the junior officer who has served only 24 hours is not already at least a brigadier-general [and] in such a mood in a large part does the public condemn the author, composer, actor, performing artists.[1]

Concert etiquette was very different in earlier times, as illustrated by Mozart's delight at a respectful audience responding freely rather than passively during the premiere of his 'Paris' Symphony in July 1778. He noted that during the first Allegro, there was a tremendous burst of applause, with further clapping of hands just after the start of the finale.[2] More than a century later, a painting now in the archives of the Royal Opera House shows the inaugural concert of London's Queen's Hall in 1893: conductor and audience are in full flight; yet, conversation is also flowing freely in the front rows of the audience.[3] Less controlled was the celebrated riotous premiere of Stravinsky's *Rite of Spring* in Paris in 1913, one of the last documented instances of active audience reaction within the Western concert tradition. A freely responding audience is nowadays more characteristic of a pop

DOI: 10.4324/9781003281573-28

concert, where performers tend to display their own carefully cultivated set of behaviours. In many other cultures, the artificial divisions between performer, composer, and audience have never existed; as the player or singer improvises, the audience responds, whether by toe-tapping, finger drumming, hand clapping, singing, or dancing. Musicians are as likely to be found in streets, markets, or public and community spaces as in more formal surroundings, since music has remained intimately associated with such ritual events as weddings, funerals, or the agricultural calendar, dealing with such perennial subjects as the wounds of love. Western Art conventions are thus only part of the global picture.

If walls could speak . . .

Many historians of any subject (and especially students of historical performance practice in music) must have indulged in the fantasy of old evidence brought to life by the buildings themselves. After all, it is the human element as well as the music itself that is ill-served by communication in mere words. How one would relish having witnessed the difficult conversations between the Director Cherubini and his brilliant pupil Berlioz during the early years of the Paris Conservatoire. To take an example from RCM's teaching studios, what was the nature of interactions between Vaughan Williams and his composition pupils such as Ina Boyle, Ruth Gipps, Peggy Glanville-Hicks, Dorothy Gow, and Elizabeth Maconchy? Much of this activity remains undocumented and mysterious. The RCM's main building acts as an important connection to the historical presence of these individuals, reinforced by physical artefacts such as portraits. There can be something quite powerful for young musicians about studying in an environment with such a history of forerunners. Whether this is inspiring or stifling may well depend on the individual.

It is worth recalling that historical working environments were in many ways unrecognisable from today's perspective: for example, we can scarcely imagine how everyone coped with the ubiquitous palls of cigarette smoke that were a natural part of everyday life until relatively recently. At the RCM, only a few decades ago, white-gloved waiters served tea in the Senior Common Room, and everyone was expected to stand when a professor entered the room. That deferential age is well reflected in the RCM building, with its three entrances for female students, professors, and male students. There is a sense in which this reminder of bygone times jars with our behaviours and student expectations today, though in practice, few members of today's RCM give the matter a great deal of consideration.

Buildings and music

As long ago as 1954, Thurston Dart made an explicit link between acoustics and musical style that had been rarely investigated in earlier histories. He laid out some fundamental principles, which if generalised remain pertinent:

> Even a superficial study shows that early composers were very aware of the effect on their music of the surroundings in which it was to be performed, and that they deliberately shaped their music accordingly. Musical acoustics may be roughly divided into 'resonant', 'room' and 'outdoor'. Plainsong is resonant music; so is the harmonic style of Leonine and Perotin. . . . The intricate sophisticated rhythms and harmonies of the fourteenth century *ars nova* . . . are room music; pieces written in the broader style of the

fifteenth century . . . are resonant music. Gabrieli's music for brass consort is resonant, written for the Cathedral of St. Mark's; music for brass consort by Hassler or Matthew Locke is open-air music, using quite a different style from the same composers' music for stringed instruments, designed to be played indoors. Purcell distinguished in style between the music he wrote for Westminster Abbey and the music he wrote for the Chapel Royal; both styles differ from that of his theatre music, written for performance in completely 'dead' surroundings. The forms used by Mozart and Haydn in their chamber or orchestral music are identical; but the details of style (counterpoint, ornamentation, rhythm, the layout of chords and rate at which the harmonies change) will vary according to whether they are writing room-music, concert music or street music. . . . Our own age has grown very insensitive to nuances of this kind; but there is plenty of evidence (quite apart from the evidence of the music itself) to show that they were taken very seriously in earlier times.[4]

More granular evidence from primary sources is provided by Andrew Parrott:[5] a collection of writings under the heading 'Acoustical matters' addresses spaces, empirical understanding, design, and enhancement. 'Placement of performers' then presents sources associated with church, concert, spectacle, and general. A variety of evidence from across Europe between 1432 and 1768 is concerned primarily with how the different genres of music may best be served.

Michael Forsyth's *Buildings for Music* provides a valuable background to the buildings for which Western music was composed from the seventeenth century onwards, while outlining some of the influences that architectural acoustics exert on musical style and, conversely, tracing the importance of musical factors in auditorium design. As an architect himself, Forsyth wrote his text with the benefit of experience in designing concert halls; importantly, he was also a violinist. *Buildings for Music* begins with a description of purpose-built music rooms in Britain, Austria, and Germany before analysing the evolution of the opera house in Italy and France, especially in relation to eighteenth-century Classical style. There follows an appraisal of the great concert halls and opera houses that arose during the nineteenth century. The twentieth century witnessed the development of acoustic science, influenced by recording techniques and electronics. The concept of adjustable acoustics gradually became taken for granted.

At the beginning of his book, Forsyth observes that:

[T]he urge to sing in the shower or to whoop in a tunnel, the ability of even unmusical people to sing in tune in a reverberant space – these suggest a relationship between music and the acoustics of a hard-surfaced enclosure. . . . Auditoria with the acoustics of the open air, on the other hand, have traditionally lent themselves to events where the intelligibility of speech is important, whether spoken or sung; that is, where clarity is necessary as opposed to fullness of tone.[6]

Concert halls evolved from the acoustically intimate rooms of the eighteenth century, such as the Altes Gewandhaus in Leipzig, where members of the small audience faced each other across a central aisle. There was doubtless a social element that involved being seen and noting the presence of others. Much chamber music repertory was composed for domestic performance, and the music may suffer when played in a very reverberant acoustic, not only because the associations are wrong but also because the musical textures are blurred.[7] The boomy halls of the later nineteenth century, such as the Concertgebouw in Amsterdam, made for a somewhat different experience. When the sermon became a major element in the Protestant service, many churches in Germany (including the Thomaskirche in Leipzig) were remodelled by the addition of drapes, radically reducing reverberation times and thus enabling Bach's string parts to be more clearly heard, allowing brisker tempi and faster rate of harmonic change.

Until the late nineteenth century, little was understood about the principle of room acoustics; success depended on a combination of intuition, experience, and luck, both in overall planning and in the use of construction materials. Theatres and opera houses tended to be lined with thin wood panelling to absorb the boomy medium- to lower-frequency sounds so as not to mask both the elaborate aria and the secco recitative. Concert halls were generally constructed of thick sound-reflective plaster, necessary for the fuller tone required of orchestral music. The fine reputation of some older concert halls may be ascribed to a process of natural selection.[8] In our own day, there is often a mismatch between (for example) a small band playing historical instruments in a concert hall that can accommodate thousands of audience members. In any event, the reason and clarity inherent in the formal structures of Haydn and Mozart undoubtedly benefit from a less reverberant acoustic than would be appropriate for Berlioz, Liszt, or Wagner, whether in a concert space or the opera house. Liberated from church or private patronage, the democratisation of music and the accumulation of music from different periods led to performances in a range of circumstances and locations.[9] Gradually came experiments in sound absorption and the discovery of a mathematical formula by which the reverberation time of a room could be predicted. A further development (whose origins date back more than 350 years) was to model graphically the way in which sound travels, by analogy with light rays reflecting off the surfaces they meet. The architectural acoustician Wallace Clement Sabine's experiments and conclusions led to the huge success of the iconic 2,600-seat Boston Symphony Hall (1900).[10] A later tendency towards clarity can be ascribed not entirely to musical requirements but to accommodating larger audiences in comfort.[11] London's Royal Festival Hall (1951) was a controversial example. Ongoing research by Professor Tapio Lokki of Aalto University and colleagues is enhancing the understanding of room acoustics by investigating auralisation, spatial sound reproduction, binaural technology, and novel objective and subjective evaluation methods.[12]

Various methods of adjustable acoustics have been a design feature over the past 40 years or so. Examples from the 1980s include the Royal Concert Hall in Nottingham and the Roy Thomson Hall in Toronto. The point is well made that:

> [T]he sound quality of the home hi-fi system, where the soloist's technical virtuosity is heard with extreme clarity in the upper register against a strongly reverberant bass accompaniment – a combination almost impossible to achieve in live performance – became for the listener a measure against which to judge acoustic excellence in the concert hall.[13]

The relative strength of sound at different frequencies is important in determining the tone of a hall – whether it sounds bright, muffled, harsh, mellow, and so on.

More recently, the world of electronics and digital media has been complemented by a less regimented approach to concertising, embracing (for example) street music, car parks, or nightclubs. The place of music in society is ever-changing, harnessed to composers' innovatory practices; performers too are increasingly curating programmes for specific spaces. Might one ultimately imagine a situation in which the traditional concert hall becomes a museum for old 'masters'? In any event, there has been a recent move towards heightened awareness of space, not least as an extension of one's own musical sound.

Building(s) for the future: Royal College of Music in context

Conservatoires are often considered to be hubs of creativity, but what is it about their physical (and, more recently, virtual) spaces that shape the creative interactions in these learning environments? As might be deduced from the rich history of buildings and music, the physical spaces that conservatoire musicians inhabit can be hugely influential in terms of the learning experience. Indeed, for many music students, the conservatoire is a second home. For as many as eight years, they will spend significant portions of their time there, practising, performing, and growing as artists. This is a very different relationship compared with the experience of a typical university student. Specialist facilities play an important part in supporting student musicians; furthermore, the very architecture of any conservatoire brings a certain cultural symbolism that is indirectly reflected in daily life. More recently, increased online teaching and performance have impacted radically on traditional interactions. The potential and limitations of remote teaching, auditions, and assessments were subject to greater scrutiny than ever in the context of the 2020 pandemic. The acknowledged benefits of in-person auditions overseas are now increasingly considered in the context of obligations relating to climate change. It is an important challenge to optimise physical space for tomorrow's musical learning while imagining what the relationship between embodied, physical, and virtual spaces might look like for artists of the future. Beginning in 2022, the London virtual concert residency *ABBA Voyage* brought those icons of pop culture back to life via digital recreations of their younger selves. Critics declared the experience unreal but thrilling. Does the generation of digital avatars (in this instance reflecting five years of technological development) herald the possibility of extraordinary performances of classical repertory without a single musician being present?

A conservatoire must accommodate hundreds of students finessing their individual technique, while providing high-quality performance spaces as well as study areas and hubs of experimentation and innovation. Even a lightning review of such institutions around the world reveals a huge variety of architectural and acoustic environments. Provision within London alone provides ample evidence. The Guildhall School of Music and Drama (founded in 1880) moved to its present purpose-built premises in the heart of the City of London's Barbican Centre in 1977; the building itself is very much of its time, its architecture showing the influence of the contemporary brutalist style. In contrast, Trinity Laban Conservatoire of Music and Dance has since 2001 occupied accommodation within the Old Royal Naval College at Greenwich, originally built between 1696 and 1712 as the Royal Hospital for Seamen. However picturesque, the accommodation it provides for music has manifold limitations. Royal Birmingham Conservatoire promoted its 2017 building as a perfect fusion of traditional and contemporary, with audio and digital infrastructure reflective of twenty-first-century creative life, facilitating new ways of teaching, learning, and practising. One might note in passing that those conservatoires housed in very traditional buildings face an increasing pressure to adapt to modern needs, a challenging task.

Beyond the UK, Yong Siew Toh Conservatory of Music in Singapore (founded 2003, completed 2006) has a modern design, whose concept focuses on the main theme of light, as well as acoustics and music. The architects took the opportunity to design spaces and rooms that have non-parallel opposing walls, with the aim of obviating disruptive flutter echoes and bestowing each space with its own unique acoustic character. In terms of modernity, a global competitor to Birmingham or Singapore is the Royal College of Music in Stockholm (2016), whose institutional origins date back as far as 1771. The new composition of the campus interweaves old and new buildings, again with an emphasis on acoustic versatility and isolation, as well as the inclusion of public spaces. Even more recently, the new building (Amare) at the Royal Conservatoire The Hague (2021) houses culture, meetings, education, and events in four large theatre and concert halls and a host of smaller spaces. Students benefit from the residencies of a professional orchestra and dance theatre, within which collaborations can be made and connections forged. Acoustic isolation is an important feature of the main spaces.[14]

Little more than a decade after its foundation, London's RCM moved into its present purpose-built home in 1894, a magnificent building designed by Sir Arthur Blomfield that reflects Victorian society in several important respects. There was little provision for social networking within the building, even after the Concert Hall was added in 1901. On the other hand, the proximity of the Royal Albert Hall, Royal College of Art, Imperial College London, and the Natural History, Science, and Victoria and Albert Museums serves to mitigate some of potential limitations of study at a specialist monotechnic institution. A significant later addition to the RCM site took place in the 1980s. At the beginning of that decade, the Casson Conder Partnership undertook a study of the condition and uses of the fabric of the College.[15] From the list of identified priorities, came a proposal for a new opera theatre. Consultants and specialists were drafted onto the Steering Committee, interviews were held with eminent musicians, and visits made to commercial opera houses and other conservatoires. The aim was to establish the essential criteria and requirements for the ideal spatial relationship between singer, conductor, and orchestra; the benefits of backstage facilities; and so on. The Committee laid special emphasis on the musical qualities of the auditorium, with the acoustics of the space a prime consideration. The shape and form of the auditorium were governed by acoustic demands – particularly, the need for a theatre with a distinctive reverberation time – approximately 1.1 seconds in performance conditions and 1.3 seconds without audience. Curved auditorium galleries, with solid and massive enclosing walls, would contribute to the diffusion of sound:

> Lime has been incorporated in the finishes of the auditorium, and a soft 'floated' surface has been used, with goat hair beaten in, in the traditional manner. The purpose of this is to create a better reverberation characteristic than would be achieved using a thin-walled structure and a hard wall plaster. Although carpeting is provided in the stalls and dress circles, all surfaces have been kept fairly tough and hard, to keep the reverberation period high.[16]

Over a quarter of a century later, the architect John Simpson was commissioned to add to the site, as part of what became known as the More Music project. He noted that the original campus had been built well and followed a coherent strategy, using a clear hierarchy between the public areas and the private teaching rooms. But over the years, access and circulation had gradually become more of a challenge because of surrounding buildings, as well as accretions to the site that were added in the 1960s and 1970s. Simpson aimed to identify the RCM's main architectural assets to evolve a scheme that used the heritage and traditions of the place to create an environment which is architecturally harmonious and timeless, with a balance between outdoor and indoor facilities. His declared aspiration was to make the campus an inspirational whole, where old and new blend seamlessly, to attract those who love music and to allow members of the RCM to realise their full potential.

More Music: Reimagining the Royal College of Music was an associated campaign that extended for the best part of a decade from 2012 (see also Chapter 5). The building element was literally a reimagining of the College in which everyone was to be actively welcomed through the doors; this significant change to a combination of student-facing and public-facing areas is more generally a defining feature of today's conservatoire. A variety of spaces in different combinations would accommodate the needs of multiple users – rooms large and small with single, double, and triple height. Step-free access and institutional welcome had not been a priority in the Victorian era but are now a priority for all public institutions. For a conservatoire, the handling and moving of large musical instruments are further considerations. In addition, the RCM has important Collections – both of manuscripts and instruments – which in prior times had not been showcased to optimal effect. Last, the reprovisioning of outdoor space would mitigate any feeling of oppression from an intensively used internal environment.

Acoustic properties are an important element in any building, especially where there is a demand for the flexibility of use and new models of performance. The same performance space may need to be used as a recital hall, orchestral rehearsal room, and recording studio. Adjustable sidewall panels are one solution to provide a very wide range of variability of sound reflection, diffusion, and absorption. Absorptive acoustic drapes in the upper part of the room can be supplemented by suspended reflectors, which at the RCM have already proved successful in the main Amaryllis Fleming Concert Hall, which was extensively refurbished (and soundproofed) in 2008–2009. Its distinctive ambience retains some alignment with the great civic halls of the nineteenth century, offering a rare immediacy of sound that encourages close audience engagement.

As outlined in other chapters within this book, future-proofing of conservatoire spaces is clearly an important agenda, which was given a major impulse by the COVID-19 pandemic. Investment in the physical environment must now be matched by a commitment to a vibrant and interactive virtual RCM. Recording studios, streaming, and remote masterclasses with other schools around the world are already a central part of the student experience; in a digital environment, performances, research, and special collections can be made available to a much richer cross-section of stakeholders. The hardware surrounding such ambition ranges from well-equipped control rooms, access terminals, and reliable wireless connectivity. Expectations of sound insulation have radically increased since the RCM's Concert Hall was built. New performance spaces incorporate a surrounding shell, within which each is constructed as a floating box. The associated control rooms are critical listening environments, requiring low services noise, good sound insulation, and considered acoustics. A new Digital Innovation Lab comprises a state-of-the-art recording and mixing suite, equipped with a Dolby Atmos 7.4.1 Genelec monitoring system; Avid S6 control surface; Apple Mac Mini workstation; and Blackmagic video switching, monitoring, and broadcast equipment. Cutting-edge digital technology complements the RCM's profile as guardian of a priceless musical heritage, underpinning an ambition to lead, as well as reflect, musical life in the twenty-first century.

Although many challenges facing the conservatoire sector have remained constant over more than two centuries, the threat of climate change has recently received unprecedented attention as one of the greatest challenges facing the world today. As a specialist higher education institution, the RCM aims to be a centre of excellence in environmental management and always to promote the best practices in the sector. On a day-to-day basis, many of the RCM's stakeholders remain unaware of the underlying agenda or even of the effort involved to improve the situation within an old building. Governments all over the world have pledged their commitment to tackle climate change, and the UK has committed to legally binding targets. Unsurprisingly, current generations of students are taking a keen interest in this investment in their future well-being. The RCM is fortunate to inhabit purpose-built facilities, but the main building offers some challenges. Carbon emissions from gas use and electricity are a natural target for reduction, and radical progress has been made, although the RCM's carbon footprint is in fact dominated by indirect emissions from sources including procurement, business travel, staff and student commuting, investments, water use, and waste. Indeed, procurement emissions contribute the vast majority of the total, dominated by construction and purchased goods and services. The RCM is working towards a target of net zero carbon.

Building online communities

Can one extend the strong essence of physical space into the virtual sphere? The COVID-19 pandemic of 2020 was an important catalyst in propelling many arts organisations to embrace new opportunities. It also highlighted the importance of buildings for our activities, whether for access to instruments, performance spaces, or for rehearsals. Indeed, what is a conservatoire without its physical spaces? How does an institution migrate online? What does it mean to be part of an online community, and can this ever replace the immediacy of an in-person experience? Traditionally, community might be defined as a group of people living in one particular area. More broadly, it could refer to a group of people who are considered a unit because of their common interests, social group, or nationality. The term is used to convey the idea of caring; the phrase 'there is a real sense of community' is often heard as a positive affirmation. Online, perhaps a true definition is more elusive. Would one treat those in your online community in the same way as a physical neighbour? Is it indeed a possibility? These are of course big questions that are applicable beyond the confines of the musical environment.

The online experience offers participants choice and the power to determine their level of engagement. Some might outwardly engage regularly and visibly demonstrate that they feel connected to an institution or to other members of the community. Others might wish to remain anonymous, silent 'lurkers' whose opinions will never be known. At the end of an online concert, the anonymous listener might press the clapping-hands emoji to signal appreciation before quietly logging off; but is this more personal, meditative experience an adequate alternative to being among a live audience, with its pre-concert chatter and eruption of applause as the final notes are struck? Does the digital experience really foster community? The answer is positive only if an organisation is honest about its values, speaks in an authentic voice, and is audience-/person- rather than institution-centric.

The RCM has endeavoured to build a flourishing community and over the last decade has continued to strengthen its digital communications, which have grown to incorporate the full spectrum of available affordances. E-newsletters and the website arguably allow the strongest experience, as both are data-rich platforms that are truly owned by the institution. Popular social media platforms have a part to play, too. In each case, content, curation, and conversation are key. But only when obliged to pivot activities to online during the pandemic did many at the RCM appreciate the true extent of its online reach. A creative campaign across social media channels revealed global engagement and provided the much-needed support during such a challenging time.

Institutions often struggle with a robust audience-centred approach and are hesitant to relinquish the status quo. One might argue that for too long, the classical music world has talked down to audiences, both existing and new. We are experts in announcing our news from the top and telling people what they should know, without developing an ability to promote the benefits of the experience. Engaging with new audiences requires the marketeer to help inspire curiosity; only messaging that resonates on a deeper, more personal level will entice new people to experience this potentially life-changing art form. Rather than telling people what they should know we might instead show them what they might *feel*.

Organisations must be clear about their values, formulate a compelling mission that communicates them, and still resonate with the target audience. In our time-pressured society, helping digital followers quickly get a sense of who we are, what we stand for, and what they can expect in engaging with us, all serve to make the digital offer as real as possible. For example, at the RCM, our communication strategy is to aim to be authentic, to engage with those who take the time to reach out to us, and to encourage people to leave comments to share how a performance made them feel. We hope that this allows us to humanise, personalise, and to be wholly present for our community. At the time of writing, the format of most of the RCM's internet traffic is video – and, as the amount of content increases, the focus must remain on quality. RCM has actively pursued a strategy that produces and disseminates high-quality, wide-ranging content on YouTube, all carefully curated and intended to inspire viewers and bring them closer to the College experience. A major further aspiration is to develop the sense of connection that will keep viewers returning, not just for the content, but because they are connected to the community itself, sometimes as an initial step to more regular interaction.

While the digital community has its limitations, recent exigencies have shown that it does have the power to reach across the globe and bring together those with common interests. For organisations (not least, conservatoires), the challenge is to engage with these groups in a convincing way that helps to elevate and create advocates for the brand. Comparisons of in-person with digital are largely unproductive, since the two must work together in the new hybrid world, which functions way beyond the traditional confines of bricks and mortar.

- Key take-away 1: the acoustical and physical dimensions of a space can have a significant effect on the musical experience of both performers and audiences.
- Key take-away 2: until the late nineteenth century, little was understood about the principle of room acoustics; ongoing research is enhancing the understanding of room acoustics by investigating auralisation, spatial sound reproduction, binaural technology, and novel objective and subjective evaluation methods.

- Key take-away 3: the challenges and opportunities of online communities are in a constant state of development. Migration online offers the possibility of global reach; yet, personal interaction is likely to remain a vital element of the communication and power of music.

Bibliography

Anderson, Emily. *The Letters of Mozart and His Family: Chronologically Arranged, Translated and Edited with an Introduction, Notes and Indexes*. London: Palgrave Macmillan UK, 1997. https://doi.org/10.1007/978-1-349-10654-7.

Beranek, Leo. *Music, Acoustics and Architecture*. New York: Wiley, 1962.

Brooks, Jeanice, Matthew Stephens, and Wiebke Thormählen, eds. *Sound Heritage: Making Music Matter in Historic Houses*. *Routledge Research in Music Series*. London: Routledge, 2022. https://doi.org/10.4324/9780429281327.

Dart, Thurston. *The Interpretation of Music*. Watford: Brendon & Son, 1954.

Forsyth, Michael. *Buildings for Music: The Architect, the Musician, and the Listener from the 17th Century to the Present Day*. Cambridge, MA: MIT Press, 1985.

Lachenmayr, Winfried, Nils Meyer-Kahlen, Otavio Colella Gomes, Antti Kuusinen, and Tapio Lokki. 'Chamber music hall acoustics: Measurements and perceptual differences'. *The Journal of the Acoustical Society of America* 154, 1 (2023): 388–400. https://doi.org/10.1121/10.0020066.

Parrott, Andrew. *The Pursuit of Musick: Musical Life in Original Writings & Art: c1200–1770*. 1st ed. London: Taverner, 2022.

Poulin, Pamela L. 'A view of eighteenth-century musical life and training: Anton Stadler's "Musick plan"'. *Music and Letters* 71, no. 2 (1990): 215–24. https://doi.org/10.1093/ml/71.2.215.

Ramsay, David. 'Constructing the Britten Opera theatre'. *RCM Magazine*, 1987, 74–82.

Rink, John, ed. *Musical Performance: A Guide to Understanding*. Cambridge; New York: Cambridge University Press, 2002.

PERSPECTIVE: CHAPTER 13

Lucy Noble

Introduction

The foregoing chapter reveals many historical issues relating to the impact of physical and virtual spaces on musical events. For me, the contemplation of such matters could not be more timely. Having worked at the Royal Albert Hall for 22 years, culminating in the position of inaugural Artistic Director, I have now moved to new pastures, recently starting at the Anschutz Entertainment Group (AEG), also as their first Artistic Director. AEG is known among other things for its ownership and management of venues, alongside the promotion of concerts. I have been recruited in this new position to expand their repertoire and broaden their horizons outside the world of rock and pop. In their own words, 'orchestras and classical music scare them'. It is a whole new world for me, as it is for them. I am hopeful that I can influence them and others to think differently about classical music, and I intend to prove that it can be interwoven into everything we do. I am writing this at the Royal College of Music (RCM), where I studied in the late nineties, and I am here today because my 12-year-old daughter attends the Junior Department. There could be no better place or time to consider my thoughts on this topic. The preservation and presentation of classical and orchestral music are something I feel passionately about – but preservation doesn't mean keeping it in a museum but rather finding new ways to protect it as we move forward.

Perspectives

My personal ambition in the realm of classical and orchestral music is to bring it back to all, with integrity. I have witnessed the decline in ticket sales for classical music in recent years at the Royal Albert Hall. It is a challenging time, and most organisations, whether they be orchestras or concert halls, would be the first to say that they have also been impacted. This has become particularly apparent since the COVID-19 pandemic.

Recalling the wonderful venues all around the world and their glorious acoustics conjures up images of great resonance. It is all too easy to remember the surroundings rather

DOI: 10.4324/9781003281573-29

than the music. I recall a time travelling with a friend to Tuscany. He was performing early music in various churches; I remember the journey, the setting, and the lovely food and wine – yet, I don't remember the repertoire apart from the fact that it was Baroque music. There's another moment that comes to mind, when I was a student and was invited to play in a private house in the New Forest. We drove through thick fog to get there – we couldn't see more than a metre ahead of us with the car lights on – and we arrived and played to a small group of guests in a room with the dullest acoustics you could imagine; it was hard work. Again, I can't remember what I played but can remember the surroundings, the journey, the atmosphere. I also remember my first time walking out onto the Royal Albert Hall stage – but can't remember what piece I played in the orchestra. My point is that the concert halls and the surroundings are just as important as the music, and they evoke emotions that help you connect with the performance.

All that said, sadly, we can't afford to be choosy in this current climate. The notion of performing in venues that are suited to a particular kind of music is aspirational, but I feel we are in a situation where the genre we love is in decline, and something must be done to save it. If the surroundings are perceived to be stuffy and traditional by those who haven't yet engaged with this genre, we could be in serious trouble. For me, this means thinking about it differently – new venues, new ways of presenting it but with the same content and repertoire at the heart. 'Classical' music hasn't always been played in the concert hall; for example, the tango and wonderful music of Astor Piazzolla were first performed in brothels.

Have we moved into a space where classical music is considered so hierarchical that it is suffocating itself? During a concert, if someone dares clap or cough at the wrong place, it can be frowned upon (I've seen it over and over again). I attended a harp competition with my daughter recently, and each competitor played two pieces. A very young girl, obviously extremely nervous, opened proceedings. I attempted to clap after her first piece, and the stares I received from around the room because this wasn't the 'done thing' reinforced my feelings around the presentation of classical music. When did classical music become so gentrified? Composers such as Mozart would be turning in their graves to think that people could no longer spontaneously react to music that was always intended to entertain. I love Yuja Wang for her fierce approach to her piano playing – knocking down those walls while wearing mini dresses and stilettos. What's not to love? Sadly, not everyone agrees with me, and she has been criticised by purists for what she wears – but it is people like her who will save this genre. Alongside this, the population at large associates an orchestra with classical music. We know that orchestras and various other ensembles can be used in many different ways to promote all styles of music. I am currently helping another music promoter to put on their first concert, which will have an orchestra accompanying a rap artist – and everyone is very excited. They just didn't know how to do it, but fortunately I could help – and it is through activities like this that we will start to bring the genre back to life – because it is also about the instruments as well as the repertoire.

I am certainly looking to where I can take orchestras to perform, and I'm looking at non-traditional platforms, thinking carefully about how I can attract new audiences to this wonderful genre. I am absolutely clear that we must communicate in a different way – the concerts will be more immersive, and respected hosts will talk to the audiences and tell them about the wonderful music and the background to the pieces rather than remaining silent. Participation will be encouraged – engagement is key.

Thinking about the future more, undoubtedly digital platforms play a significant, if not overwhelming, part in our modern day lives. Billions are constantly consuming content online and on demand. There is so much to devour that people rarely dwell in one place for any length of time. In fact, most people will watch something for 20 seconds maximum and then move onto the next vacuous meme or reel. Many of us receive our weekly reports on our phones which tell us how long we've been engaged in the digital sphere that week, and I have to say that I'm more often than not horrified at how many hours I've spent scrolling through inane content. Where does that leave us? This new kind of content is not only competing for our time but also develops an increased lack of concentration and ability to focus for any meaningful amount of time. Alongside that, many schools aren't engaging with music full stop. My children attend a primary school that has zero participation in music. They have no idea that one of their pupils attends the RCM Junior Department, despite my having attempted to tell them several times. They have no music, no interest in music, and one can only assume they therefore place no value on music. It is very concerning, and this is being seen across the country and well beyond the UK.

However, there are positives to the digital world; for example, I have recently worked with the inspirational organist and TikTok sensation, Anna Lapwood. At the Royal Albert Hall, I made her an Associate Artist, as we endeavoured to celebrate our astonishing organ and to bring it to new audiences – and I can honestly say it was a huge success. The Hall became Anna's second home, and she comes in by night to rehearse on the organ (because of the busy schedule of performances). She documented every step on social media, some short films from the Hall getting millions of views at a time. Suddenly, we were being noticed by a whole raft of new people and everyone was talking about it. At the heart of it, Anna is an amazingly accomplished musician and that is of course key. Get those two things right, and we're back on track.

Digital recordings of music are fabulous, and you hear everything with clarity and perfection – but more often than not, I do enjoy listening to an analogue recording (preferably on vinyl) knowing that it has probably been recorded in one take with no digital influences or tweaking afterwards. It feels more real, and you feel more connected; it feels special.

Summary

I am in a privileged position. I have the knowledge and know-how when it comes to classical music and presenting concerts. Alongside that, I am now working in a supportive organisation which has not previously engaged with this area, who are willing to back me to bring it back to the forefront. I will seize this opportunity with both hands and do everything I can to sustain classical music both in the UK and further afield. My initial concert will be an orchestral performance to open the famous British Summer Time Hyde Park Festival. It is the first time classical music will be a part of this festival. It will be packaged differently, and we will have some fun at the same time – everyone will be welcome! This will not and cannot of course detract from the music which will always remain at the heart, but if you'd like to clap in between movements, I'm okay with that (shock; horror!). Never must we condescend to those who haven't yet had the pleasure of interacting with this genre, and we must understand that they may listen and consume and react differently from those of us who are deemed experts – that's also okay, and we will also perform this kind of music in any place we feel fit. The future is optimistic and extremely exciting!

Chapter Notes

1 Poulin, 'A view of eighteenth-century musical life and training', 220.
2 Anderson, *The Letters of Mozart and His Family*, 558.
3 Forsyth, *Buildings for Music*, 229.
4 Dart, *The Interpretation of Music*, 56–57.
5 Parrott, *The Pursuit of Musick*, 459–63.
6 Forsyth, *Buildings for Music*, 3.
7 See Rink, *Musical Performance*, 190, where Eric Clarke notes that in the antiphonal music of Andrea Gabrieli or in Karl Stockhausen's spatially distributed music such as *Gruppen*, the 'geometry' of the space is exceptionally important as a component of the music's structure.
8 See Beranek, *Music, Acoustics and Architecture*, 11:

> Good and bad halls exist in every age, and good and bad halls have probably been built in every period. It is more than likely that the old halls that are still standing are among the best that were built. Very few halls that compared badly with their contemporaries are still with us.

9 As Forsyth, *Buildings for Music*, 129 suggests: 'The kinship that had in previous centuries existed between nondramatic music and its visual-stylistic context became in the nineteenth century somewhat tenuous.' Certain aspects of programme music (Berlioz, Liszt, Richard Strauss) transcend the concert hall, making any attempt at a fusion of aural and visual styles superfluous.
10 The excellence of Boston Symphony Hall was initially ascribed to its optimal reverberation time. Yet, it also became clear that the spatial impression in a concert hall is also of great importance, that is, the awareness of the direction of arrival of sound in each ear. The impression of space depends on sound reflections arriving from the sides rather than the ceiling overhead. Once understood spatial factors were to have an important influence on twentieth-century design.
11 As Forsyth observes in *Buildings for Music*, 259, such an approach suits the pungent, percussive music of Stravinsky and his contemporaries.
12 See https://research.aalto.fi/fi/persons/tapio-lokki/publications/. For example Lachenmayr et al., 'Chamber music hall acoustics'.
13 Forsyth, *Buildings for Music*, 298.
14 As the website suggests,

> The architecture of the Amare building is impressive and unique. The columns on the outside, which look like tuning forks, have an important function: they are the foundation of the building. The foundation has been deliberately placed on the outside, so that the number of vertical connections in the building is kept to a minimum. This prevents noise travelling between the different halls.
> www.noahh.nl.

15 Ramsay, 'Constructing the Britten Opera theatre', 74–82.
16 Ramsay, 'Constructing the Britten Opera theatre', 82.

14

TOWARDS THE CIVIC CONSERVATOIRE

Dave Camlin, Hayley Clements, and Rosie Perkins

Introduction

This chapter posits that a civic conservatoire must incorporate a civic community. This requires dialogue across the institution that encourages questioning and critical interrogation of what we do, why we do it, and hence what our relevance and function are in society. Such concerns are important not only to conservatoires but also to higher education more broadly. The Civic University Commission of 2018/2019, for example, asked 'what it means to be a "civic university"',[1] listing such activities as understanding and working with local populations, understanding ourselves as institutions, working with other local organisations, and having a clear set of priorities.[2] To do so necessitates thinking beyond the 'rational community'[3] or, in other words, the 'common language and logic'[4] of the conservatoire. Thinking beyond the rational community is not necessarily straightforward, though, as the conservatoire's population is heavily invested in the reproduction and conservation of its 'rational' and often passionately held practices. However, we argue that what we call a 'dialogic' approach can help the move towards civic responsibility and a civic conservatoire. Who is involved in such a dialogue – literally who gets to speak and be heard – is a crucial factor in advancing the notion of a civic conservatoire. Attending to and amplifying quieter and hidden voices within and around the conservatoire – the perspectives of support and facilities staff, for example, as well as the students in general and the perspectives of those in the local community who might view the conservatoire as 'not for the likes of me' – can offer valuable insights into how such civic dialogue might be broadened. In this chapter, we explore what a 'dialogic' approach could offer the conservatoire and how to uncover hidden voices, and provide three examples of work that might (constructively) disturb the conservatoire's rational community. We conclude with some critical reflections on infrastructures to support the civic conservatoire.

Dialogue in the civic conservatoire

What do we mean by a 'dialogic' approach to civic responsibility? This could mean several things but centres on considering dialogue as a form of pedagogy. In educational terms, a

DOI: 10.4324/9781003281573-30

dialogical approach might simply imply that some discussion of the subject is necessary to 'mediate the cognitive and cultural spaces between . . . teacher and learner'.[5] In other words, it means using dialogue and discussion as a pedagogical tool to foster understanding. However, dialogic approaches can also be about more than 'education *through* dialogue', and also 'education *for* dialogue',[6] by which is meant preparing students to participate in a world of plurality and difference. Dialogue in this sense is about engaging with – or even 'becoming-with'[7] – the wider world and dealing with the contradictions that ensue when one encounters difference or resistance to one's expectations or assumptions. In pedagogical terms, a dialogic attitude represents a curiosity about the perspective of the 'other' and a willingness to account for that perspective in the development of a curriculum and/or pedagogy.

The conservatoire is perhaps less well-disposed to voices that do not contribute to or recreate its rational discourse, steeped as it is in traditions that require conformity to particular musical standards: 'untune that string, and, hark, what discord follows!'[8] In general, students undergo rigorous training to ensure that they are able to communicate musically in ways that are consistent with the rational discourse of well-established musical traditions. Hence, learning to hear utterances (musical or otherwise) that deviate from such rational discourse – without judging them by the standards implicit in that discourse – is not an easy undertaking. However, it is through such dialogic processes – learning to attend to the utterances of another and articulating one's own 'truth' in response[9] – that we come into a richer relationship with a world of plurality and begin to examine critically not just what we do but also *why* we do what we do. This process of self-knowledge and self-actualisation through dialogue could lie at the heart of educating musicians to be critically reflective. It allows students to address complex questions about how to be authentically themselves in different situations, with different people. Through dialogue, asking ourselves *'what is music for me?'* encourages us to also ask *'what is music for other people?'* and therefore naturally leads us to consider the more complex issue of what role musicians and conservatoires play in society, and what responsibilities come with such a role.

Dialogic approaches to educating musicians are motivated by an ethical intention to give students the best possible start in their professional careers, supporting them to think about and question what they do and why, to facilitate or catalyse their development as unique musical individuals (see also Chapter 10). Such approaches also have potential benefit to the institution of the conservatoire but only when there are clear ways for insights that students develop in their encounters with less familiar musical practices – in educational, community, and health settings, for example – to become part of a wider discourse. When students engage in practices other than those central to the reproduction of the conservatoire's own rational community, they potentially become the 'civic ear' of the conservatoire, attending to the ways in which music comes to mean something in the wider society beyond the conservatoire's boundaries. It is therefore incumbent upon the institution not just to provide students with the necessary tools and skills to make sense of the kinds of musical experiences they may have outside of the rational community of the conservatoire, but also to develop feedback systems that allow for those experiences and insights to flow back into the conservatoire, influencing its own civic future. Such dialogues are always emergent, never finished. There are always new and/or different voices to be attended to, and for the conservatoire to be a truly civic institution, these new voices need to be welcomed, amplified, accounted for, and integrated within its discourse, as part of an ongoing and ever-evolving polyphony.

Uncovering hidden voices in the civic conservatoire

How, then, do new, quiet, dissenting, or hidden voices get heard? We have hinted above that one place we can look is to our students. Conservatoire students are at the chalk face of the conservatoire's civic responsibilities through their encounters with different parts of the wider community, whether through their performances, compositions, research, teaching, or work in community or health settings. During these encounters, they undoubtedly develop new insights, but it is not always clear whether or how these insights align with, and can shape and alter, the norms within the conservatoire. Developing ways to amplify the student voice is one way of broadening dialogue within the conservatoire by encouraging students' questioning about aspects of rational discourse that might otherwise be taken for granted. Indeed, we recognise that some students are deeply embedded in the rational discourse of the conservatoire. Where are the opportunities to question this or expand it? Where are there spaces to reflect on the *purpose* of music in a conservatoire? How do students know there are other opportunities to develop as human beings with musical skills? Rather than encouraging students to focus their attention *exclusively* on musical and spoken/written utterances that conform with the expectations of the rational community, we suggest that through their studies – if they are supported to find ways to develop a greater awareness of the questions, uncertainties, ambiguities, tensions, and discomfort that characterise professional practice – they will benefit from such an expanded awareness. This means giving students voice, without the fear of judgement, censorship, or disapproval. After all, expressing heterodox views might be an effective way of identifying oneself as existing outside of the rational discourse of the conservatoire, with all the concomitant loss of cultural and social capital that such a position might entail.

Anecdotally, undergraduate students sometimes develop such critical insights into their conservatoire experiences only once they have graduated and are no longer part of the rational community in quite the same way. However, such insights can be nascent during their undergraduate studies but often unexpressed or unexplored, because of the constraints on rational discourse noted above.[10] The question then becomes how to make it easier for these critical insights to be expressed and explored as part of their conservatoire education, rather than after they have finished. A potential way of supporting this is through facilitating students' encounters with more participatory musical traditions,[11] whose practices might initially seem to be unfamiliar or even strange to musicians steeped in the aesthetic traditions of the conservatoire. Students (and teachers) working with different materials – such as musical *participants* as well as different and/or unfamiliar musical instruments and musical works – introduce a different set of musical practices to the conservatoire that can ultimately help align its future with more sustainable and inclusive ways. In the following section, we introduce some recent examples of initiatives that may constructively 'disturb' the rational discourse, allowing different voices and practices to emerge in support of the development of a civic conservatoire.

Constructively disturbing the rational discourse of the conservatoire

Bringing the community into the conservatoire

The civic conservatoire has a direct responsibility to shape a future musical landscape that is both inclusive and diverse. *Sparks Juniors* is an example of the Royal College of Music

(RCM) London's commitment to this agenda and offers an access pathway for young people (and their families) from under-represented groups.[12] Launched in October 2009, the programme offers a bespoke learning experience for a cohort of up to ten participants per year, who access half a day per week of learning as part of the RCM Junior Department (RCMJD).[13] RCMJD runs on Saturdays during term time, offering one-to-one lessons, chamber music, orchestra, choir and, musicianship to talented young musicians, with the aim of preparing them for happy, successful, healthy, and entrepreneurial musical lives. Participants for *Sparks Juniors* are recruited from local schools with higher-than-average levels of free school meals and with whom the RCM's Learning and Participation team have long-term relationships. The recruitment process is informed by creating a picture of the child's musical interest in school, home support network, and musical potential shown through informal assessment workshops. All participants must also fulfil at least one of the access criteria.[14]

The *Sparks Juniors* programme is intended to go beyond the opportunity to widen access to the RCM, directly positioning a diverse community population at the heart of the RCMJD offer, developing the foundations for a truly civic conservatoire. The culture is rich, fostering dialogical models of knowledge exchange across multiple areas of practice – delivery, monitoring and assessment, evaluation – and, importantly, it has started to embed a socio-ecological approach to diversifying the RCM and our ways of thinking around course provision and access. As illustrated in Figure 14.1, by putting the individual learner at the starting point of the process, the conservatoire aims to grow the exchange of knowledge ecologically (rather than in a top-down fashion). Individual participants feed in knowledge

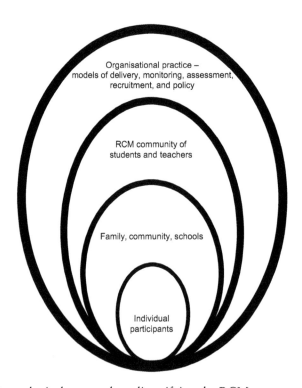

FIGURE 14.1   A socio-ecological approach to diversifying the RCM.

BOX 14.1 *SPARKS JUNIORS* PARENT TESTIMONIALS

Thank you for this amazing opportunity for my daughter! We all love the enthusiasm that the teachers bring each week, we feel very lucky to be taking part. All the sessions have been well pre-pared and delivered to a high standard. I cannot express how grateful I'm as a parent to see the development of [my daughter].

B has grown and learnt so much. This programme inspires her and allows her to learn and grow not only as a musician but in herself. The music learning is brilliant with all teachers. This is a com-mitment that we did not take on lightly and we are committed as a family for B to succeed as much as possible. We are so thankful for B to be able to have this experience and fantastic opportunity that we happily prioritise our lives around it.

It has been an awesome experience and we are grateful and glad to be able to have this chance of being a part of the RCM. Thank you and we look forward to the future.

---

around their family, community, and education, which in turn provides a fuller picture to inform the RCM environment of learners. Only at this point can inclusive organisational processes, including delivery and assessment, be successfully developed.

The core focus of *Sparks Juniors* is to develop foundational-stage musical training while building confidence and community with the participants and their family members. The children have three to four hours of weekly tuition including group Dalcroze exploring expression and musical feeling, group musicianship with family members laying the build-ing blocks of theoretical learning, an individual instrumental lesson, and mixed ensemble. Importantly, reflection sessions are timetabled into the year in the Spring and Summer terms to inform teacher planning and encourage a culture of sharing and creating an environ-ment where learning is a dialogue between all parties. This provides essential interpersonal context and allows culture, community, and experience to flourish. Parent testimonials for *Sparks Juniors* are shown in Box 14.1, demonstrating the immersion into the conservatoire environment that facilitates the development and inclusion of the young people and their families taking part.

A civic conservatoire centres around a sense of belonging, and *Sparks Juniors* brings a space for musicians of different levels to share and learn, including RCM undergraduate and postgraduate students as mentors and role models. Through focusing on pathways to inclusion, dialogue, and opportunities for (musical) development, *Sparks Juniors* provides an example of how the conservatoire can celebrate diversity and learn how to be truly inclu-sive in its policy and practice.

Bringing the conservatoire into the community

Most professional musicians are likely to teach music as part of a portfolio career,[15] and hence developing the skills and aptitudes for teaching is increasingly an essential part of the undergraduate music curriculum. The undergraduate music education modules at the RCM are about preparing and supporting students to engage in the musical development of others, to reflect critically on the practices and processes of doing so, and thereby to develop not just their own music education capabilities but also a more holistic understanding of both the general value of music in society and of themselves as musicians. All undergraduate students undertake modules in music leadership where they have opportunities to observe and reflect critically on a wide range of music education practices, from music classrooms and instrumental studios to community and healthcare settings. They have the opportunity to develop their own capabilities as music educators in these diverse settings, working alongside more experienced practitioners, and to reflect critically on these experiences in order to develop and strengthen their own practice.

For many of them, these encounters with a diverse range of music education practices help them to understand not just the broader value that music has in wider society but crucially, also develop insights into their own musical development, ambitions, and purpose *as* musicians. A recent study of a small group of students found that engaging in participatory musical practices helped them to 'develop a more holistic understanding of music's power' and to '"think differently" about music and what it "means" from the perspective of participation'.[16] This echoes previous research, which found that such engagement, including in community settings, supports students to 'see the power of music more directly and to gain a stronger perception of what it means to be a musician, both individually and collectively'[17] (see also Chapter 10). Starting a career as a musician with a more holistic understanding of what music is and what music does for people in broader society might be considered a form of professional 'career creativity',[18] a philosophical and psychological understanding of the complex ways in which music and, more importantly, *being musical* come to 'mean' something to people in their everyday lives.

In addition to modules delivered in music education, RCM undergraduate students can access a module focused on *musical care*; how music can provide care for people throughout their lives, responding to people's health, education, and social needs.[19] Delivered through practice sharing, seminars, and observational visits, students are supported to reflect critically on their own musical care experiences and their future potential work in musical care. Through curricula such as this, the idea is that students are introduced to content that flexes and expands the ideas of what it means to train as a musician at a conservatoire and are encouraged and supported to try new practices and to reflect on 'who they are' as a musician. We know that, for some students, experiences such as these will be transformative,[20] potentially paving the way for career decisions that will prioritise ways of making and sharing music that are reflective, socially aware, and with a strong sense of civic responsibility.[21]

Building the civic conservatoire through new programmes

A third way in which a dialogic community can be developed is through reflecting on and changing the material that students (and staff) engage with via new programmes. In 2011, the RCM launched its MSc (Master of Science) in Performance Science programme,[22] which was the first significant departure from the more traditional performance- and composition-based provision. The MSc, hosted by the Centre for Performance Science,[23] equips students with a scientific understanding of how music is created, learnt, performed, and perceived. It explicitly puts science within the conservatoire, using scientific methods to encourage students to reflect on and critique the existing knowledge and to ask and answer questions related to performance psychology, performance education, performers' health, and the role of the arts in health and well-being. Students typically enter the MSc programme with questions that have arisen from real-world contexts, perhaps as performers, educators, and/or arts administrators. Through the programme, they develop the contextual knowledge and research skills to facilitate answers to these questions, working collaboratively within an interdisciplinary context that includes students of many different ages and from a range of disciplines including music, education, performing arts, health, and natural sciences. Evaluation of the programme indicated that students embark on the MSc in order to 'engage in processes of self-reflection and questioning', learning 'new study and research skills as well as applied content knowledge that enable reflexivity'.[24] Situating this approach within a conservatoire not only diversifies the student body – entry is based on suitability for a research-led academic programme based on critical enquiry, rather than practical music skills – but it also provides a forum where a constructive scrutiny of music and its place in society is fostered, encouraged, and supported.

In 2018, the RCM also extended its postgraduate provision with its first Master's programmes in music education, aimed at musicians with previous experience as music educators in the broadest sense, as a way for them to deepen their professional capabilities through critical reflection and also to develop their research capabilities. These postgraduate programmes provide a valuable context for 'musicians who think of themselves also as teachers'[25] to interrogate their practice critically – to turn it into a 'praxis' through the fusing of theory and practice[26] – in order to refine it and thereby make more of a difference in the world through it. Using dialogic approaches, students explore some of the philosophical and practical tenets of their own professional situation, developing research skills in order to examine their own educational practice more critically. Questioning assumptions, and addressing questions which arise directly from practice, their enquiries also therefore represent a critical perspective on the rational community of the conservatoire, both broadening and deepening its rational discourse.

Infrastructures to support the civic conservatoire

A key question is how the sorts of practices illustrated above make their way (or not) back into the rational discourse of the conservatoire. The insights that students develop through such encounters can be profound, but unless there are feedback mechanisms within the conservatoire to make sense of these experiences, there is a risk that such pockets of dialogue – of which there are many more examples – do not become part of the wider discourse of the conservatoire. Further questions therefore arise: How does the conservatoire foster a culture of sharing and dialogue that shifts the discourse? And how do such shifting discourses intersect with the conservatoire's focus on artistic excellence?

There are many possible responses to these questions. One route is to 'disturb' consciously the rational community by showcasing different types of musical practices. For example, providing opportunities for undergraduate performance students to work with students on other programmes, creating a dialogic space for knowledge exchange between people with different musical backgrounds and roles. Or by introducing prizes and scholarships that spotlight civic musical engagement, recognising the situational musical excellence[27] required to lead an effective and meaningful musical encounter in a community or health setting. Additionally, ensuring that issues of equality, diversity, and inclusion are part of the discourse of the conservatoire at every level – from policy through to delivery – is more likely to support the evolution of a culture where people are more sensitively tuned to *differences* in perspectives and experiences, rather than similarities. Finally, as noted in Chapter 6, governing bodies in conservatoires can advance their institutions by 'continuously interrogating institutional success'. Part of this can include space for dialogue around what the agendas laid forth in this chapter mean for our understandings of musical excellence (see also Chapter 4). Indeed, 'these issues are complex and difficult, but it is surely no longer sustainable to operate as if the teaching of individual musical excellence can be set apart from a broader social context'.[28]

As well as a conservatoire perspective on the local/civic community, a community perspective on the conservatoire is also required. This 'subjectification' of the conservatoire's civic community requires us to acknowledge that 'those at whom our educational efforts are directed are not to be seen as objects but as subjects in their own right; subjects of action and responsibility'.[29] It requires a mindset different from the one which positions the conservatoire at the centre of discourse, rather than as one voice within a much broader cultural dialogue. Even then, because of the nature of the rational discourse of the conservatoire, there is always a risk that this subjectification of the civic community is only ever partially accomplished – 'enough about the conservatoire, let's talk about you; what do *you* think of the conservatoire?'. When it comes to thinking about the conservatoire's civic community, moving beyond potential 'deficit models'[30] of culture takes patience, humility, and a good deal of vigilant listening to people's creative aspirations and ideas. Hence, the musicians of tomorrow – the conservatoire's civic ambassadors – need opportunities to practise these dialogic skills, and these opportunities therefore need to be threaded through the fabric of the curriculum and more generally represented in the rational discourse of the conservatoire itself.

Summary

This chapter has put forward the idea that a civic conservatoire must include a civic community, where a dialogic approach amplifies different voices and perspectives that help to advance the 'rational community'. Three examples (of the many that could have been chosen) have been given to illustrate how different dialogic initiatives can help to disturb (constructively) the rational community. Acknowledging that there is much work still to do, we conclude with three takeaways for the next steps towards a civic conservatoire:

- Key take-away 1: disturbing the rationale discourse through dialogue can facilitate critical interrogation of what conservatoires do, what our relevance and function are in society, and why. Yet, we do not know how much or what types of 'disturbing' are actually happening. A first step is to search for and champion examples, using them to develop and advance the civic conservatoire.
- Key take-away 2: the student (and, indeed, staff) body is a promising site for disturbing rational discourse to evolve conservatoire culture to be more civic-minded. Voices from diverse practices – including less orthodox and more socially engaged perspectives – need amplification to be heard and included and require supportive spaces where they can become part of a broader civic discourse within the conservatoire.

- Key take-away 3: conservatoires have an ethical responsibility to ensure that structures are in place to attend to and amplify the hidden voices of their students, teachers, and communities to foster broader dialogues about the value of music to people and society. The civic conservatoire is therefore both an internal and external responsibility. Internally, we aspire to civic communities *within* the conservatoire. Externally, we aspire for the conservatoire to contribute to civic communities *beyond* the conservatoire, playing a leading role in shaping the role of music in society.

Acknowledgements

We gratefully acknowledge our colleagues in the music education team, RCM Sparks, and the Centre for Performance Science, whose work has contributed to the ideas presented in this chapter.

Further information and reading

Camlin, David A. *Music Making and Civic Imagination*. A Holistic Philosophy. Intellect, 2023.
RCM MMusEd. www.rcm.ac.uk/mmused.
RCM MSc in Performance Science. www.rcm.ac.uk/msc.
RCM Sparks. www.rcm.ac.uk/sparks.

Bibliography

Alexander, Robin. *Essays on Pedagogy*. London; New York: Routledge, 2008.
Ascenso, Sara. *Finding Meaning in Music: The Impact of Community Engagement for Professional Musicians*. London: Royal College of Music, November 2016. https://londonmusic masters.org/wp-content/uploads/2018/04/Finding-Meaning-in-Music-an-LMM-RCM-research-project-2016.pdf.
Bennett, Dawn. *Life in the Real World: How to Make Music Graduates Employable*. Champaign, IL: Common Ground Publishing, 2012.
Bennett, Dawn, and Pam Burnard. 'Human capital career creativities for creative industries work: Lessons underpinned by Bourdieu's tools for thinking'. In *Higher Education and the Creative Economy: Beyond the Campus*, 123–42. Abingdon, Oxon: Routledge, 2016.
Biesta, Gert. 'The community of those who have nothing in common: Education and the language of responsibility'. *Interchange* 35, no. 3 (September 1, 2004): 307–24. https://doi.org/10.1007/BF02698880.
Biesta, Gert. *The Beautiful Risk of Education*. Boulder: Routledge, 2014.
Bull, Anna, and Christina Scharff. 'Classical music as genre: Hierarchies of value within freelance classical musicians' discourses'. *European Journal of Cultural Studies* 24, no. 3 (2021): 673–89. https://doi.org/10.1177/13675494211006094.
Burnard, Pamela. 'Working with Bourdieu's cultural analysis and legacy: Alignments and allegiances in developing career creativities'. In *Bourdieu and the Sociology of Music Education*, edited by Pamela Burnard, Ylva Hofvander Trulsson, and Johan Soderman. Burlington, VT; Farnham, Surrey, England: Routledge, 2015.
Camlin, David A. 'This is my truth, tell me yours: Emphasising dialogue within participatory music'. *International Journal of Community Music* 8, no. 3 (2015a): 233–57. https://doi.org/10.1386/ijcm.8.3.233_1.
Camlin, David A. 'Whose quality is it anyway? Inhabiting the creative tension between presentational and participatory music'. *Journal of Arts and Communities* 6, no. 2–3 (2015b): 99–118.
Camlin, David A. 'Mind the gap!' In *Community Music at the Boundaries*, edited by Lee Willingham, 72–95. Waterloo, ON: Wilfrid Laurier University Press, 2021. www.wlupress.wlu.ca/Books/C/Community-Music-at-the-Boundaries.

Camlin, David A. 'Encounters with participatory music'. In *The Chamber Musician in the 21st Century*, edited by Mine Dogantan-Dack, 43–71. Cambridge University; OUP, 2022. www.mdpi.com/books/pdfview/edition/5783.

Camlin, David A. *Music Making and Civic Imagination*. A Holistic Philosophy. Intellect, 2023.

Comunian, Roberta, and Abigail Gilmore, eds. *Higher Education and the Creative Economy: Beyond the Campus*. Abingdon, Oxon; New York, NY: Routledge, 2016.

Doğantan-Dack, Mine, ed. *The Chamber Musician in the Twenty-First Century*. MDPI, 2022. https://doi.org/10.3390/books978-3-03897-563-2.

Gaunt, Helena, Celia Duffy, Ana Coric, Isabel R. González Delgado, Linda Messas, Oleksandr Pryimenko, and Henrik Sveidahl. 'Musicians as "makers in society": A conceptual foundation for contemporary professional higher music education'. *Frontiers in Psychology* 12 (August 3, 2021): 713648. https://doi.org/10.3389/fpsyg.2021.713648.

Gross, Jonathan, Nick Wilson, and Anna Bull. *Towards cultural democracy*. London: Kings College, 2017. www.kcl.ac.uk/cultural/resources/reports/towards-cultural-democracy-2017-kcl.pdf.

Hadley, Steven. 'Towards cultural democracy: Promoting cultural capabilities for everyone'. *Cultural Trends* 27, no. 1 (January 2018): 52–55. https://doi.org/10.1080/09548963.2018.1415417.

Haraway, Donna J. *Staying with the Trouble (Experimental Futures): Making Kin in the Chthulucene*. Illustrated ed. Durham: Duke University Press Books, 2016.

Nelson, Robin. *Practice as Research in the Arts: Principles, Protocols, Pedagogies, Resistances*. New York: Palgrave Macmillan, 2013.

Perkins, Rosie, Lisa Aufegger, and Aaron Williamon. 'Learning through teaching: Exploring what conservatoire students learn from teaching beginner older adults'. *International Journal of Music Education* 33 (2015): 80–90.

Perkins, Rosie, and Aaron Williamon. 'Creative leadership-in-action through a conservatoire-based MSc in performance science'. In *Leadership of Pedagogy and Curriculum in Higher Music Education*, edited by Jennifer Rowley, Dawn Bennett, and Patrick K. Schmidt, 97–114. Routledge, 2019.

Renshaw, Peter. *Being – In Tune*. Guildhall School of Music & Drama and Barbican Centre, September 2013a. www.gsmd.ac.uk/fileadmin/user_upload/files/Research/Being_In-tune_report_2013.pdf.

Renshaw, Peter. *Being in Tune, a Provocation Paper: Seeking Ways of Addressing Isolation and Dislocation through Engaging in the Arts*. London: Guildhall School of Music & Drama, 2013b.

Rowley, Jennifer, Dawn Bennett, and Patrick K. Schmidt, eds. *Leadership of Pedagogy and Curriculum in Higher Music Education*. ISME Global Perspectives in Music Education Series. New York; London: Routledge, 2019.

Shakespeare, William. *Troilus and Cressida: Third Series*. Revised and 2nd ed. Edited by David Bevington. London; New Delhi; New York; Sydney: Bloomsbury Arden Shakespeare, 1609.

Spiro, Neta, and Katie Rose M. Sanfilippo, eds. *Collaborative Insights: Interdisciplinary Perspectives on Musical Care Throughout the Life Course*. Oxford University Press, 2022.

Swanwick, Keith. *Teaching Music Musically*. London; New York: Routledge, 1999.

Tregear, Peter, Geir Johansen, Harald Jørgensen, John Sloboda, Helena Tulve, and Richard Wistreich. 'Conservatoires in society: Institutional challenges and possibilities for change'. *Arts and Humanities in Higher Education* 15, no. 3–4 (2016): 276–92. https://doi.org/10.1177/1474022216647379.

Turino, Thomas. *Music as Social Life: The Politics of Participation*. Chicago: University of Chicago Press, 2008.

The UPP Foundation. *Truly Civic: Strengthening the Connection Between Universities and Their Places*. The UPP Foundation Civic University Commission, 2019. https://upp-foundation.org/wp-content/uploads/2019/02/Civic-University-Commission-Final-Report.pdf.

Wegerif, Rupert. *Dialogic: Education for the Internet Age*. Abingdon: Routledge, 2012.

Willingham, Lee, ed. *Community Music at the Boundaries*. Waterloo, Ontario, Canada: Wilfrid Laurier University Press, 2021.

PERSPECTIVE: CHAPTER 14

Brydie-Leigh Bartleet

Introduction

The valuable perspectives shared in this chapter resonate strongly with the work I have undertaken in Australia over many years. By way of introduction, I am a Professor and Australian Research Council (ARC) Future Fellow at the Creative Arts Research Institute and Queensland Conservatorium at Griffith University. I am currently working on two ARC-funded projects which have striking synergies with the ethically minded, socially oriented focus of this chapter. Our ARC Creative Change Project is examining the role community music can play in addressing entrenched social inequity, and our ARC Remedy Project is exploring music as a primary cultural determinant of health for First Nations' Peoples. Communities are the heartland of both projects, as we seek to critically explore how music can bring about positive social and cultural changes. These projects are built on many others I have undertaken over the past 20 years, which have aimed to explore the cultural, social, economic, and environmental benefits of music and the arts in First Nations' Communities; prisons; war-affected cities; areas of extreme socio-economic disadvantage; and educational and industry contexts. This research has been highly interdisciplinary, connecting music and the arts with areas as diverse as regional development, criminology and corrections, health equity, and human rights. Relatedly, as a long-standing Faculty Member of the Queensland Conservatorium Griffith University, over the years, I have been responsible for leading engagement initiatives, which have worked at the interface of the conservatoire and communities, mobilising and connecting colleagues, students, community partners, and industry stakeholders both inside and outside the university walls. My work is primarily grounded in dialogue and relationships, recognising music as a powerful force for interpersonal connection and engagement between people, cultures, communities, and institutions. The notion of a civic conservatoire has been at the heart of many of these initiatives, and it is an honour to share this response.

DOI: 10.4324/9781003281573-31

Perspectives

This chapter is vital reading for anyone working, studying, or engaging with a conservatoire. It begins with the premise that a civic conservatoire must incorporate a civic community. How that civic community is defined remains an open question, allowing readers to consider their own cultural and geographical contexts. The authors contend that this process requires dialogue across the institution in a way that encourages a critical interrogation of what we do, why we do it, and what our relevance and function within society could be. In Brink's (2018) words, these dialogues need to focus on not only what we are 'good *at*' but also what we are 'good *for*'.[31] If done well, this dialogic approach has the potential to amplify different voices and perspectives that can open up conservatoire practices to become more civically minded in their purpose/s. As the authors suggest, this can foster a culture of sharing that shifts current discourse beyond artistic excellence, positioning the conservatoire within a much broader cultural dialogue. While conceptually challenging, this chapter is eminently practical, offering three examples of Royal College of Music (RCM) programmes that illustrate how these dialogic initiatives can lead a conservatoire to become more civically aware.

The word 'Towards' in the title of this chapter is striking and challenges us reflect on the steps we need to take to become a truly engaged civic conservatoire. The authors suggest that there is still much work to do, for as Lord Kerslake suggests, not all civic engagement automatically results in a civic university. While the sorts of activities conservatoires customarily undertake as part of their engagement programmes might generate civic awareness and civic responsibility, these do not necessarily result in a truly civic conservatoire.[32] Rather, a civic conservatoire needs to have a clear strategy, rooted in analysis, which explains what, why, and how its activity adds up to a civic role.[33] As Goddard et al. (2016) explain, in the civic university 'there is no perception of a core or periphery: engagement is seen as embedded and relevant to other areas of activity'.[34] In other words, there needs to be a 'root and branch' approach where civically minded strategies and activities are holistically integrated into *all* aspects of a conservatoire's purpose and practices, rather than being seen as a peripheral concern.

In order to move closer towards being a civic conservatoire, the authors of this chapter emphasise the need for deeply relational ways of working. This includes making space for different community members with their perspectives to not only participate but also have a voice, agency, and an active role in the co-design of a conservatoire's civic activities. This requires a shift from outdated notions of one-way 'outreach' towards a much more relationally focused, reciprocal approach to participatory music-making. As the chapter suggests, this could allow conservatoires to challenge and change dominant norms and expectations and shift their ways of working. In doing so, conservatoires would be prompted to reflect on who is driving these civic activities, and on whose terms, and whether they are simply inviting select community members into their buildings to fit in with the status quo.

The chapter gives a compelling account of the vital role students play in this process, evocatively describing them as the 'civic ear' of the conservatoire. The authors see the potential that students hold for attending to the ways in which music comes to mean something in wider society beyond the conservatoire's boundaries. They suggest it is therefore incumbent upon the institution to not only provide students with the necessary tools and skills to make sense of these musical experiences but also to develop feedback systems that allow for those experiences and insights to flow back into the conservatoire, influencing its own civic future. Beyond the student body, the challenge for those of us working in conservatoires is to also consider the multifarious ways in which civic engagement might occur. Goddard (2009) argues that university leaders need to foster an institution-wide strategy for civic engagement, a strategy that reaches across teaching and research rather than being boxed off as a third stream of activity.[35] This would involve conservatoires working in new ways with businesses, government, and civil society at both global and local levels. It would also require conservatoires to critically reflect on who the communities are that they seek to connect with. These may be locally focused, linked to a strong sense of the place where the conservatoire is geographically located. Or these communities might be culturally and musically focused, bound by shared creative interests, drawing community members from a much wider geographical area. Of course, communities are not static entities but rather highly dynamic, meaning that this endeavour of creating a civic conservatoire is always evolving.

Summary

This chapter offers an open and generous invitation to consider how a civic mindset might enhance a conservatoire's role in the social fabric of civil society, and how a conservatoire might work in more relational ways with their surrounding communities. It offers conceptual and practical reflections from within the RCM context, which have a strong international relevance and resonance. It challenges us to consider *how* conservatoires might move from being civically aware to being truly engaged civic institutions, and, in doing so, how they might critically understand and define their surrounding communities. Most importantly, this chapter invites us to consider how conservatoires might engage in a 'root and branch' approach to widening their social purpose in society in the future and, in turn, amplifying the vital role that music can play in addressing the most pressing social issues facing our local and global communities.

Bibliography

Brink, Chris. *The Soul of a University: Why Excellence Is Not Enough*. Bristol, Chicago: Bristol University Press, 2018.
Goddard, John B. *Reinventing the Civic University*. NESTA, September 2009. https://media.nesta.org.uk/documents/reinventing_the_civic_university.pdf.
Goddard, John B., Ellen Hazelkorn, Louise Kempton, and Paul Vallance, eds. *The Civic University: The Policy and Leadership Challenges*. Cheltenham, UK; Northampton, MA, USA: Edward Elgar Publishing, 2016.
Truly Civic: Strengthening the Connection between Universities and Their Places. The UPP Foundation, 2019. https://upp-foundation.org/wp-content/uploads/2019/02/Civic-University-Commission-Final-Report.pdf.

Chapter and Perspective Notes

1 https://upp-foundation.org/about-us/civic-university-network/.
2 The UPP Foundation, *Truly civic*.
3 Biesta, *The beautiful risk of education*.
4 Biesta, 'The community of those who have nothing in common', 315.
5 Alexander, *Essays on pedagogy*, 92.

6 Wegerif, *Dialogic*, 28.
7 Haraway, *Staying with the trouble*, 168.
8 Shakespeare, *Troilus and Cressida* Act 1, Scene 3.
9 Camlin, 'This is my truth'.
10 For further recent discussion on how institutional discourses can shape how particular musical practices are (de)valued, see Bull and Scharff, 'Classical music as genre'.
11 Turino, *Music as Social Life*; Camlin, 'Encounters with participatory music', 43–71.
12 See www.officeforstudents.org.uk/advice-and-guidance/promoting-equal-opportunities/our-approach-to-access-and-participation/.
13 See www.rcm.ac.uk/junior/.
14 Current criteria include the following: children eligible for Pupil Premium (and their families); children looked after by the local authority or in foster care (and their families); Black, Asian, and minority ethnic children/young people and families*; participants who have Special Education Needs and Disabilities*; families who live in social housing; families who are eligible for Universal Credit; families/individuals who are eligible for disability benefit; service families*; families from Gypsy, Roma, and Traveller communities*; young carers and their families*; refugee families/families with migrant status. (* denotes having a household income of less than £31,139.)
15 Bennett, *Life in the Real World*; Camlin, 'Mind the gap!', 72–95; Renshaw, *Being – In Tune*, 42; Burnard, 'Working with Bourdieu's cultural analysis and legacy'.
16 Camlin, 'Encounters with participatory music' 64, 56.
17 Ascenso, 'Finding meaning in music', 4.
18 Bennett and Burnard, 'Human capital career creativities', 123–42.
19 Spiro and Sanfilippo, *Collaborative Insights*.
20 See Perkins et al., 'Learning through teaching'; see also Chapter 10.
21 See Gaunt et al., 'Musicians as "makers in society"'.
22 See rcm.ac.uk/msc.
23 See www.PerformanceScience.ac.uk.
24 Perkins and Williamon, 'Creative leadership-in-action', 97–114.
25 Swanwick, *Teaching Music Musically*, x.
26 Nelson, *Practice as Research in the Arts*.
27 Camlin, 'Whose quality is it anyway?'.
28 Tregear et al., 'Conservatoires in society', 283.
29 Biesta, *The Beautiful Risk of Education*, 10.
30 Gross et al., *Towards Cultural Democracy*.
31 Brink, *The Soul of a University*, xvi.
32 The Upp Foundation, *Truly Civic*.
33 The Upp Foundation, *Truly Civic*.
34 Goddard et al., *The Civic University*, 7.
35 Goddard, *Reinventing the Civic University*.

15

DIVERSIFYING MUSICAL PRACTICES

How to address the need for change within conservatoire training

Florence Ambrose and Wiebke Thormählen

With contributions from Elena Dubinets and Helen Wallace

Introduction

The last few years have presented the cultural sector with unprecedented challenges that are forcing the 'classical' music industry into a reckoning with its values and its modes of operation.[1] Questions around the accessibility of music education and of professional training in 'classical' music and of this music as a pastime or entertainment for anyone wishing to engage with it, are exposing deep-rooted hierarchies that many regularly engaged in the classical music business are finding at best challenging to act on and at worst difficult even to acknowledge. Yet, the renewed and enhanced call to 'diversify music' is one that educational institutions have a particular duty to address. This brief, however, is a wide one, embracing anything from rethinking the repertoire we teach and perform to investigating our musical practices, our teaching practices, and the ideological foundations on which both our traditional concert craft and the current system for conservatoire education are built.

Several recent reports have laid bare the extent of the problem we face, showing for instance that music in higher education settings is disproportionately white even in comparison to other arts subjects, or that a pathway into classical music as a profession is available only to those from a socioeconomically privileged background.[2] Bull et al. (2021)'s recent edited collection *Voices for Change in the Classical Music Profession: New Ideas for Tackling Inequalities and Exclusions* brings together writers to reflect on the challenges that current social justice movements are inspiring the classical music industry to address; it is essential reading for anyone interested in questions of equality, diversity, and inclusion in the industry.[3] Like the editors of this collection, in this chapter, we use the term 'classical music' as one that adumbrates a musical practice which a general public recognises as a particular category or set of practices. Similarly, we use the term 'diversify' as currently

DOI: 10.4324/9781003281573-32

accepted terminology to describe the desire to effect change in the classical music sector in such a way as to become more open and inclusive. Reflecting on this term critically would reach beyond the confines of this chapter, but we offer some thoughts below with respect to our observations on what it means and how it is deployed in current practice.

Our chapter offers a reflection on the responses to the desire to diversify within the conservatoire setting. Due to the vastness of the topic, we focus on a particular aspect of conservatoire training: the training of orchestral musicians for an orchestral workforce. That this is a reasonable limitation to impose will become apparent during the opening pages of the chapter where we briefly revisit the historic entanglement of the conservatoire with the orchestra as a representational tool for high art music. In order to look at this entanglement today, we invited two industry professionals – directors of an internationally renowned venue and an orchestra – to discuss with us how they go about seeking change in their programming. Together we reflected on their perceived needs and desires for 'the future musician'. While these two substantial conversations by no means present a comprehensive study of the professional needs of musicians or of the future-proofing of conservatoire training, they nonetheless offer valuable insights into the changing demands of a profession in flux. They open up two of the three areas of 'diversification' which we then go on to illuminate through examples from recent conservatoire practice in our third section. Here, finally, we provide examples of changing practice from within the Royal College of Music (RCM). While these examples refer to one conservatoire only, others are undertaking similar work, and frequent cross-institutional collaboration is crucial to fostering much-needed change.

The conservatoire and the orchestra – a legacy of entanglement

The origins of the twentieth-century conservatoire as an education system and training model have been the subject of many books and articles in recent years. They are of significance here as they go some way to explaining what the conservatoire is designed to teach and how. The RCM was founded in 1882 on the basis of a belief in music's 'civilising powers' and its benefits to society, values that its first Director, Sir George Grove, put to good use in lobbying for the establishment, and which he had prepared well through his previous enterprises.[4] Grove, like many, considered music a tool to educate the masses and to control and direct their leisure activities. A training place, therefore, was needed to equip musicians with the skills to teach, to direct choral societies, amateur bands and orchestras, and to perform at concerts that could fulfil music's moral and educational purpose.[5] Key in this 'musical workforce' were orchestral musicians and organists, the latter providing key music services in 'the provinces' in churches and as choir leaders, and the former staffing the musical institutions that showcased 'excellent' music: the orchestras. Indeed, conservatoires today remain largely structured along orchestral fault lines with the student body assigned to a particular faculty or school such as strings, woodwind, brass, or percussion. Through these schools, key training in orchestral repertoire and etiquette is delivered to prepare students for 'the profession'. The modern conservatoire's origins, then, institutionalised what one might refer to as the orchestra's 'performance modi operandi': how interactions between musicians work, how the audience interacts with the musicians, and how an audience listens. Musicians today continue to be trained in these traditions.

Second, these origins cemented *what* music is traditionally learnt in a conservatoire, thereby perpetuating particular canons of music. Victorian ideologies that music could function as 'this greatest of all civilisers', and unite people across class divides by 'cultivating their imaginations', were wedded to a hierarchy between different types of music and to a faith-like belief in particular bodies of musical works that formed a canon of high art.[6] These works were produced almost exclusively by white men; yet, they were celebrated for having a universality and perfect ingenuity in their construction that marked them out as 'classical'. A music conservatoire had to train three things: the composition of such works, their performance, and their understanding. It had to equip its students to understand and impart to their disciples and audiences in turn the intellectual engagement that was deemed to be required of the audience.[7]

Through these origins, then, three key parameters are enshrined throughout the conservatoire's history, which form barriers to diversity and inclusion. A canon of works sits at its heart – the 'what' we play;[8] particular performance modes and particular modes of assessing quality in a musical work and excellence in its performance are coupled with this canon – the 'how' we play; finally, deep-rooted hierarchies – gendered, racialised, and class-based – that create the senses of belonging and exclusion from cultural and educational spaces. The orchestra – more specifically the symphony orchestra – as an institution and sound ideal is central to this. With its own rites, it forms the professional companion to much of conservatoire training and is therefore modelled throughout the educational journey.

Arguably, there remain pragmatic reasons even today to keep repertoire and the broad modes of operation stable. The idea of a core repertoire facilitates the delivery of a comprehensive education in this repertoire that allows students to step out of the conservatoire and into orchestras that function often on minimal rehearsal time.[9] Indeed, conservatoire orchestral programming until recently was customarily created along a list of key pieces with the aim of performing the majority of 'core works' over the four-year cycle of an undergraduate student's time in the conservatoire. 'Concert craft' remains a staple in the students' weekly learning activities with – until recently – comparatively little space allocated to encourage creativity or explore alternative formats of performance. Orchestral performances often followed the common overture, concerto, symphony format, and little was done to attract and engage new audiences, while the list of pieces that formed the 'core' remained largely unquestioned. In tandem, any academic teaching in music theory, aural skills, and music history relied on examples taken from this core list with style histories, genre narratives, and technical parameters used to explain aesthetic value woven around this canon of works.

Yet, whether these pragmatic reasons truly are the cause for repertoire's remarkable resistance to being replaced is highly questionable as, arguably, ideological reasons exert far greater influence here than pragmatic ones. As suggested above, the conservatoire's training system is founded on an ideological agreement on the meaning of 'excellence' in repertoire and on excellence in performance skills; indeed, the latter mapped firmly onto the nature of the former: the excellent French horn player masters the melancholy solo in Stravinsky's *Firebird* flawlessly (and against their instrument's odds) with a sound moulded to tug at heart strings, while each orchestral section in Bartok's *Concerto for Orchestra* is treated in a soloistic manner to create a virtuosic mix of orchestral textures that requires absolute unanimity within each of the groups; it requires similar excellence in having control over one's instrument as over one's section collaboration to perform the fiendishly difficult ending of Strauss' *Also sprach Zarathustra* and so on. Here, particular sonic ideals and particular modes of listening are prioritised, and they determine the 'excellence of skill' required from each individual performer.

Ideals of excellence and exclusivity are mapped closely onto exclusion here in several ways: the limits of the canon and its – for long – unacknowledged privileging of white male creation are perhaps easy to address. Yet, the sonic ideals arising from this 'core repertoire' and the often unthinking attempt to assess all other music – music regularly written for different spaces or performance modes precisely because its creators were excluded from certain spaces – continue to present a skewed mode of assessing 'quality' in music. Different ways of approaching music-making, then, need to be acknowledged as equally valid, not least because access and exposure to the white-male-canonic model of excellence at an early age vary. As recent studies across sociology and music pedagogy have shown, socio-economic background and the educational pipeline have a disproportionate impact not only on musical training but, crucially, on a person's sense of belonging in particular cultural spaces, as the recognition of the broad modes of operating within, for instance, the orchestral or choral space is established long before students enter the higher education (HE) space of the conservatoire.[10]

At the heart of much conservatoire training sits one-to-one tuition in technical facility, artistic intuition, and aesthetic understanding measured through the performance of particular repertoire.[11] It is a model of deep mentorship that could, one might think, lend itself to help students overcome pre-HE lack of exposure to classical repertoire and modes of behaviour; yet, this appears not to be case. With the student–professor relationship at its centre, the training has often been compared to the master–apprentice or master–disciple model, a model that is highly functional in retaining a status quo and perfecting a particular art;[12] it lends itself less well to a creative, root-and-branch re-assembly of values. Indeed, as highlighted in Chapter 7, it is a model that tends to veer from its traditions only if presented with a significant challenge, normally forced by external circumstances.[13] Crucially, a sense of 'belonging' within the conservatoire is often beholden to the rapport between professor and student. Representation of professors with different ethnic backgrounds remains the exception.[14] Similarly, professors with different educational and socio-economic histories which they explicitly and proudly own within the conservatoire space rather than enacting assimilation or deploying masking techniques to avoid their visibility are a significant minority. Recent scholarship has highlighted the problematic aspects of exclusivity permeated through the one-to-one training system as starting with the audition process itself during which professors – consciously or unconsciously – are drawn to students who they sense a rapport with, a rapport that is frequently based on a common socio-economic and/or educational background.[15] From the very beginning of a student's journey, then, a sense of belonging is affirmed or undermined.

Within conservatoires, the desire to 'diversify' until recently focused on reaching new and different audiences and, next, on broadening the student body. The latter in particular was seen as 'challenge enough' as the entrance audition process by which 'talent' is selected limited the pool of applicants in most instrumental groups to those with financial and educational access to private tuition from an early age coupled with parental support and regular sociocultural exposure to Western classical music.[16] The fact that sociocultural gatekeeping around an education on Western classical instruments has been exacerbated by cuts to music education funding in UK schools and Local Education Authority music hubs coupled with other factors such as the impact of Brexit can become utilised as excuses that absolve educational institutions from tackling the real issues. Here, reports such as Tamsin Cox and Hannah Kilshaw's, commissioned by Arts Council England in 2019 and investigating routes into the orchestral profession in England, can become halting points rather than driving momentum.[17] This report, executed together with the Association of British Orchestras, the BBC, the Musicians' Union, and Conservatoires UK, affirmed that the sector suffered from severe pipeline issues and did not offer routes into the profession for any but a small, elite section of society. It is complemented by the report conducted by EDIMS (Equality, Diversity and Inclusion in Music Studies, a cross-organisational network) that provided data on demographic patterns alongside actual experiences. It also presents case studies on diversity issues in Music in Higher Education more broadly.[18] Both reports highlight that conservatoires, orchestras, and cultural venues face three challenges in tackling the homogeneity of their participants and engagement with what diversity actually means: what is performed/offered; how it is offered – here, both the adherence to score-based music-making and concert halls as habitualised and habitualising sites for music-making need to be investigated; and, most pertinently, the 'sense of belonging'. All three require engagement with fundamental ideological challenges that come together in the concepts of belonging and cultural ownership.

The conservatoire and the cultural sector – identifying training needs and models for interaction

Conservatoires have always prided themselves on training students to perform at the highest level and on preparing them for the music profession. But recent incisive events – the COVID-19 pandemic, Brexit, and renewed Black Lives Matter protests – have left both conservatoires and the industry in a state of flux. To be sure, professional orchestras and conservatoires had already begun to dabble in digital technology, with trials of programme notes on mobile phones and explorations of new lighting configurations to attract new audiences, when all activity had to shift online in 2020. Streaming services had already put paid to the concert hall's central place while the wider digital revolution had begun to blur the boundaries between creators and audiences, 'artistes', and amateur music lovers. Programmers had ventured out to explore new performance spaces including concerts in popular public spaces with high footfall such as Trafalgar Square and the Imperial War Museum North; classical gigs started to pop up in pubs and car parks; and partnerships with hospitals, schools, and prisons emerged.[19] These programmes, although tentative at first, started to grow as institutions saw the value in reaching out to new audiences and new funding possibilities. This work focused primarily on bringing more diverse audiences to classical music. Nevertheless, these endeavours sowed some seeds for the crucial work of changing students' outlook on music performance in the 'classical' space, and with that presented an essential stepping stone to creating greater space for 'belonging'.

To discuss such work, to explore its challenges, and to understand better how the music industry might view the conservatoire's educational provision with regard to the change of 'key skills' or 'excellence' required, we invited Dr Elena Dubinets, Artistic Director of the London Philharmonic Orchestra, and Helen Wallace, formerly Executive Artistic Director at Kings Place Music Foundation and now Head of Music at the Barbican, to contemplate these questions with us. The following section is indebted to their contributions.

The wider classical music industry is currently experimenting with a variety of different models to better represent the communities they serve and increase their audience numbers. In the orchestral field, the London Philharmonic Orchestra recently announced their two new Conductor Fellows in a scheme designed to support the development of conductors from backgrounds currently under-represented in the industry in the early stages of their careers. The London Symphony Orchestra's Half Six Fix is a series of concerts designed to appeal to a different audience; the concerts last for a maximum of 60 minutes without interval, audiences are welcome to take a drink into the auditorium, and the conductor will introduce the music supported by digital programme notes. Many orchestras offer chamber concerts in smaller venues – an initiative born out of necessity during the COVID-19 pandemic but now accepted as a successful method of connecting with audiences who may not have visited a concert hall in the past.

Venues are in a position to think beyond the traditional constraints of particular professional groups, such as an orchestra, which has a particular workforce and particular working methods. Recent initiatives have indeed focused on seeking out other professional music ensembles that may represent different population groups within the urban landscape. A recent project at King's Place, for instance, recognised London's heritage as a migrant city and sought to bring in a much wider variety of performing groups. While this brought different audiences into the cultural centre, the next challenge is one of bringing communities together through collaborations between different performance groups, performance styles, and listening/experience expectations. This is the space where new performance modes can be explored – modes that truly diversify music performance by placing different practices on an equal footing rather than presenting one as the norm and others as the tributaries, a practice with unpalatable remnants of exoticism.

In order to prepare music students for these changing workspaces and conditions, various key requirements emerged during the course of our conversations. The first – and perhaps most impactful – key topic focused on the fundamental change in the musicians' approach to their work. In the past, musicians themselves might have thought of the essence of the profession as the reverence and communication of works of art that had a universal value. Increasingly, it appears that music's social agency has greater significance for musicians regardless of their regular performance circumstances. While core skills of collaboration and communication within working groups (such as 'The Orchestra') to achieve unique products (such as musical works) remain, questions and discussions around the purpose of such production and communication have become much more prevalent. Here, it seems that the industry and the education sector are in sync as students increasingly enter their educational journey demanding training that helps them to think about and develop the social relevance of their music-making. Within the profession, it appears that increasing numbers of musicians are seeking out professional training to improve their skill set for public engagement work, for instance, and to increase their awareness of music's role in relation to topics of wider cultural and social relevance such as the Black Lives Matter movement or environmental issues.

This shift in the perception of music, music-making, and the sociocultural relevance of the profession led both our interview partners to express the need for much wider training to prepare musicians for situations, contexts, and performance plans that require flexibility.

Changing audience expectations and concert platforms make new demands on venues and organisations in terms of programming which requires a flexible approach to performance group sizes and make-up. Orchestral musicians, therefore, need to be able to change roles from being a section player to taking on a chamber music or even a soloistic function. Anecdotally, orchestral players report that this takes them beyond their zone of expertise and that they are therefore uncomfortable with such changing roles. Training musicians today, then, requires a wide bandwidth of approaches that prepares them to change roles and performance modes even within a single concert.

Flexibility was also identified as a key skill in a separate field: classical musicians are traditionally trained to perform notated pieces of music. The skill of assured sight-reading takes up key training time and is of the essence in most classical rehearsal contexts. Solo and chamber music performances work on the basis of the same ideological model which suggests that the classical musician is a spokesperson – albeit one who recites with and through an individual voice – for the intentions of a composer as captured in a score.[20] The desire to diversify performance today, in contrast, has rightly brought with it the exploration of different performance models not least from the world of jazz, in which improvisation skills are central. Our conversations with Helen and Elena confirmed that these skills are indeed highly desirable, not to say essential in today's music market with examples ranging from stylistic collaborations across jazz and early music to topic-driven projects such as King's Place's recent 'Venus unwrapped'.[21]

But our conversations also suggested that at present, many classically trained musicians still struggle with these skills. Examples include difficulties during rehearsals when Western classically trained musicians and Indian classically trained musicians collaborate, a process that requires a significant amount of rehearsal time for those involved to become familiar with each other's styles and ideologies so as to be able to collaborate. While such projects offer much-needed space for cultural communication, they also require considerable preparation and support for all involved. On one hand, then, further professional training in improvisation skills is a necessity; on the other – and more difficult yet crucial to address – entirely different approaches to performance and music-making are called on here that require a change in mindset as the players have to approach the idea of 'excellence' in music and musicianship in new ways. Fear factors around 'perfection' and its deeply ingrained definition within 'Western classical music' often present hurdles here. Such journeys need to start at conservatoire level, and space has to be made to investigate often uncritically accepted notions of excellence and perfection. Ideally, the gradual infiltration of the workforce by recent graduates as well as continuous active collaboration between HE and cultural institutions helps to grow these mindsets to embrace different models of music-making.

Finally, and as discussed in Chapter 8, a key part of any musician's skill set today and in the future will be 'digital fluency', a concept that implies confidence in the use of a variety of digital platforms to create, record, and produce art and to disseminate it; having expertise in the strategic use of social media; and, finally, exercising circumspection in the digital space as a key part of the work arena. Our conversation partners both stressed the significance here and communicated that such digital fluency entails aspects of copyright and intellectual property (IP) as well as understanding the representation and the negotiation of individual voices with the 'corporate' and institutional voices of performing groups, concert promoters, venues, and educational institutions. This will become increasingly significant if traditional performing groups such as orchestras are rethinking their make-up and identity while professional musicians are already playing catch-up in these fields. Conservatoire training, both agreed, must ensure that students are at the forefront of these developments and can act as role models, ambassadors, educators, and leaders in these fields.

Training in a new excellence – sites to challenge current practice

Where can the conservatoire education address these particular points? To what degree is this already happening? To what degree does the conservatoire's view of 'diversification' coincide with the points raised by our collaborators? Crucially, what are the sites and routes that allow for a reckoning with heritage and ideology within the conservatoire? These are questions that the conservatoire sector collectively is grappling with at present. In the following, the RCM serves as our case study, with the acknowledgement that a wide range of activities around diversification are currently being explored across the UK conservatoire sector with each institution contributing a range of research and expertise. Ideas sharing is facilitated via cross-sector groups such as Conservatoires UK and the Royal Musical Association's Equality, Diversity, and Inclusion in Music initiative (see report discussed earlier).

A key element in the conservatoire's journey towards greater diversity has been the institutional acknowledgement that not all voices are heard equally within the educational institution and that spaces need to be created to allow these voices to contribute and to impact on the conservatoire's operations. Embedding this within the institutional governance, therefore, was a key step and one that, in line with the HE sector more widely, at the RCM as elsewhere included the establishment of an Equality, Diversity, and Inclusion policy, and of a committee briefed with devising, implementing, and monitoring the work thus started. In addition, working groups drawn from the staff and student body would promote this work throughout the learning and teaching activities within the conservatoire, often challenging areas where there was insufficient engagement. Increasingly over the last three years, the demand for diverse materials, practices, and viewpoints has come from the student body – an encouraging sign that students are taking ownership of their learning and seeking to shape the sector in a new image.

The real work, however, has to happen in the teaching spaces as in the daily interaction with each other and with ideals of music-making. Significant starting points here have focused on access to different repertoire, addressing the 'what' described above. In response to student and examiner observations, initially around the imbalance of gender in the classical music world, the Performance and Programming team at the RCM set about addressing the problem that comparatively little repertoire by women composers was readily available in good editions and perhaps even recordings. To help staff and students, they started a compilation project beginning with a list of solo repertoire by women composers for each instrument. Next, they acknowledged the issue that repertoire lists emerging across the internet often included works unavailable for repeat performances, a fact that would leave performers returning to the old tried-and-tested instead. Here, the RCM library became involved in sourcing editions and recordings. Lists were expanded to include chamber music, and professors were contacted to help build the lists, revealing interesting gaps in what they themselves had been taught and were therefore regularly teaching their students. A new database for students and professors to 'Find Something New' was first shared on International Women's Day in March 2020, shortly before the world paused due to

COVID-19. The Black Lives Matter momentum after May 2020 resulted in new attention and a new database to help students discover works by ethnically under-represented composers. With each small step, students were discovering new works and sharing them with their peers in performance classes and through chamber music.

Student initiative increased significantly, and their discoveries became more visible across the College's music-making activities, from exam syllabuses to programmed performance opportunities. Crucial in these developments was the strong financial support from the RCM library which committed to stocking the library with repertoire from under-represented composers at a rapid pace. Frequently, this revealed how entirely sensible and necessary music industry rules and regulations can nonetheless hamper progress: for the story doesn't end with the acquisition of single copies of music but, often, the addition of previously unedited repertoire resulted in difficulties in hiring sets of parts, while, at times, clearing performance rights became complicated. Building diversification into strategic planning, then, was crucial so as to have the necessary support financially, procedurally, and in sheer person-power.

Other areas of musical training, however, remained wedded to perceived ideas about the profession, seeking to emulate the latter so as to prepare the students for it. Audition excerpts are one such example: students prepare these based on the probability with which they will encounter them in auditions for professional orchestras. When questioned in 2021, several orchestras had not updated their audition excerpts for many years, so works by under-represented composers were well-nigh absent. The RCM's annual orchestral auditions for its own orchestras now reflect the increasing diversity of its performance programme but until the current trend of exploring previously neglected repertoire beds in across the professional sector and new pieces become audience favourites that are regularly performed, professional orchestral audition excerpts may be slow to change.

Another significant change in training musicians towards greater creative initiative and therefore diversification is the acknowledgement that orchestras mark only one portion of the professional musicians' workplace. Conservatoires, including the RCM, have begun to emphasise entrepreneurial musicianship, giving it greater space in the curriculum and the performance diary. At the RCM, a specific festival – the FestivALL (born in 2021) – has allowed students to explore and perform repertoire in new ways through their own initiatives. Such showcase spaces for individual and new curation of music are essential in allowing students to investigate how inherited modes of performance may have perpetuated exclusion zones and what different modes can crack these open. Students relished the opportunity: applications to perform in the FestivALL rose from 12 in 2021 to 44 in 2022, demonstrating increased awareness and engagement among the students. In addition, academic programme revisions included an enhanced focus on improvisation and practical acquisition of harmony and counterpoint skills; the creation of project spaces that allowed a greater number of students to engage in research-driven, creative projects around their personal areas of interest; and the creative use of library resources and museum artefacts beyond traditional learning settings.

Facilitating a broad culture change, though, to create spaces 'belonging' to a greater variety of students remains perhaps the area most resistant to change, as it requires honest investigation of latent ideologies undertaken by each individual and as a collective. At the RCM, we address this by implementing it in the music history curriculum. The new curriculum (revised in 2020) reversed the traditional order of knowledge acquisition, followed by analysis/understanding/investigation, and finally by creative application, instead placing the central section first, allowing this to drive the material for knowledge acquisition individually. This revised journey was based on the acknowledgement of the culturally uniquely diverse student body at the point of entry. It acknowledges and capitalises on the fact that students enter the conservatoire typically from a wide variety of cultural-political backgrounds as they are recruited around the globe; yet, on entering the conservatoire, they often select to show only the portion of their musical heritage that they deem to belong there. Instead of affirming perceptions of what a conservatoire education would teach them, we asked them to investigate the cultural and musical richness that they brought with them as whole people and whole musicians. The new history curriculum is designed to encourage students to explore their own musical roots and any preconceptions around different types of music. From here, recent history becomes a lens through which students are encouraged to investigate the cultural conditions under which the (classical) music industry operates and to question received listening practices as well as assumed relationships between performer, composer, text, and audience. Students are led to refract this through London's international and ethnically diverse landscape and to reflect and exchange experiences that explore their own, diverse experiences of a 'Western classical music culture'.[22]

Conclusion: keeping conservatoire education relevant

In our quest to address the lack of diversity in the classical music sector, the last few years have been significant. The sudden stop of all concert activity as the sector had known it coincided with the increased awareness of systemic racism as a result of failures to address the colonial past. If the student protests demanding the removal of the statue of Cecil Rhodes from university campuses since 2015 appeared to leave much of musical life – at least in this country – untouched, the toppling of Edward Colston's statue and its highly symbolic dumping into Bristol Harbour in 2020 set off waves that for a while seemed unstoppable. The recognition that colonial history and its legacies of racism are rife was spurred on, of course, by the horrifying murder of George Floyd, an event that was memorialised through creative practice responses such as paintings, murals, songs, poems, and at least one opera. Audience interest in seeing and hearing artists – non-white and non-male – increased overnight. Such impetus, however, has a habit of waning rapidly, and the key work of investigating how and where the music industry has been implicated in upholding colonial and male-dominated hierarchies remains far from complete. Key now is not to allow these events to fade into the background.

Here – our observations show us – we can take our cue from the student body. Many graduating from conservatoires are increasingly excited by the breadth of possible careers, hoping no longer to step into a full-time orchestral job where what and how they play are largely determined by others. Instead, entrepreneurship is on their radar, and experience shows us that they relish the much wider skill set that these educational institutions have begun to offer, be that as presenters or producers, working in healthcare settings, or developing their own programmes and new models for chamber groups and ensembles. The shift from an aesthetics of universal art to an aesthetics based on social relevance is a significant one, yet one that does not sit easily with current modes of perceiving the field of Western classical music.

Still, we may have made fair strides in the 'what' and, to some degree, the 'how', even if here we need to continue to ask whether taking away the walls of the concert hall, for instance, really opens up performance modes and audience access. In other words, are we doing enough to leave our own comfort zones as musicians and teachers emerging from this system so as to invite others in for whom this has so far not been a comfortable space? We need to remain vigilant in our new curation of physical, virtual, and conceptual spaces so that we leave behind notions of wanting to bring 'great music' to 'the masses'. Only if we critically engage with Western classical music's civilising heritage can we begin the true journey to diversity.

Within the conservatoire, there is one key blind spot that needs to be brought into the folds of any work we do around inclusivity: the prominent and in many ways dominant one-to-one teaching space. Not only is this a crucial space in which that essential ingredient – *Belonging* – is cultivated or undermined, but this is also the space where the serving workforce – our large body of principal study professors – are the ones who are active participants in the orchestral and wider cultural working space beyond the conservatoire. Rarely, though, have we addressed them as a group directly so far. Yet, the risk is high that any discomforts felt in new demands in their working life in orchestras, for instance, may result in an assertive behaviour within the conservatoire teaching space as a way of self-reassurance that the values one once learnt continue to hold relevance somewhere.

This group of participants must start to play a vital role in any open development of new skill sets that are based on the intricacy of collaboration and attunement. Such attunement to myriad ways of perceiving and conceiving of music can represent key avenues into cultural understanding and therefore reach far beyond concert spaces. Such attunement also demands that excellence is rearticulated away from its singular mapping onto the 'specialness' of Western classical music, recognising instead that 'excellence' resides in the expertise with which musical interactions are conducted. It resides in all musical cultures the moment ideas, skills, and coordination across those involved in the experience are aligned. While it is unrealistic that one institution can train in a wide variety of musical cultures, it has to be the prerogative of any specialist training institution to recognise and raise awareness of this plurality. What this means in practice is to equip students in 'excellence skills' beyond the traditional mastery of the instrument so as to provide core skills for a multitude of social and artistic interactions through music.

Summary

- Key take-away 1: all four contributors share the perception that musicians, professionals, and conservatoire students alike are increasingly considering the social implications and values of their profession. This development is intricately linked to the desire to practise greater inclusion, equality, and diversity within the classical music sector.
- Key take-away 2: professional musical training should include wider musical skills such as improvisation; adaptability to different musical settings, ensemble constellations, and audiences; and key entrepreneurial and research skills leading to cultural understanding and socio-political openness.

- Key take-away 3: the need to acknowledge the dominance of white, middle-class, often male hegemonies in classical music education persists. This acknowledgement needs to permeate all aspects of a conservatoire's processes, training, pedagogy, and self-understanding so as to influence decision-making and create spaces where any student can belong.

Further information and reading

Bull, Anna, Diljeet Bhachu, Amy Blier-Carruthers, Alexander Bradley, and Seferin James. *Slow Train Coming? Equality, Diversity and Inclusion in UK Music Higher Education*. Equality, Diversity and Inclusion in Music Studies Network, 2022.

Bull, Anna, Christina Scharff, and Laudan Nooshin, eds. *Voices for Change in the Classical Music Profession: New Ideas for Tackling Inequalities and Exclusions*. Oxford: Oxford University Press, 2023.

Dromey, Chris, and Julia Haferkorn. *The Classical Music Industry*. New York: Routledge, 2018.

Gaunt, Helena, Celia Duffy, Ana Coric, Isabel González Delgado, Linda Messas, Oleksandr Pryimenko, and Henrik Sveidahl. 'Musicians as "makers in society": A conceptual foundation for contemporary professional higher music education'. *Frontiers in Psychology* 12 (2021): 1–20. https://doi.org/10.3389/fpsyg.2021.713648.

Bibliography

Bower, Bruno. 'Stories about music: The program notes of the crystal palace Saturday concerts, 1865–1879'. *The Musical Quarterly* 105, no. 3–4 (2022): 406–32. https://doi.org/10.1093/musqtl/gdac007

Bull, Anna. *Class, Control, and Classical Music*. Oxford: Oxford University Press, 2019.

Bull, Anna, Diljeet Bhachu, Amy Blier-Carruthers, Alexander Bradley, and Seferin James. *Slow Train Coming? Equality, Diversity and Inclusion in UK Music Higher Education*. Equality, Diversity and Inclusion in Music Studies Network, 2022.

Bull, Anna, Christina Scharff, and Laudan Nooshin, eds. *Voices for Change in the Classical Music Profession: New Ideas for Tackling Inequalities and Exclusions*. Oxford: Oxford University Press, 2023.

Burwell, Kim. 'Apprenticeship in music: A contextual study for instrumental teaching and learning'. *International Journal of Music Education* 31, no. 3 (2013): 276–91. https://doi.org/10.1177/0255761411434501

Carey, Gemma, and Don Lebler. 'Prior learning of conservatoire students: A Western classical perspective'. *Proceedings of the 17th International Seminar of the Commission for the Education of the Professional Musician (CEPROM)* (2008): 15–20.

Cox, Tamsin, and Hannah Kilshaw. *Creating a More Inclusive Classical Music. A Study of the English Orchestral Workforce and the Current Routes to Joining It. Executive Summary*. Arts Council England, 2021. www.artscouncil.org.uk/sites/default/files/download-file/Executive_Summary.pdf.

Dromey, Chris, and Julia Haferkorn. *The Classical Music Industry*. New York: Routledge, 2018.

Harrison, Scott, and Catherine Grant. 'Exploring of new models of research pedagogy: Time to let go of master-apprentice style supervision?'. *Teaching in Higher Education* 20, no. 5 (2015): 556–66. https://doi.org/10.1080/13562517.2015.1036732.

Hughes, Meirion, and Robert A. Stradling. *The English Musical Renaissance, 1840–1940*. Manchester: Manchester University Press, 2001.

Musgrave, Michael. *The Musical Life of the Crystal Palace*. Cambridge: Cambridge University Press, 1995.

Porton, Jennie Joy. 'Social inclusion in contemporary British conservatoires: Alumni perspectives'. In *Voices for Change in the Classical Music Profession: New Ideas for Tackling Inequalities and Exclusions*, edited by Anna Bull, Christina Scharff, and Laudan Nooshin, 42–53. New York: Oxford University Press, 2023. https://doi.org/10.1093/oso/9780197601211.001.0001.

Prokop, Rainer, and Rosa Reitsamer. 'The role of music conservatoires in the making of classical music careers'. In *Voices for Change*, edited by Anna Bull, Christina Scharff, and Laudan Nooshin, 31–41. Oxford: Oxford University Press, 2023.

Thormählen, Wiebke. 'Music & dance'. In *Bloomsbury Cultural History of Emotions. Vol. 5: The Age of Romanticism, Revolution and Empire*, edited by Susan Matt, 55–74. London: Bloomsbury Publishing, 2019.

Welliver, Phyllis. *Mary Gladstone and the Victorian Salon: Music, Literature, Liberalism*. Cambridge: Cambridge University Press, 2017.

Wright, David C. H. 'The South Kensington music schools and the development of the British conservatoire in the late nineteenth century'. *Journal of the Royal Musical Association* 130, no. 2 (2005): 236–82. https://doi.org/10.1093/jrma/fki012.

Wright, David C. H. *The Royal College of Music and its Contexts: An Artistic and Social History*. Cambridge: Cambridge University Press, 2020.

PERSPECTIVE: CHAPTER 15

Roger Wilson

Introduction

I am Director of Operations at Black Lives in Music, an organisation co-founded by myself and Charisse Beaumont. Our organisation highlights the narrative of change needed for the Black and global majority community to thrive in the music sector. We have a sector-wide approach to driving change, in consideration of the endemic issues of inequity and discrimination throughout the music ecology.

I am formerly a professional musician, having enjoyed a portfolio career spanning nearly three decades. Having grown up in an area of considerable socio-economic deprivation, my musical story starts as a child, the grateful recipient of free music education – a unicorn now, but a wonderful thing for so many people of yesteryears. That gift took me on to study at a conservatoire of music, (again, free of charge!), before embarking on a long and rewarding career in the profession.

Perspectives

When I think of a conservatoire, I think of a community. It is after all, very simply that. You can of course extrapolate the concept to include all stakeholders existing beyond its walls. Be they children and young people at first access stage or, indeed, the professional ensembles and organisations that they will go on to join or for that matter the audiences who will come and hear those same artists at all points in their development. To think about the conservatoire community from the macro perspective lets us focus on the experience of the individual, the person whose life is in some way touched by the business of a conservatoire. It is in fact my view that in recent times, the conservatoire has actually stopped being about the individual and more about a particular concept of excellence, as recognised in the preceding chapter. To my mind, that suggests a narrow train of thinking and, most importantly, one that diminishes the sense of community rather than enhances it. Like Thormählen and Ambrose, I support the call to reimagine excellence in the conservatoire.

DOI: 10.4324/9781003281573-33

Thinking from the macro perspective in terms of equipping students in preparation for the business births some important questions. There can only be tension in relation to road maps for learning like the National Plan for Music Education and modern music curricula if aspects of our sector are slow to acknowledge the modern societal landscape. Conservatoires may, in contemporary times, wish to champion a wider talent pool of music creators, but the tension arises when the profession insists on lagging behind while maintaining a focus on traditional canonical repertoire. Ambassadors for change, like the indefatigable Chi-chi Nwanoku, maintain their crusade to champion diversity by shining a light on diverse composers with ensembles like the celebrated 'Chineke!'. Meanwhile, inspirational visionaries like Charles Hazlewood and the pioneering Paraorchestra blaze a path for the evolution of the inclusive orchestra. Thought leaders like Fabienne Krause provide important spaces for discussion on the future of classical music at conference expo events such as Classical: NEXT. Meanwhile, the majority of professional orchestras trail in their wake on account of their own preference of traditional repertoire as chosen by their conductors and musicians. There even exists an unfounded narrative that audiences will diminish with a change of focus to embrace inclusive programming. We should not forget: these conductors and musicians are the backbone of our pedagogical workforce in today's conservatoires, as they always have been. Consequently, the rate of change in revising the curriculum and repertoire on offer can only be seen as underpowered. We cannot ignore the gatekeepers of tradition who continue to have a not insignificant footing in both spaces of high-level performance and learning.

It is more important than ever that aspects of our music ecology do not work in silos and, instead, join up their conversation. Repertoire in orchestra training at a conservatoire level cannot change if the professional orchestras fail to sufficiently revise their programmes. The work being done by instrumental examining boards including ABRSM, TCL, and RSL to diversify their repertoire is important. Students will otherwise expect to play solo and chamber repertoire penned by the 'great' composers as part of a 'good' education. There is much work to do if we are to escape the shackles of tradition.

Gatekeeping and gatekeepers are two words that are seemingly becoming unpopular due to their hackneyed use, but still, they could never be more appropriate in the context of diversifying musical practices. The first person we meet when entering the conservatoire building – be it the physical gatekeepers or teachers, directors of faculty, Principal, or board – they are all gatekeepers of tradition. With the exception of the physical gatekeepers, all have an uncomfortable entanglement with the profession for which they are equipping tomorrow's professionals – today's conservatoire students. All at some point will have been subject to maintaining the traditions of the profession as performers, administrators, as audience members, perhaps even as season subscribers. Until we can successfully diversify this group, it will be difficult to realise our aspirations of a relevant art form for a representative community – lived experience informs change.

The traditions of a long-gone era continue to reign in the conservatoire while perpetuating much that is bad about this model as well as the good. After all, this community could easily be mistaken to be the result of an ongoing eugenically crafted experiment. It continues to be largely monocultural and unrepresentative of wider society. Notably, there is a near-complete absence of physically disabled music makers studying in these institutions. The conservatoire curriculum largely still reflects this streamlined sense of identity.

Effectively, this micro-community continues in failing to serve the macro-community – our wider society. While this continues to be the case, the conservatoire will fail in its every attempt to fend off the sticky label that is elitism. Currently, under 3% of teaching staff in UK conservatoires are from Black, Asian, and ethnically diverse backgrounds. I can't imagine the number of physically disabled teaching staff to be even a third of that figure. Frustratingly, data is thin on the ground in this respect. Workforce development is key to building a wider stakeholder base and reclaiming high-level music education for a twenty-first-century multicultural society. Teaching staff from that current and very monocultural community need to go beyond using empty phrases like 'I don't see colour' or 'I am a liberal thinker' and become proactive ambassadors in the interests of a modern and relevant approach. Unfortunately, their thinking is often still centred on the premise that talent always rises to the top and that the best musicians will succeed – the concept of an equitable pathway from the point of first access is yet to be successfully internalised. As highlighted earlier in this chapter, these challenges are further exacerbated by the existing one-to-one teaching model. Conservatoire teachers who themselves as students will likely have done little more than a brief module on pedagogy are, in turn, teaching tomorrow's professionals. This is largely on the basis of their reputation as performers. Within this sacrosanct space, they continue to pass on the established best practices while sharing their own personal thoughts and views. This heralded but flawed model must be reviewed. Rigour must permeate the exemplar of teaching at this level. Appraisal and monitoring must be fit for purpose and supportive of an inclusive culture as well as of a high-level learning experience.

Summary

At Black Lives in Music, we believe there are four pillars that are mission critical. *Governance and leadership* – without exception, the wider community continues to be unrepresented at this level in today's conservatoires. Those without lived experience will struggle to be invested enough to expedite change. *Recruitment* – perception of the conservatoire is perpetuated on the basis of facts. Today's conservatoire must strategise to recruit from a wider talent pool in all areas – from governors down to those all-important people we first meet when walking through the front door. We must work harder to recruit a wider and more talented community of students, making crucial considerations of equity and reasonable adjustments. *Curriculum* – we must tell it like it is, not as some of us want it to be. The purification of our art form renders the wider community disengaged, dispassionate, and, most importantly, disenfranchised. The conservatoire of music is synonymous with the genre of classical music. Yet, we know there is so much more wonderful music to celebrate and learn about, not to mention, value! *Marketing and communications* – well, if we can address the first three pillars, then this one enables us to talk passionately about what we do with real integrity and humility to a wider community.

Community is a word you will find purposely threaded throughout this Perspective. We must never forget the concept; it should underpin our every thinking in this context.

So, who says conservatoire training needs to change? Many in our community see there is a need, crucial for so many reasons – some are in fact the gatekeepers of tradition with the power to make that change, others lack the authority. So, what's stopping us making that change? Is it an invisible force? I'm afraid the reality is much less sinister. The only thing stopping us? Ourselves.

Chapter Notes

1 The term 'classical music' is understood in public discourse to denote a particular genre and practice of music. In line with recent scholarship, the inverted commas employed throughout the chapter call attention to the term's problematic assumptions of status and value.

2 See particularly Cox and Kilshaw, *Creating a More Inclusive Classical Music*, and Bull et al., *Slow Train Coming?*

3 Bull et al., *Voices for Change in the Classical Music Profession*.

4 Wright, *The Royal College of Music*; Wright, 'The South Kensington music schools'. On Grove's previous endeavours, see Bower, 'Stories about music'.

5 Hughes and Stradling, *The English Musical Renaissance*.

6 Grove (1882) in Hughes and Stradling, *The English Musical Renaissance*, 28–30. On betterment through art, see Bower, 'Stories about music'; Thormählen, 'Music & dance'; and Welliver, *Mary Gladstone and the Victorian Salon*.

7 The idea that instrumental music forms the pinnacle of high art and that it requires some knowledge to understand this goes back in Britain at least as far as the foundation of the Philharmonic Society in 1813.

8 New music included in conservatoire training is commonly conceived as having a heritage within the space of 'classical' music.

9 Another key factor, of course, is the implicit transferability across different orchestras and across national boundaries: working in a symphony orchestra will be much the same whether in the UK, in mainland Europe, or in the United States for instance.

10 Porton, 'Social inclusion'.

11 Notions such as 'faithfulness to the text' (the musical score) and received ideas about composers' 'intentions' permeate conversations about excellence among students. This has long gone hand-in-hand with particular presentation formats: the concert hall as a reverent space, the audience listening in darkness and in silence while the performer(s) – usually distanced by their elevation onto a stage – impart as 'interpreters' the beauty of 'great works'.

12 Burwell, 'Apprenticeship in music'; Carey and Lebler, 'Prior learning of conservatoire students'.

13 Harrison and Grant, 'Exploring of new models of research pedagogy'.

14 Comparison between reports from 2015 and 2022 shows little progress. Compare 'Slow train coming' with www.impulse-music.co.uk/wp-content/uploads/2017/05/Equality-and-Diversity-in-Classical-Music-Report.pdf.

15 Prokop and Reitsamer, 'The role of music conservatoires'. The authors here coin the concept of 'social cloning', 38.

16 Bull, *Class, Control, and Classical Music*.

17 Cox and Kilshaw, *Creating a More Inclusive Classical Music*.

18 Bull et al., *Slow Train Coming?*

19 Dromey and Haferkorn, *The Classical Music Industry*.

20 This performance model – essentially born of the ideology surrounding the romantic artist as an inventive genius – has been at the heart of classical music performance for around 200 years. To be sure, much 'new music' since the second half of the twentieth century has required the reading of new notation techniques and at times has dictated flexibility in the execution of such notation. Nonetheless, the standard composition-text-performance model has remained comparatively stable and central to much classical music performance and training.

21 www.kingsplace.co.uk/magazine/media/videos/venus-unwrapped-2019-official-trailer/.

22 Thormählen, Curriculum rationale and teaching plan for Music History, BMus Review 2020, RCM internal documents.

16

THE GLOBAL CONSERVATOIRE

Tania Lisboa and Diana Salazar

Introduction

In recent decades, the conservatoire sector in the United Kingdom and beyond has engaged with a wide range of pedagogical and technological innovations. Chapters 7–12 have highlighted many initiatives that are enriching the conservatoire learning culture and preparing students for a world that needs resilient and versatile artists. Projects like the Virtual Conservatoire, the Global Audition Training Programme, the Centre for Performance Science (CPS) performance simulator, and the use of livestreaming technology are harnessing emerging technologies, revealing to students new understandings of performance today.[1] These types of initiatives demonstrate reorientation towards progressive and differentiated methods of teaching and learning that extend or reimagine traditional face-to-face forms of elite music performance training. However, even today, such projects are typically peripheral in the curriculum or 'extracurricular' in status.

While many scholars have critiqued the 'master–apprentice' model, its dominance in conservatoire education persists.[2] At the RCM, like many UK conservatoires, students from all over the globe travel to the UK to receive in-person one-to-one lessons with professors who are seen as the great 'masters' of their instruments. This physical uprooting and relocation in search of a highly respected professor are a rite of passage for many young musicians, providing them with access to world-leading expertise that is individually tailored to their needs and aspirations. Around their principal study lessons, students study complementary subjects such as aural skills, music history, and musicianship, as well as more professionally focused areas, for instance health and well-being, 'musicians in the digital age', entrepreneurship, and music education. Finally, for musicians-in-training, students develop professional skills and understanding through collaboration with other students on group projects and performances. These projects, from chamber ensembles to large-scale symphony orchestra or opera productions, are often led by visiting professional conductors, directors, composers, or performers.

Arguably, it is this rich layering of embodied experiences and encounters, from one-to-one guidance to immersion in large-scale ensembles, that characterises the 'true' conservatoire

DOI: 10.4324/9781003281573-34

experience. However, in an online world where digital connectivity is ubiquitous, it is essential to examine the role of online, 'disembodied' interactions in our conservatoire ecologies. The limitations of consumer-level videoconferencing technology for professional instrumental or vocal training are widely recognised,[3] but in a multifaceted learning environment like the conservatoire, we propose that with careful design, learning that centres on online experiences can complement and even enhance traditional, face-to-face experiences. In this chapter, we present a short summary of research in online music education before exploring the potential of one such transnational model of online learning – the Global Conservatoire. The main findings of a research project associated with the Global Conservatoire are discussed before concluding with reflections and recommendations based on an analysis of teachers' and students' experiences.

Online teaching and learning

Online teaching and learning is not a new field of research in music. There is a significant body of research on instrumental teaching and learning experiences, much of which has focused on synchronous online teaching. This includes studies by Richard Dammers and Nathan Kruse and colleagues on delivering trumpet and piano lessons using Skype videoconferencing software and work by Pamela Pike and colleagues on teaching piano using a Disklavier and internet MIDI software in distance learning.[4] The literature also includes important studies on low latency systems in collaborative music-making;[5] on classroom videoconference music lessons;[6] examples of specific online teaching methods and outcomes;[7] student and teacher behaviour in distance learning;[8] and finally, technologies for curriculum enhancement in higher music education institutions.[9]

The year 2020 brought a rapid shift in music education due to the COVID-19 pandemic and the worldwide-imposed social isolation. The prohibition of in-person communication led to online teaching and learning as the principal tool for social communication and for education. Researchers responded quickly, and numerous studies were published focusing on the experiences of teachers and students, pointing to the benefits as well as challenges posed by the online medium. An entire special issue of the *Music Education Research journal* was published on 'The Digital Turn in Music Education' to explore such experiences.[10] Now, post-pandemic, higher education is in an 'emergent context'.[11] Without the pressures of the pandemic, there is an opportunity to develop more considered approaches to online learning. But uncertainty remains about the value of online learning, the optimum balance of in-person and online, and the expectations of future students, especially in practice-led disciplines. In addition, there is work required to overcome some negative perceptions of online learning which have been reinforced by media and political narratives.[12]

Prior to this, conservatoires around the world have been exploring synchronous online teaching with state-of-the art low latency videoconferencing technology for decades. Since the early 2000s, the RCM has run several projects using high-speed network technology such as *LoLa* (Low Latency Audio Visual Streaming System) and *Polycom* (currently, 'Poly') to facilitate international collaborations in teaching and performance. These projects have included international masterclasses, research seminars and conferences, and public remote performances. An example of one particularly innovative project is the Global Audition Training Programme which began in 2014. This initiative develops students' understanding of international orchestral auditioning techniques by bringing together a panel of experts from several locations around the world simultaneously, in real time, to work with students on understanding the differences in playing style and audition requirements between different continents, so that they can be prepared to compete more effectively worldwide. During the pandemic, these types of specialised projects also ceased to exist, as such technology relies on high bandwidth that is only available on institutional or campus networks. Like many other higher education institutions, conservatoire teachers and students had to be creative with the consumer technology that was available, adapting to the pandemic scenario.

Despite considerable interest and activity in myriad forms of online teaching and learning within conservatoires pre-, during, and post-pandemic, there have been very few projects focused on *global and collaborative* teaching as proposed in the Global Conservatoire model set out in this chapter. Furthermore, there is no research to date on *transnational* online teaching and learning within the conservatoire environment. The Global Conservatoire project therefore occupies a unique place in digital learning in higher education, enabling investigation of the ways in which an international frame might enhance online learning in the conservatoire.

The Global Conservatoire

Launched in 2021, the Global Conservatoire (GC) was initially a consortium of four world-leading conservatoires: the Royal College of Music, London (RCM); the Royal Danish Academy of Music, Copenhagen; the University of the Performing Arts, Vienna; and the Manhattan School of Music, New York City.[13] Together, these four partner schools (now five with the recent addition of the Conservatorium van Amsterdam) have been collaborating to design and deliver a suite of online transnational courses specifically planned for conservatoire students. Recognising the limitations of fully online delivery for the teaching of advanced instrumental and vocal tuition, GC online courses are designed to complement core principal study provision in conservatoires. The GC course portfolio aims to develop professional awareness, digital fluency, and cultural understanding, applying an online learning model that recognises the practice-led focus and learning needs of conservatoire students. To date, 15 GC modules have been developed, each reflecting a shared set of educational values and online design principles, while providing a flexible format for institutions to share their distinctive strengths.

At the heart of the GC delivery model is the concept of sharing institutional expertise in an online transnational classroom. Each online course is delivered by one of the consortium partners to a class comprising students from all four institutions. Not only is the GC partnership an international consortium representing Austria, Denmark, The Netherlands, the United Kingdom, and the United States, but furthermore all five institutions attract students from around the globe, with a combined average of 60% international students from over 50 countries.

Typically, each GC class of 20 students includes 4–5 students from each of the four partner institutions. To provide maximum access and flexibility across time zones and students' busy timetables, the ten-week courses are delivered through a series of asynchronous 'units' hosted on a virtual learning environment (VLE), accompanied by three to four synchronous Zoom meetings spaced evenly through the course. The courses are run as electives at undergraduate or postgraduate level, with two ECTS,[14] two US credit hours, or ten UK credits awarded for successful completion. This enables the courses to occupy a significant and credited position in the curriculum, running alongside the more traditional, face-to-face provision.

These specially designed courses draw upon the digital expertise, digital resources, prior experience of delivering technology-enhanced learning, and unique subject expertise of each conservatoire. This means that students are afforded access to subjects that would not otherwise be available to them at their 'home' institution. For instance a 'Nordic Noir' module reflects the unique Nordic Music research specialism of the Royal Danish Academy of Music. 'The Harlem Renaissance' module draws upon Manhattan School of Music's position as a New York City institution with deep connections to jazz through its location, history, and staff research culture. And 'Music and Racism' reflects MDW's interdisciplinary research expertise that focuses on the humanities, cultural studies, and social sciences to enrich our understanding of the arts in society today.

'The Digital Musician' course builds on the RCM's many years of digital innovation in livestreaming, distance learning, and composition with technology. Aimed at postgraduate performers and composers, it seeks to prepare students for a digital music career informed by current theory and practice. Topics range from digital content creation to online teaching using home platforms, to rehearsing and performing relying on state-of-the art technology, to composing in the digital age, and reaching new global audiences. The course concludes with forward-looking workshops that explore what innovation in the international arts context means today, prompting students to reflect on career opportunities as a digital musician. Following the GC delivery framework, four synchronous sessions via Zoom are delivered at regular intervals. These enable student networking between themselves and also with working professionals from around the world, who present and demonstrate their unique applications of technology and discuss their own careers in a digital world. The synchronous 'anchors' are interspersed with asynchronous learning units that enable learning through a variety of multimedia resources, for example, videos, podcasts, or interactive presentations that are released through the VLE on a weekly basis. Students complete weekly interactive tasks submitted through the VLE, and they have access to weekly 'office hours' with the course leader (an active researcher in the field of digital learning) if they wish to discuss any aspect of the course. Lastly, assessments are designed flexibly with the option to demonstrate learning through a combination of digital media including text, video, or a podcasts. This enables students from all institutions to work to their strengths.

The Global Conservatoire: research, evaluation, and insights

In parallel to the development of the GC online courses, a large research project led by the RCM has explored the following question: *'what constitutes best practice in online transnational learning environments within conservatoires?'*. This research was designed to: (i) highlight challenges and benefits of online teaching practices that will inform innovative models, going beyond the COVID-19 pandemic emergency teaching; (ii) share best teaching practice in online course design, delivery, and assessment; (iii) demonstrate best approaches to expanding student access to a wider range of subject areas; iv) reveal best practices to foster global artistic citizenship in our students; and (v) share students' and teachers' experiences of the development of a global online learning community that aims to promote artistic innovation, inclusion, collaboration, and excellence. While the goals were ambitious, engaging with these dimensions of online pedagogy could transform approaches to conservatoire education.

Following ethical approval from the Conservatoires UK Research Ethics Committee, the research applied a mixed-method approach comprising surveys, focus groups, and semi-structured individual interviews, with both students and staff from across the four institutions. Questions explored challenges as well as new opportunities in content delivery (for teachers) and in online learning (for students), as well as whether teaching and learning approaches had to be modified and, if so, how; and finally, how teachers and students co-construct effective transnational teaching and learning environments in an online setting.

Drawing upon the first-hand experiences of teachers and students in this way allowed us to understand the interaction of conservatoire cultures in the online transnational space. While the student experience is often the primary focus in learning and teaching projects, exploring this in tandem with the staff experience shines a light on the symbiotic relationship between institutional structures, staff support, and online student success.

The teacher perspective

The interviews with teachers not only revealed their motivations for joining the GC project but also gave detailed reports of challenges they experienced, with suggestions for future developments. The teachers' motivations for joining the GC mostly matched the students' motivations: teachers and students expressed their desire to belong to a transnational community, to have access to international expertise, and to meet peers from around the globe. Teachers also took pride in being selected to participate. The teachers collectively spoke about their previous experiences in online teaching and learning, which were mostly based on the pandemic emergency teaching and learning scenario, the majority of which was delivered synchronously (i.e. via Zoom, Skype, and other platforms). Very few teachers had the experience of planned and specifically designed asynchronous content delivery. This scenario led to considerable levels of anxiety about how best to plan and prepare for a class of students that they had never met before, nor could they seek immediate feedback from, as would be the case in face-to-face classroom teaching. The following quote illustrates some of these points:

> [O]nline teaching started mostly because of the shutdown for COVID here . . . trying to understand what that [the Global Conservatoire] entailed, and then especially with teaching [mentions course], how is that going to work? . . . Okay, . . . well that's not gonna work . . . and I probably changed the syllabus like . . . I changed it five times in two weeks, to make it work as best as I could.
>
> *(Teacher 6)*

The teachers collectively brought passion and energy to this project – but at the start, they felt overwhelmed by trial-and-error processes in order to develop a curriculum that 'worked' for the students. This points to a gap in staff development. Even post-pandemic, there is still a need to develop new pedagogical approaches coupled with basic technical expertise in digital learning design in order to work more efficiently in the asynchronous environment. Here, teachers are working with students they have not previously met and without the immediate feedback common in face-to-face scenarios. This is a situation that poses challenges.

During discussions of the challenges encountered, there were several references to the overwhelming workload related to the design of online resources, the new technical under-standing required to produce various formats of delivery (e.g. text, videos, multimedia, podcasts), and the need for availability to give timely feedback to students. Some of these challenges are illustrated below:

[A] *colleague of mine, who was also supposed to give a class this semester, dropped out, because she then learned that it would be actually much more work.*

(Focus group interview)

[E]*verything had to be more orchestrated. And thought-through beforehand . . . you have to define all of the content beforehand.*

(Teacher 7)

The interviews underlined the paradigm shift in the teaching approaches required for the Global Conservatoire, before and during delivery, compared to 'standard' face-to-face courses. Teachers needed to work to a radically different timeline to prepare for a GC course. This raises important questions related to issues of financial recognition for those staff involved in delivery and whether courses are financially viable when such significant investment of staff time is required. It also became clear that teachers found it challenging to plan courses when there were so many unknown factors (for instance not meeting students beforehand; not knowing students' levels of expertise from other institutions; not meeting peers; not having experience of asynchronous teaching). The research highlighted that sub-ject expertise and teaching experience on their own were not necessarily sufficient for staff to adapt to this radically different, and intensive, method of delivery.

Teachers themselves observed that there was a notable and unexpected difference between their GC teaching and the 'emergency' online teaching of the pandemic. The asynchro-nous and transnational teaching environment also presented quite different demands to the face-to-face classroom situations they were used to. It became clear that simply delivering content in the usual way but via a screen was not good practice and led to reduced engage-ment and motivation in the students. Online teaching must be seen as a different medium for which 'teachers as designers have to address both product-oriented and process-oriented aspects of strategic planning'.[15] In response to this realisation, all GC teachers expressed a desire for deeper reflection on best teaching practices, and this included learning about resource development that was also inclusive. Accessibility was soon at the forefront of the discussions, as illustrated in the following quote:

[T]*he book [course resource] must be in digital format . . . maybe it should also be trans-lated. Because the learning curve alone in the synchronous time is difficult for people who aren't natural English speakers.*

(Teacher focus group interview)

This is a situation routinely encountered in all five GC conservatoires, which have high pro-portions of students with English as an additional language. It is, however, exacerbated in the online space, where there is reduced scope for clarifications if resources and delivery are not planned well. Curriculum design and delivery must recognise not only different levels of English but also other important issues related to equality, diversity, and inclusion (EDI), many of which are amplified in an online and transnational context.

As a result, the GC team quickly identified the need for staff development activities in the first year of the project, which were specifically focused on universal principles for learning, to raise awareness around EDI in digital learning and to train staff towards best practices for resource development. Examples included discussions around resources for visually impaired students and for those with dyslexia as well as other learning differences; resources that responded to a range of individual preferences (e.g. text *and* videos), new delivery approaches such as microlearning to avoid cognitive overload; and a choice of submission formats for assessments to allow students to showcase their strengths. Although training focused on the needs of GC courses, it became clear that many of these inclusive teaching practices were equally important and transferable to other areas of conservatoire delivery, whether online, blended, or even face-to-face.

It was also noted that participation in the first year of the GC project was a steep learning curve for all involved. The interviews highlighted some of the limitations faced by teaching staff, the need for a closer collaboration with digital learning teams, and dedicated time for experimentation. This distributed and experimental approach may have felt uncomfortable at first, but it led to deeper reflection upon one's own teaching (i.e. a metacognitive approach to teaching) not often present in day-to-day in-person teaching:

> [T]*he whole preparation of the course was totally new and for me it was a new way of having to think about how I teach and what the topics are that I want to teach, and what are the points I want to bring across.*
>
> *(Teacher 5)*

> [S]*hould I now – because I've been challenged, should I now incorporate this into everything that I do, even performing?*
>
> *(Focus group interview)*

> *I changed . . . asking the students to evaluate, and so – from the start . . . And I've never done that before. But this is really, the way of approaching and making sure that they are that present and open, I will do that in the physical teaching as well.*
>
> *(Focus group interview)*

The first cohort of GC teachers spoke of expanding their teaching knowledge in new directions and developing their resilience as educators, which included being more open to experimentation, developing greater awareness and responsiveness to cultural difference, rethinking their teaching approaches in general (not simply for online teaching), and engaging with technology as an innovative medium for their work.

The desire to create a strong transnational community of practice was evident, but such a community did not emerge automatically. The interviews revealed the need for strong peer collaborations and more active efforts to connect with colleagues for feedback and 'sense-checking'. Both teachers and students expressed feelings of isolation and loneliness, which is somewhat expected in asynchronous learning environments:

> *I must admit that we received an immense amount of technical support . . . but I had no peer evaluation of my stuff. We are so . . . even today I'm sitting here I feel a little . . . very lonely, with yourself in this thing.*
>
> *(Focus group interview)*

> *[T]he kind of abstractness of it was somehow an obstacle for me. But now, you know, sharing and seeing that others are going through the same stuff is actually a kind of motivation that, that's somehow an impulse for, yeah, further steps.*
>
> *(Focus group interview)*

In summary, the first cohort of GC teachers experienced a steep learning curve. Although all were highly experienced teachers in conservatoires, they identified considerable challenges adapting their practice to the asynchronous and transnational online environment of the GC. This raises questions for conservatoires about how institutions can best prepare and support their teaching staff for increasingly digital and global teaching approaches.

The student perspective

As is the case with teachers, students' prior online learning experiences were mostly related to the emergency synchronous learning during the pandemic of 2020:

> *In my school before the pandemic, we had a few lectures that were shifted online and then I also attended a summer program in 2020 that was all held online using a Facebook group – on a private group page in my school we used Zoom.*
>
> *(Participant 3)*

While most online teaching during the pandemic was imposed upon students by necessity, the GC offers a different prospect. Students may opt in to the GC, choosing to participate in a course that they understand from the outset will be delivered fully online. Interviews with students revealed enthusiasm for the novel concept of GC, and some were attracted to the 'prestige' of the programme as a distinctive addition to their musical CV.

Students were also attracted to the prospect of studying in an international classroom, with students from other international conservatoires. They stated that they opted for these courses because they wanted to find out '*what the atmosphere was like at other institutions*', to know other students and other places as well as other cultures. Some students also wanted to attend courses delivered in English. Their motivations were also related to having access to international expertise and to new subjects that went beyond their home institution curricula, as illustrated here:

> *I am curious to learn subjects that aren't offered at my school.*
>
> *(Participant 3)*

I thought that was really nice to not just have the perspective of our teacher but also other guest speakers that was, I think, very interesting.

(Participant 3)

The asynchronous learning format was new to most students, and the challenges and benefits of this were clearly stated in the interviews. The flexibility of learning offered by the asynchronous delivery was perceived as very positive by most students. They had continuous access to course materials for revision and for studying at their own pace and in their own time. Many saw this as advantageous for working around their intensive in-person conservatoire schedules. However, it also presented students with unanticipated challenges and demands on their organisational and time management skills:

I felt that it was very nice that we had to deliver something every week, also quite tough to have to manage that every week. But that's part of what I liked about the course that there were like high standards.

(Participant 13)

Students dealt with the high volume of independent learning in different ways. Some students mentioned that they usually prioritised their rehearsals and performances, and, if they did not access course materials regularly, it led to an overwhelming volume of materials to be studied all at once. In this scenario, students had to accept that increased flexibility meant taking increased responsibility for their learning. This also highlighted the importance of a well-planned course design, presented through clear and well-structured platforms, which guided students through each step of the programme in a coherent manner.

The synchronous sessions were important to establish more personal contact between teachers and students as well as to make peer-to-peer connections. These sessions allowed direct access to international speakers as well as discussing points of online materials with the teacher (i.e. based on flipped learning pedagogy).[16] Furthermore, the synchronous sessions were crucial for networking and socialising, for obtaining feedback, and for getting to know one another more closely. This also points to some of the challenges in the design of the courses. For instance teachers and students commented on how they embarked on this project with the desire to be part of a global music community, but, in contrast, they felt somewhat isolated behind their own computer screens. Teachers highlighted the importance of the synchronous sessions to meet their students *before* they planned the delivery – in fact, in the second year of the GC project, the timing of these sessions was changed to frontload them in the early weeks of each course. Students mentioned that they would like to meet their peers in advance and noted that more coursework in groups would be beneficial to develop the international community of learning that they were seeking. The quotes below highlight not only their appreciation for group work within the courses but also how this was developed outside the GC:

I love doing the group project. It works really well, and I think it's so, so cool to connect to people from all around the world, and to see how yeah different we are, but we have so much together, so I loved it.

(Participant 8)

[N]ow I have some new Facebook friends from New York and Vienna, which is nice. Yeah, I mean we only had to do like, one thing together where all the students were involved.

(Participant 10)

This points to some misalignment between teacher and student goals in the first delivery of GC courses. While teachers initially focused on delivering high-quality materials, in practice students were more interested in *social* forms of learning with students from other institutions and cultures. In some respects, this should come as no surprise, as collaboration is one of the cornerstones of conservatoire education and a familiar form of learning for our students. However, in online learning, it is all too easy to become preoccupied by technical considerations. It is clear that the focus needs to shift towards the design of *peer learning* activities to maximise the potential of the online transnational learning environment.

The Global Conservatoire: reflections

The research shone a light on the combination of cultural and educational expectations that shape students' learning in this online transnational environment, representing multiple interacting dimensions (see Figure 16.1).

In such a complex web of learning experiences and expectations, there is a risk of students experiencing a type of 'dissonance'. The word is applied here in a similar way to Burwell, who employs this metaphor to imply 'a want of resolution without suggesting single causes, instead evoking a confluence of forces and the tensions among them'.[17] Tensions may occur when students experience the confluence of different and unfamiliar learning cultures in a digital space that is already quite detached from their usual learning environment. At the outset, the GC classroom stands in direct contrast with the immediacy and personalised experiences of students' typical conservatoire experiences. To overcome this isolation and unfamiliarity, it is therefore critical for social connections and community building to be

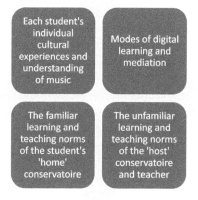

FIGURE 16.1   Multiple interacting dimensions representing the confluence of cultural and educational expectations of transnational students in the GC.

woven into curriculum design. This work needs to be intensive and sustained to build student motivation and maintain engagement.

The GC research project, running in parallel to the teaching and learning, sets out a new model for conservatoire transnational online teaching and learning. Although in its infancy at the time of writing, initial findings suggest that there can be significant long-term benefits for conservatoire students and staff when this type of transnational education is used to complement in-person activities. Digital upskilling, promoting a global outlook, and fostering new international connections with peers are all significant outcomes for students and staff. However, the ambitiousness of this project has revealed gaps in conservatoire infrastructure and areas for development to optimise student engagement, outcomes, and the long-term sustainability of the project. For instance a mature approach to transnational online course design requires a careful planning of group activities and assessments to foster international collaboration between students, as well as stimulate the development of a transnational community of teaching and learning. Looking ahead, there is scope to expand the co-creative possibilities of this model, for instance through the co-teaching of new courses across the partner institutions. On a practical level, the timing of synchronous 'contact time' in the online transnational environment requires careful planning to maximise social cohesion at the outset of courses and lay solid foundations for asynchronous learning to take place. And while the concept of students as practitioners has informed all GC courses to date, there is room for further exploration of the relationship between conservatoire students' personal artistic development and the online transnational experience.

Next steps

This chapter highlights an urgent call to work towards the development of a new approach to online teaching within the conservatoire sector, an approach which we term 'global pedagogy'. This stems from the shared set of values developed for the GC online transnational teaching environment. Global pedagogy embraces and responds to cultural diversity in the online transnational space; it seeks to find common and inclusive approaches to assessment across institutions; it fosters staff and students' international collaborations to a higher level of co-creation; it uses social connections to promote student motivation and engagement in online learning; and above all, it broadens students' access to a variety of subjects and international expertise in a common way across institutions around the globe. A further impact of this exploration is seen in increased reflection upon teaching and learning approaches adopted by the team and the impact of this on teaching that happens in-person within the conservatoire.

The implications of this for the conservatoire sector could involve significant recasting of the conservatoire vision of learning and teaching excellence. The GC project points to three areas where conservatoires could prepare for global pedagogy to become a cornerstone not just of GC courses but also of their institution-wide learning and teaching ethos:

- Key take-away 1: the GC research identified clear gaps in staff development for twenty-first-century teachers in the conservatoire. To develop more agile forms of learning and teaching, spanning face-to-face, blended, and fully online modes, teachers need access to regular training and time for development that recognise the emergent nature of pedagogy in the digital age. Our conservatoire learning cultures should promote co-creation between teaching staff and digital learning teams, focusing on facilitating social and practice-led forms of learning rather than basic 'technical' training in VLE and media tools. Coordinating this training with other conservatoires would help to promote innovative practices and improved resilience among teachers.

- Key take-away 2: the model of compartmentalised learning, where individual modules exist independently in the curriculum as silos that are designed, delivered, and assessed by one teacher, may not be sustainable. In recent years, much artistic practice has exhibited a distributed approach to creativity, and conservatoire pedagogies can undoubtedly learn from this reimagining of agency and authorship. But to enable this, conservatoires will need to adopt more coordinated approaches to enabling learning, investing in effective infrastructure, systems, and communication across the institution. Meaningful and sustained collaboration between teachers, managers and administrators, learning technologists, IT staff, and indeed students themselves is critical to ensure that online and blended learning can be delivered to the same quality as in-person elements in the curriculum.
- Key take-away 3: by normalising online learning experiences in the core conservatoire curricula, students can become more digitally fluent and resilient. In doing so, conservatoires can enable students to move smoothly between face-to-face and online contexts, equipping them with the tools and the confidence to flourish as digital artists, collaborators, and learners.

To reshape our curricula in this way, we need to set aside some outdated conceptions of the limitations of online teaching, for instance that it is of lower quality, only suited to theoretical subjects, and is low cost to deliver. With the necessary investment in staff training, infrastructure, and curriculum design, conservatoires are in an ideal position to develop innovative, socially driven approaches that place practice, collaboration, and cultural responsiveness at the heart of digital learning.

Bibliography

Ahmed, Hanaa Ouda Khadri. 'Flipped learning as a new educational paradigm: An analytical critical study'. *European Scientific Journal, ESJ* 12, no. 10 (April 2016): 417. https://doi.org/10.19044/esj.2016.v12n10p417.

Burwell, Kim. 'Dissonance in the studio: An exploration of tensions within the apprenticeship setting in higher education music'. *International Journal of Music Education* 34, no. 4 (November 2016): 499–512. https://doi.org/10.1177/0255761415574124.

Burwell, Kim. 'Issues of Dissonance in Advanced Studio Lessons'. *Research Studies in Music Education* 41, no. 1 (April 2019): 3–17. https://doi.org/10.1177/1321103X18771797.

Burwell, Kim, Gemma Carey, and Dawn Bennett. 'Isolation in studio music teaching: The secret garden'. *Arts and Humanities in Higher Education* 18, no. 4 (October 2019): 372–94. https://doi.org/10.1177/1474022217736581.

Camlin, David A., and Tania Lisboa. 'The digital 'turn' in music education (editorial)'. *Music Education Research* 23, no. 2 (March 15, 2021): 129–38. https://doi.org/10.1080/14613808.2021.1908792.

Dammers, Richard J. 'Utilizing internet-based videoconferencing for instrumental music lessons'. *Update: Applications of Research in Music Education* 28, no. 1 (August 19, 2009): 17–24. https://doi.org/10.1177/8755123309344159.

Duffy, Celia. 'ICON: Radical professional development in the conservatoire'. *Arts and Humanities in Higher Education* 15, no. 3–4 (July 2016): 376–85. https://doi.org/10.1177/1474022216647385.

Duffy, Sam, and Patrick Healey. 'A new medium for remote music tuition'. *Journal of Music, Technology and Education* 10, no. 1 (2017): 5–29. https://doi.org/10.1386/jmte.10.1.5_1.

Dumlavwalla, Diana. 'Transitioning from traditional to online piano lessons: Perceptions of students, parents and teacher'. *MTNA e-Journal* 8, no. 3 (2017): 2.

Dye, Keith. 'Student and instructor behaviors in online music lessons: An exploratory study'. *International Journal of Music Education* 34, no. 2 (2016): 161–70. https://doi.org/10.1177/0255761415584.2.

Global Audition Training. *Global Audition Training*, 2016. Accessed April 11, 2023. www.dkdm.dk/en/news/global-audition-training.

The Global Conservatoire Global Conservatoire, 2021. Accessed December 23, 2022. https://global-conservatoire.com/.

Jarvis, Alistair. *Making the Political Case for Online Learning*. Accessed December 9, 2022. www.london.ac.uk/news-opinion/making-political-case-online-learning.

Johnson, Carol. 'Teaching music online: Changing pedagogical approach when moving to the online environment'. *London Review of Education* 5, no. 3 (2017): 439–56. https://doi.org/10.18546/LRE.15.3.08.

Johnson, Carol. 'Preparing for change: Getting ready for offering online music courses'. In *Pedagogy Development for Teaching Online Music*, 1–19. IGI Global, 2018. https://doi.org/10.4018/978-1-5225-5109-6.ch001.

Koutsoupidou, Theano. 'Online distance learning and music training: Benefits, drawbacks and challenges'. *Open Learning: The Journal of Open, Distance and e-Learning* 29, no. 3 (2014): 243–55. https://doi.org/10.1080/02680513.2015.1011112.

Kruse, Nathan B., Steven C. Harlos, Russell M. Callahan, and Michelle L. Herring. 'Skype music lessons in the academy: Intersections of music education, applied music and technology'. *Journal of Music, Technology and Education* 6, no. 1 (April 1, 2013): 43–60. https://doi.org/10.1386/jmte.6.1.43_1.

Long, Marion, Andrea Creech, Helena Gaunt, Susan Hallam, and Linnhe Robertson. 'Blast from the past: Conservatoire students' experiences and perceptions of public master classes'. *Musicae Scientiae* 16, no. 3 (November 2012): 286–306. https://doi.org/10.1177/1029864912458848.

Maki, Jukka. *Is It Possible to Teach Music in a Classroom from Distance of 1000 km? Learning Environment of Music Education using ISDN-Videoconferencing*. Association for the Advancement of Computing in Education (AACE), 2001.

Office for Students. *Blended Learning Review*, October 2022. Accessed December 9, 2022. www.officeforstudents.org.uk/media/dc1c3c84-269a-4c40-8f87-15bfae0fcced/blended-learning-review-panel-report.pdf.

Park, Yeil. 'High school of online cello playing: A quantitative analysis of online music instruction via video conferencing application'. PhD dissertation, Arizona State University, 2019.

Pike, Pamela D. 'Improving music teaching and learning through online service: A case study of a synchronous online teaching internship'. *International Journal of Music Education* 35, no. 1 (June 23, 2016): 107–17. https://doi.org/10.1177/0255761415613534.

Pike, Pamela D., and Kristin Shoemaker. 'The effect of distance learning on acquisition of piano sight-reading skills'. *Journal of Music, Technology and Education* 6, no. 2 (August 1, 2013): 147–62. https://doi.org/10.1386/jmte.6.2.147_1.

Rapanta, Chrysi, Luca Botturi, Peter Goodyear, Lourdes Guàrdia, and Marguerite Koole. 'Online university teaching during and after the Covid-19 crisis: Refocusing teacher presence and learning activity'. *Postdigital Science and Education* 2, no. 3 (October 2020): 923–45. https://doi.org/10.1007/s42438-020-00155-y.

Riley, Holly, Rebecca B. MacLeod, and Matthew Libera. 'Low latency audio video: Potentials for collaborative music making through distance learning'. *Update: Applications of Research in Music Education* 34, no. 3 (2016): 15–23.

Rumiantsev, Tamara W., Wilfried F. Admiraal, and Roeland M. van der Rijst. 'Conservatoire leaders' observations and perceptions on curriculum reform'. *British Journal of Music Education* 37, no. 1 (March 2020): 29–41. https://doi.org/10.1017/S0265051719000214.

PERSPECTIVE: CHAPTER 16

Joachim Junghanss

Introduction

As Deputy Director of the most recent partner of the Global Conservatoire consortium, the Conservatorium van Amsterdam, it is a pleasure to share my perspective following such insightful work by Tania Lisboa and Diana Salazar. My perspectives are informed by my role as part of the institute's board of directors, as well as heading the Jazz, Pop and Electronic Music departments and 'CvA Online', the institution's own digital branch.

What drives me as a musician, educator, and administrator is a holistic view of music practice, connecting genres and opening up to the possibilities of technology and music production. As a pianist trained in jazz and classical music, education, and composition/arrangement, I was fortunate to study under the guidance of excellent musicians in Germany, the United States, and around the globe. I earned a DMA degree as a Fulbright grantee in the United States at the Manhattan School of Music, researching the interaction between humans and computers in musical improvisation.

In my view, music performance and education do not only have transformative power within future societies. It is also the role of musicians to act as inspiring and empathic leaders and activists, connecting cultures and driving future societal development. Driven by this conviction, I embraced several non-traditional roles that broadened my cross-cultural experience, including launching a grassroots music education project in Ghana, setting up a pop and production music academy in India, establishing a digital-only music school, and working as a management consultant at the Boston Consulting Group.

I am particularly fascinated by the potential of technological evolution and digitalisation in music. While being aware of pitfalls and challenges, I believe that digitalisation is one of the cornerstones of future global music education. As CvA has built years of expertise in digital music education, I am particularly excited that it recently joined the Global Conservatoire and am convinced it will add value to this promising initiative.

DOI: 10.4324/9781003281573-35

Perspectives

Futuring: the global conservatoire

Why a global conservatoire?

Global demand for music and for music education is increasing, and conservatoires provide music education to the top segment in the field. As our world becomes increasingly digitally interconnected, the need for online collaboration is growing around the globe. A shared, digital collaboration between established music academies, the Global Conservatoire (GC) can serve as a key initiative to take up this challenge and meet this demand.

What are the implications of being 'global' and yet a 'conservatoire' in general? What are future challenges and opportunities in higher music education for the Global Conservatoire in particular? What role could the GC play in a global society of the future?

The conservatoire as a model for progress

The word 'conservative' is often connotated with being 'averse to change or innovation'. Why would a rapidly changing and progressing, global society need a global 'conservatoire' in this sense at all? I will argue that, in contrast to their name, conservatoires have in fact been developing and transforming music education throughout history.

A *conservatorio* was an orphanage during the Italian Renaissance period and earlier. Such orphanages, like the ones in Venice in the seventeenth century, developed into musical training centres as girls and boys received regular musical training, and they educated outstanding musicians. As the forerunners of European music academies, they therefore soon became role models for the continent. Conservatoires were founded in cities all over Europe and later also northern America. The term 'conservatoire' is thus merely a historical reference on a transformational path coined by venture, effort, and development in music education.

The transnational conservatoire

What potential arises from being 'global' for the GC and for each partner academy? Academies are traditionally closely embedded into their specific geographical location. Music academies very often carry their city's or country's name in their titles, as do all partner academies of the GC. In an increasingly digital and interconnected world, the term 'global' omits such defined, physical location. The GC is not an online branch of an already existing institute such as 'Berklee online' for the Berklee College of Music. The GC is a separate, online entity and therefore can develop its own identity. In my opinion, it is the structural, transnational nature of collaboration within this shared entity which bears its potential for partners, their faculty, and their students.

Being 'global' coins two characteristic aspects of the GC: transnational collaboration and worldwide accessibility. Within its partnership, the GC shares the faculty of each institution on a structural basis. It develops a common course offering, which integrates the specific expertise of each academy. Furthermore, the administrative staff of all partner academies collaborate regularly, from student recruitment and registration to documentation and grading. Thereby, students, faculty, and institutions themselves learn from each other.

Such committed and structural collaboration provides the GC its strength within the higher music education landscape. The GC offering is available to all students of the participating academies. This allows students not only to benefit from the expertise of the partner but also to increase their network, meet peers, and form learning communities outside their home institute and across the globe. 'Global' furthermore stands for access to students, who can take part in online courses despite their respective locations. Through this regular, transnational collaboration of five established academies, the GC brings new value to students, faculty, and the institutions themselves.

The transformative conservatoire

I have argued that conservatoires are places of venture, effort, and development. Let's think of conservatoires as places of transformation. On their journey through history, conservatoires have been developing new educational models in music and widening their course portfolios. For example, the traditional master–apprentice model itself was gradually transformed by music academies. Before the conservatoire, the master embodied the curriculum, the master's house was the institution, and the student was a subordinate. Translating it into an institutional context, the conservatoire implicitly altered this strict relation. Further educational strategies, such as team teaching, peer learning and evaluation, and feedback, gradually transformed the traditional model. Online education, such as that practiced in the GC, provides room to experiment with the latest models of learning and teaching music. Furthermore, students follow academic curricula with a multitude of courses. Conservatoires have continually developed and innovated their curricula, creating an ever-widening portfolio of disciplines and choices. By adding variety to the academy curricula, the GC can add valuable opportunities to widen choices for students.

Transformative ventures such as the GC are necessary to progress into the future of music education. Our globalised society undergoes an accelerated technological transformation, and music education makes no exception. On the other hand, music is still a deeply inter-human art form which has immediate sensual, physical, and social characteristics, for example when visiting a live concert or stepping into a physical classroom. So far, it has been arguably challenging to duplicate those experiences technically, yet technology is catching up. If conservatoires are institutes of transformation, they need to collaborate and experiment with technology. Offering music education in technologically driven environments is one way of doing so.

Being an online entity, the GC is a key initiative to branch out conservatoire education into the digital and also the virtual realm. The tech market is progressing to connect people around the globe virtually with an improved experience. Immersive technologies will capture and reproduce sensual experiences more and more convincingly, such as 3D vision, immersive sound, and low-latency connections. Other senses, such as haptics, will follow. While virtual reality experiences and gaming are widely available first applications, more areas of use will follow.

The virtual conservatoire

As technology will provide for more immersive, memorable, and profound experiences, music performance and education will also be available in virtual reality environments and metaverses. Education using those technologies will therefore become part of the music education offering, and conservatoires will need to pivot their education also towards these emerging technological environments. As a shared, digital initiative, the GC can play an important role in this technological transformation of conservatoire education.

Technological development is an obvious, yet certainly not the only future challenge to conservatoires for which the GC can help to develop answers. The GC can also stimulate the development of strong communities within music education more sustainably, since it does not rely on travel. Furthermore, it can extend access to conservatoire education to more diverse groups of students. Students from remote and less-affluent regions could access higher music education while not having to travel to and live in major metropoles. Therefore, the GC model offers the potential to connect talent across the globe to benefit from its educational offering.

Summary

Higher music education is challenged to develop at a quick pace and to develop within a global, collaborative context. Despite their name, conservatoires have proven to be institutes able to transform music education; future societies demand progressiveness, collaboration, and agility. The GC offers promising potential to transform conservatoire education towards a global future.

Chapter Notes

1 See www.rcm.ac.uk/about/news/all/2019-04-01otisandeunice.aspx; www.dkdm.dk/en/news/global-audition-training; https://performancescience.ac.uk/simulator/.
2 See Long et al., 'Blast from the past'; Duffy, 'ICON: Radical professional development'; and Burwell et al., 'Isolation in studio music teaching'.
3 Park, 'High school of online cello playing'; Dammers, 'Utilizing internet-based videoconferencing'.
4 Dammers, 'Utilizing internet-based videoconferencing'; Kruse et al., 'Skype music lessons in the academy'; Pike, 'Improving music teaching and learning'.
5 Riley et al., 'Low latency audio video'.
6 Maki, *Is It Possible*.
7 Dumlavwalla, 'Transitioning from traditional to online'.
8 Duffy and Healey, 'A new medium for remote music tuition'; Dye, 'Student and instructor behaviors'.
9 Johnson, 'Teaching music online'; Johnson, 'Preparing for change'.
10 Camlin and Lisboa, 'The digital 'turn' in music education'.
11 Office for Students, *Blended Learning Review*, 3.
12 See Jarvis, *Making the Political Case for Online Learning*.
13 The project 'GloCoDA: A Global Conservatoire for the Digital Age' was initially supported by a two-year Erasmus+ Strategic Partnership Grant, which provided start-up funding for staff training, course development, technical support, and research-led evaluation. For more information, see https://globalconservatoire.com/. Since the time of writing, the Conservatorium van Amsterdam (CvA) has joined the Global Conservatoire Consortium.
14 European Credit Transfer and Accumulation System – a system used to recognise work completed by students on exchanges with institutions outside their home institution country. See https://education.ec.europa.eu/education-levels/higher-education/inclusive-and-connected-higher-education/european-credit-transfer-and-accumulation-system.
15 Rapanta et al., 'Online university teaching', 925.
16 Ahmed, 'Flipped learning as a new educational paradigm'.
17 Burwell, 'Dissonance in the studio', 4.

17

WHAT NEXT FOR CONSERVATOIRES?

Rosie Perkins, Diana Salazar, and Colin Lawson

Introduction

Inside the Contemporary Conservatoire has juxtaposed a range of voices from both within and beyond the Royal College of Music, London (RCM). Over the course of the preceding pages, we have moved from rethinking conservatoire identities and values (Part I), to exploring learning and teaching in the conservatoire (Part II), to considering conservatoires of the future (Part III). Readers will have observed myriad different views, informed by those working in a multitude of roles and with varied musical, educational, and professional backgrounds. Reflecting on key themes from across the book, this short conclusion foregrounds some of the potential areas for development as we continue to shape and reimagine the contemporary conservatoire.

The external national and international environment is a major factor in determining institutional health and well-being. In particular, the fiscal landscape has become more challenging for many conservatoires. While the balance of government support, student fees, endowments, and sponsorship vary, the global financial crisis of 2008 heralded an era of general austerity. In the United Kingdom, an infrastructure of institution-led fundraising has been necessary to support capital projects and scholarships (see Chapter 5), while Brexit (2016) has led to more consideration of the applicant pipeline, adversely impacting musicians' mobility and opportunities such as the Erasmus exchange network. Furthermore, the English Baccalaureate (EBacc, 2010) excluded the performing arts, leading many schools to downgrade (or even abandon) these subjects when faced with ever challenging budgets. Such a policy disadvantages pupils who may have a special talent outside traditional academic subjects. Controversially, the EBacc was defined as 'a set of subjects . . . that keeps young people's options open for further study and future careers'.[1] Moreover, the British government has increasingly linked the value of degrees with the earning potential of their graduates, an unwelcome development for the musical community. The UK government publishes Longitudinal Educational Outcomes data, which shows 'employment and earnings outcomes of higher education first degree graduates by provider, subject studied and graduate characteristics'.[2] Furthermore, the COVID-19 pandemic brought a new set of

DOI: 10.4324/9781003281573-36

challenges, especially for students but also for institutions, and the unstable political situation around the world may have unexpected consequences at any moment. Against this complex external background, we return to the question posed at the end of Chapter 1: what should be our next steps? In what follows, we offer four areas in which we argue the contemporary – and future – conservatoire must focus.

Broadening musical excellence

Excellence is one of the RCM's founding principles and is at the core of our strategy and identity. But what do we – and can we – mean by it? As noted in Chapter 4, musical excellence is varied, nuanced, and personal. It is a journey for everyone involved in the conservatoire, and it is, and needs to be, constantly evolving. The plurality of voices in the preceding chapters hints at varying views on musical excellence inside the conservatoire. This is perhaps not surprising, given that 'excellence' is not easy to define in any domain. As John W. Gardner put it:

> I find that 'excellence' is a curiously powerful word – a word about which people feel strongly and deeply. But it is a word that means different things to different people. . . . As the individual contemplates the word 'excellence' he [sic] reads into it his own aspirations, his own conception of high standards, his hopes for a better world. And it brings powerfully to his mind evidence of the betrayal of excellence (as he conceives it).[3]

Musical excellence in the conservatoire is often imbued with similar strength of feeling. As we have read in this volume, questions about musical excellence relate not only to the specificities of musical processes and products but also to wider discussions about what sorts of activities 'count' when we talk about excellence within specialist music institutions. In particular, balancing and assessing the art and craft of musical performance and composition provoke a broad range of musical opinion.

Looking to the future, one way we can protect this breadth is by creating the conditions needed to enable excellence for each *individual* student. This means that we aim to create a culture where students have the agency to explore what being an excellent musician means for them, within a space where they trust that their excellence will be valued. This last point is key – if we are to encourage students to curate their own views on excellence, we must be able, willing, and ready to respond in kind. This means listening and reacting to student imperatives as well as maintaining an openness to change. Enacting change in complex environments is challenging when there is such an array of different views, yet no one should feel disenfranchised. Of course, conservatoires have institutional structures – such as the expertise of staff and the regulations of programmes – that shape and put boundaries around the types of excellence that we can realistically support. But we must also acknowledge the view that 'institutional structures and training routes need to valorise the creative musician with a wide set of competencies'[4] and that this requires openness to recognising and celebrating excellence in domains or activities that will expand and challenge some of our more long-standing practices.

To achieve this relies on maintaining a porous rather than a sealed environment, in which the student voice plays a seminal part. It requires recognising that our institutional structures need to be adaptable to allow a dynamic and curious approach to new practices within the conservatoire. This might include, for example, establishing new programmes (such as those described in Chapter 14), facilitating meaningful ways in which students can experiment with new genres and repertoire (see Chapter 15), and finding new ways of encouraging students to explore their artistry and musical futures (see Chapters 2, 3, and 12 in particular). A further important element in maintaining excellence has recently been a renewed emphasis on students' mental health (see Chapter 11). We are obliged to offer a balance of empathy with expectations of and support for the resilience that will be needed in the profession.[5] Helping students to overcome adversity and disappointment is a significant element in effective mentoring. With all of this comes reflection on how we assess excellence and decide upon what counts as 'success'.[6] Camlin argues that:

> [I]n order to understand how to assess the quality of any specified instance of musicking, we have to understand what it is for, in terms of the degree to which it aspires towards realization of presentational/aesthetic qualities, praxial/participatory qualities and its transformative social impact on listeners and/or participants.[7]

In other words, excellence differs depending on the nature and the purpose of the musical activity in question; there are 'multiple excellences'.[8] If we are to facilitate these multiple excellences as defined by the members of our community, then we need to have dynamic admissions and assessment processes that encourage and actively celebrate the demonstrations of excellence in and across diverse musical practices and domains, so that '"experimenting" with new ideas becomes an inherent rule of the game for higher music education'.[9] With the age of deference in sharp decline, a top-down approach can no longer carry conviction.

Social engagement and civic responsibility

In the 1980s, Peter Renshaw argued that professional musicians were failing to recognise the potential role of music in a society in crisis. Against this backdrop, he articulated a vision for a new conservatoire course that would, among other things, invite musicians to reappraise their role in the community, raise awareness of the musical demands of a multicultural society, and foreground the imperative for music-making to be accessible and responsive to changing societies.[10] In the decades that have followed, some of this vision has undoubtedly permeated conservatoire and higher music education practices around the world. Student perspectives on social engagement, while being diverse in many ways, include imperatives such as engaging in social change agendas, extending interests and connections beyond music, sharing musical skills with others, and cultivating personal values that benefit others.[11] Yet, Tregear and colleagues remind us that many questions remain about the extent to which conservatoires meaningfully engage with society, arguing that 'it is both timely and necessary for conservatoires to reconsider, reinvigorate and re-articulate their capacity to contribute to broader social goods'.[12] As articulated at the beginning of this volume, many members of society are simply unaware of the breadth of endeavour to which most conservatoires aspire.

These issues are grappled with by many involved in higher music education. Authors of several chapters in this volume refer to Helena Gaunt and colleagues' proposition of musicians as 'makers in society',[13] a paradigm that positions three domains as being central to higher music education: musicians' visions and identities, musical craft and artistry, and need and potential in society. This final point opens central questions for the conservatoire. What should conservatoires (as particular forms of higher music education) and their inhabitants contribute to larger society? How can this be inclusive and relevant? What role can the conservatoire play in demonstrating – through both practice and research – how music contributes not only to cultural life but also to well-being, health, and flourishing? How can the conservatoire actively shape new professional possibilities, so that students are not only prepared for 'the profession' but also can in fact reshape and redefine what that profession is, in ways that are socially oriented and responsive?

As Gaunt et al. point out, evolving curricula to enable musicians to live up to their potential as 'makers in society' brings into play many creative tensions, not least between cultural heritage and innovation that connects to society. It is imperative that these creative tensions be given space within the conservatoire, so that wide-ranging musical activities can sit side by side in a diverse and socially engaged musical ecology. This, in turn, requires meaningful two-way partnerships that connect students and institutions with other musicians and communities.[14] Empowering students to seek and find these communities and to consider how their music can make a difference are a key part of moving towards a more civic conservatoire: 'conservatoires may then become better known as institutions that support and nourish not just the dreams and hopes of the talented, elite, performers fortunate to enter their doors, but ultimately the dreams and hopes of us all'.[15] Alongside access and excellence, advocacy was a founding principle of the RCM. This is today more important than ever, not just in a narrow conservatoire context but also in terms of Western art music as a whole. As Nicholas Kenyon has so powerfully written,

> [C]lassical music has had to contend in recent years with a change from its privileged position in our society to one in which it is repeatedly, and in my opinion rightly, challenged by pop music, world music and a range of alternative mass entertainment. . . . If it means that classical music has more strenuously to argue its case and earn its place in our society and prove every day the insights and excitements that it can bring, then surely that is absolutely positive.[16]

Equality, diversity, and inclusion (EDI)

Chapter 15 explored the ways in which conservatoires are taking concrete steps to develop curricula and learning experiences that critique the canon and better reflect the diversity of society today. But as Roger Wilson points out, institutions with strong roots in the traditions of classical music are especially slow to change. Today, there are still very serious issues of representation in the student and staff bodies of conservatoires, as well as their audiences, boards, and donors, a situation that can perpetuate 'acts of self-affirmation and self-reproduction', a type of echo chamber in the conservatoire.[17] Reflecting on the many themes in this volume, this poses a risk for all aspects of conservatoires' work. Questions about inclusion arise, implicitly or explicitly, in nearly every chapter. We can trace this thread back to a fundamental question for all conservatoires today: who are we for?

We could optimistically suggest that a conservatoire can be for everyone, but in practice at present, this remains an aspiration. Even a student who has won a hard-fought place at a conservatoire may sense that they do not belong. On entering the conservatoire, students may bring with them musical and sociocultural experiences that deviate considerably from the dominant experiences of 'typical' conservatoire students. A young Black musician might not see themselves reflected in the community, and a state-educated student might feel isolated from those who experienced a specialist music education. Unintentionally, conservatoire norms can erode individuals' sense of belonging and introduce psychological barriers through what Porton describes as a 'them and us divide'.[18] And this divide can be amplified by physical aspects such as grand, unfamiliar buildings that portray esteem, privilege, and wealth, issues explored in Chapter 13. As a result, staff and students can also easily succumb to imposter syndrome, surmising that they are operating in an environment to which they do not really belong.[19]

To take a more meaningful and arguably overdue step forward, we should ask ourselves what *real inclusion* looks and feels like in the conservatoire. True inclusion not only celebrates efforts to represent women, ethnically diverse, and disabled composers and artists in the artistic programme but also recognises these initiatives as just one step in a process of culture change. While widening participation initiatives is important, genuine inclusion acknowledges that diversifying recruitment does not automatically create an inclusive space. A strong sense of belonging is key, and to build this, we must recognise and respect the lived experiences and identities of everyone in the conservatoire community. A truly inclusive conservatoire gives a voice to everyone, not simply those who have traditionally been located at the top of the hierarchy. Such a community is conscious of the ways in which tacit (i.e. 'inside') knowledge and assumptions can exclude and isolate others and critically reflects on the ways in which traditional values and dominant discourses can inadvertently perpetuate inequities. To realise this kind of inclusive environment, our conservatoires need to become 'bold spaces' 'in which [acting] students feel empowered to take risks and 'make bold choices' whilst feeling safe in the knowledge of their right and ability to set boundaries which will be respected'.[20] Indeed, the issue of *respect* has recently been foregrounded, reflecting the #MeToo movement and a greater awareness of LGBTQ+ rights, both nowadays embedded in the wider fabric of society.

EDI should not exist in isolation, and it is important not to view EDI initiatives as box-ticking exercises but as essential goals for any conservatoire that is committed to responding to the needs of society today. In this way, inclusion is deeply connected to the starting point of this chapter: the recognition and celebration of multiple forms of excellence. To address the world's challenges at local and global levels, our conservatoires must embrace divergent thinking. This requires an environment where diverse voices are present and heard (see Chapter 14). Those diverse voices might include not only individuals from traditionally under-represented groups in classical music but also musicians with expertise in different musical styles or based in other disciplines. At this juncture, we can extrapolate a further connection: the vital link between divergent thinking and a thriving research culture (see also Chapter 10). A research mindset embraces divergent thinking and, in doing so, drives bold new ideas and innovation. The importance of the feedback loop connecting a research mindset, divergent discourses, and positive cultural change in the conservatoire should not be underestimated by conservatoire leaders.

Innovation and heritage

Many traditions of our music conservatoires are a source of inspiration and pride, but we should take care that they do not become a burden to innovation. This is especially important in monotechnic conservatoires like the RCM, where classical music history defines much of the institutional identity, including its brand identity in a global market-place. As Kenyon asserts,

> [P]erformance today . . . is based on a wealth of varying traditions which are rapidly being challenged by a multiplicity of new forms of listening, creation and reception. For not all these performances depend on fidelity to a score, a skill acquired over years, and the active participation of a listening, concentrating audience. . . . They can be posted on the web without the mediation of agents, producers or record companies. Around the world, there are radically different situations in both performance and education, in America, in Africa, in East Asia, particularly in the emergingly powerful and influential musical world of China.[21]

Students themselves increasingly do not embrace traditional genre barriers and naturally gravitate to a more fluid understanding of music of all types. So, to remain relevant, conservatoires today require a broader outlook and renewed clarity of purpose. As explored in Chapter 8, this includes situating conservatoire creativity in a world that is mediated by digital technologies. There is a great potential to leverage emerging technologies to extend our reach and reimagine classical music experiences for the twenty-first century. It is this agility and openness to new models of performance that will strengthen conservatoires' resilience and relevance for twenty-first-century students, audience, and funders.

Concluding remarks

As we reflect on the chapters in this collection, we as editors are struck by the extraordinary complexity of conservatoires, despite their compact size and seemingly restricted remit as higher education institutions. This rich learning environment is fascinating for the way in which it combines so many skills and expertise in the pursuit of creating and sharing musical knowledge. The range of different views in this collection reflects the conservatoire's position today: a place where institutions are making sense of their histories, their values, and their relevance in the world. Conservatoires find themselves at the crossroads of tradition and innovation, on the cusp of internal renewal, and ready to establish a stronger, more persuasive position in wider society. This volume underlines that conservatoire communities are indeed evolving and, despite the enduring perception that conservatoires are highly traditional institutions, there is emerging evidence of progressive and critically informed attitudes to learning and teaching. While there is undoubtedly a need for more rapid, concrete change, especially in the areas of access and inclusion, the act of curating and publishing these views on the current position of the RCM and conservatoire education today is itself a step towards more authentic reflection, improved transparency, and progress in conservatoire discourses. We are optimistic that this is an early move towards enabling change.

Bibliography

Bartleet, Brydie-Leigh, Christina Ballico, Dawn Bennett, Ruth Bridgstock, Paul Draper, Vanessa Tomlinson, and Scott Harrison. 'Building sustainable portfolio careers in music: Insights and implications for higher education'. *Music Education Research* 21, no. 3 (2019): 282–94. https://doi.org/10.1080/14613808.2019.1598348.

Bull, Anna. *Class, Control, and Classical Music*. Oxford: Oxford University Press, 2019.

Camlin, Dave. 'Whose quality is it anyway? Inhabiting the creative tension between presentational and participatory music'. *Journal of Arts & Communities* 6, no. 2–3 (2014). https://doi.org/10.1386/jaac.6.2-3.99_1

Conservatoires UK. *Conservatoires UK Strategic Plan 2024–2029*. Accessed November 2024. https://conservatoiresuk.ac.uk/wp-content/uploads/2024/08/CUK-Strategic-Plan.pdf

Department for Education. *Guidance English Baccalaureate (EBacc)*. Accessed November 2024. https://www.gov.uk/government/publications/english-baccalaureate-ebacc/english-baccalaureate-ebacc

Department for Education. *LEO Graduate Outcomes Provider Level Data*. Accessed November 2024. https://explore-education-statistics.service.gov.uk/find-statistics/graduate-outcomes-leo-provider-level-data

Gardner, John W. *Excellence: Can We be Equal and Excellent Too?* NY: Harper Colophon Books, 1961.

Gaunt, Helena. 'Introduction to special issue on the reflective conservatoire'. *Arts and Humanities in Higher Education* 15, no. 3–4 (2016). https://doi.org/10.1177/1474022216655512.

Gaunt, Helena, Duffy Celia, Coric Ana, Isabel R. González Delgado, Messas Linda, Pryimenko Oleksandr, and Sveidahl Henrik. 'Musicians as "makers in society": A conceptual foundation for contemporary professional higher music education'. *Frontiers in Psychology* 12 (2021). https://doi.org/10.3389/fpsyg.2021.713648.

Gaunt, Helena, and Heidi Westerlund, eds. *Expanding Professionalism in Music and Higher Music Education*. SEMPRE Series in The Psychology of Music. Abingdon: Routledge, 2022.

Grant, Catherine. 'What does it mean for a musician to be socially engaged? How undergraduate music students perceive their possible social roles as musicians'. *Music Education Research* 21, no. 4 (2019): 387–98. https://doi.org/10.1080/14613808.2019.1626360.

Kenyon, Nicholas. 'Performance today'. In *The Cambridge History of Musical Performance*, edited by C. Lawson and R. Stowell, 1–34. Cambridge University Press, 2012.

Perkins, Rosie. 'Learning cultures and the conservatoire: An ethnographically-informed case study'. *Music Education Research* 15 (2013): 196–213. https://doi.org/10.1080/14613808.2012.759551.

Porton, Jennie Joy. 'Social inclusion in contemporary British conservatoires: Alumni perspectives'. In *Voices for Change in the Classical Music Profession: New Ideas for Tackling Inequalities and Exclusions*, edited by Anna Bull, Christina Scharff, and Laudan Nooshin, 42–53. New York: Oxford University Press, 2023. https://doi.org/10.1093/oso/9780197601211.001.0001.

Prokop, Rainer, and Rosa Reitsamer. 'The role of music conservatoire in the making of classical music careers'. In *Voices for Change in the Classical Music Profession: New Ideas for Tackling Inequalities and Exclusions*, edited by Anna Bull, Christina Scharff, and Laudan Nooshin, 31–41. New York: Oxford University Press, 2023. https://doi.org/10.1093/oso/9780197601211.001.0001.

Renshaw, Peter. 'Towards the changing face of the conservatoire curriculum'. *British Journal of Music Education* 3 (1986): 79–90. https://doi.org/10.1017/S0265051700005143.

Rushton, Eleanor. 'Facilitators of each other's development: An exploration of the relationship dynamics experienced by acting students during their training in UK Drama Schools'. Unpublished MSc thesis, Royal College of Music, 2023.

Tregear, Peter, Geir Johansen, Harald Jørgensen, John Sloboda, Helena Tulve, and Richard Wistreich. 'Conservatoires in society: Institutional challenges and possibilities for change'. *Arts and Humanities in Higher Education* 15, no. 3–4 (2016): 276–92. https://doi.org/10.1177/1474022216647379.

Notes

1 Department for Education, *Guidance English Baccalaureate*.
2 Department for Education, *LEO Graduate Outcomes Provider Level Data*.
3 Gardner, *Excellence*, xii.
4 Bull, *Class, control, and classical music*, 236.
5 The current strategic plan of Conservatoires UK aims 'to develop the resilience and knowledge needed to flourish in an increasingly challenging and complex landscape for the performing arts'. Conservatoires UK, *Strategic Plan 2024–2029*, 4.
6 Perkins, 'Learning cultures and the conservatoire', 196–213.
7 Camlin, 'Whose quality is it anyway? Inhabiting the creative tension between presentational and participatory music', 115.
8 Gaunt, 'Introduction to special issue on the reflective conservatoire', 15.

9 Gaunt and Westerlund, *Expanding Professionalism in Music*, xiii.
10 Renshaw, 'Towards the changing face of the conservatoire curriculum'.
11 Grant, 'What does it mean for a musician to be socially engaged?'.
12 Tregear et al., 'Conservatoires in society', 276.
13 Gaunt et al., 'Musicians as "makers in society"'.
14 Bartleet et al., 'Building sustainable portfolio careers in music', 289.
15 Tregear et al., 'Conservatoires in society', 288.
16 Kenyon, 'Performance today', 33–34.
17 Prokop and Reitsamer, 'The role of music conservatoire in the making of classical music careers', 41.
18 Porton, 'Social inclusion in contemporary British conservatoires', 48.
19 See Bull, *Class, Control, and Classical Music* for further discussion of music and inequality.
20 Rushton, 'Facilitators of each other's development', 42.
21 Kenyon, 'Performance today', 6–7.

INDEX

www.ingramcontent.com/pod-product-compliance
Ingram Content Group UK Ltd.
Pitfield, Milton Keynes, MK11 3LW, UK
UKHW052339070325
455956UK00013B/112